LATIN AMERICA:

An Introductory Survey

LATIN AMERICA:
An Introductory Survey

edited by
Brian W. Blouet
Olwyn M. Blouet
University of Nebraska

JOHN WILEY & SONS
New York
Chichester
Brisbane
Toronto
Singapore

1807 1982

Library of Congress Cataloging in Publication Data:

Main entry under title.

Latin America, an introductory survey

Includes bibliographical references and index.
1. Latin America.   I. Blouet, Brian W., 1936–
II. Blouet, Olwyn M., 1948–
F1408.L386   980   81-7451
ISBN 0-471-08385-2   AACR2

Printed in the United States of America

10   9   8   7   6   5

Preface

In 1941 Carl Sauer wrote that the "two most important things to know about Mexico still are the patterns of life that existed before the coming of the white men and the changes that were introduced during the first generation or two of the Spanish period."[1] This remark still applies to much of former Spanish America. In 1941 Sauer recognized that a period of transformation was underway but that the great economic changes of the second half of the twentieth century would certainly not be unrelated to the previous experience of cultural evolution.

Most of the contributors to this textbook would agree that the present situation in Latin America cannot be understood without knowledge of the past. This may seem trite, a mere recitation of conventional thoughts as a polite prelude to the real study of the present. However, Anglo-Americans constantly underestimate the vastness of the socioeconomic changes that traditional societies must make in the process of modernization. The United States was in many senses a modern country when it achieved independence. The Constitution is a foundation document for a modernizing society intent on utilizing fully its human resources. Just as important, the greatest part of the country's resources had not been preempted by elite landowning classes. There was a region with the values and structure of a traditional society in the Old

---

Carl O. Sauer, "The Personality of Mexico," *Geographical Review*, Vol. 31, 1941, pp. 353–364. Reprinted in *Land and Life*, Berkeley, University of California Press, 1967.

South, but much of this structure was dismantled as a result of the Civil War. The point is that in the process of economic development the United States did not have to modify a traditional society in order to modernize. This was not the case in Latin America, where a traditional agrarian society is still in the process of modernization.

Latin American cultural history is complicated because the colonizing Iberians only established enclaves where the values of traditional agrarian societies prevailed. Elsewhere the life-style of the Indian community dominated, and now both patterns are being subjected to the processes of industrialization and modernization.

It is important to remember that industrialization and modernization are not the same thing, although modern societies are frequently industrialized. Modernization implies a group of characteristics such as universal literacy, low infant mortality, broad participation in political processes, good educational standards, and high per capita incomes. Basic industrialization can take place utilizing a work force that enjoys few of the attributes of a modern society. In Britain, for example, industrialization took place in the nineteenth century; since then there has been a constant battle to modernize. In late eighteenth-century England the greatest part of the land was owned by less than 10 percent of the population. The average inhabitant was a farm laborer, fitfully employed and dependent on decisions made by members of a small, powerful, landowning elite. The right to vote was denied to all but property holders. In this traditional, agrarian society the process of industrialization was started by a small group of entrepreneurs. Eventually the mass of people migrated from rural to urban areas to hire themselves out as laborers in factories and live in mean, overcrowded, unsanitary hovels in towns frequently visited by epidemics. By 1861 England had an urban majority, but the transition from rural field laborer to urban factory worker left many things unchanged. The illiterate mass of the population still suffered poor living conditions and was denied access to the political process. For a great part of the nineteenth century trade union activity was illegal; universal franchise for men did not come until after 1867, and the first attempt to create a national system of education was not begun until 1870.

One reason that U.S. citizens cannot understand Britain's twentieth-century problems is that they do not appreciate how the values, class structure, ignorance, and social relationships of a traditional society were carried out of the countryside and into the cities of the nineteenth century, and that many of the scars of battles fought long ago are still fresh. The intransigence of labor organizers when dealing with management, the still pervasive social distinctions, the attitudes toward education, and many other facts of present-day life in Britain reflect a society that has very imperfectly made the transition, over 200 years, from a traditional to a modern society.

In Latin America the situation is more complex than in Western Europe. A region characterized by Indian communities was overwhelmed in the sixteenth century by Iberians who came from an area that displayed the values of a traditional agrarian society. In fact, at least as far as Castile was concerned, the society still retained many feudal elements. Land was the resource that determined wealth and standing in society. The Iberians (and their heirs) were the nucleus of an elite, landowning group in Latin America, and the majority of the population was unable to gain control of resources or influence political processes. Early in the twentieth century the distribution of landownership throughout most of Latin America was not dissimilar to that described for Britain in the late eighteenth century. Since the start of World War II, many Latin American regions have undergone economic transformation, and at a faster pace than experienced by Western Europe in the nineteenth century. Within a few decades the traditional agrarian societies created in the colonial period, which imperfectly incorporated the Indian communities, have been altered as the major cities of the region have grown from provincial towns to sprawling metropolitan areas. But the people who have migrated from small towns, Indian communities, or *haciendas* have not been totally transformed and they bring with them various value systems. How these systems will be adapted to urban living in centers of economic change is not well understood, but a surprisingly large number of cultural traits have been carried from rural to urban communities.

We have been prone to undervalue the persistence of traditional beliefs and ethnic values in the process of urbanization and modernization, but we will no longer do so. In the United States we have rediscovered many of the ethnic value systems of migrant groups who entered the country in the nineteenth century; it is surprising how persistent certain attributes are, long after direct contact with the homeland has been lost. No one can be certain how the varied ethnic groups in Latin American cities are going to respond over the long term to the development process, but there will be responses; this will insure that the economic transition in the region will be distinctive and not merely a later version of a process already generated elsewhere.

The persistence of folkways in the urban areas of Latin America has been part of the anthropological literature for several decades. In an article published in 1952 Oscar Lewis observed how many rural traits survived in Mexico City, and in a 1965 study he commented on the similarity of many aspects of rural and urban life in Mexico, at least for the poor.

> I found no sharp differences in family structure, diet, dress, and belief systems of the *vecindad* tenants according to their rural-urban origins. The use of herbs for curing, the raising of animals, the belief in sorcery, and spiritualism, the celebration of the Day of the Dead, illiteracy and low level of education, political apathy

and cynicism about government . . . were just as common among persons who had been in . . . Mexico City . . . for over thirty years as among recent arrivals.[2]

The availability of more wealth in Mexico and more resources for education as a possible result of expanded oil production may not remove the underlying cultural differences that exist in the urban areas. The folkways, many of them pre-Hispanic in origin, will continue to persist, and it may be difficult for modernized educational systems to penetrate the cultural barriers involved. Within the context of economic development the implications of this are immense; it implies that the benefits of growth will not be equally spaced in the future. It may well be that just when aggregate wealth in Mexico begins to increase rapidly, the cities will be marked by social unrest. The modernizing part of the nation could become more affluent and educated, while those locked into the "culture of poverty" and its folkways may become more aware of the inequalities. The same scenario could well be witnessed in other Latin American countries.

FURTHER READING

This textbook uses a predominantly historical and systematic approach to studying Latin America; other books approach the topic in different ways and use, for example, the regional approach.

The following is a partial list of valuable geography texts.

Blakemore, Harold, and Cliffort T. Smith (eds.), *Latin America: Geographical Perspectives*, London, Methuen, 1971.
Butland, Gilbert J., *Latin America: A Regional Geography*, 3rd ed., New York, Wiley, 1972.
Gilbert, Alan, *Latin American Development, A Geographical Perspective*, Harmondsworth and Baltimore, Pelican, 1974.
James, Preston E., *Latin America*, 4th ed., New York, Odyssey Press, 1969.
Odell, Peter R., and David A. Preston *Economies and Societies in Latin America: A Geographical Interpretation*, New York, Wiley, 1973.

The following journals are devoted primarily to Latin America.

Journal of Inter-American Studies, Coral Gables, Fla.
Journal of Latin American Studies, Cambridge University Press, England, twice a year.
Latin American Perspectives, Riverside, Calif., four times a year.
Latin American Research Review, Latin American Studies Association, three times a year.
Hispanic American Historical Review, Duke University Press, N.C., irregularly.

[2]Oscar Lewis, "The Folk-Urban Ideal Types," in Philip M. Hauser and Leo F. Schnore (eds.), *The Study of Urbanization*, New York, Wiley, 1965, p. 496.

Other sources of value are *The South American Handbook* published annually by Rand McNally, Chicago, *Bolsa Review* published by the Bank of London and South America, and the *Latin American Newsletter*. An excellent source of statistics for any country in the world is the *Statesman's Yearbook*, New York, St. Martin's Press, annually since 1864. The following U.N. annual publications are of value: *The Demographic Yearbook, The Statistical Yearbook,* and the *Economic Survey of Latin America*.

Brian W. Blouet
Olwyn M. Blouet

Contents

CHAPTER 1

Physical Environments of Latin America

Tom L. Martinson

[handwritten annotation:] Diverse physical environment. Range of climates from tropical, temperate to tundra. Various crops.

Latin America is a region of diverse physical environments. Latitudinally it extends from northernmost Baja, California (32.30° N), to the southern islands in the Tierra del Fuego group (55° S). South of Cape Horn is the Drake Passage, the South Shetland Islands, and the Graham Land peninsula of Antarctica. The climates of the region range from tropical to temperate to tundra. However, the configuration of the land area is such that the greatest part of the region lies within the tropics although, in the mountains, tropicality is modified by altitude. South of the tropic of Capricorn South America tapers, and the area of temperate lands is not great when compared with the tropical core of the region. The tapering means that oceanic influences are progressively more important toward the south. Unlike North America, there is no higher latitude landmass to sustain continental, climatic influences.

Even within countries of the region the range of environments is immense. In Peru the greatest part of the coastal region is a desert, punctuated by cultivated valleys that are watered by streams descending from the western versant of the Andes. In the mountains themselves the environment ranges from snow-covered peaks to high grazing country to valleys and basins of varying altitude in which various crops can be grown. In some of the deeper Andean valleys it is possible to travel from lush, tropical forest to high grasslands that lie above the practical limit of cultivation. To the east of the Peruvian Andes lies the *oriente*, a predominantly tropical region drained by the Amazon system.

Changing Perceptions of the Environment

The diversity of the physical environment of Latin America is equaled only by the different ways in which it has been perceived and used. Amerindians, European conquerors, African slaves, travelers, and contemporary inhabitants have all developed images of segments of this vast region, and their ideas are reflected in literature, music, and art as well as in everyday affairs.

The Environment as God. Native Americans revered the environment. The high cultures of the Aztecs in the Valley of Mexico, the Mayas of the tropical lowlands around the Yucatan, and the Incas of highland Peru all attained their status, at least in part, by successful relationships with the environment.

One reason for the success of the high cultures was their close philosophical association with the physical world. According to Ralph Nelson in his introduction to the Mayan *Popul Vuh*:

> Nature is often considered to be the prime source of early contemplation, and in Mesoamerica, cultural development was most likely affected by a world-view carried down from hunting-gathering times. Fate (symbolized by the reed) seems to be a concept central to Mayan thinking. Also, the cyclical view of existence that formed an important part of later religion probably took its lead from nature, where seasons come and go, and life follows death. Nature also suggests a unity, and the idea may have existed, too, that all elements of life are an intricate part of the whole. The bug on the leaf and the passing cloud are brothers, in this sense, parts of the same absolute identity. This view is close to the pantheistic idea that the world *is* god.

This view is not limited to people of the past. Indeed, there is still a significant proportion of the people of Latin America, especially descendants of Indians in their isolated mountain communities, who subscribe to these beliefs.

The Environment as Prey. Iberian conquerors saw the New World as pristine and ripe for the plucking. The Indians were not strong enough to resist European technology, and the land yielded to the European pick or plow. The results were spectacular: great wealth and prestige began to flow into the hands of *conquistadores* and on to Spain and Portugal, further firing the spirit of adventure. According to Picon-Salas:

> Even accepting the pursuit of gold as the ideal, the Spaniard loved the adventure of the quest almost more than its monetary value. Distasteful to him were purely commercial enterprises like the Portuguese colonies in Asia or later those of the English that were primarily coastal trading ports where the natives brought their wares from the interior to be weighed, measured, and haggled over. To achieve eminence, to become a nobleman . . . and to wield influence in affairs of state— these were the real reasons why he craved gold.

The struggle to gain wealth by plundering the environment remains a common theme throughout contemporary Latin American history. Whether the perpetrator has been soldier or landowner, foreigner or native, the region's water resources, landforms, soils, and vegetation have suffered greatly over the centuries. Some of the damage is irreparable.

Beautiful landscapes

The Environment as Illusion. From the beginning of the age of discovery, the New World appeared as a mirage, too good to be true. This early fascination is reflected in the journals of Christopher Columbus. As Sauer writes in *The Early Spanish Main* (1966, p. 29):

> The beauty of the islands moved Columbus greatly. . . . The trade-wind shores he found as tropical nature at its best, and he reveled in praise of their charm and beauty. The perfume of the trees and flowers, he said, was carried out to the ships at sea. The islands were lands of perpetual spring. Birds of many forms and colors sang sweetly in a vast garden of innocent nature, inhabited by the gentlest and kindest natives.

This image of the New World as a sort of Garden of Eden persisted throughout the conquest and colonial period and, to some degree, to the present day. For example, the great traveler, writer, and geographer Alexander von Humboldt (1769-1859) found it difficult to describe the places he saw as a visitor to Mexico and South America during his expedition of 1799-1804, so he encouraged artists to travel to Latin America to paint and draw the region's landscapes and display these pictures to a fascinated European audience.

Even then the image of Latin America remained clouded. Johann Moritz Rugendas, perhaps the most famous of the European artists whom Humboldt persuaded to come to the New World, saw the continent in romantic terms. He was trained in reportorial art and was attracted to scenes illustrating the great conflicts between nature and people. His paintings are powerful statements of environmental relationships, illustrations colored by excitement engendered by the unfamiliar and the tension of conflict.

The Environment as Obstacle. Certainly both Indians and invaders found the physical environment of Latin America difficult to handle. The broad sweep of the Amazon Basin and the crags of the Andes are formidable impediments to travel, even in the age of the airplane. Some writers, such as historian Hubert Herring, have gone so far as to say that the environment has determined the region's development.

> The mountains and their high plateaus have largely determined the political, economic, and social patterns of much of Latin America. The Andes' high barriers established the boundaries of Chile and Argentina. The plateaus and inaccessible valleys furnished refuge to aboriginal peoples, delayed their conquest by European invaders, and helped to preserve their ancient ways.

Painting by Johann Moritz Rugendas (1802–1858), *Distant View of Orizaba* is provided by Staatliche Graphics Sammlung, Munich.

Most geographers would disagree with Herring's assertion of environmental dominance, preferring to outline the basic problems posed by the environment and then indicate how people have responded to these challenges. This view is expressed by Preston James when he says:

> There is, after all, only one basic compulsion in the relations of man to the land—if a group of people is to remain for a long time in any area, some kind of workable connection must be formed with the earth resources. Not even city people are free from this necessity. From the land must come the fundamental needs of human life—food, clothing, and shelter; and from the land, also, must come the material means by which a human community can raise its standard of living above the minimum essentials of existence. To the problem of making a living however, or of creating wealth from the resources of the earth, the earth itself remains essentially passive and indifferent.

diff to t moisture due to location

CLIMATE

Climate differs greatly from place to place in Latin America. Generally, variations in temperature and moisture result from differences in the amount of solar energy received at different locations on the earth's surface and the disposition of this insolation after it is received. Because of Latin America's size, position, and configuration, these factors are subject to many regional and local influences.

Temperature and Moisture Characteristics. Solar energy received at the earth's surface is the fuel that stokes Latin American climatic machinery. Temperature, the measure of this energy and one of the two major elements of climate,

Seasonal changes due to rotation in orbit around the sun.

Painting by Johann Moritz Rugendas (1802–1858), *Bivouac in the Chilean Andes* is provided by Staatliche Graphics Sammlung, Munich.

varies with the nature of earth-sun relationships. The distribution of moisture, the second major element of climate, reflects the energy available to operate the hydrologic cycle.

The amount of insolation received by Latin America's land and water surfaces is controlled by earth-sun relationships. The sun produces a more or less constant supply of energy, and the amount captured by the earth as a whole varies little, but the concentration of this energy changes from season to season because of the variation in the angle at which the sun's rays strike the surface of the earth as it proceeds in its orbit around the sun.

tropics intense head o local variations, different
temperatures in different latitudes, altitudes +
elevations. Rainfall -200m. per yr. some areas

The rays of the sun are most direct and intense between the tropic of Cancer in the Northern Hemisphere and the tropic of Capricorn in the Southern Hemisphere: at higher latitudes the sun's rays are oblique and diffused over a wider area. Accordingly, the parts of Latin America's land and water that lie within the tropics are subject to more intense heating over the year than extratropical locations, where seasonal temperature changes are common. The irregularly warmed earth then provides heat to the atmosphere to fuel other processes.

The amount and rate of energy transferred to the atmosphere for other purposes often depends on the physical nature of the surface material. If water bodies are at the surface, as in the oceans adjacent to Latin America, heating or cooling occurs much more slowly than in the case of land surfaces. Air masses overlying water may then be warmer in winter or cooler in summer than those over land.

Local variations in this broad pattern of temperature distribution result from several factors. Some solar energy, especially that striking the high latitudes where snow and ice are found, is reflected. Elevation affects the distribution of surface temperature. High locations then have lower temperatures than places at low elevations, even though they may be located at the same latitude.

One of the best examples of the effect of altitude on temperature is in Ecuador, where Quito (9300 feet), in the Andes has an average annual temperature of 54.6 °F, while Guayaquil, on the Pacific coast, has an average annual temperature of 78.2 °F, a difference of 23.6 °F.

Some of the most active and complex of the physical systems on earth serve to redistribute heat energy. The primary air circulation system is one example of this process (Figure 1-1). The major air circulation cells prevalent over Latin America are the trade winds that, at the surface, blow from the subtropical high-pressure belts at about 30° N and S latitudes toward the equator, and the westerlies that prevail from about 30° N and S latitudes to the subpolar lows at about 60° N and S latitudes. The trade winds converge on the equatorial region and, in this zone of intertropical convergence (I.T.C.), unstable air tends to rise and promote numerous showers and storms. Weather activity can be particularly intense when "waves," or disturbances, form in the I.T.C. Rainfall totals are high in equatorial regions, particularly where unstable air is raised by passage over mountain chains. Rainfall totals of 200 inches per year are recorded on the eastern flanks of the Andes in areas where the trade winds are forced aloft by relief.

The passage of water through the hydrologic cycle in Latin America is a reflection of the receipt and disposition of solar energy there. Evaporation, condensation, and precipitation processes depend on the availability of moisture and energy. Evaporation occurs where there is sufficient energy to change water to a gas: water vapor. In high latitudes and high altitudes there is little

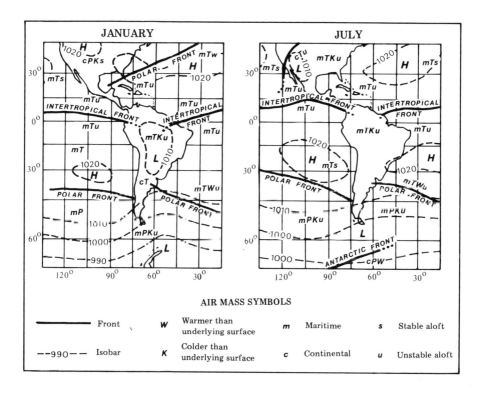

Figure 1.1   Seasonal Distribution of Air Masses

precipitation but also little evaporation because less energy is available. At low elevations in the tropics, precipitation and average temperatures are higher, and evaporation is maximized. The air over Patagonia is dry compared to the high relative humidities experienced in the Brazilian Amazon Basin, for example.

Once evaporated, water in vapor form can be carried long distances by the prevailing winds. Areas such as the tropical eastern flanks of the Andes owe their high rainfall totals to the constant importation of large amounts of moist air from the warm South Atlantic Ocean and then its movement over the continent by the southeast trade winds.

Condensation, the second stage in the hydrologic cycle, is the direct precursor of precipitation. Condensation results from the adiabatic cooling of moist air masses by convective, cyclonic, or orographic lifting. This change of water vapor to a liquid occurs when air parcels are cooled by lifting to the dew point, the temperature at which their relative humidities are at 100 percent. The daily convective showers that characterize the lowland tropics of Latin

America result from local heating and subsequent uplift and then adiabatic cooling of these air parcels.

Cyclonic and orographic processes provide moisture to much larger areas of Latin America. Cyclonic precipitation, resulting from the uplift of warm, moist air along a boundary with cooler, drier air, occurs in the Latin American middle latitudes that come under the seasonal influence of the polar front, where these two types of air masses meet. Some parts of Mexico in the northern middle latitudes are subject to spring or autumn showers because of periodic invasions of dense polar air into buoyant warm air from the tropics. These storms may travel hundreds of miles, depending on their intensity, the strength of the prevailing winds, and the location of barriers to air movement. Orographic precipitation depends on the location of mountain barriers in relation to prevailing winds because the adiabatic cooling process is triggered by moist air rising up mountain slopes.

A band of clouds along a mountain slope or a plume of clouds extending over a mountain peak are familiar sights in lowland tropical Latin America and, in some seasons and locations, middle-latitude locations.

On a hemispheric scale most rain falls in the convergence zones, where large masses of moist air are uplifted, or in the belts, where prevailing winds meet great mountain barriers. As a result, practically all the lowland tropics of Latin America are wet, at least seasonally, and zones of moisture penetrate the middle latitudes along the windward slopes of major mountain ranges such as the Sierra Madre Oriental and Sierra Madre Occidental of Mexico and the Andes of Chile. Some dry lands are found in the continental interiors far from

Cumulus Clouds Building over the Andean Front in Eastern Colombia

assured sources of moisture and where subtropical high pressure prevails, at about 30° N and S latitudes. The Sonora Desert of Mexico and the Atacama Desert of Chile are examples of the latter, while the seasonally dry *chaco* of interior Argentina-Bolivia-Paraguay results from its interior continental position, far from the oceans. The Atacama Desert is one of the driest in the world and owes its extreme aridity to a high combination of factors such as subsiding air within a stable high-pressure system centered offshore and the upwelling of cold water associated with the north-flowing Peruvian current. The cold water causes frequent fogs and low stratus clouds, but the air is stable and rainfall is a rarity.

An anomalous arid region exists on the Caribbean shore of Venezuela and Colombia. Here descending, stable air that is warming (and thus tending to absorb instead of give up moisture) seems to be at least a partial cause of aridity. The annual rainfall of La Guaira, on the Caribbean shore of Venezuela, barely exceeds 10 inches.

The *caatinga* zone of northeast Brazil suffers from droughts that cause, from time to time, tens of thousands of farmers to seek refuge in other parts of the country. The Brazilian author Euclides da Cunha, in *Rebellion in the Backlands*, has written vividly of this plight.

> The cautery of the droughts is adjusted on the backlands; the burning air is sterilized; the ground, parched and cleft, becomes petrified; the northeaster roars in the wilderness; and, like a lacerating haircloth, the caatinga extends over the earth its thorny branches . . .

The Distribution of Climatic Types

Several schemes have been developed to generalize the distribution of temperature and moisture conditions on a hemispheric scale. Indians and conquering Spaniards utilized informal climate classification systems based on altitude in the tropics. Although this technique ignores many of the processes just outlined, it accentuates the influences of elevation on temperature that are apparent to the casual observer today. Conditions vary with latitude but, within the tropics, generally places from sea level to about 3000 feet lie within the *tierra caliente*; from 6000 feet within the *tierra templada*; 12,000 feet within the *tierra fria*; and, in the highest elevations, *tierra helada* prevails (Figure 1-2).

Conventional wisdom is supplemented and extended by other classifications based on aggregate climatic data (Figure 1-3) and on the temperature and moisture characteristics of the large air masses that dominate the region. Generally, there are four major types of air masses controlling temperature and moisture conditions over large areas: the cold, dry continental polar (cP) air masses that originate over the continental high-pressure cells of the polar lati-

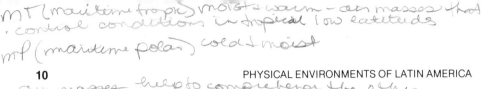

[handwritten marginalia: mT (maritime trop.) moist + warm – air masses that control conditions in tropical low latitudes. mP (maritime polar) cold + moist]

[handwritten marginalia: air masses help to comprehend the other physical patterns of L.A. – provides insight into seasonal weather conditions.]

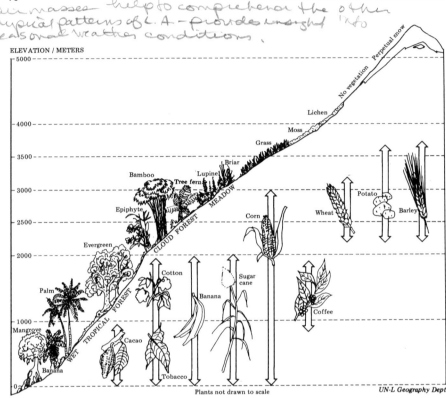

Figure 1.2 The Effects of Altitudinal Zonation

tudes; the warm, moist maritime tropical (mT) air masses that control conditions in the tropical low latitudes; the hot, dry continental tropical (cT) air masses that are spawned over the landmasses and their margins in the subtropics distant from infusions of moisture; and the cool, moist maritime polar (mP) air masses. The three air masses that dominate Latin America's climate in both winter and summer are the hot dry (cT), warm moist (mT), and cool moist (mP). In January warm, moist air masses control temperature and moisture conditions over the Caribbean area and the central core of the South American continent and the Central American isthmus; cold, moist (mP) air masses of the South Atlantic meet the hot, dry (cT) air masses of central Argentina along the polar front. In July warm, moist air still dominates the Caribbean and the South American continent, but hot, dry air has moved over the Mexican north, and cool, moist air prevails in southernmost South America, carrying as far north as the Rio de la Plata along the polar front. These air masses are keys to comprehending other physical patterns in Latin America (Figure 1-1).

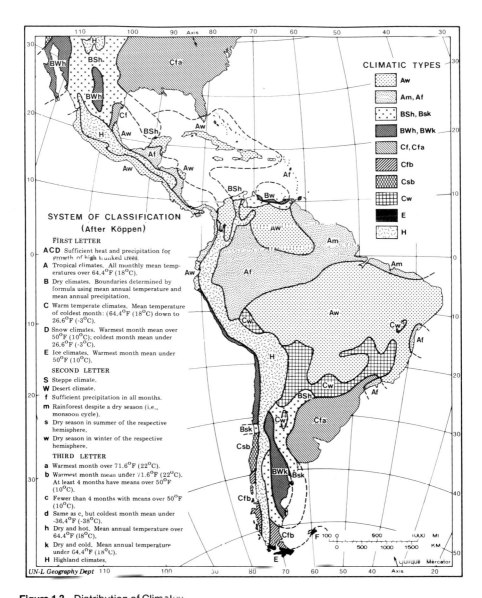

Figure 1.3 Distribution of Climates

Understanding the general pattern of air mass distribution also provides some insight into seasonal weather conditions in Latin America. The Amazon lowlands, for example, are predictably warm and wet all year, but Mexican border towns in the cT realm expect hot, dry conditions in July and cool, dry conditions in January. The Argentine west, by contrast, experiences warm, dry conditions in January and cool, moist weather in July. Locations in the low latitudes at low elevations hardly need weather services because conditions are eminently predictable; in the middle latitudes and altitudes forecasts are more difficult because the extent, characteristics, and interactions of air masses there constantly change. These changes may produce violent weather such as that described by Jorge Icaza in *Huasipungo*.

> The fury of the storm obliterated all the human voices with a single roar. Like mute, blind shadows the Indians clung to each other in a childlike desire to banish the loneliness and fear from their hearts and heads. It rained with a seemingly tireless fury, and, in only thirty or forty minutes, which was a whole century to the drenched *mingueros*, the lashing water flooded the earth, littering through the gorges of the hill, through the cracks in the rocks, through the winding ravines, and over the jutting edges of the boulders. . . .

People–Climate Controversies in Latin America

Climate is a pervasive factor in the human affairs of Latin America to the extent that some people equate the area's relative underdevelopment with its tropical location. Climate stereotypes such as this date back at least to Plato's time and entered into the popular mythology concerning place and people differentiation. Although compelling, this hypothesis has never been supported by all the facts. Placed in contemporary world perspective, Latin America's economy does offer lower per capita incomes than the developed world centered on the North Atlantic, but it is more advanced than most of Asia or Africa. In addition, much of Latin America, because of latitude or altitude, falls outside the tropics. Another argument against strict climatic determinism is that, although individual human bodies do react to changing temperature and moisture conditions, there is no direct evidence that conditions within the tropics have ever retarded cultural achievement.

A number of high cultures developed in the American tropics, including the little-known Olmecs of the Mexican Gulf coast, said to be cultural forebears of several later groups including the Toltecs and Aztecs of the Mexican highlands and the illustrious Mayas of the Central American tropics. Artifacts and historical documents indicate that these groups were sophisticated and, in some respects, superior to the later conquerors, the middle-latitude Spaniards and Portuguese.

WATER

Some of the world's lushest tropical rainforests and most arid deserts are found in Latin America. These environments are reflections of water surplus and water deficiency, extremes on the continuum of water supply on the continent.

The Hydrologic Cycle

Both extreme and intermediate supplies of water may be investigated using the hydrologic cycle. The hydrologic cycle illustrates the interrelationships among evaporation, condensation, and precipitation as well as the many other roles played by water.

The oceans off Latin America and its extensive tropical rainforests are great reservoirs of water for evaporation. Because of the warm temperatures and abundant water supply, the highest annual evaporation rates occur over the tropical and subtropical oceans. Land and plant surfaces also provide water for evaporation, either directly from the soil or through the leaves of plants by transpiration. In some places, especially near the subtropical high-pressure belts where the energy available for evaporation exceeds the amount of water available to be evaporated, dry lands are found.

Condensation occurs when air is adiabatically cooled to its dew point temperature in the presence of sufficient nuclei (such as dust particles or salt spray) so that water drops form. Several mechanisms in the skies over Latin America result in precipitation.

Rapid local uplift of air, such as that occurring over warm places in the "heat" of the day, causes the showers of convective precipitation that contribute substantially to the heavy rainfall totals in the Amazon Basin and other lowland tropical areas in the warm season.

Cyclonic processes, occurring when relatively warm, moist air is forced to rise over relatively cool, dry air, produce light to moderate rainfall over extensive areas of the hemisphere. This type of precipitation is more prevalent in the Latin American middle latitudes where air masses of different characteristics are more likely to meet, but it does also occur in the tropics, along the zone where the trade winds converge. Cyclonic precipitation often occurs seasonally in Latin America in the zone over which air mass convergence extends, following the high sun. Incursions of cold air masses and related showers occur as close to the equator as Costa Rica or central Brazil in their respective winter seasons, causing agricultural disasters such as the loss of important coffee crops. In the extreme northern or southern fringes of high-altitude margins of Latin America snowfall accompanies these cold air outbreaks.

Orographic precipitation results when adiabatic cooling is induced by the rise of relatively warm, moist air over mountains. Because there are substantial mountain ranges in Latin America, there are massive orographic precipitation belts along windward slopes throughout the continent. This process extends to lower mountains such as those in Central America and causes "fingers" of heavy precipitation to extend up the east-facing Caribbean valleys of Honduras. Even small Caribbean islands carry cloud plumes on their windward flanks.

Saba Island in the Caribbean

Cactus in the Balsas Depression

Where all three types of precipitation (convectional, cyclonic, and oro-graphic) are found in Latin America, the precipitation totals are likely to be greatest. Accordingly, places such as the east-facing Andean rim of the Amazon Basin are abundantly watered. Where these processes are circumvented, as in cooler places under the influence of semipermanent high-pressure cells and on the leeward sides of significant mountain barriers, water deficit is common. Many intermontane depressions also are dry, as is the Balsas depression of Mexico.

Although it is complex, some generalizations can be stated about the distribution of precipitation in Latin America. There is an equatorial zone of maximum precipitation, related to the convergence zone of the trade winds. Rainfall is high on windward slopes throughout the continent. Storms of the Latin American middle latitudes are related to incursions of relatively cold, dry air into areas usually dominated by warm, moist air. Snow is commonly confined to the high latitudes and high altitudes of the continent. The dry areas of Latin America generally are found in places dominated by high pressure and on the leeward sides of mountains or mountain systems. Examples include coastal Peru, northern coastal Venezuela, and northeast Brazil.

Surface Water

After precipitation reaches the ground, it may be redistributed by runoff, percolation, and/or evaporation. Alternatively, it may be stored for short terms as ice and snow or for long terms in chemical combinations with other substances.

Where there is a great deal of precipitation, the water is highly visible on the landscape as lakes, streams, and rivers. As will be shown in the following section on landforms, this surface water accomplishes most of the erosion in Latin America. Controlled surface runoff that remains in established channels or is impounded poses no problems for human activities, but uncontrolled runoff that results from deforestation or urban waterproofing threatens agriculture and settlement in some localities.

The water that percolates into the subsurface also may accomplish solution and remove materials. In areas where the subsurface rock is easily dissolved, such as where thick, jointed layers of limestone are found, subsurface erosion takes expression in the form of disappearing streams, underground caverns, and sinks. These sinks, called *cenotes* in the Mexican Yucatan peninsula, have become famous archeological sites because they contain relics from the city-states of the late Mayan Empire.

Erosion accomplished by surface water (or groundwater) is a particularly serious problem where rainfall is intense or prolonged, and people have taken steps to deal with this problem. Many tropical agricultural practices, for example, have evolved specifically to deal with the threat of water erosion. Terracing (or *tablon* agriculture, as it is known in Guatemala), for example, reduces the possibility of topsoil erosion and permits irrigation during a dry season. The Inca terraces of Peru were frequently built to facilitate irrigation and to offer a flat surface for planting crops.

Many modern agricultural practices also depend on the elimination of surplus water from the soil. Therefore drainage ditches are a common sight in the lowland tropics of Latin America, especially where modern commercial agriculture is practiced. The ancient ridged fields of the Amazon and Orinoco basins and parts of Middle America were precursors of these attempts to solve the problem of excess soil moisture.

In comparison with other large continental masses, not a great deal of water is retained on land surfaces in Latin America. This is due to its general location and surface configuration. Moreover, the South American landmass tapers as it approaches the South Pole. There is no great "continental" influence, and the possibilities for snow accumulation, glacier development, and ice formation are small when compared with North America or Asia. The high altitudes of Latin America offer some opportunities for snow accumulation and glacier growth, but the record shows that glaciers were more common during the Pleistocene than at present. Flowing water are the most prominent expression of this.

Water Movement

Although snow and ice are important in some Latin American localities, streams, rivers, and lakes are the most prominent expressions of water on the landscape.

In areas dominated by continental tropical (cT) air masses, such as interior northern Mexico, permanent streams are often absent because potential evaporation exceeds precipitation. The only major rivers are those that originate in wetter places and pass through deserts on their way to the ocean. Perhaps the most famous example of such an exotic stream in Latin America is the Rio Bravo del Norte (or the Rio Grande, as it is known in the United States) because it serves a relatively dense population dependent on this water for the production of agricultural specialty crops that are grown for sale to foreign markets. This river takes on added significance because it is also the political boundary between the United States and Mexico.

In high-altitude locations stream flow may be limited in winter while the snowmelt of summer insures high runoff. The supply of Andean meltwaters in the summer greatly benefits the agriculture of places such as the adjacent Central Valley of Chile, where summer irrigation is often necessary to produce crops. Even though water is available in major streams during the summer, extensive areas cannot be irrigated and therefore lie fallow during this season.

The maritime polar (mP) air mass regions receive adequate rainfall in all seasons and thus exhibit extensive river development. Noteworthy among such places are southern Brazil, northern Argentina, Paraguay, and Uruguay, where surface waters converge to form the Parana-Paraguay-Uruguay river system that discharges at the Rio de la Plata estuary. This region of Latin

America is relatively small compared with the extensive mP zones in counterpart latitudes in the Northern Hemisphere that foster great rivers such as the Mississippi or the Rhine.

The hot, wet conditions of the maritime tropical (mT) air mass regions promote extreme river development. Here the great annual rainfall totals generate vast amounts of surface water that are discharged in innumerable streams and several major rivers. The Amazon and Orinoco lowland river complexes are among the largest in the world, reflecting the climatic conditions that caused them. This is a pluvial environment; water pervades every aspect of life, adding to the mystery and attraction of the region.

Ocean Water

Ocean water is a valuable natural resource for Latin America, but sometimes it acts to restrict human activity. As indicated, oceans influence the distribution of climate by acting as heat and moisture reservoirs. They may be such effective storage fields for heat that they contribute most of the energy for the destructive hurricanes that plague the Caribbean lowlands and sometimes extend to the middle latitudes of the U.S. Gulf and Atlantic coasts. These periodic storms are accepted stoically by at least some of the natives, as portrayed by Thomas Hudson in Ernest Hemingway's *Islands in the Stream*.

> Thomas Hudson had studied tropical storms for many years and he could tell from the sky when there was a tropical disturbance long before his barometer showed its presence. He knew how to plot storms and the precautions that should be taken against them. He knew too, what it was to live through a hurricane with the other people of the island and the bond that the hurricane made between all people who had been through it. He also knew that hurricanes could be so bad that nothing could live through them. He always thought, though, that if there was ever one that bad he would like to be there for it and go with the house if she went.

Many locations in the oceans adjacent to Latin America offer sources of food for people and animals. Notable in this regard is the cold Peruvian current that provides a hospitable environment for plankton and the fish that feed on them. Large fish catches, especially of anchovies, have recently entered into world trade and feed chickens in the United States and Europe.

Water provides the opportunity for trade, and much local, national, and international commerce passes over water routes. Landlocked countries such as Bolivia and Paraguay are greatly disadvantaged by their poor access to international commerce; even El Salvador suffers because it does not have a Caribbean port and therefore cannot participate directly in the sea trade of the Gulf of Mexico.

On the other hand, water does separate people and retard commerce in some Latin American areas. The small islands of the Caribbean, for example, are isolated by their surrounding waters. It is one of the greatest ironies of South American economic life that the mighty Amazon, offering passage to oceangoing ships for 3000 miles along its course, is a commercial backwater. Even though the Amazon is much larger than the Mississippi or Rhine systems, its trade volume is virtually insignificant from a world standpoint.

Human Intervention in the Hydrologic Cycle

Perhaps the most widespread human activities that cause change in the hydrologic cycle are the deforestation and seasonal burning practiced in the Latin American grasslands. These activities result in a loss of plant surfaces for evapotranspiration and contribute greatly to the supply of nuclei for condensation. The burning of the tropical rainforest, which approaches conflagration proportions in the pioneer zones on the eastern flanks of the Andes and now along the Amazon penetration roads in Brazil, threatens to deplete one of the world's last remaining stands of virgin timber.

The localized human activities that alter the hydrologic cycle are agriculture (now easier with modern machinery) and urbanization. Vegetation clearing and plow agriculture reduce the storage capacity of the soil, resulting in quick and sometimes destructive runoff. Urbanization changes the temperature and moisture characteristics of local areas by introducing new heat

Grassland Burning in the Western Orinoco

sources and encouraging precipitation with the introduction of dust and other forms of pollution that act as hygroscopic nuclei. In addition, the weather-proofing of cities retards absorption of water by the soil and also reduces cooling by evaporation because the rainfall is quickly directed away through sewers and other underground channels. New construction in the city accelerates erosion and increases the sediment load of streams.

In some cases large cities have outgrown their local supplies of water and now reach out to surrounding moist places in search of more. Mexico City, located in a relatively dry interior basin, offers the opportunity to observe the effects of this problem. Over a long time span the city, originally located by the Aztecs on an island in Lake Texcoco, grew to occupy a much larger area, and the lake was drained. Removal of the groundwater for urban uses as the Spanish city grew caused not only massive dust storms but also compression and "shrinking" of the underlying soil. The result has been an unstable base on which to build and a dependence on more and more distant water supplies today.

LANDFORMS

Latin America's varied and spectacular topography is the product of continental displacement (which may be explained with reference to plate tectonics) and the action of erosion agents such as water, ice, wind, and gravity. The top 60 miles of the earth's surface, the lithosphere, consists of at least six plates that float on top of a plastic layer. One of these plates, the American, is bounded on the east by the Mid-Atlantic Ridge and on the west by a trench that extends from Tierra del Fuego to beyond the Mexico-U.S. border (Figure 1-4).

The Mid-Atlantic Ridge is a divergent plate boundary that acts as a conveyor belt to push the Americas westward into the convergent trench at the western boundary, where the plate is subsumed. At the trench is a zone of crustal instability along which the Andes and other mountain systems have developed. This area is known for its seismic activity; many destructive earthquakes occur along the west coast of Latin America.

Volcanic activity, because of its violence, has been a persistent theme in the history of Latin American settlement. It is impossible to think about Latin America without the eruption of Mt. Pelée, the growth of Paricutín, the repeated seismicity in Managua, or the tremors in Quito. As Simpson so effectively relates about southern Mexico:

> Frequent earthquakes, some of them very destructive of life and property, keep the pious in a continual state of bewilderment over the inscrutable ways of Providence. In February, 1943, for example, after preliminary tremors and subterranean explosions, a fissure opened in a cornfield near the little village of Paricutín,

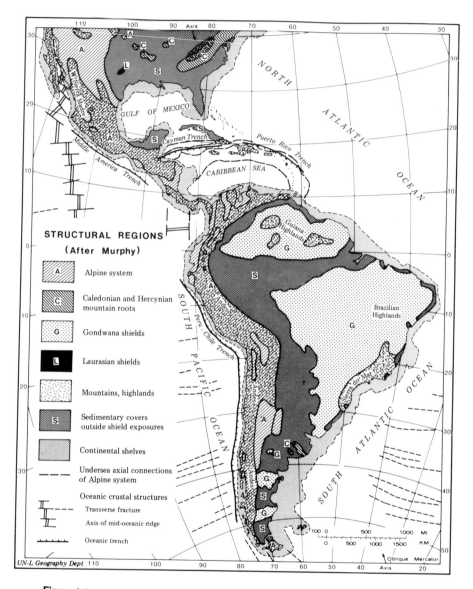

Figure 1.4

Michoacan, through which an immense stream of molten lava poured and inundated the countryside. The village of Parangaricutiro was completely burned, and ten villages and towns in the vicinity suffered varying degrees of damage. Up to its quiet death, on March 2, 1952, Paracutín had vomited a billion or so tons of lava, which probably did less damage than the vast amount of volcanic sand and ashes it spewed over the countryside, killing crops and trees, and rendering the land useless for cultivation. In time the ashes will make new and fertile soil, but meanwhile the destitute population makes a living guiding the swarms of scientists and tourists who come from all parts to observe or exclaim.

Perhaps the most spectacular volcanic explosion in Latin America took place in 1902 when Mt. Pelée exploded on Martinique. The eruption was preceded over several days by ashfalls and a flood of boiling mud but, on May 28 at 7:30 A.M., a black cloud of superheated steam and dust particles issued from the volcano, practically obliterating the city of St. Pièrre and killing nearly all its 30,000 inhabitants within a few seconds. Even ships in the harbor were capsized or burned to the waterline. Only two inhabitants of the city survived, one because he was a prisoner in an underground cell. Mt. Pelée continued erupting for several months, finally stopping on August 30. Destroyed not only was St. Pièrre, the "Paris of the West Indies," but also five other towns on Martinique.

More recently, seismic activity has resulted in the destruction of villages in Guatemala and the virtual elimination of the downtown business district of Managua, Nicaragua. In Managua disaster struck between midnight and 1:00 A.M. on December 23, 1972. The earthquake, recorded at 6.5 on the Richter scale, had its epicenter in the center of the city. The quake reactivated nine parallel faults trending northeast-southwest, practically destroying Managua. After the quake, official reports said there were 8000 to 10,000 people dead, more than 20,000 injured, and 220,000 to 250,000 homeless.

It is impossible to calculate the total destruction in terms of lives and property that has taken place over the course of Latin American history. The cost has been enormous, and greatest where human population is concentrated. Often human influences have increased potential for destruction, since buildings are fragile in the face of powerful tectonic forces. On the other hand, it is becoming obvious that more and more small-scale landforms in Latin America are being created entirely by people. People have been making flat land in the mountains by terracing for thousands of years, but more modern examples also illustrate human ingenuity. The open-pit copper mine at Chuquicamata, Chile, and the strip-mined landscape in parts of Jamaica are good examples of human ability to change Latin America's topography radically.

Landform Diversity in the Ecological Realms

Many of the factors responsible for the diversity of Latin American landforms may be understood if they are grouped according to ecologic realm while remembering the great importance of plate tectonics in setting the stage for these activities.

Sods saturated forming large rivers

Chilean Andean Front from the Air

The cP air mass realm, dominated by cold, dry air most of the year, occurs only in southernmost South America and from place to place in the mountains. During winter, low temperatures in many places cause ice and snow accumulation to exceed ablation, so mechanical weathering by alternate freezing and thawing and ice erosion then prevail in this realm. During summer, temperatures may increase enough for some chemical weathering through solution and some erosion by water or gravity.

The mP realm, found in the moist middle latitudes of Latin America, is a zone of chemical weathering and water erosion all year. Here temperatures are moderate, and moisture is enough to produce extensive river systems with low interfluves. Included here are the lowlands of the Parana-Paraguay-Uruguay river system whose broad valleys also reflect their origin in a structural depression.

Areas dominated by cT air masses throughout the year have become the deserts of Latin America. This desert climate is dominated by an environment with little, none, or undependable rain. In general, gradation is slower in the cT air mass realm, and the effect of the wind as an agent of erosion is relatively greater. The deserts of northern Latin America (including the Sonora and Chihuahua) and southern Latin America (including the Atacama and Patagonia) are related to the semipermanent, subtropical, high-pressure belts located at about 30° N and S latitudes or to their effective distance from the oceans.

The mT realm is distinguished by warm temperatures and heavy rainfall. Here chemical weathering predominates, creating a deep waste mantle. Because of the excess moisture, soils are saturated and mass movement is com-

Each enviro. defs distinct land form as a result of geologic processes + of the climate + H2O conditions in that area.

mon. Large river systems such as the Orinoco and the Amazon occupy structural depressions in this realm. Their landforms are low and rounded, with gentle slopes.

Each of the environmental realms contains distinctive landforms, the result of geologic processes and of the climate and water conditions prevalent in each area. In depressions where temperatures are warm and moisture is abundant, over the course of time landforms have come to exhibit low relief, and broad river valleys dominate the landscape. At the other end of the environmental scale in mountainous areas where moisture is scarce, wind erosion is accentuated and landforms are much rougher and more angular. In intermediate locations or in zones of recent crustal movement, stream profiles are steeper, valleys are more vee-shaped, and the topography is highly dissected. Each of these environments presents special difficulties and offers distinct opportunities for human use.

SOIL

Humans have also altered soil processes. Differences related to climate, H2O, landform + vegetation. Both organic + mineral. Soils are found in L.A.

Soil is a biological laboratory that is closely related to climate, water resources, landforms, and vegetation in the Latin American environmental complex. Human beings have altered soil processes as they have interfered with other physical processes in the region.

Both organic and mineral soils are found in Latin America, but mineral soils are better known, cover a wider area, and are more important agriculturally than organic soils. These mineral soils, containing only about 5 percent organic material, deserve further attention.

Controls of Soil Development

Climate influential control over soil development + organic matter in soil. As to ↑ amount of organic soil material ↓ + as moisture ↑, the amount ↑. ↑ organic material leads to higher soil fertility + greater crop productivity.

Mineral soils in Latin America may be analyzed in terms of their composition and properties as they have developed in response to environmental controls. Climate is an influential control over soil development. Soil develops slowly on sloping land where water erosion is prominent. Erosion is accelerated where the natural vegetation cover is removed, as in cultivation. Serious erosion occurs on arable land that has been planted to row crops without considering slope.

Perhaps most important, climate exerts a dominant influence on the development of organic material in the soil. In general, as temperature increases, the amount of organic soil material decreases and as effective moisture increases, the amount of such material increases. Increased organic material leads to higher soil fertility and greater crop productivity. The high humus content of the grass-covered loess soils of Argentina's humid *pampas*, for example, is responsible for their high productivity (Figure 1-5).

Tine also effects soil

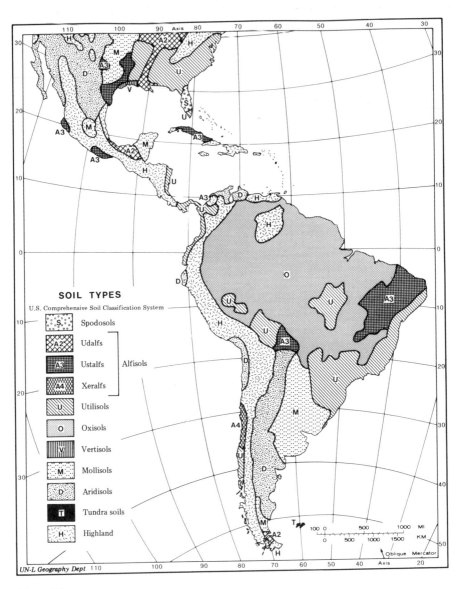

SOIL TYPES

U.S. Comprehensive Soil Classification System

S	Spodosols
A2	Udalfs
A3	Ustalfs Alfisols
A4	Xeralfs
U	Utilisols
O	Oxisols
V	Vertisols
M	Mollisols
D	Aridisols
T	Tundra soils
H	Highland

UN-L Geography Dept

Figure 1.5

Although climate is the most important control of soil development over extensive areas, other factors are important in small areas or over limited time. For example, in a young soil that has not lain in place long enough to be radically changed by exposure to the elements of climate, properties are determined by its parent material. Sedentary parent materials eventually are weathered to great depth, and their soils may be leached of their dissolvable mineral and plant nutrient constituents. This is generally true of soils developed on sedentary parent materials in the humid tropics of Latin America, particularly over igneous rocks. Alternatively, soils developed from parent materials newly transported by water, ice, or wind have not lain in place long enough to be severely leached and therefore the soil may contain more plant nutrients. The floodplains of major streams in Latin America are prized for agriculture because their soils are "new," contain more plant nutrients, and may be flooded seasonally to infuse a new layer of soil material containing more plant nutrients and minerals. The banks of the Amazon and its tributaries are more densely populated than interior locations because of the ease of transportation and the availability of fish and other aquatic life for food and also because soils here, if properly drained, are generally more fertile and more productive of crops than the higher, more severely leached soils on the interfluves.

The properties of a soil also are influenced by vegetation. As plants grow and die, they are incorporated into the soil's supply of organic material or humus. Where there is little vegetation, as in Latin America's arid regions, little humus accumulates. The wet lowland tropics of Latin America also have humus-poor soils, because high temperatures lead to rapid decomposition of organic debris and encourage the rapid utilization of this material by fast-growing vegetation. Where environmental conditions are more moderate, as in the middle latitudes of Latin America's mP realm, humus and nutrients are allowed to accumulate, and a more fertile and productive soil results.

Topography affects soil development because slope and contour permit or restrict the growth of the soil profile. Obviously, no soil is permitted to develop on the sheer faces of mountains. Even gently sloping land may allow sheet erosion and gullying to occur, quickly stripping away layers of soil that may have taken thousands of years to develop. Such erosion is especially severe where the vegetation has been altered, as in the case of forest removal. On the other hand, there are many places in Latin America, as in the humid *pampas* of Argentina or the high basins of Mexico, where interior drainage is prevalent and water accumulates. This waterlogging in some local areas is enough to cause the development of an organic bog soil instead of a mineral soil.

The activities of people are crucial in soil formation. Agriculture and settlement, in particular, may disturb the natural development of soil. Some soils may benefit from human influences, since their agricultural potential may be improved by the elimination of pests or the addition of certain minerals necessary for healthy plant growth. Other soils suffer from misuse through erosion of their top layers or the depletion of essential minerals or nutrients by improper cultivation or poor conservation practices. These changes are especially pronounced where people are concentrated, and they will become more widespread as the demand for food in Latin America increases in the coming decades. The time may have already arrived when all arable soils are cultivated and have become "acculturated." Succeeding generations of Latin American farmers will be obligated to use better conservation methods and more scientific management techniques if they are to equal current agricultural output, much less keep pace with expected population increases.

Soil Orders

Mineral soils in Latin America that develop similar composition and properties under the influence of similar controls may be grouped into soil orders. There are three general great soil orders: zonal, intrazonal, and azonal.

Zonal soils are those occurring over large areas that have similar properties developed mainly under the long-term influence of climate. These soils are widespread, having within them recognizable zones, layers, or horizons that are grouped together into a complete soil profile. The layers may be distinguished on the basis of color or constituent material. The top, or *A*, horizon, for example, may be darker in color than the lower horizons because more humus has accumulated. The next deeper, or *B*, horizon may be lighter in color because of the lower humus content and because it has received deposits of easily dissolved minerals (often lighter-colored minerals such as the calcium carbonate) carried by water passing down through the soil profile, the leaching process. The *A* and *B* horizons, constituting the solum, overlie the *C* horizon, where soil is being developed from the original parent material.

Zonal soils in Latin America result from at least four processes: gleization, podzolization, laterization, and calcification. One of these processes dominates each environmental realm of Latin America.

Gleization, the accumulation of organic materials in the top layers of the soil, occurs primarily in the cP realm. Here, under cold, dry conditions, the soils tend to be shallow, acidic, and rich in humus. Gleization is the soil-forming process that dominates in the southern reaches of the South American continent as well as in high elevations throughout the region. These soils are not particularly fertile; this, together with the climatic extremes of the areas in which they develop, precludes their intensive use.

Podzolization, the accumulation of silica in the top layers of the soil, is dominant in the cool, wet mP realm. Biochemical activity of the soil here is slow as the result of cool temperatures, and there is likely to be great concentrations of humus here under the mixed forests of the middle latitudes. Consequently, these soils tend to be more fertile and more agriculturally productive than other types. Over time, seasonal rains percolate through the organic debris of the forest, forming weak acids that leach out the easily dissolved minerals and leave behind gray silicon oxides. In warmer, wetter places this process intensifies.

Laterization, the accumulation of iron and aluminum oxides in the top layers of the soil, occurs in the hot, wet tropics of Latin America's mT realm.

[handwritten annotations at top: "Intrazonal - develop horizons under influence of climate, H2O conditions for parent material. Isolated pockets in wide zone. Conform to environ, take on local characteristics. Azonal - do not have well-developed profiles due to limited time or specialized topographic conditions"]

Here organic debris quickly decays through bacterial action, making possible rapid absorption of nutrients by plants. This quick nutrient cycle leads to the accumulation of nutrients in the vegetation itself instead of in the soil and, under the hot, wet conditions, nutrients not absorbed by plants are carried away by the large volumes of water. Agriculture is poor, except on the floodplain soils, because of the few plant nutrients available. The end product of this process is an infertile soil covered by lush natural vegetation, an environmental paradox whose complexity is exceeded only by the myths surrounding it.

[handwritten: Zonal] Calcification, the accumulation of carbonates in the top layers of the soil, is accentuated in the hot, dry areas of the cT realm. The relative absence of water and, therefore, the reduced leaching make the characteristically whitish soil rich in dissolved salts but low in humus. The white color results from the evaporation of water at the soil surface and the resultant deposition of its minerals there. Where water is supplied under carefully controlled conditions, these soils may become highly productive of agricultural crops, as in the booming oases of Mexico's northwestern border region.

Intrazonal soils are different from zonal soils in that they develop horizons principally under the influence of local climate, water conditions, or parent material. They usually form isolated pockets of distinctive soil within the more widely distributed zonal soil orders. They take on the local characteristics because of their environments, becoming hydromorphic if waterlogged, halomorphic if subjected to salt concentrations, or calcimorphic if developed on calcium-rich parent materials, for example.

Azonal soils, like intrazonal types, are limited in extent. They are called azonal because they do not have well-developed profiles, perhaps because of limited time or specialized topographic conditions. Lithosols, for example, are the thin soils that cling to the steep mountain slopes of the Andes. Alluvial soils and aeolian soils are of great agricultural significance on river floodplains and in the *pampas*, respectively, because they are young, transported soils and therefore are likely to contain more plant nutrients.

[handwritten: Human interaction + interference alters the soil. Agriculture is a pervasive factor in soil development]

Acculturated Soils

People are important agents of soil development in Latin America and can be responsible for climate, water, landform, and vegetation change. Alterations in these aspects of the physical environment influence changes in soil, and the soil itself is changed by direct human interference.

Agriculture is a pervasive factor in soil development, even when traditional techniques of cultivation are employed. For example, fire is often used in clearing fields for shifting cultivation in the tropics, and this may bake the top layer of the soil, changing its physical structure, or eliminate certain microorganisms, affecting the development of other soil characteristics. Replacement of natural vegetation by cultivated crops may draw plant nutrients from the soil more quickly and lead to quick depletion of the soil's fertility. Consequently, farmers must move to new plots as their yields decline. Although shifting cultivation is perhaps the most environmentally sound method of farming in the tropical realm, contemporary population and economic pressures now force agriculturalists to use more land, leaving less time for necessary fallowing. The conflict between environmentally acceptable and economically desirable uses of the soil is likely to grow in the coming years.

The "acculturation" of soils is taking place in all of Latin America's environmental realms as people use fertile (and marginally fertile) soils wherever they are found in the region. In general, the greatest changes have been in and around urban areas. Urbanization is related to soil use in that fertile soils attract farmers and allow food surpluses to be produced for sale to the residents of growing agricultural service centers. Many of these agricultural centers have then become foci of further economic development, resulting in a greater demand for agricultural goods to supply the expanding urban populations. This cycle continues as long as farmers in the city's hinterland are capable of generating necessary food and other agricultural goods. Although Latin American cities are expanding rapidly in the present century and are likely to continue growing for some time, their ultimate economic base lies in an agrarian countryside that has suffered for centuries from severe exploitation and neglect.

vegetation - indicator of environmental relationships + human activities

VEGETATION ASSOCIATIONS

Vegetation is a corollary and useful indicator of environmental relationships and human activities in Latin America. Natural vegetation is a mirror for the distribution of climate, water resources, landforms, and soils in the region and is the first factor of the environment influenced by human settlement and economic activities (Figure 1-6).

most important factor influencing distribution of natural vegetation is climate, as reflected by

Environmental Influences
temp + moisture. Solar @ is vital force behind plant growth (photosynthesis)

The most important environmental factor influencing the distribution of natural vegetation in Latin America is climate, as reflected in temperature and moisture conditions. Solar energy is the vital force behind plant growth because it supplies the power for photosynthesis. Biochemical activity in plants increases with higher temperature when moisture is adequate. As a result of variations in temperature and moisture conditions in Latin America, there are several more or less homogeneous natural vegetation associations.

Specially adapted plants occupy each environmental realm. Hydrophytes (water plants) are common in lakes, swamps, and other poorly drained areas, for example, while xerophytes (desert plants) populate arid regions. Usually

Hydrophyte plants commonly found around water. Common in lakes, swamps + other wet, poorly drained areas
Xerophytic - desert plants - dry arid regions

Figure 1.6

the number and variety of plants that compose a vegetation association are great, so the association is named after the dominant vegetation. For example, trees are the dominant plants in a forest association even though there may be many other plant types there, such as bushes, grass, reeds, or vines.

4 types ① broadleaf evergreen ② broadleaf deciduous
③ needleleaf evergreen and ④ needleleaf deciduous.

30   PHYSICAL ENVIRONMENTS OF LATIN AMERICA

Forest Associations. Water must be present in large amounts and temperatures should be warm during most of the year for trees to be dominant in any natural vegetation association. Trees may cope with seasonal temperature or moisture stress by suspending some physical functions (such as dropping leaves, thus reducing evaporation to a minimum) or by one variety of tree being replaced by a sturdier type (broadleaf evergreen trees are replaced by broadleaf deciduous or needleleaf evergreen trees as environmental conditions become less favorable over space).

On the basis of temperature and moisture conditions, at least four principal types of forest can be distinguished: those dominated by broadleaf evergreen trees, by broadleaf deciduous trees, by needleleaf evergreen trees, or by needleleaf deciduous trees. In some places these trees are found in pure stands; in other places mixed forest predominates.

The tropical rainforest is the most luxuriant of all the Latin American forest types. It is found in places such as the Amazon Basin and other wet tropical lowlands where temperatures are consistently high (usually about 65 °F or above), leading to rapid biochemical activity, and there is no pronounced dry period (rainfall usually exceeds 200 inches annually), allowing growth to occur without interruption.

The structure of the tropical rainforest may consist of as many as three layers of forest trees and several other plant components. At the top is a discontinuous grouping of crowns as high as 90 to 120 feet. The second set of crowns, at 50 to 90 feet, tends to be a continuous canopy, shading the lower vegetation. The lowest set is much shorter, between 15 and 50 feet in height, and much less dense. Thousands of different tree species may be found over limited areas. Where sufficient light penetrates the canopy, other lower plants such as herbs, vines, saprophytes, epiphytes, and parasites are found. The variety of species and luxuriance of the tropical rainforest is legendary, as this selection from naturalist W.H. Hudson's *Green Mansions* (1904) illustrates.

> Here Nature is unapproachable with her green, airy canopy, a sun-impregnated cloud—cloud above cloud; and though the highest may be unreached by the eye, the beams yet filter through, illuming the wide spaces beneath—chamber succeeded by chamber, each with its own special lights and shadows.

Forests at the tropical margins and continuing on through Latin America's middle latitudes are dominated by broadleaf deciduous or needleleaf evergreen trees. Where rainfall is seasonal or temperatures are lower or change markedly with the seasons, deciduous trees are common. Needleleaf trees survive in places too cold or dry for the adaptive mechanisms of deciduous types; their thick, needlelike leaves reduce moisture loss by transpiration, their thick bark and sugar-rich sap resist the cold, a shallow root system enables them to grow in thin soils, and they are tolerant of highly acid conditions. In the mid-

dle-latitude forest there is only a single story and little undergrowth because of
the lower temperature and moisture levels.

Grassland Associations. Latin American grasslands, which may be the result of
natural or cultural influences, have a typically continuous vegetation cover
only occasionally interrupted by isolated trees. The grasslands are composed
of either perennials or annuals that vary in height from a few inches to several
feet, depending on climate and soil conditions.

The tropical grassland (savanna) is found at the dry margins of the forest,
although there is no direct evidence that it is the result of climatic influence. It
is believed that most of this grassland has been formed by repeated burning by
people or is due to local soil conditions that promote rapid percolation.

Further toward the South Pole or at higher elevations somewhat shorter
grass prevails, ranging from tall prairie to short steppe. Meadow grass is found
above the tree line on high mountain slopes or in the high basins of the central
Andes in Colombia, Ecuador, Peru, and Bolivia.

Desert Associations. As dryness increases in the environmental realms of Latin
America, grassland gives way to desert vegetation. The vegetation of both the
cool, dry deserts and the warm, dry deserts is sparse and specialized. All plants
in the true deserts are xerophytic, adapted to a limited water supply.

Among the special qualities insuring the survival of desert plants are a
short growth period among the perennials, a quick life cycle among the annuals, the ability in both to store moisture over extended periods of time, small
size, special root structure (extending to deep water sources or spreading out
over an extensive area near the surface), and seeds designed to withstand prolonged drought. In spite of these characteristics, vegetation is nearly absent in
places such as the Atacama, one of the driest deserts in the world. The northern Mexican deserts seem lush by comparison, but rainfall is seasonal and
must be supplemented by irrigation if the deserts are to be farmed.

The Distribution of Vegetation

Because natural vegetation is the mirror image of other environmental factors,
particularly climate, its distribution correlates well with the environmental
realms already outlined.

The tropical rainforests, composed of broadleaf evergreen trees, are
found in the mT environmental realm where temperature averages and moisture totals are high. Associated with the rainforests are extensive rivers, chemical weathering, and transportation of soil nutrients. Laterization processes
have produced the infertile soils that support these luxuriant forests.

In the cT environmental realms are the xerophytic plants of the deserts of
Latin America. Here is little moisture, and soils produced by calcification

processes are prominent. Physical weathering and the combined effects of wind and water erosion have produced the angular landforms of this realm.

Needleleaf evergreen and broadleaf deciduous trees predominate in the mP environmental realms of Latin America. Here adequate moisture and cool temperatures encourage chemical weathering, and podzolization processes produce the soils associated with forest conditions.

In the cP environmental realms are some hardy trees, mountain grasses, and low, xerophytic plants. Physical weathering is dominant in this realm, and gleization processes have produced thin soils in locations where soil development is possible.

Transitional vegetation types, primarily grasslands, occupy marginal areas between major environmental realms. Tundra vegetation is the transitional type between the cold desert of the cP environmental realm and the needleleaf evergreen-broadleaf deciduous forest of the mP environmental realm. The altitudinal counterpart of the tundra is meadow grass vegetation, found above the tree lines and below the snowswept high slopes. In the middle latitudes prairie grasses form the boundary zone between the tropical rainforests and the subtropical deserts.

Vegetation as a Resource and a Barrier

The four principal vegetation associations of Latin America offer advantages and disadvantages for resource development. Forests result from complex environmental conditions but disappear rapidly under human attack such as they are experiencing in the Amazon rainforest. Grasslands in extensive areas such as the *pampas* may be the product of repeated burning by people. Deserts may be among the driest in the world, but they do bloom under careful management, as in the Peruvian coastal oasis settlements. Domesticated plants are replacing native vegetation at every turn, accentuating once again the growing influence of people in environmental affairs and underscoring the delicate balance between population and natural resources in Latin America.

New Environmental Relationships?

Over the course of space and time in Latin America, people have interacted with the environment to project at least four images: environment as God; environment as prey; environment as illusion; and environment as obstacle. There are still many people in Latin America whose relationships with the environment are based on ritualized reverence, and many views of the region are illusions based on incomplete evidence or biased perception, but today it seems that there is a strong adversary relationship between people and environment. The specters of advanced technology and increasing population menace the environmental base of Latin American life and may also threaten world environmental stability.

Unfortunately, there is no ready prognosis for the future of Latin American environmental relations. If the recent past is a reliable guide, environmental deterioration is likely to continue, and at an increasing rate. Arresting this trend will be difficult. If, on the other hand, a workable marriage can be arranged between piety and progress, Latin America's environment will survive and will sustain the region's rapid population growth.

BIBLIOGRAPHY

Blume, H. *The Caribbean Islands*, London, Longman, 1974.

Fittkau, E. J., et al., *Biogeography and Ecology of South America*, The Hague, Junk, 1968.

Hill, A. D. (ed.), *Latin American Development Issues*, East Lansing, Mich., CLAG Publications, 1973.

James, P. E., *Latin America*, 4th ed., New York, Odyssey Press, 1969.

Lentnek, B., R. L. Carmin, and T. L. Martinson (eds.), *Geographic Research on Latin America: Benchmark 1970*, Muncie, Ind., Ball State University, 1971.

Lowenthal, D., "The Caribbean Region," in M. W. Mikesell (ed.), *Geographers Abroad: Essays on the Problems and Prospects of Research in Foreign Areas*, Chicago, University of Chicago Press, 1973, pp. 47–69.

Momsen, R. P., Jr. (ed.), *Geographical Analysis for Development in Latin America and the Caribbean*, Chapel Hill, N.C., CLAG Publications, 1975.

Parsons, James J., "The Contribution of Geography to Latin American Studies," in C. Wagley (ed.), *Social Science Research on Latin America*, New York, Columbia University Press, 1964, pp. 33–85.

———, "Latin America," in M. W. Mikesell (ed.), *Geographers Abroad: Essays on the Problems and Prospects of Research in Foreign Areas*, Chicago, University of Chicago, 1973, pp. 16–46.

Platt, R. S., *Latin America: Countrysides and United Regions*, New York, McGraw-Hill, 1942.

West, R. C., and J. P. Augelli, *Middle America: Its Lands and Peoples*, 2nd ed., Englewood Cliffs, N.J., Prentice-Hall, 1976.

West, R. C. (ed.), *Natural Environment and Early Cultures: Handbook of Middle American Indians*, Vol. 1, Austin, University of Texas Press, 1964.

CHAPTER 2

Aboriginal and Colonial Geography of Latin America

Robert C. West

[handwritten annotation: L.A. + the aboriginal civilization - like that of a 16th century European society, European occupation has longest cont. record]

Latin America has the longest continuous record of European occupation of any part of the New World. It was also the locale of the aboriginal civilizations of America—the Aztec, Mayan, and Incan cultures, whose way of life in some respects equaled or excelled that of sixteenth-century European society. The aboriginal and colonial heritage of Latin America is strong still today, and many aspects of the contemporary scene are difficult to comprehend without some knowledge of the developments of the past 500 years.

This chapter points out some of the salient features of aboriginal and colonial life that have strongly influenced the land and people of Latin America. The aboriginal scene on the eve of European conquest is first considered, followed by the story of the European invasion and its influence on the native inhabitants. In dealing with the historical geography of the colonial period, emphasis is placed on the exploitation of human and natural resources by the three main groups of European settlers—Spaniards, Portuguese, and North Europeans. *[handwritten annotation: European colonial development - aboriginal pattern in L.A.]*

Aboriginal Patterns on the Eve of Conquest

The aboriginal background is basic to understanding European colonial development in Latin America. In most of Spanish America, especially, the aboriginal element was as significant as the European in the evolution of colonial life and landscape. Today, the people of southern Mexico, Central America, and the central Andean countries are still considered to be largely Amerind in character, although they have been variously modified by European culture.

On the eve of European conquest Mexico, the West Indies, and Central and South America were occupied by many aboriginal groups that varied greatly in cultural attainments; they ranged from extremely primitive bands who still practiced Stone Age culture to highly civilized states such as the Aztec and Inca. Generally, the influence of aboriginal groups on European colonial development varied with their degree of cultural attainments and population densities. The civilized, densely peopled states of Mexico and the central Andes obviously fashioned the pattern of Spanish colonial settlement and economic development in those areas differently and more thoroughly than the simple forest tribes influenced the course of Portuguese occupation of Brazil.

Two fundamentally different types of aboriginal economies, or patterns of livelihood, prevailed in Latin America just prior to European contact: (1) the *nonagricultural economies*, characterized by gathering, hunting, and fishing, which occurred mainly in the extratropical zones of the southern and northern peripheries of Latin America, and (2) the *agricultural economies*, which were practiced mainly in the tropical highlands and lowlands (Figure 2-1). Because the farming areas contained the great bulk of aboriginal population, including the two centers of civilization (Mexico and the central Andes), they were far more significant in European colonization than the nonfarming sectors.

The Nonagricultural Economies

Low population densities, impermanent settlement, and rudimentary technology characterized most of the nonfarming peoples. Many inhabited isolated refuge areas into which they may have been pushed by invaders having a higher culture. Among the most primitive of these groups were the Fuegian shellfish gatherers of the cold, wet southern end of South America. Probably never more than 15,000 in number, these Stone Age people inhabited one of the least desirable parts of the continent. Europeans delayed effective contact with them until the nineteenth century and, since then, these primitives have become practically extinct. In the West Indies a similar shellfish-gathering group, the Ciboney, who once occupied all of the Greater Antilles, had been almost wholly replaced by more sophisticated farming peoples at the time of Spanish contact.

North of the Fuegian peoples of southernmost South America there extends a large area that was inhabited by small bands of hunters, whom anthropologists have termed the "*pampean* Indians." This region includes most of Argentina and all of Uruguay. Physically it is composed of the arid, bush and grass-covered Patagonia plateau and the grassy plains of the *pampas*. Little is known of the Indians who occupied this area until after they had acquired cer-

addition of horses hunters became mobile & wealthy, hunting techniques highly specialized population grew. social organ. complex. Probably changed w/ horse.

36   ABORIGINAL AND COLONIAL GEOGRAPHY OF LATIN AMERICA

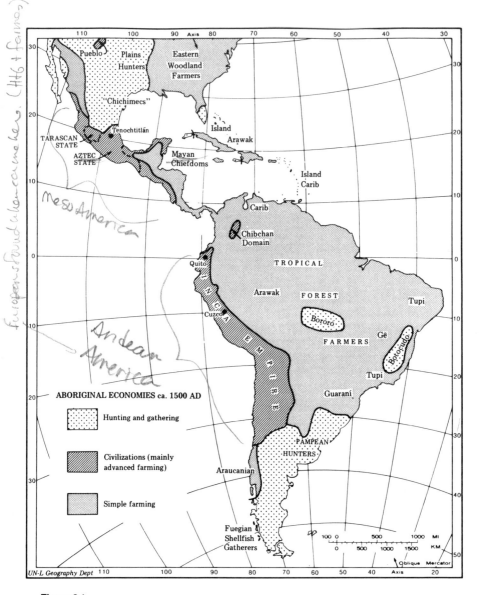

Europeans found when came here. (H+6 + farmers)

Meso America

Andean America

ABORIGINAL ECONOMIES ca. 1500 AD

Hunting and gathering

Civilizations (mainly advanced farming)

Simple farming

Figure 2.1

tain European traits, such as the horse for riding, in the middle of the seventeenth century. It is known that they hunted the guanaco (one of the American camels related to the domesticated llama of the Andes), the rhea (or American ostrich), and several small mammals. Spears and bolas were the main weapons, and the *pampeans* apparently wandered from place to place seeking animals and plants for food. After the acquisition of the horse, these hunters became mobile and warlike, their hunting techniques became highly specialized, their population grew, and their social organization became complex. Aided by Indian horsemen who had migrated from Chile, they evolved into a formidable aboriginal military force who helped delay European occupation of the fertile *pampas* of Argentina until well after independence. Not until the 1850s were the last of the *pampean* bands subdued and placed on reservations. Interesting parallels can be drawn between the *pampeans* of Argentina and Uruguay and the Plains Indians of the United States and Canada. Both hunted large mammals in similar natural environments; the culture of both was profoundly changed along similar lines by the adoption of the European horse at about the same time; and the subsequent relations between native and European evolved similarly.

Throughout the vast forested and grass-covered Brazilian highlands, small groups of hunters and gatherers formed enclaves within a large area of farming economy. Examples include the Bororó of interior Brazil and the Botocudo near the Atlantic coast. The Bororó and the Gê-speaking bands who occupied much of the Brazilian plateau seem to have been hunters and gatherers who occasionally dabbled in farming, having either learned incipient cultivation from their agricultural neighbors or having given up a former agricultural skill in their habitat of difficult soils by the time of Portuguese contact in the sixteenth century. Many of the present-day primitives who inhabit the headwaters of rivers within the Brazilian plateau are descendants of the once widespread Gê-speaking bands.

Hunting and gathering peoples occupied a large territory on the northern periphery of Latin America, especially in the deserts of northern Mexico and the peninsula of Baja California. The inhabitants of the peninsula were the least numerous and culturally the least advanced of any Mexican aboriginal groups. After Spanish missionary contact in the seventeenth century, the lowly Baja Californians quickly disappeared because of culture shock and disease. The desert nomads of north-central Mexico, however, were more numerous and more culturally advanced than the Californians, particularly in social organization. Warlike and mobile, especially after the acquisition of the horse from the Spaniards in the seventeenth century, these people, collectively called "Chichimecs," became a partial barrier to northward expansion of Spanish settlement from central Mexico during the colonial period. The hunting and gathering economy of northern Mexico can be considered a southern extension of a similar culture that covered much of the arid portion of western North America, which included groups such as the Apache, Piute, and Shoshone. Hunting and gathering bands also extended to the Pacific coast of North America, where the "Digger" Indians of southern California and the acorn gatherers of central California formed a relatively dense population that was missionized during Spain's political expansion into upper California in the late eighteenth century.

¹⁄₃ LA. agriculture - occupied by farmers more settled.
more abundant food supplies + plant cultivation, pop ↑.
Great part of land for agri + farming ½ coming from hunt /
gather.

The Agricultural Economies

More than two-thirds of Latin American territory was occupied by farmers prior to the conquest. In contrast to the nomadic hunters and gatherers, most of the farmers were sedentary people, settled in hamlets or villages ranging in size from perhaps a dozen to several thousand inhabitants. With a more reliable and abundant food supply through plant cultivation, the densities of farming populations were usually much greater than those of nonagricultural peoples. By far the greater part of the land devoted to agriculture was occupied by simple farmers whose cultivation techniques were rudimentary, at least one-half of whose food came from hunting and fishing, and whose social organization was based largely on tribal affiliations. The use of more advanced agricultural practices and nearly complete reliance on domesticated plants and animals for food was found mainly among the aboriginal civilizations in highland Mexico and the Andean area.

The Simple Farmers. Most of the simple farmers used a type of tillage system called slash-and-burn, or swidden, one of our most ancient farming techniques. In the Americas it was practiced on steep, wooded slopes in the highlands and on both slopes and level land within the lowland forests. Today this simple aboriginal method still prevails in subsistence farming in many areas from Mexico to Chile.[1]

Tropical Forest Farmers of South America. The simple farmers who inhabited the tropical forest of Brazil and northern South America cultivated starchy root crops, such as manioc (both bitter and sweet varieties), sweet potatoes, and arrowroot as their main staples. Except for the peanut, few protein-yielding crops were grown and, in most areas, maize (corn) was secondary or absent. Such crops were raised in temporary clearings along riverbanks, where the more fertile alluvial soils occur. Interfluves, characterized by highly leached, infertile soils, were rarely cropped. Protein foods consisted almost wholly of fish and game obtained from the river and forest.

Because they were riverine people and expert canoers, these tropical forest people easily migrated long distances. Thus, long before Portuguese contact, the Tupi-speaking bands of the lower Amazon Basin had spread southward

---

[1]Slash-and-burn farming involves the following procedures. Small plots are cleared within the forest and the brush is burned. Seeds or tubers are then planted in holes punched into the ash-covered soil with a sharpened stick, or dibble. However, after 2 or 3 years of cultivation, yields usually decline because of loss of soil fertility and weed competition. The plot is then abandoned for perhaps 10 to 20 years to permit soil rejuvenation and the reestablishment of second-growth forest. After that time, the same plot may be recleared and the cycle repeated. Meanwhile, in the surrounding forest, the farmer has cleared new plots that go through the same cycle of cropping and abandonment. Thus the farmer is continually shifting small fields and, occasionally, an entire village may be moved to a new site when land around it has become overcropped.

along the Atlantic coast and inland as far as southern Brazil, and the related Guaraní had occupied the fertile lands of eastern Paraguay. The Arawaks of the upper Amazon had settled along most of the western tributaries of that vast basin and, by the beginning of the Christian era, had migrated into the Greater Antilles as far as Cuba and the Bahamas, taking their manioc–sweet potato farming complex with them. Likewise, bands of Caribs from the Guianas and Venezuela had island-hopped into the Lesser Antilles by A.D. 1400. Moreover, groups speaking languages related to Chibchan pushed northward by land from Colombia into the tropical forests of southern and eastern Central America, carrying South American life-styles into that area. Such migrations caused Amazonian-type farming based on slash-and-burn cultivation of root crops to become the most widespread agricultural complex in aboriginal America. Manioc and other tubers are still the basic foodstuffs throughout this vast region.

Aboriginal population densities within this area, although they varied greatly, were much above those of nonagricultural peoples. Because of an abundant and stable food supply from land and water, the riverbanks and sea coasts had densities up to 30 persons per square mile (Denevan, 1966a, 1976). The account of Orellana's renowned journey down the Amazon River in 1542 mentions the large and almost continuous villages along it, and the Tupi settlements on the Brazilian coast were probably just as numerous. The Greater Antilles, however, was the most densely settled area occupied by natives of Amazonian culture. The island Arawak developed a completely sedentary type of farming characterized by the construction of permanent, raised, circular beds (or mounds) for planting surfaces that produced prodigious crops (Sauer, 1966). At Spanish contact (1492) more than 1 million natives inhabited Hispaniola (presently Haiti and the Dominican Republic), giving it an overall population density of 35 persons per square mile.[2]

A minor area of simple farming occurred in Central Chile, well outside the tropics, forming the southernmost extent of agriculture in South America. Inhabited by Indians of Araucanian speech, the northern, sparsely wooded part of the area was under Incan rule, while the southern, heavily forested sector from the Maule River to Chiloé Island was held by independent tribes at the time of Spanish contact. Using slash-and-burn methods, the Araucanians cultivated maize and potatoes as the main staples, supplemented by beans, squash, and various local grains. In contrast to the docile tropical forest farm-

[2]Estimates of the aboriginal population for Hispaniola have been reviewed by Cook and Borah (1971), who suggest that the island contained as many as 7 to 8 million inhabitants on the eve of Spanish contact. Recently, extensive areas of raised beds in the form of ridges have been discovered in the wet Mamoré plains in northeastern Bolivia and northern Colombia. Preliminary study indicates that such beds were used for cultivation and could have supported a dense population; their age, however, has not yet been determined (Denevan, 1970).

ers of Brazil and the Greater Antilles, the Araucanians were fiercely warlike, and they succeeded in blocking permanent Spanish settlement in their forested land until the nineteenth century. The modern descendants of these people, called Mapuches, still practice slash-and-burn farming on reservations in south-central Chile.

Simple Farmers of Mexico and Central America. A major area of simple farming covered the mountain slopes and adjacent lowlands of northern Central America and southern Mexico, with an extension into northwestern Mexico. In these areas the slash-and-burn farmers cultivated mainly seed crops; maize, beans, and squash were the most important ones. Root crops, such as the sweet potato and sweet manioc, were secondary. The crop triad of maize, beans, and squash affords a fairly well-balanced diet; partly for that reason, hunting and fishing were less important than among the forest Indians of South America. Maize furnishes the starch element and is also rich in oil and certain proteins; beans provide most of the protein component; and squash offers a variety of essential vitamins. Indians cultivated all three crops together in the same plot, as many do today. Aboriginal maize foods, such as tortillas, tamales, and atole, still form the basic food staples throughout Mexico and most of Central America.

Although they are classed as simple farmers, most of the lowland inhabitants of southern Mexico, such as the Huastec and Totonac of the Gulf coast, were descendants of older civilizations or had been engulfed by Aztec conquests at the time of European contact. Slash-and-burn farming was the rule in the Yucatan peninsula, even during the height of Mayan civilization several centuries previous to the coming of the Spaniards. It is still the rule among Mayan subsistence farmers throughout the peninsula.

The simple farmers of northwestern Mexico practiced slash-and-burn cultivation on hill slopes and along stream bottoms. Within the Sierra Madre Occidental, the Tarahumar and Tepehuan formed the largest groups, while along the coast various tribes, such as the Yaqui and Mayo, planted along the river floodplains, utilizing the moist alluvial soil when the annual floods receded. Farther north in Sonora, the Ópata and Pima groups had some knowledge of irrigation, and the Pueblo Indians along the upper Rio Grande in New Mexico had evolved a sophisticated system of canal irrigation. Having a sizable population, such groups would later attract Spanish conquest and settlement into what is now U.S. territory.

The Aboriginal Civilizations. At European contact, two main areas of aboriginal civilization had evolved in the New World. The northern area, which anthropologists call *Mesoamerica*, included southern Mexico and northern Central America. The southern area, called *Andean America*, covered the central Andean highlands and adjacent Pacific coast of South America. At least three-quarters of the total aboriginal population south of the Rio Grande was concentrated within these two areas, which comprised less than one-fifth of the total land surface of Latin American territory.

The inhabitants of these two areas had developed several key cultural attributes that gave them civilized status. Among these were (1) a highly stratified social class system, in which a small group of nobles and priests held tight control over a large proletariat for public labor, tribute, or civic duties; (2) the concept of a political state, forged by organized military operations; (3) intensive cultivation techniques, which could produce an abundant and stable food supply; (4) the use of metals, primarily gold and silver for ceremonial ornamentation and secondarily some of the lesser metals (copper and bronze) for utilitarian purposes; and (5) the growth of true cities, characterized by large concentrations of population, urban functions such as manufacturing and various public services, and the presence of monumental architecture. Such attributes, especially the great mass of organized and subservient manpower and the presence of precious metals, attracted European conquest and gave rise to the two great centers of Spanish exploitation and settlement in the New World: Mexico and Peru.

Mesoamerica. By A.D. 1500, two strong military states existed in the highlands of central Mexico. These were the Aztec realm in the east and the Tarascan state in the west. The Aztecs had established the larger and more populous of the two states and, when the Spaniards arrived in 1519, the Aztecs had extended their political hegemony from the Pánuco River in the northeast to the modern frontier of Guatemala in the south. The Aztec domain was not an empire in the modern sense; instead, it was a tribute state. All conquered towns were subject to the payment of tribute in the form of various economic products of the land. Political power emanated from the Aztec capital, Tenochtitlán (in the valley of Mexico), a city of perhaps 100,000 inhabitants.

Although not comparable in size and wealth to that of the Aztecs, the Tarascan state was a cohesive political unit that corresponded roughly to the present state of Michoacan in west-central Mexico (Stanislawski, 1947). The Tarascan state was probably more of a political empire than that of the Aztec. The Tarascans exacted tribute from conquered areas and also colonized their own people along the frontiers; by this means, they spread their language and culture through methods not used by the Aztecs. Both peoples had strong armies, and there were frequent military clashes along the frontier separating the two realms.

Southernmost Mesoamerica was organized into small independent chiefdoms instead of states. Despite their high attainments in religious art, science, and architecture, the Maya of the Yucatan peninsula never developed a true political state and, at Spanish contact, their territory consisted of 18 small chiefdoms. A similar political structure characterized the Guatemalan highlands and the Pacific lowlands of Central America as far as northwestern Costa Rica.

During preconquest times, Mesoamerica formed one of the most densely settled areas of the New World. Recent studies present convincing evidence that central and southern Mexico alone may have supported as many as 25 million people on the eve of Spanish conquest (Borah and Cook, 1963). Rural population densities in the Valley of Mexico and other highland basins in the eastern part of the Aztec state may have been as great or even greater in A.D. 1500 than at the present time. The inhabitants of highland Guatemala may well have numbered over 1 million; of the Yucatan peninsula, 500,000; and of southernmost Mesoamerica, perhaps another 250,000 or more.

The sustenance of such a large population required farming techniques that were more productive than the primitive slash-and-burn method of the simple farmers. As indicated previously, most of the tropical lowland dwellers within Mesoamerica practiced slash-and-burn, but more sophisticated techniques of cultivation had evolved in the highlands. Among these were permanent fields that were fallowed every 2 or 3 years; terraced fields on hillslopes; and, in places, irrigation. The latter was employed as far south as the Pacific lowlands of Nicaragua, especially for tree crops. The most productive cultivation method, however, was the *chinampa*, or so-called "floating garden," still used in the southern part of the Valley of Mexico. A type of land reclamation technique, *chinampas* are raised, elongated plots constructed along the margins of shallow, freshwater lakes. Irrigated and heavily fertilized, a single *chinampa* plot can produce as many as three crops annually. This technique was used mainly in the Valley of Mexico, but it also occurred in other parts of east-central Mexico (Wilken, 1969; West, 1970; Armillas, 1971).

Like other Mesoamerican farmers, the Aztecs and their neighbors relied on maize, beans, and squash as their staple foods; other crops included the chili pepper, a grain called amaranth, cotton, maguey (from which the native alcoholic drink, pulque, is made), and many tropical fruits. Among the latter, cacao, or chocolate bean, was the most important tree crop; the bean was used widely as currency and formed an important item in long-distance trade.

Inca Empire — lgest aboriginal state in New World.

Andean America. At the beginning of the sixteenth century, Andean America was dominated by the Inca Empire, the largest aboriginal state in the New World. Expanding outward from the high Andean valley of Cuzco (11,000 feet elevation), Incan armies, led by able rulers, within a period of 90 years (1438–1526) had conquered a vast area that extended 2800 miles from southern Colombia to central Chile. The empire included the central Andean highlands (presently Peru, Ecuador, Bolivia, and northwestern Argentina), and also the productive oases of the Peruvian coastal desert and the tropical coastal lowlands of Ecuador.

[handwritten annotations in top margin:] near state - true empire. Natural resources + farmland belonged to state. The State kaly fueling imposed on the people. Prod + dist. organized according to tripartite system whereby farms produced crops for seed. Inca nobility + State priesthood. Surplus was stored + distributed to needy.

[handwritten right margin:] The Andean America Less densely pop than mesoamerica - because of aridity, high altitude, mountainous terrain. Advanced farming techniques & crop complexity. Domesticated animals. Root crops dominant.

Unlike the Aztec tribute state in Mexico, the Incan state was a true empire. It was tightly controlled by the Incan nobility through one of the most highly organized sociopolitical systems known in the ancient world. All natural resources, including farmland, in theory belonged to the state. The state language, Quechua, as well as the state religion of sun worship, was imposed on most of the conquered peoples. (The widespread use of the Quechua language today in Ecuador, Peru, and Bolivia stems from ancient Incan policy.) Production and distribution of agricultural products were organized according to a tripartite system whereby the farmers of each village produced crops for themselves, the Incan nobility, and the state priesthood. Surplus production was stored and distributed to areas in need, precluding food shortages or famine. A well-maintained road system and the use of llama pack trains insured proper food distribution and effective military control throughout the empire. Moreover, through a labor system called the *mita*, all able-bodied males in every village were obliged to serve a few weeks of each year in the army or on public works. (After the conquest, the Spaniards continued the *mita* labor system, extending it particularly to the mining industry, much to their advantage.)

Cuzco, the center of Quechua nobility, was the chief administrative seat of the Inca. Early in the sixteenth century a second capital was established in Quito (Ecuador) to help control the northern part of the empire.

Although highly organized, the Incan imperial structure was extremely fragile, and disruption of even one of its key components, such as succession of political power within the royal family, could bring disaster. This is seen in the civil war over rights of royal succession that was in progress when the Spanish conquerors arrived in 1531.

In the northern Andes, north of the Inca Empire, at least one other aboriginal culture was sufficiently advanced to be classed as a civilization. This was the Chibchan domain in the eastern *cordillera* of present-day Colombia. At conquest, several chiefdoms of Chibchan-speaking Indians living in the highland basins had confederated to form a rudimentary political state. Unlike the Inca, however, the Chibchans built no monumental architectural structures, and there was little tendency to expand territorially outside the eastern *cordillera*. Nonetheless, Chibchans had established a well-organized trade with the simple farmers living in the Magdalena and Cauca valleys to the west, exchanging their salt and cotton cloth for the lowlanders' gold and gold ornaments.

Andean America was less densely populated than Mesoamerica. Between 6 and 12 million people lived within the Inca Empire at Spanish contact (Rowe, 1946; Smith, 1970), and no more than 500,000 inhabited the Chibchan domain (Eidt, 1959). Because of aridity, high altitude, and mountainous terrain, the central Andean environment is harsh. There are relatively few valleys in the mountains, and many of these, being over 10,000 feet in elevation, are subject to killing frosts 8 months of the year. In the high Bolivian *altiplano* (11,500 feet elevation), the best arable land clusters around Lake Titicaca, whose shores were densely settled in Inca times, as they are today. Other small spots of dense population occurred in the river oases within the Peruvian coastal desert. As in parts of Mesoamerica, population in most of the Inca Empire probably had reached maximum densities in terms of available arable land and the agricultural technology developed at the time of the Spanish conquest.

The Indians of Andean America developed many advanced farming techniques and a large crop complex. In addition, they domesticated more animals than any other aboriginal group in the Americas. Root crops were dominant, as they were in most of South America. In the highlands, the potato was the staff of life. Frost-tolerant tubers, including the potato, were preserved by drying, forming the light, easily transportable substance called chuñu, which would last years without spoiling. Native plants, such as quinoa, could be grown at elevations as high as 14,000 feet. Maize was a secondary crop in most highland areas. It had been introduced into the Andes from Mesoamerica as early as 3000 B.C. (MacNeish, 1970) but, because it does not mature well in areas over 10,000 feet in elevation, it never replaced the native tubers as the main staple. In pre-Spanish times maize was used in Andean America chiefly for making chicha, a ceremonial beer. In the coastal oases of Peru the dominant crops were tubers such as sweet manioc and sweet potatoes (both introduced at an early date from the Amazon Basin), and maize, beans, and squash. Animal domesticates of the Andean area included the guinea pig, raised for its meat (and thus the main source of protein among the highlanders); the llama, reared for its wool and as a beast of burden; the alpaca, a close relative of the llama, bred for its fine fleece; the muscovy duck, probably introduced from the Amazon Basin; and several varieties of dogs.

In aboriginal America irrigation reached its height of development in the coastal oases of Peru where water was diverted from streams and carried in long canals to fields far down-valley. In the highlands stone-faced terraces were laboriously constructed on steep mountain slopes to increase the amount of cultivable land; water from springs and small streams was diverted by canals onto the terrace surfaces. In many parts of the Peruvian highlands Incan terraces are still maintained for cultivation. The most widespread farming technique in the highlands, however, was the *era*, or permanent ridged fields on hillslopes made for the cultivation of potatoes and other tubers. The ridges were constructed with the Andean footplow, or *taclla*, and today they are still made in the same way as in pre-Spanish times (West, 1959; Gade and Rios, 1972). Without such sophisticated agricultural practices the Andean peoples might never have evolved their high civilization, nor would their population densities have been maximized to the ultimate carrying capacity of the land.

European conquest & settlement of Mid + S. Amer. began in late 15th century landing of Columbus in W. Indies. Spain + Portugal - major conquerors ① Spain → Mexico, Cent. Am + W.S.A for wealth + minerals ② Portugal → Brazil coast - sugar plantations Indians as slaves ③ European → L.A as pirates + settlers in W. Indies (like Portugal) — the 3 spheres evolve. Spanish L.A largest + richest + most diverse culturally.

THE EUROPEAN INVASION

The European conquest and settlement of Middle and South America began in the late fifteenth century with the landing of Columbus in the West Indies. Spain and Portugal were the major conquerors. The Spaniards managed quickly to occupy the populous areas of aboriginal civilization in Mexico, Central America, and western South America—all of prodigious wealth in people, land, and minerals. The Portuguese, on the other hand, slowly gained a foothold on the Brazilian coast, where they established sugar plantations among the tropical forest Indians; these they enslaved, eventually obliterated, and replaced with African blacks. A third European force, composed of North European nations (mainly England, France, and Holland), entered the Latin American scene first as pirates and later as settlers and entrepreneurs in parts of the West Indies and in the Guianas. Like the Brazilian Portuguese, they established sugar plantations and brought in African slave labor.

Thus three spheres of European influence evolved in colonial Latin America. The Spanish sphere was the largest, potentially the richest, and the most diverse culturally and physically. Spaniards tended to look inland toward the highland areas of dense aboriginal population and mineral wealth; except for a few ports and the dry littoral of Peru, they generally neglected the coastal zones. In the interiors the Spaniards developed the semifeudal, *hacienda*-type agricultural estate, using aboriginal serf labor to supply food to a local market—mainly the Spanish towns and mining centers. In contrast, both the Brazilian Portuguese and the North Europeans in the West Indies and the Guianas developed the capitalistic plantation, using black slave labor to produce sugar for an overseas market. The interiors of both Brazil and the Guianas were neglected until late. To this day a coastal orientation dominates the economy and culture of most of the West Indies and Guianas. In Brazil effective settlement of the immediate interior did not occur until the eighteenth century, and occupation of the far interior still lies in the future, despite a recent spate of road building and political slogans to encourage frontier settlement. Spain, Portugal + N. Eur. → wanted to gain quick wealth. Spain esp precious metals + Port + NE gold + silver, but settled for agric.

Centers of Conquest and Settlement Spread

Within each of the colonial spheres of influence particular areas emerge as foci that, once firmly held by Europeans, became centers or hearths for new conquests and settlement of adjacent areas. The motives for the establishment of such centers and for the movements from them were varied. For Spaniard, Portuguese, or North European the pervading reason to conquer and settle was economic—the desire to gain quick wealth. The Spaniards in particular were attracted by precious metals. The Portuguese and North Europeans also sought gold and silver, but most settled for the more prosaic agricultural pursuits such as sugar, tobacco, or indigo production. After initial conquest, the spread of the Christian faith by missionary endeavor became another motive for conquest and settlement, particularly by Spain and Portugal, but less so by the North European nations. Finally, political considerations led to frontier expansion, such as the Spanish settlement of upper California to thwart encroachment of Russian influence from Alaska or the occupation of the Banda Oriental (Uruguay) to meet the southward expansion of Portuguese from Brazil.

The Spanish Centers. In their conquest and settlement of the vast areas of the New World that eventually came under their control, the Spaniards established several different centers for territorial expansion (Figure 2-2).

Conquest of Middle America. The West Indian island of Hispaniola, discovered and occupied by Columbus on his initial voyage, was the first center. Attracted by the island's gold deposits and dense native population of docile Arawaks, in 1496 the Spaniards founded the city of Santo Domingo on the southern coast as the first permanent European settlement and administrative center in the New World. For almost one-half century (1493-1530) mining gold with native labor was the main Spanish activity on the island. Rapid decline of the Indian population, however, led the Spaniards to adjacent islands, the Gulf Coast, and the mainland of northern South America to recruit by force Indian labor for the Hispaniola mines. Gold deposits were also discovered in Cuba and Puerto Rico; for that reason Spanish settlement and culture in those islands became well established. Hispaniola was an early proving ground for many social and economic institutions, as well as crops and livestock, that the Spaniards introduced from their homeland and later transferred to mainland Latin America. The island thus functioned as a stepping-stone for conquest and settlement of the mainland.

By the first decade of the sixteenth century, the Spaniards on Hispaniola had made themselves familiar with the north coast of South America, where they sought Indian slaves to replenish the declining population of the island. Most of the Colombian and Venezuelan coast was then called Nueva Andalucía, and only a few impermanent settlements were made along the coast to serve as bases from which to raid the interior for slaves, around the coastal islands of Margarita and Cubagua to exploit pearl oyster deposits, and at various points inland to mine gold. One of the latter was Santa María la Antigua del Darién, founded in 1510 near the present Panama-Colombia border. From this small settlement Balboa crossed the isthmus and discovered the Pacific, or South Sea, in 1513.

The Spaniards quickly realized the strategic value of the Panamanian isthmus as a transit zone between the Atlantic and Pacific oceans. Mainly for that reason the city of Panama was established in 1517 as the capital of Castilla del

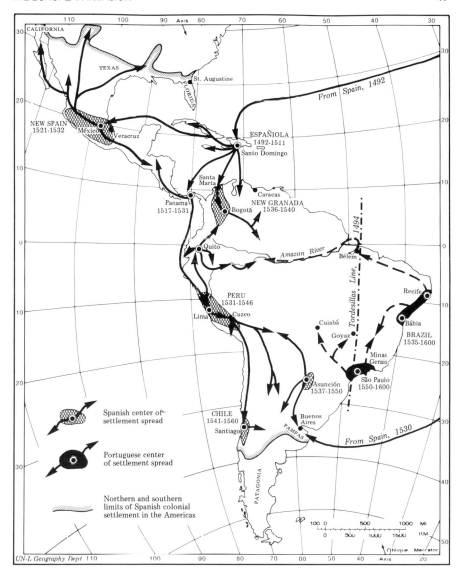

Figure 2.2 Spanish and Portuguese Conquest and Settlement of the New World

Oro, as the isthmus was then called. Panama became the second major point of dispersal for Spanish conquest and settlement in the New World. From the isthmus the southern part of Central America was explored and settled. But, more important, Panama was the departure point for exploration and conquest by sea to the coast of Peru, where the Spaniards discovered the vast Inca Empire.

The Spaniards established a third major center of conquest and settlement in central Mexico, the focus of Mesoamerican Indian civilization and the locale of the Aztec and Tarascan tribute states. Landing in the vicinity of Veracruz after a short voyage from Cuba, in 1519 the Cortés party quickly discovered the extent and wealth of the Aztec realm. The fall of Tenochtitlán, the Aztec capital in the Valley of Mexico, occurred 2 years later; on its ruins the Spaniards slowly built the city of Mexico. This city became the administrative center of New Spain, the name given to colonial Mexico and most of Central America. Spanish expansion from the Valley of Mexico occurred in two phases, each encompassing a definite geographical area. The first was characterized by an easy and rapid overrunning of heavily populated Mesoamerica, which included central and southern Mexico and the northern third of Central America. Within 10 years after the fall of the Aztec state, Cortés and his men had taken control of the native people by means of the *encomienda*, a system of tribute[3]; they had staked out claims to gold and silver deposits and some of the choice agricultural areas; and they had founded several Spanish towns, or *villas*, in strategic spots to control the Indians.

The second and later phase of expansion dealt chiefly with the slow conquest of northern Mexico, an arid region inhabited by the Chichimecs, nomadic Indians of low cultural status. In contrast to the rapid overrunning of Mesoamerica, the effective occupation of northern Mexico took 200 years. The discovery of rich silver deposits, beginning with that of Zacatecas in 1546, was the magnet that drew Spaniards northward. Beyond Zacatecas, one line of northward advance followed a series of silver deposits along the western side of the Mexican plateau, through Durango and Chihuahua, where grassy plains afforded abundant forage for livestock. Continuing further north, farmers and stockmen in 1599 made initial settlements among the Pueblo Indians in the upper Rio Grande Valley, within present U.S. territory. Another route of advance led northeastward from Zacatecas across the interior desert to the mines of Mazapil, Saltillo, Monclova and finally into Texas, where San Antonio was founded in 1718, mainly to thwart French designs for expansion from Louisiana. In the seventeenth century a third line of northward movement was made into Sonora in northwestern Mexico by Jesuit missionaries, who were followed by Spanish stockmen and miners. From Sonora this line of settlement reached into southern Arizona. The last northward thrust of Spanish settlement into what is now U.S. territory was the occupation of upper California by Franciscan missionaries, stockmen, and the military in order to counter Russian advances from Alaska.

Conquest of South America. The Spanish occupation of South America is overshadowed by the conquest of the Inca Empire. In Panama Spaniards first

---

[3]For definition and discussion of the *encomienda*, see p. 63.

heard tales of a high civilization to the south, and several exploratory trips along the rain-drenched Pacific coast of northwestern South America were made beginning in 1524. Finally, in 1531, the Pizarro-Almagro party landed in northern Peru, where the coastal desert begins.

The story of this conquest, including its fortuitous timing with civil strife within the Inca Empire, is well known. By 1533, both Cuzco, the capital city of the Inca, and Quito, the seat of the northern part of the Incan realm, had fallen to the Spaniards with little resistance. Almost invariably the Spaniards built their highland towns on the foundations of the looted Incan cities, among which Cuzco, Quito, Cajamarca, and Jauja were the more important. In Peru, however, the Spaniards did not choose an interior highland site within an area of dense Indian population for their main administrative city. Instead, Pizarro founded as the capital Lima, or Ciudad de los Reyes, in one of the coastal oases called Rimac, or Limac, at the terminous of the easiest route to the sea from Cuzco. Such a choice may have resulted from the tenuous hold that the Spaniards held over the potentially rebellious Incan nobles and the danger of committing the main administrative seat to a vulnerable place far into the mountainous interior. At any rate, Lima eventually became the political center of the extensive viceroyalty of Peru and one of the most opulent cities of the Spanish colonies. With its port of Callao it was also the main collecting point for the great mineral wealth of highland Peru.

In Peru as in Mexico the search for precious metals was the attracting force behind much of the Spaniards' efforts at conquest and settlement. However, the looting of the gold and silver artifacts from Incan temples and the debilitating civil war between the Pizarro and Almagro factions in Peru may have delayed for perhaps a decade the discovery of rich silver deposits in the high *altiplano* (upper Peru) south of Cuzco. Although small Incan silver mines such as Porco continued to be exploited after Spanish conquest, not until 1545 were the rich Potosí mines discovered in the *cordillera* east of the *altiplano*. The finding of many other deposits in the central Andes followed. Thereafter the mines in the *altiplano* and its surrounding areas became the main focus of Spanish economic activity and settlement in South America.

Both before and after the discovery of silver riches of upper Peru, two highland cities within the conquered Incan realm—Cuzco and Quito—were departure points for further Spanish conquest and settlement of western South America. With these conquests the Spaniards blocked out a vast area that was placed under the jurisdiction of the viceroyalty of Peru. Chile was occupied by a party of settlers led by Pedro de Valdivia, who left Cuzco in 1540 and in the following year founded Santiago as the capital of the province. During the remainder of the century, other Spanish towns and gold placer camps were laid out in the fertile central valley of Chile, which eventually became a land of Spanish farmers and stockmen of the southern frontier. But permanent settlers pushed no farther south than the Bío-Bío River, the beginning of dense, mid-latitude forests and the locale of warlike Araucanian Indians. For nearly 250 years the Bío-Bío marked the southern frontier of Spanish settlement in South America. Santiago de Chile itself became a point of departure for settlement when in 1561 a group of Chilean farmers crossed the Andes over the high Uspallata Pass (12,650 feet elevation) to found the vineyard towns of Mendoza and San Juan in the province called Cuyo, in what is now part of Argentina.

Most of northwestern Argentina was also occupied by stockmen and adventurers from Cuzco, such as those who in 1553 founded the town of Santiago del Estero in the lowland plains bordering the eastern foothills of the Andes. From this settlement other Spanish towns such as Tucumán, Córdoba, and Salta, were formed during the last third of the sixteenth century, mainly to furnish livestock and other supplies to the mines of upper Peru.

From Quito, the former northern Incan city, Spanish control expanded in many directions. Guayaquil on the Pacific coast was founded in 1537 as the port for Quito. In 1536 Sebastián de Benalcazar forged northward to found Popayán and Cali in present-day Colombia. From Cali a part of the group pressed far down the Cauca Valley, where rich gold deposits were found.

Centers of Spanish conquest and settlement in the northern Andes were, however, approached mostly from the Caribbean. The major penetration was carried out by the expedition of Jiménez de Quesada that, in 1536, left the small port of Santa Marta to seek gold and conquer the Chibcha Indian domain in the fertile highland basins within the Cordillera Oriental (present-day Colombia). Two years later Jiménez established the Spanish town of Santa Fé de Bogotá as the capital of the New Kingdom of Granada. Instead of rich gold deposits, the Spaniards found a dense population of docile Indian farmers whom they quickly appropriated in *encomiendas*. Later in the sixteenth century a series of towns, including Tunja, San Cristóbal, and Mérida (the latter two in present-day Venezuela), were founded in the highlands, all of which became centers of farming and stock raising on large *haciendas* worked by native labor. Westward from the New Kingdom of Granada the province of Antioquia was opened up in the 1540s by gold seekers from Cartagena and other Caribbean ports. Exploitation of rich placer mines on the Cauca River and its tributaries made this area the foremost gold-producing district of the Spanish colonies. In 1546 Santa Fé de Antioquia was established near the Cauca River as the administrative center of the province. Late in the seventeenth century the administrative function was moved to Medellín, today Colombia's second largest city.

The Caribbean coast of South America was the scene of perhaps the most dismal record of early European occupation in the New World. As indicated previously, this coast was the first part of South America that the Spaniards controlled, mainly for the purpose of exporting Indian slaves to Hispaniola and elsewhere. The only permanent Spanish settlements were those of Cumaná

[handwritten notes at top of page:] expansion ① search for metal ② spread of Christian Faith ③ stem Portuguese move ⁕ ments westward into areas claimed by Spain

(founded in 1516) and Coro (1527) along the Venezuelan coast, and Santa Marta (1525) and Cartagena (1533) along the coast of present-day Colombia. Most of these began as slaving stations, and the continuation of slaving for many decades resulted in the desolation of the entire coastal region. Not until the last half of the sixteenth century were the highland basins of northern Venezuela opened to Spanish settlement, and the capital of the province was moved from Coro to Caracas (founded in 1567). Cattle ranches were established in various highland centers such as Valencia, Barquisimeto, and Tocuyo from which the stock-raising industry moved into the vast plains (*llanos*) of the Orinoco Basin, bringing that isolated region under firm Spanish control. The province of Venezuela was the only large area of Spanish South America that fell outside the direct administration of the viceroyalty of Peru. Until the eighteenth century its political ties were with the *audiencia*[4] of Santo Domingo (Hispaniola), a part of the viceroyalty of New Spain.

From nearly all of the main Andean centers of South America the Spanish crown encouraged expansion eastward into the hot lowlands of the Amazon and Orinoco basins. Reasons for this expansion were threefold: to search for precious metals, to spread the Christian faith, and to stem Portuguese movement westward into areas claimed by Spain. Spanish penetration into the eastern Andean slope and adjacent Amazonian and Orinoco lowlands during colonial times is reflected today in the eastern boundaries of Colombia, Ecuador, Peru, and Bolivia. During the sixteenth century, several expeditions set out from Cuzco to explore the southwestern tributaries of the Amazon and, for 100 years (1668–1768), the Jesuit order missionized among the Mojos Indians who lived in the wet lowlands of northern Bolivia (Denevan, 1966b). In 1539 an expedition left Quito (Ecuador) to seek gold in the forest-covered eastern slopes of the Andes. One of the members, Francisco de Orellana, continued down the length of the Amazon River, claiming for Spain a vast eastern realm that was later occupied mainly by the church orders. One of these eastern areas settled from Quito was the province of Quijos (along the Napo River), famed for its cotton production in the sixteenth and seventeenth centuries. Another was the mission province of Maynas on the upper Amazon; here forest Indians were indoctrinated in 80 missions founded by the Jesuits in the seventeenth century (Rippy and Nelson, 1936). Santa Fé de Bogotá (Colombia), seat of a large archbishopric, was another departure point for Jesuit missionaries who, in the seventeenth century, moved eastward into the Orinoco lowlands, where they founded 42 mission towns along the Meta, Casanare, and upper Orinoco

[4]Within the Spanish colonial political system an *audiencia* was a tribunal composed of a president and generally four judges having administrative and judicial jurisdiction over a particular geographical area. Such an area was also known as an *audiencia*. The tribunal was subordinate only to the viceroy and the Council of the Indies in administrative and judicial matters.

rivers. Despite vigorous missionary activity, the eastern Andean slopes and adjacent lowlands attracted few Spanish settlers, and most of the missionized Indians succumbed to disease. Only today are pioneer farmers from the highlands slowly penetrating these nearly empty areas.

The southeastern part of South America was the major area of the Spanish colonies that lacked mineral wealth. Chiefly for that reason, until the eighteenth century, the Paraná-Paraguay river basin and the *pampas* that border the La Plata estuary were lightly settled by Spaniards and largely ignored by the Spanish crown, save for the famous Jesuit missions of Paraguay. As early as 1536, Spaniards attempted to found a colony called Buenos Aires on the La Plata estuary in order to open a direct route from the east to the newly conquered Inca realm in the Andes and to forestall Portuguese designs to expand southward from Brazil. Indian hostilities defeated this venture. But, in 1537, Spaniards succeeded in ascending the Paraguay River for a distance of 800 miles from the sea. On the high east bank of the river, within a rich agricultural zone densely inhabited by Guaraní Indian farmers, they established the town of Asunción as the capital of the La Plata area. Asunción was a center for further exploration and settlement of Paraguay and northern Argentina. In 1573 Spaniards from Asunción founded the stock-raising center of Santa Fé on the northern edge of the *pampas* and, in 1580, they reestablished Buenos Aires as a small port. Thereafter the northern *pampas* became a source of dried meat and hides for the mines of upper Peru, and Buenos Aires degenerated into a smuggling station through which contraband merchandise found its way to Potosí and even Lima. The rolling grasslands of the Banda Oriental (Uruguay) directly across the La Plata from Buenos Aires were not occupied by Spaniards until the eighteenth century, mainly to stem Portuguese penetration from the north. In 1680 the latter had established the port of Colonia on the La Plata across from Buenos Aires as a point for shipping meat and hides to their sugar plantations along the Brazilian coast. In 1726 the Spaniards founded a garrison town called Montevideo (present capital of Uruguay) farther eastward on the estuary and succeeded in expelling the Portuguese. Most of the *pampas* of Argentina and the desolate scrub and grass-covered plateau of Patagonia that stretches for 1000 miles to the south were not effectively occupied until the middle of the nineteenth century, well after the close of the colonial period.

In contrast to the slow Spanish colonization of most of southeastern South America, the province of Paraguay in the fertile Paraná-Paraguay Basin was quickly overrun by *encomenderos* exploiting the large Guaraní population for food and labor. To protect the remaining Indians, in 1610 the Jesuits began to settle the Guaraní in mission towns, hoping eventually to form a utopian "republic." The first missions were founded in the Guairá area within the present Brazilian state of Paraná and along the lower Paraná and Uruguay rivers within the present Paraguay-Argentine borderland (Caraman, 1976). Because of Portuguese raids the Jesuits and their charges retreated southward from the Guairá area but, by 1730, 30 missions containing 140,000 Guaraní in what is now southern and eastern Paraguay made up the thriving christianized Indian community, tightly controlled by the Jesuit fathers. After the Spanish crown expelled the Jesuits from the New World in 1767, the mission towns gradually disintegrated but, by then, the native culture had been sufficiently protected to have preserved much of the Guaraní folkways. Today, Guaraní is the household language spoken in rural areas and among many urban families in Paraguay.

The Portuguese Centers. Portuguese claims to New World territory were based on the Treaty of Tordesillas of 1494[5] and on Cabral's chance landing on the Brazilian coast in 1500. But, fully occupied with its Asian commitments, Portugal failed to colonize Brazil for three decades thereafter. During that interval, French and Portuguese adventurers ranged along the Brazilian coast, trading with Indians and cutting brazilwood (hence the place name, Brazil), a source of dyestuff for use in Europe. In 1532 permanent Portuguese settlements first appeared on the coast, the crown previously having divided the territory into 12 large proprietary land grants called *capitanias*, each given to a *donatario* (a private individual of noble rank) who was responsible for its development at his own expense. Each *capitania* fronted on a sizable stretch of coast (100 to 400 miles) and extended inland for an undetermined distance. Finding no precious metals on their lands, the *donatarios* turned to cutting brazilwood and cultivating sugarcane and tobacco along the tropical and fertile coastal lowlands. Only a few of the original *capitanias*, however, were successful and, in 1549, all of them were transferred to the crown. Among the successful ones were Pernambuco and Bahía in the northeast and São Vicente in the south. These two areas later became hearths from which Portuguese conquest and settlement spread to other parts of Brazil (Figure 2-2).

The Northeastern Center. For nearly two centuries Portuguese settlement in the northeast was confined chiefly to the coastal plain. The most prosperous sugar plantations and tobacco farms of Brazil were in the *capitanias* of Pernambuco and Bahía. There the coastal forest was completely cleared for agriculture and stock raising. The native Tupi Indians, at first enslaved, either fled into the interior or died, and black slaves were imported from Africa to provide labor in their stead. From Pernambuco sugarcane cultivation spread into

[5]The treaty gave to Portugal exclusive rights to regions of the New World east of a north-south line drawn 370 leagues west of the Cape Verde Islands and to Spain all lands west thereof. This line intersected eastern South America from approximately the mouth of the Amazon to the São Paulo coast, Brazil.

other *capitanias* as far north as that of Maranhão. But in those of Ilheus and Porto Seguro, south of Bahía, invading Indians in 1560 wiped out the thriving plantations, and Europeans did not succeed in resettling that area until the nineteenth century. Two main port cities developed in the northeast: Salvador (Bahía) and Pernambuco (Recife). Because of its wealth in sugar and its large harbor, for more than 200 years Salvador was the political capital of all colonial Brazil, a rank held until 1763, when the capital seat was shifted to Rio de Janeiro. In the northeast the Brazilian plantation, or *fazenda*, based on black slave labor and the export of sugar, reached its apogee. The rich plantation owners formed a social aristocracy from which came many of the political leaders, writers, and entrepreneurs of colonial Brazil. For these reasons the northeastern center is sometimes regarded as the "culture hearth" of the Brazilian nation (Schmieder, 1929).

So lucrative were the northeastern sugar plantations that for a short period (1624–1654) Holland wrested the *capitania* of Pernambuco from the Portuguese and operated the sugar industry with efficiency and profit. The Dutch introduced improved methods of refining sugar and developed the port city of Olinda (near Recife), which still reflects Dutch influence in much of its colonial architecture.

There were at least two periods of significant emigration from the densely populated coastal lowlands of the northeast in colonial times. Early in the seventeenth century, many Portuguese and mixed bloods began to settle the higher and drier backlands—the *sertão*. Most of these people engaged in stock raising on large ranches located no more than 200 to 300 miles from the coast. A second movement occurred on a much larger scale in the eighteenth century, after gold was discovered in the backlands of Minas Gerais, 200 miles from the coast. For most of that period gold vied with sugar as Brazil's most valuable export.

During the seventeenth century, a third movement out of the northeastern center resulted in territorial claims and tenuous occupation by Portugal of a large part of northern Brazil. Permanent port settlements were made in the northernmost *capitanias* and beyond: Fortaleza in Ceará (1609), São Luis de Maranhão (1612), and Belém at the mouth of the Amazon (1616). Belém, in turn, was a base for occupation of the Amazon Basin. Portugal used the expedition of Pedro Teixeira (1637–1639) up the Amazon River as a basis to claim this vast forested area, deep into Spanish territory west of the Line of Tordesillas (Phelan, 1967, p. 32). Moreover, for more than a century (1637–1755), various church orders based in Belém established missions among the Indians along the Amazon and its lower tributaries, further consolidating Portugal's claim on the territory (Rippy and Nelson, 1936, p. 237). However, despite missionary activity, the Portuguese used the Amazon area mainly as a source of Indian slaves for the coastal sugar plantations, and slave raids continued there well into the eighteenth century, forcing the Indian population to flee into the upper tributaries.

The Southern Center. During the sixteenth century, the plantations established on the narrow coastal plain of São Vicente, the southernmost of the early *capitanias*, were second only to those of the northeast in sugar production. The significance of the southern center for Portuguese expansion, however, did not derive from sugar but from the rise of a large group of mixed Portuguese-Indian stockmen on the plateau of São Paulo, immediately inland from the coast. Called *Paulistas*, or *bandeirantes*, these mixed bloods became more adept at enslaving Indians than raising livestock. They wandered far into the interior, capturing Indians for export to the coastal plantations, especially during the first half of the seventeenth century (Morse, 1965). After the expulsion of the Dutch from Pernambuco in the 1650s, slaves from Africa once more became available, Indian slavery declined, and the Paulistas turned to seeking deposits of gold and diamonds in the interior. They discovered the goldfields of Minas Gerais in 1693, of Cuiabá in 1718, and of Goiaz in 1725, and the diamond deposits of Minas Gerais were found in 1729. These discoveries resulted in Portuguese settlement of widely separated points within the south-central part of the colony—the first successful penetration of the Brazilian interior. Other than mining camps, the *Paulistas* made few permanent settlements. Their role was that of pathfinders, not settlers.

The North European Centers of Settlement. As settlers, the North Europeans came to Latin America late. Edged out by prior Iberian territorial claims, the English, French, and Dutch were first attracted to the Caribbean in the middle of the sixteenth century as pirates preying on Spanish galleons richly laden with gold, silver, and other products from Mexico and Peru. The more successful pirates, abetted by their mother nations, established bases on a few unoccupied islands within the Caribbean. The French and English, for example, operated from Tortuga, off northern Hispaniola; later, the English used Jamaica, especially Port Royal, for privateering; and, during the eighteenth century, the Bahamas, lying close to the main Spanish homeward route through the Florida straits, were bases for various North European pirates.

In general, areas claimed and later settled by North Europeans within Latin America were those that initially were of little interest to Spain or Portugal. Devoid of gold and inhabited by warlike Caribs, the Lesser Antilles held little attraction for Spaniards, but these small islands had become prized possessions of England and France by the end of the seventeenth century. Although Spain considered all of Hispaniola as its rightful territory, there were few Spanish settlements in the western third of the island, which in 1697 was transferred by treaty to France as the colony of St. Domingue (modern Haiti). Again, Spain had occupied Jamaica as early as 1509, but England captured

Jamaica in 1655 and later developed it into one of its most valuable possessions in the Americas. On the other hand, Spain kept a strong hold on Santo
Domingo (the eastern two-thirds of Hispaniola), Cuba, and Puerto Rico,
where Spanish lifeways had been firmly entrenched during the period of gold
mining in the early sixteenth century. On the northern coast of South America,
between Venezuela and the Amazon mouth, the hot, forested Guiana coast
was a no-man's-land until colonized by the Dutch, English, and French in the
seventeenth and eighteenth centuries.

Permanent English and French colonization of the Lesser Antilles began
in 1624 on St. Christopher (St. Kitts) with the settlement of peasant farmers
who grew tobacco and cotton for export. From there English settlement spread
to other islands of the Leeward (northern) group, such as Nevis and Anguilla in
1628 and Antigua and Montserrat in 1632. Farther south the English colonized
Barbados in 1627 (Dunn, 1972). French colonists occupied Martinique and
Guadeloupe as well as several islands of the Windward (southern) group and,
in the 1640s, began settlement of the western part of Hispaniola, long before it
became legal French territory. The Dutch also colonized some of the Leeward
islands and those of Aruba and Curaçao in the southern Caribbean. In the
1640s sugar cultivation and black slavery were introduced from Brazil into the
North European holdings of the Caribbean. For nearly two centuries sugar
was the prevailing crop of these small islands, making them the most lucrative
eighteenth-century possessions of France and England in the New World.

Of the several North European nations that colonized within the Caribbean area, England carried its influence and culture farthest. Outside the sugar
islands of Jamaica and the Lesser Antilles, English-speaking whites, mulatto
freedmen, and black slaves occupied the Bahamas, several small islands in the
western Caribbean, and some parts of the Caribbean shores of Central America that were ineffectively held by Spain. The British colony of Belize (British
Honduras) had its origin in English exploitation of dyewoods along the coast
during the seventeenth century. The influence of English smugglers was so
strong along the Caribbean coast of Honduras and Nicaragua that until the
middle of the nineteenth century much of that area (the mosquito coast) was a
virtual protectorate of Great Britain.

The first colonizers of the Guiana coast were the Dutch, who early in the
seventeenth century established small settlements on some of the rivers of present-day Guyana (former British Guiana). The English followed in the 1650s
when peasant farmers from Barbados, squeezed out by the sugar barons, settled along the Suriname River. After several attempts, the French finally established a small colony on the Cayenne River in 1674. Ravaged by disease and
based on the cultivation of tobacco and indigo, none of these initial settlements was economically successful. In the early eighteenth century the Dutch
began to move settlement to the coast, where swamps were drained and sugar

plantations established with some success on rich organic soils. As in the Caribbean islands, the Guiana colonies changed hands between the North European powers several times, and final claims were not established until the beginning of the nineteenth century.

In Latin America the Spaniards blocked out their sphere of influence quickly, having accomplished initial conquest and settlement of the richest, most heavily populated, and most civilized parts of the New World by the middle of the sixteenth century. The Portuguese, having occupied the coastal fringe of Brazil about the same time, waited until the late seventeenth century to expand inland. The North European countries, starting late with what Spain and Portugal considered to be the less favorable of New World lands and beset by continual international wars, finally consolidated their respective spheres in the Caribbean and Guianas early in the nineteenth century.

Effects of the European Conquest on the Aboriginal Population

The European conquest of Latin America clearly affected the native peoples both physically and culturally. Spaniards, Portuguese, and North Europeans introduced into their respective spheres of influence their own lifeways, including food crops and habits, farming methods, language, social organization, and religion. These they imposed on the aboriginal peoples and landscapes with varying degrees of effectiveness. In turn, the indigenous cultures influenced the Europeans, so that in many parts of Latin America elements of Old and New World peoples and cultures fused to form an amalgam that characterizes the human scene in those areas today.

One of the most far-reaching effects of European conquest is seen in the physical change of native peoples that occurred during the colonial period. One of these was the drastic reduction of the Indian population immediately following European contact. Another was that of miscegenation, or race mixing, which increased progressively during the colonial period and continues to the present. These changes have greatly reduced the aboriginal element in Latin America as a whole in both relative and absolute terms. Indian peoples and cultures still persist, however, in some areas of the ancient civilizations (e.g., Guatemala, Peru, and Bolivia) or in isolated sections (e.g., parts of interior Brazil).

Decrease of the Indian Population. Table 2-1 gives examples of the abrupt decline of the aboriginal population, based on recent estimates. The most disastrous collapse of any indigenous New World population occurred on Hispaniola, locale of the first European settlement in the Americas. By 1508, only 16 years after Spanish contact, the native population had dropped from more than 1 million to 60,000; by 1518, to about 12,000; and, in 1570, only 50 Indi-

Table 2-1   Decline of the Indian Population in Three Selected Areas of Latin America

	Estimated Population at European Contact	1570	1650	1800
Hispaniola	1,100,000[a]	100[b]	?	0 (?)
Central and Southern Mexico	25,000,000[c]	2,600,000[d]	1,500,000[e]	2,500,000[f]
Central Andean Area	12,000,000[g]	1,500,000[h]	?	600,000[i]

[a]Columbus census of 1496, cited in Sauer, 1966, p. 66, and in Cook and Borah, 1971, pp. 388–389.
[b]Cook and Borah, 1971, p. 401.
[c]Borah and Cook, 1963, p. 88.
[d]Borah and Cook, 1963, p. 4.
[e]Dobyns, 1966 (Gerhard, 1972, p. 24, gives 1 million for 1650).
[f]Gerhard, 1972, p. 24. *Incredible decline in Tijuana.*
[g]Smith, 1970. *Shipped from elsewhere + they*
[h]Lipschutz, 1966. *died too.*
[i]Patch, 1958.

ans were left (Cook and Borah, 1971, pp. 397-401). The rapid decline of labor for the gold mines in Hispaniola prompted the Spaniards to import Indian slaves from the neighboring islands, and they, too, died. By the close of the sixteenth century, most of the West Indies had lost their native population—a case of near extinction of a large human group within a century. A similar pattern of population decline occurred among some of the simple farmers, such as the Quimbaya of northern Colombia, who had been exterminated by 1570 (Friede, 1963).

The conquest also took an appalling toll of civilized Indians in Mesoamerica and the Andean area. Within 50 years after contact the natives of both central Mexico and the central Andes were decreased to one-tenth of their original numbers (Lipschutz, 1966). The low ebb in the central Mexican population came at the beginning of the seventeenth century, when about 1 million Indians are estimated to have survived (Borah and Cook, 1963); thereafter the Indian population began a recovery that lasted into the nineteenth century. The nadir of the Andean peoples, however, came about a century later before an increase set in. The conquest decimated the civilized Indians, but it did not obliterate them as it did the Arawak of the West Indies.

Various factors contributed to this dreadful mortality. Warfare took many native lives, especially during the conquest of the Aztecan and Incan civilizations and other groups who resisted the Europeans. Enslavement of Indians also contributed to death and dislocation of population. Spaniards made traffic in Indians a lucrative business in the Caribbean, Mexico, and Central America until the practice was outlawed in 1542. In Brazil enslavement of Indians occurred on a large scale for much of the colonial period and may have been the prime cause for the disappearance of the Tupi population from the eastern part of the colony. Morse (1965, p. 24) estimates that during the sixteenth and seventeenth centuries the Paulista slave hunters of southern Brazil took more than 350,000 Indian prisoners, most of whom were trekked to the coastal sugar plantations, where they died. Aside from actual enslavement, other factors such as harsh treatment, disruption of normal food supply, and psychological despair may have contributed to the death rates. The *encomienda*, a system of tribute and forced labor instituted by the Spaniards, especially contributed to such conditions. Sauer (1966, p. 203) believes that disruption of the native economy by Spanish demands for Indian labor caused the demise of the aborigines of the Caribbean islands.

Perhaps the most important cause of Indian mortality, however, was Old World diseases. The most virulent killers were smallpox, measles, and typhus, against which the American Indians had no immunity. The first smallpox epidemic broke out in Hispaniola in 1518, spread to Mexico with the initial Spanish conquest and, by the late 1520s, had become pandemic over much of Middle America and western South America (Crosby, 1967). Subsequent epidemics of Old World diseases occurred throughout Mesoamerica and the Andean area at frequent intervals for the rest of the colonial period, but the worst ones came in the sixteenth century, causing the precipitous decline of the native population. Indians gradually developed partial immunity to smallpox and measles and, by the end of the colonial period, their numbers had begun to increase. Little is known of other Old World diseases that Europeans and their African slaves carried to the Americas. Malaria probably took its toll in the tropical lowlands of Mexico and the coast of Peru, where in many sections the native population practically disappeared during the sixteenth century.

Serious consequences in culture and economy resulted from the great decrease of Indian population, especially among the native civilizations. Indeed, the ability of the Aztec, Tarascan, and Incan states to resist Spanish invasion may have been weakened by the first great smallpox pandemic. After the conquest, the declining population brought about decreased tributes and a scarcity of labor so severe that, according to some authors (Borah, 1951), a long period of economic depression ensued in Mexico and Peru during the seventeenth century. Moreover, into areas that suffered nearly complete extinction of native population, as in the Caribbean islands and portions of the Brazilian coast, Europeans imported large numbers of African slaves, whose descendants have marked the racial and cultural complexion of those areas to this day.

Racial Mixing. The most lasting biological effect of the conquest on the native population was the gradual dilution of Indian blood with that of the European whites and the African blacks. The interbreeding of these three races has produced the present mixed bloods that now predominate in much of Latin Amer-

Blacks more resistant to disease + enviro. conditions

ica, one of the major world areas in which effective racial mixing has been achieved.

In Spanish America the mixing of European and Indian began slowly. By law the Spanish crown discouraged mixed unions and, compared to the large native population, there were relatively few Spaniards in the colonies during the sixteenth century (Table 2-2). In Mexico and Central America, a sizable mixed, or *mestizo*, element did not exist until after the beginning of the eighteenth century. Thereafter the number of *mestizos* increased rapidly, accounting at the close of the colonial period for about 35 percent of the total population. Race mixing occurred mainly through the custom of concubinage, especially in the Spanish towns and mining centers, where white males and Indian women were in close contact.

During the colonial period, large numbers of African slaves were imported into Middle and South America (Mellafe, 1975). Black slavery had been a tradition among Iberian peoples for centuries. Moreover, in the tropical lowlands of the New World blacks proved to be more or less resistant to disease,

Table 2-2   Changes in the Racial Composition of the Population in Selected Areas of Latin America During the Colonial Period

	Mexico and Central America		
	1570	1650	1825
Whites	60,000 (2%)	120,000 (6%)	1,000,000 (14%)
Mixed bloods	36,000 (1%)	260,000 (14%)	2,500,000 (35%)
Indians	3,000,000 (97%)	1,500,000 (80%)	3,600,000 (51%)
Total	3,096,000	1,880,000	7,100,000

	West Indies (North European and Spanish Possessions)		
	1570	1650	1825
Whites	7,500 (12%)	80,000 (13%)	482,000 (17%)
Blacks	56,000 (85%)	400,000 (66%)	1,960,000 (69%)
Mixed bloods		124,000 (21%)	400,000 (14%)
Indians	2,000 (3%)	(nearly extinct)	(nearly extinct)
Total	65,500	604,000	2,842,000

	Brazil		
	1570	1650	1825
Whites	20,000 (2%)	70,000 (7%)	920,000 (23%)
Blacks	30,000 (4%)	100,000 (11%)	1,960,000 (50%)
Mixed bloods		80,000 (8%)	700,000 (18%)
Indians	800,000 (94%)	700,000 (73%)	360,000 (9%)
Total	850,000	950,000	3,940,000

Source. Based on data modified from Rosenblat, 1954, Vol. 1.

especially malaria, and they survived longer than the Indians at hard labor under hot, humid conditions. Most of the Africans brought to Latin America were shipped to Brazil, the West Indies, and the Guianas, where Indian labor had disappeared or was greatly depleted. From 1650 to 1830, the North European sugar barons brought to their West Indian possessions perhaps 4 million blacks; from 1540 to 1860 the Portuguese may have shipped 3 or 4 million to the Brazilian coast (Curtin, 1969). By the close of the eighteenth century, blacks dominated the population of these two areas, and a large group of mulattoes from black and white unions had evolved. Moreover, Portuguese in Brazil bred freely with Indian women in the backcountry, giving rise to the *mameluco* mixed blood; on the coast, black and Indian interbred to form the *cafuso* element. In Brazil more racial mixture occurred than in any other area of Latin America, possibly because of the paucity of white women and the economic structure of the colony.

Black slaves were imported into Spanish America in smaller numbers (about 1.5 million), but they were used in nearly every Spanish area of the New World. Most were sold in the Greater Antilles, but many were taken to Mexico and Central America, where they worked in mines, on stock ranches, in port towns, in sugar mills, and at other pursuits thought to be too arduous for Indians (Palmer, 1976). Others were used as farmhands in the oases of the Peruvian coastal desert, which had been depleted of its aboriginal population by disease. Again, a large contingent of blacks in Spanish America was sent to New Granada (present-day Colombia) to work in the lowland alluvial gold deposits because the natives of the area quickly perished under Spanish rule or were too recalcitrant to control.

Wherever there were black slaves in Spanish America they interbred with Indians and whites, in spite of regulations to the contrary. Many blacks escaped to Indian villages, and other runaways formed isolated settlements, taking Indian wives with them. Black and mulatto freedmen also mixed freely with the other races, so that a complex racial caste system had evolved in Spanish society by the close of the colonial period. Except in Colombia, Venezuela, and northern Ecuador, however, black blood in Spanish America today has been almost completely absorbed into the *mestizo* element.[6]

Because of the high death rate and miscegenation, the percentage of the native population declined almost everywhere in Latin America during the sixteenth, seventeenth, and eighteenth centuries. Since the close of the colonial period, Indian groups have been reduced to pockets of varying extent in southern Mexico; northwestern Guatemala; the highlands of Ecuador, Peru, and

---

[6]The dominant black population along much of the Caribbean coast of Central America is not a Spanish colonial development but stems mainly from relatively recent migrations from the West Indies.

Bolivia; south-central Chile; and a few small areas in the Amazon and Orinoco basins. Even the "Indians" of these areas have today been "mestizoized" to varying degrees in culture and blood.

THE COLONIAL ECONOMY

The European activities in the New World that most thoroughly affected the geographical landscape were economic in nature. Spaniards, Portuguese, and North Europeans exploited human and natural resources within their respective realms of influence in various ways. In the early formative years of occupation Spaniards emphasized the exploitation of the native population through formal institutions such as the *encomienda*, labor levies, and enslavement of rebelling Indians. Formal establishment of industries based on the exploitation of natural resources such as mining and agriculture followed. The Portuguese in Brazil and the North Europeans in the West Indies were less concerned with native peoples, who were far less numerous and civilized than those in the Spanish realm. As indicated previously, Portugal and the North European countries relied on slaves imported from Africa to exploit the land.

The colonial exploitation of natural resources in Latin America was dominated by two great industries: (1) the mining and processing of precious metals, and (2) the cultivation and manufacture of sugar. Mining, localized in the mountainous interior, formed the economic core of Spanish America. The sugar industry, best developed on fertile soils along tropical coasts, was the main economic basis for the Portuguese in Brazil and the North Europeans in the Caribbean. The products of these two industries furnished the most valuable exports shipped from the Latin American colonies to their respective mother countries. Around the two industries revolved most of the other economic activities within the colonies, including staple food production, stock raising, and transport. Both industries required a large, cheap labor force, supplied by native Indians in the case of mining and by imported African slaves in the case of sugar. In short, within their respective areas, the two industries were instrumental in shaping the form of the geographical landscape of colonial Latin America, including settlement and land use patterns, as well as distribution and racial composition of the population. Much of this landscape is retained today, and even the present export orientation of most Latin American countries may stem from the nature of the colonial economy.

To be sure, the geographical limitation of mining to the Spanish realm and sugar to the Portuguese and North European areas was not absolute. Gold mining was important in colonial Brazil, but not until the eighteenth century. Sugar was widely grown in Spanish America, but mainly for internal consumption, except in Cuba, which became a major sugar exporter late in the eighteenth century. Moreover, colonists exported other products, such as dyestuffs, hides, and tobacco but, by value, these were comparatively insignificant in the export economy.

The Colonial Economy of Spanish America

The Encomienda. Although mining and agriculture dominated the colonial economy of Spanish America, the *encomienda* was Spain's most effective economic and social institution in the New World during the initial period of settlement in the early sixteenth century. The *encomienda* system arose in Spain during medieval times; in the Americas it was modified to suit local conditions. In brief, groups of Indians—usually several contiguous villages—were "commended" to a deserving Spaniard (the *encomendero*) who was obligated to instruct his wards in the Spanish language and the Catholic faith; in return, the *encomendero* had the right to exact tribute in the form of economic products or labor from his Indians. In theory the *encomienda* did not entail landownership. *Encomienda* grants were made throughout the Spanish realm, but they were successful mainly in New Spain and Peru, where the native population was numerous and civilized. In 1549 the rendering of labor service by *encomienda* Indians was abolished. Thereafter, by law the system became exclusively one of tribute payments by natives to their *encomendero*, and Indian labor for agriculture and mining was supplied mainly through levy systems that the Spanish authorities imposed on Indian villages. By means of their *encomiendas* many Spaniards in the New World were able to survive during the early sixteenth century because tributes consisted of agricultural products, gold, cloth, or any other product that the *encomendero* could consume or sell. The drastic decline of the native population in the late sixteenth century partially caused the demise of the *encomienda*. By the seventeenth century, tributes had so decreased that few Spaniards found their *encomiendas* profitable, and the larger ones had reverted to the crown (Zavala, 1943; Simpson, 1950).

The Mining Economy. Following the rapid exploitation of alluvial gold deposits in the Greater Antilles, Spaniards continued the search for quick wealth on the mainland, where they found both gold and silver in abundance. From Mexico to Chile gold was encountered as dust and nuggets within the sands and gravels of lowland rivers that drained crystalline rock mountains. Because such alluvial deposits were quickly depleted, requiring the frequent shifting of labor gangs along stream courses, their exploitation rarely led to the establishment of permanent settlements. Silver, and some gold, however, occurred as complex ores in veins that penetrated deeply into mountain flanks within the highlands. Since vein mining and ore refining was slow and required large investments in·machinery, reagents, and labor, such operations usually resulted in the founding of permanent mining camps, some of which grew into large and opulent cities. So great was the demand for labor, food, clothing, draft animals, and raw materials in the large mining centers that these settlements became the "dynamos" that generated much of the economic activity within colonial Spanish America.

Mexico and upper Peru (Bolivia) were the foremost producers of silver during the colonial period; New Granada (Colombia) was the source of much of the gold in Spanish America; other producing areas were minor by comparison: the Greater Antilles (gold), Honduras (silver and gold), Ecuador (gold), and Chile (gold and copper). Although Taxco, discovered southwest of Mexico City in 1526, was the first silver district to be developed by the Spaniards in the New World, large-scale production of the metal did not begin until after the opening of the Zacatecas mines in 1546 and the subsequent exploitation of rich silver lodes north and southeast thereof within the "Silver Belt" of New Spain (Parral, Guanajuato, and Pachuca). At about the same time (1544), the great silver deposits of Potosí were discovered in the high *altiplano* of upper Peru, and later finds in the same area and in the central Andes (Oruro, Castrovirreyna, and Cerro de Pasco) gave the viceroyalty of Lima even more wealth than Mexico in the sixteenth and seventeenth centuries. Between 1580 and 1670, for example, upper Peru accounted for 65 percent of all American silver shipped to Spain, whereas by the late eighteenth century, Mexico's share was 67 percent. During most of the colonial period, Zacatecas and Potosí were the largest and most productive mining centers in Spanish America. Zacatecas produced about one-third of Mexican silver and was considered the second city of New Spain; it possessed 5000 inhabitants at the middle of the seventeenth century. At that time Potosí was much larger, having 160,000 inhabitants, produced two-thirds of Peruvian silver, and was considered the leading metropolis of South America (Bakewell, 1971; Brading and Cross, 1972).

Mine Labor. The colonial mining industry in Spanish America could not have operated without a plentiful labor supply. Fortunately for the Spaniards, the silver-producing districts of Mexico and Peru lay within or near areas populated by civilized Indians. In both areas the Spaniards applied a system of forced labor for the mines. In Mexico it was called the *repartimiento*; in Peru it was the *mita*. Both derived from aboriginal systems of obligatory public service. Both were labor levies whereby Indian villages were required to furnish a given number of able-bodied males to work for various periods in the mines or in the ore-processing plants. In Mexico forced labor was largely replaced by free wage workers by the middle of the seventeenth century, especially in the northern mines, far from the densely populated central part of the colony. In Peru, however, the *mita* continued until its abolition in 1812, but it was considered an oppressive form of servitude that caused the death of thousands of Indians. A total of 13,300 Indians were obliged to work at 4-month intervals in the Potosí mines alone, some having to walk from the Cuzco district, a distance of 600 miles (Vázquez de Espinosa, 1942, p. 624). The decline of the native population through disease and other factors gave rise to frequent labor shortages. In New Granada, for example, Indians who were forced to work in the lowland gold placers through the *encomienda* system quickly died off, and Spaniards had to replace them with African slaves.

Refining Techniques and Reagents. In 1557 a new method for refining silver, called the *patio*, or amalgamation, process, was introduced into Mexico. It revolutionized the mining industry in Spanish America and caused a sharp increase in silver production. Smelting, effective for refining high-grade silver ores, was previously the sole method known to the Spaniards. Amalgamation, a simple, inexpensive means of refining large quantities of low-grade ore, involved finely grinding and puddling ore and applying mercury, salt, and copper pyrite to extract the silver. Strictly controlled by royal monopoly, quantities of mercury were shipped from Spain to Mexico for this process. Because of the distance and cost of mercury shipments, amalgamation was not introduced into Peru until 1574 after the discovery of a large deposit of mercury at Huancavelica in the central Andes, 800 miles northwest of the Potosí mines. Thereafter silver production at Potosí boomed (Bakewell, 1977). In both Peru and Mexico, maximum silver output occurred between 1580 and 1630 but, for the rest of the seventeenth century, production slumped badly, mainly because of mercury shortages. With the restoration of regular shipments of this reagent and improvements in mining technology in the late eighteenth century, silver production began to exceed that of any time previous (Brading and Cross, 1972; Fisher, 1975).

The need for large quantities of salt in the amalgamation process created an industry adjunct to that of silver mining. In Peru and Mexico salt was obtained by scraping the surfaces of dry lake beds located at varying distances from the mining centers. The Peruvian supply originated in the large salines on the high, arid *altiplano*, while the salt for the Mexican refineries came from the central desert, north and east of the Silver Belt, and from tidal lagoons along the Pacific coast. Since copper pyrite was found near most of the mining centers, its supply provided few problems for the silver refiners.

Wood was also needed for many operations within the mining centers, giving rise to other occupations such as the lumber business to supply beams and planks for buildings, mine supports, and machinery, and the manufacture of charcoal for use as fuel in smelting ore and in various operations of the amalgamation process. For miles around every mining center in Mexico woody vegetation was seriously depleted by woodcutters and charcoal makers; the effects of this are seen to this day. But in the high, treeless country of Potosí and adjacent areas, lumber and charcoal were hauled great distances, from the forested eastern slopes of the Andes and even from Ecuador. Peruvian refiners were often obliged to use llama dung and bunch grass to fuel smelters, because of the lack of charcoal.

Agriculture. Throughout the colonial period, production of food for subsistence remained primarily in the hands of the Indians and mixed bloods, who retained native crops and farming methods. Commercial agriculture, however, was directed mainly by Spaniards, using Old World plants, animals, and techniques. The development of commercial farming and stock raising was closely tied to the mining industry, since the mines were the main markets for grains and animal products. The Spanish towns were secondary markets. Moreover, large numbers of pack animals, especially mules, were required for land transport to connect ports and food-producing areas with mines and towns. Except for dyestuffs and hides, few agricultural products were exported overseas. Production for local consumption was the rule.

Although in the early years of conquest Spaniards had to rely on Indian foods, they soon introduced their own Old World plant and animal domesticates into the Americas. Wheat and barley quickly became important crops in the tropical highlands of Mexico and Peru and in the middle latitude areas of Chile. Other introduced crops significant in Spanish culture included grapevines, olives, and figs, which were grown chiefly in the desert oases of northern Mexico and coastal Peru. Such crops did poorly in the tropical lowlands, where Old World plants such as plantains, citrus, and sugarcane were successfully grown and even adopted by Indian farmers. The introduction of European domesticated animals resulted in fundamental changes in land use even more so than plants. Except for the Andean llama and alpaca, large, domesticated animals were lacking among the Indians, and a true aboriginal herding economy was unknown. The range animals—cattle, sheep, horses, and mules—became the mainstay of the livestock industry, which was established in most parts of the Spanish realm. These animals reproduced so rapidly in the New World that in some areas, such as the tropical savannas of the West Indies and lowland Mexico and the grassy *pampas* of Argentina, herds went wild and were annually "harvested" by hunting expeditions for hides until well into the seventeenth century (Coní, 1956).

In New Spain, by the 1530s, the Spaniards had established wheat farms in the basins of Mexico and Puebla on the central plateau, and cattle, sheep, and mules were being herded in the surrounding hills that were unoccupied by Indians (Gibson, 1964). At that time wheat flour and meat were supplied mainly to Mexico City and other Spanish towns; however, with the opening of the Silver Belt north and southeast of Zacatecas during the following decades, the main market for agricultural produce shifted to the mines. New wheat-farming and stock-raising areas such as the fertile Bajío of Guanajuato and the Valley of

Guadalajara in the western portion of the central plateau were opened to supply Zacatecas, Guanajuato, and smaller mining centers nearby. As Spanish
settlement progressed northward from Zacatecas along the Silver Belt, irrigated wheat and maize farms sprang up along river valleys near every mining
center, and stock ranches were formed in the surrounding grass-covered
plains. Thus in northern Mexico the mining community, the stock ranch, and
the grain farm, being economically interdependent and geographically proxi-
mate, combined to form the colonial ranch-mine settlement complex, traces of
which persist today (West, 1949). Using Indian labor, the farmers supplied
wheat and maize to the mines; the stockmen furnished mules (for mine work),
beef (for food), hides (for ore sacks), and tallow (for candles, the chief means
of illuminating the dark shafts and tunnels).

In the viceroyalty of Peru the agricultural pattern as it related to the mining industry was far more complex than in New Spain. The main market for
agricultural produce was the great mining center of Potosí and the surrounding satellite communities in upper Peru. Products from as far away as New
Granada and Quito in the northern Andes, central Chile, and the Argentine
pampas and Paraguay converged on Potosí, the major economic magnet for
the entire viceroyalty. Most of the staple foods consumed in the Potosí area,
however, came from nearby Indian lands and Spanish estates, especially (1) in
the fertile, well-watered valleys of Cochabamba, Chuquisaca (La Plata), and
Tarija on the eastern slopes of the Andean highlands (maize and wheat), and
(2) on the high *altiplano* (source of the native chuño, the main food consumed
by Indian mine labor). Food was also brought in from the irrigated farms
along the Peruvian desert coast, where land was taken over by Spanish farmers
after the Indians had perished in the smallpox epidemics of the early sixteenth
century. The most valuable exports of the southern coastal oases, such as Pis-
co, Ica, and Arequipa, were wine and brandy, products of the vineyards introduced by Spaniards and worked by black slave labor. Consumed in large quantities in the mining centers, wine and brandy also came from the vineyards of
Mendoza in western Argentina. These vineyards, as well as those of the Peruvian oases, are still today among the major wine-producing districts of South
America. In the Peruvian mining centers and administrative towns Spaniards
and *mestizos* consumed most of the wine and brandy, while the Indian workers
drank the native chicha, or corn beer, made locally from the maize brought in
from the eastern valleys. In some of these valleys Spaniards had taken over aboriginal coca farms and, with Indian labor, produced large quantities of this
stimulant for sale in the mining centers (Cobb, 1945, 1949; Helmer, 1950).

The Potosí mining district was also the major market for the products of
stock ranches: meat, hides, and tallow as well as draft and pack animals. Such
products were supplied mainly from the large ranches established in the last
half of the sixteenth century in northwestern Argentina and the northern edge

of the *pampas*. Probably the most renowned aspect of the stock-raising industry that developed through the stimulus of the Potosí market was the mule trade of northwestern Argentina, where each year during the seventeenth and eighteenth centuries 30,000 to 60,000 animals from the ranches around Córdoba and Tucumán were sold at the great mule fair of Salta and driven to upper Peru (Wrigley, 1916; Schmieder, 1928). Mules were also driven into the Peruvian mines from the Cúcuta pastures of northern New Granada, 2500 miles from Potosí (Vázquez de Espinosa, 1942, p. 323). In addition, native llamas in Peru were used as pack animals and for food; 100,000 were consumed each year in Potosí at the beginning of the seventeenth century (Jiménez de la Espada, Vol. 1, 1965, p. 308).

In other areas of the viceroyalty mines as well as port cities and administrative centers stimulated farming and stock raising. In central Peru, Spaniards established grain farms and cattle ranches in the high Andean basins, such as Huancayo, Jauja, and Huamanga (Ayacucho), to supply food for the mines of Cerro de Pasco and Huancavelica and the city of Lima. The same pattern developed in the highlands of Quito (Ecuador), where wheat, barley, maize, and cattle were shipped to the Zaruma gold mine and the port of Guayaquil. Similarly, the Spanish grain and cattle estates in the highlands of New Granada around Bogotá and Tunja depended on the gold placers of Antioquia and the upper Cauca for their main markets (West, 1952). Land Grants

Agriculture and Land Tenure. A fundamental aspect of commercial farming and stock raising in colonial Spanish America was the development of large landed estates, variously called *haciendas, estancias,* or *hatos.* The land tenure problems of many Spanish American countries since independence stem partly from adverse social and economic conditions associated with the large estates owned by elite families.

During the colonial period, Spaniards normally obtained private lands by means of the *merced,* a municipal or royal grant. Single grants for raising livestock were large, some more than 5000 acres in size. Through the accumulation of several contiguous grants by purchase or otherwise, some Spaniards came into possession of immense estates, particularly in northern Mexico and the Argentine *pampas,* where Indian population was sparse and nomadic. Original land grants were smaller in areas of dense native population, as in central Mexico and the Andean highlands, where a mixed grain-livestock economy evolved and where tracts occupied by Indians were legally protected from usurpation. Nonetheless, as Indians declined in numbers, their abandoned lands gradually were attached to adjacent Spanish holdings, creating large *haciendas.*

Moreover, the church, especially the regular orders such as the Jesuits, Dominicans, and Augustinians, by various means acquired large *haciendas* that they operated far more efficiently than the lay *hacendados.* Beginning in

1767 with the expulsion of the Jesuit order from the New World, such church lands were gradually absorbed through purchase by the private estate owners, enlarging their vast holdings still further (Bauer, 1972).

The focal point of the *hacienda* was a compact cluster of buildings called the *casco*. It included the "big house" of the owner or overseer, the huts of the workers, often a chapel, and the corrals and granaries. By the end of the eighteenth century, the *hacienda* and its *casco* had become the dominant rural settlement form in much of Spanish America. The *hacienda cascos*, some in ruins, others in use, are still a conspicuous part of the countryside in many Spanish American countries.

Inadequate labor and uncertain markets were constant problems of the estate owners. In the early colonial period the *haciendas* within areas of dense native population were often supplied with hands through government-controlled work levies, such as the *repartimiento* in Mexico. In Peru and Chile some *encomenderos* who managed to obtain land grants near the villages of their Indian wards probably used the male population for farm work long after the abolition of *encomienda* labor services in 1549 (Mörner, 1973). However, after the epidemics of the sixteenth century had reduced the Indian population, most *hacienda* owners used extralegal means to get sufficient labor. In Mexico and Central America Indians were induced to leave their villages to settle on the estate by offers of relatively high wages paid in kind. By advancing them credit, the owner was able to keep his workers in perpetual debt (debt peonage), which bound them to the *hacienda* (Chevalier, 1963). In the Andean area Indians were bound to the estates by permitting them to cultivate a portion of *hacienda* land for subsistence in return for their labor in tending the owner's crops and herds (Vargas, 1957). Bondage proved to be one of the most pernicious social aspects of the *hacienda* and helped to precipitate agrarian revolutions and reforms in various Spanish American countries during the twentieth century.

Production for a local market (mines and towns) instead of for overseas trade was one of the main characteristics of the Spanish American *hacienda*. Because of frequent fluctuations in metal production and population in mining centers, high costs of land transport, and occasional shortages of farm labor, *hacienda* owners normally underproduced to maintain high prices, and relatively small amounts of capital were invested to improve the land. Consequently, large tracts of potentially productive land were purposely retired from agricultural production, a practice that has continued in places into modern times despite the increase of population and demand for food. Furthermore, in Spanish American society the mere accumulation of large landholdings may have enhanced the social prestige and political power of elite families.

Although the Spanish American *hacienda* is usually defined according to the attributes just described, its nature varied from place to place, so that nowhere did there exist a "classical" form. Moreover, the *hacienda* as both a major institution and landscape element evolved slowly during the colonial period; in some places, such as Bolivia, it did not reach full development until the beginning of the present century (Mörner, 1973).

Manufacturing Industries. To protect industry in the mother country, the Spanish crown discouraged large-scale manufacturing in its American colonies. Besides the processing of agricultural products such as sugar, grapes, and dyestuffs, only one colonial industry—textile manufacturing—grew to sizable proportions in various parts of Spanish America. Again, the mining centers consumed the greater part of the textile products, although Spanish towns and Indian communities were also important markets. The weaving of cheap, coarse cotton and woolen cloth formed the basis of the colonial textile industry, which developed in many areas inhabited by Indians who were weavers by tradition. Three textile-making areas, however, produced most of the cloth that entered local trade: (1) east-central Mexico, especially the cities of Puebla, Tlaxcala, and Mexico; (2) the highland basins of Ecuador, where weaving was carried on in Indian towns around Quito, Riobamba, and Latacunga; and (3) the districts of Córdoba, Santiago del Estero, and Tucumán in northwestern Argentina. In all three areas cloth was woven by Indians who either paid tributes in cloth or worked as forced laborers in small Spanish-controlled factories called *obrajes* (Greenleaf, 1967; Super, 1976). The greatest cloth production occurred in the Ecuadorian highlands, where large herds of merino sheep grazed and abundant cotton was obtained from the hot lowlands of the Amazon Basin and the Pacific coast (Vargas, 1957; Phelan, 1967). From Quito textiles were shipped to all parts of the viceroyalty of Peru, but mainly to the Potosí mining district, 1500 miles away. Potosí also obtained large amounts of cotton cloth from the textile towns of northwestern Argentina. Mexican textiles were sold mostly in the northern mines, where wages were often paid in pieces of cotton or woolen cloth. Since the cloth and other textiles produced in the Americas were of poor quality and manufactured primarily for Indian workers in mines and *haciendas*, the weaving guilds in Spain made few objections to the colonial industry as long as they could export Andalusian velvets, silks, and brocades for sale to rich miners and *hacendados* in Peru and Mexico.

As mentioned earlier, of the few agricultural products raised in Spanish America for export overseas, only dyestuffs and hides were of any significance. Two native America dyestuffs were cultivated for export, both being used in the European cloth industry. One was cochineal, a crimson dye extracted from tiny insects raised on the leaves of the prickly-pear cactus by the Indians of New Spain. In Europe cochineal commanded fabulous prices; by 1600 it ranked in value second to silver among Mexican exports to Spain. The other dyestuff was native indigo, cultivated on Spanish estates by black African labor mainly along the Pacific lowlands of Central America (MacLeod,

1973). In the seventeenth and eighteenth centuries it became the main economic product of that area and was produced in El Salvador as late as 1920, when
it was finally eclipsed by synthetics. Although most of the colonial Spanish
American stockmen found their main markets for livestock in the local mines
and towns, in some areas cattle were raised or hunted chiefly for hides that
were exported to Spain for the leather industry. The half-wild herds in the
Spanish West Indies, the Gulf lowlands of Mexico, and the Argentine *pampa*
were the main source of these hides. According to Chaunu (1955, Vol. 6, p.
105), between 1562 and 1620 hides, by weight and volume, were the most important export to Spain from the American colonies. By value, however, hide
exports were insignificant when compared to the precious metals.

The Colonial Economy of Portuguese America

Just as the colonial economy of Spanish America tended to revolve around the
mining of gold and silver in the mountainous interior, that of Portuguese
America was based largely on the production of sugar along the Brazilian
coastal plain. Not until the eighteenth century did mining become significant
in the Brazilian interior, and thereafter the nature of Spanish and Portuguese
colonial economies became more similar.

The Brazilian Sugar Plantation. The decision of Portuguese *donatarios* to turn to
sugar cultivation in their Brazilian holdings in the middle of the sixteenth century was prompted by rising sugar prices in Europe. Since 1520, the price had
soared, mainly because Turkey had occupied Syria and Egypt, at that time the
main sources of sugar for Europe. Thus, already versed in sugar production on
their Atlantic islands of Madeira and São Thomé, the Portuguese turned readily to that activity in Brazil to gain enormous profits (Schmieder, 1929). By
1580 Brazil had become the leading sugar-producing area of the world, a rank
it held for more than a century until surpassed by the West Indies about 1700.

Along the wet, forested Brazilian coast, plantations were established on
large tracts of land, called *sesmarias*, each averaging about 12 square miles in
size. Such tracts were allotted to colonists who were obliged to begin cultivation and make other capital improvements on the land within a given time period, according to the Portuguese *sesmaria* land system. Because such improvements, including forest clearing and mill construction, required investment of
considerable capital, only the wealthier colonists became successful planters.
By 1570 the northern *capitanias* of Pernambuco and Bahia had become the
major sugar area and the politico-economic center of the colony.

The sugar plantation was the major settlement form along the coast; except for ports and trading centers, the Portuguese did not establish formal
towns as did the Spaniards. Each plantation usually consisted of four parts:
the cane fields, in actual cultivation or in fallow; pastureland for grazing oxen;

the *roça*, or land cultivated for food; and the woodland, left in reserve for future clearing and cultivation (Greenlee, 1943; Poppino, 1949). The grinding mill and cooking vats for processing sugar formed the plantation center, around which were the huts of the workers and the big house of the owner or overseer. The Brazilian sugar plantation was physically similar to the Spanish *hacienda*, but it was quite different in function, producing a single processed product for export to overseas markets.

Along with sugarcane and the tropical plantation concept, the Portuguese brought over oxen to power the mills and to draw cane carts and plows. Oxen were so valuable as draft animals that cattle were rarely raised for meat on the sugar plantations. Until the seventeenth century much of the dried meat and hides consumed on the plantations were imported from Portugal, the Atlantic islands, and even from the Argentine *pampas* (Mauro, 1960). Because of the tropical climate, the cultivation of wheat and other Mediterranean-type crops was never successful in Brazil. Thus the Portuguese colonists early adopted Indian crops, such as manioc and sweet potatoes, as food staples for themselves and for the plantation slaves.

The Portuguese operated their holdings almost wholly with slave labor. As indicated previously, they used both Indian and African slaves but, because the docile, forest-dwelling Tupi died quickly under forced servitude, black slaves comprised most of the work force on the plantations. The traffic in blacks was significant; each large plantation required 150 to 200 slaves, most of whom were purchased at stations along the Guinea coast of Africa and in Angola, a Portuguese colony. Relations with Brazilian natives, however, were not confined to slavery; in the southern *capitanias* an active trade developed between the Portuguese and the Tupi, who supplied manioc to the plantations and to the transatlantic slave ships in exchange for iron tools (Cortesão, 1956).

Although dominant, sugar was not the sole product of plantation agriculture in colonial Brazil. In the seventeenth century, especially during and after the Dutch occupation of Pernambuco, tobacco became an important export crop on some of the smaller holdings in the northeast. Moreover, many plantation owners with land near the coast continued to cut brazilwood for export as a secondary activity well into the seventeenth century. Exports decreased sharply after 1650, mainly because of the gradual destruction of the coastal forests (Mauro, 1960). Brazilwood has long since disappeared from commerce, but sugar and tobacco of colonial fame, together with cacao, are still the major commercial crops of the coastal plain of the Brazilian northeast.

Pastoral Activities. In Brazil the range cattle industry first evolved in response to the demand for animal products in the sugar plantations. In the northeast, the colonists who lacked the capital to establish plantations obtained large land grants to run cattle, especially in the dry scrub forests of the *sertão* from Pernambuco northward to Ceará. Cattle raising was expanded in the 1630s, when the tropical savannas of the plateau were penetrated by stockmen fleeing the Dutch occupation of Pernambuco. By 1700 there had been a remarkable development of stock raising in the São Francisco valley, which drains much of the northeastern plateau. In 1711 1.3 million head of cattle grazed on the São Francisco ranches, some of which were 40 square miles large (Poppino, 1949). Ranchers from the northeastern interior supplied livestock, dried meat, tallow, and hides to the adjacent coastal sugar plantations in return for raw sugar, cane brandy, food, and other necessities. Such transactions took place in a series of market centers, or fairs, established on the coastal edge of the *sertao* (Figure 2-3). A similar pattern developed on a lesser scale in southeastern Brazil, where large cattle ranches on the Sao Paulo plateau supplied the coastal sugar plantations of São Vicente and Rio de Janeiro. In the Brazilian northeast this simple symbiotic relationship between coast and interior continued into the twentieth century (Lasserre, 1948). Through both the sugar plantation and the cattle ranch, large holdings became the dominant form of land tenure in colonial Brazil. *Such a discovery of gold & sugar prices*

Mining. In 1693 the accidental discovery of gold in the headwaters of the São Francisco and Doce rivers greatly expanded the colonial economy of Brazil. During the eighteenth century, Brazil became the world's leading producer of gold and, for a time, the precious metal surpassed sugar as the colony's most valuable export. The initial discovery in Minas Gerais, as this highly mineralized plateau area came to be called, precipitated the world's first major gold rush. Thousands from the Brazilian coast, Portugal, and other parts of Europe flocked into Minas Gerais. Discouraged by falling sugar prices, many plantation owners of Bahia and Pernambuco liquidated their lowland holdings and moved their slave gangs into the interior to mine gold. It is estimated that during the eighteenth century gold mining attracted 800,000 Portuguese to Brazil (Webb, 1959).

Minas Gerais gold was found mainly in alluvial deposits in streambeds and on terraces or, less frequently, in weathered soils on hillsides (Boxer, 1962). Thus most settlements were ephemeral mining camps, each being shifted to a new location after depletion of a particular deposit. The few permanent towns in the mining district were administrative centers, such as Vila Rica, later called Ouro Prêto.

Food for the mining crews was imported or raised on small plots within the area. The demand for dried meat in the camps gave the stockmen of the São Francisco valley and the São Paulo plateau an expanded market, and cattle fairs, similar to those that served the sugar plantations, were soon established in various parts of Minas Gerais (Webb, 1959). Moreover, the small town of Rio de Janeiro on the southeastern coast became the main port for the mines. Because of the growing importance of gold in the Brazilian economy and the relative decline of sugar in the northeast, in 1763 the colonial capital

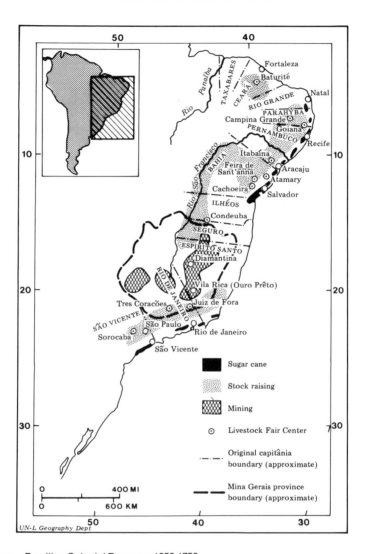

Figure 2.3   Brazilian Colonial Economy 1650-1750

was moved from Salvador to Rio de Janeiro. The subsequent discovery and exploitation of gold farther inland (Goias and Cuiabá) and of diamonds in various parts of the plateau added to the growth of Brazil's mining industry and to
the token settlement of scattered points in the far interior.

Thus, during the eighteenth century, the colonial economy of Brazil revolved around the exploitation of precious metals, paralleling the pattern earlier developed in Spanish America. Brazil's "golden age," however, was short

lived; by the early nineteenth century the major gold placers had been depleted and other boom activities, such as coffee growing, were beginning in the São Paulo area. Nonetheless, the tradition of placer mining still persists among the *garimpeiros*, the folk miners who wash gold and diamonds from stream gravels in the Brazilian interior. ~~Sugar prod. trend, shift~~

Colonial Economy of the North European Possessions

Like the Portuguese in Brazil, the English and French in the West Indies developed sugar as the main facet of colonial economy. Except for their plantations in the Guianas, the Dutch concerned themselves primarily with shipping, and their small islands in the Antilles functioned mainly as trading centers. Lacking deposits of precious metals in their islands and coastal lowland possessions, none of the North European nations, of course, engaged in mining.

Both the English and French devoted the first two decades of colonizing the Lesser Antilles (1620s-1640s) to the settlement of peasant farmers, who used white indentured servants from the homeland to cultivate small holdings planted to various tropical crops marketable in Europe. In the English islands indentured servants were mainly youths between the ages of 15 and 25 who contracted to serve from 4 to 6 years; such labor made up the bulk of North European immigration to the Leeward Islands and Barbados until the middle of the seventeenth century (Dunn, 1972). Crops grown for export included first, tobacco and cotton, and secondarily indigo and ginger (Deerr, 1949, Vol. I).

Individual farmers as well as trading companies in London and Paris subsequently saw the possibilities of large financial gains in establishing sugar plantations on the islands as the Portuguese had done earlier on the Brazilian coast. Individual farmers began sugar cultivation on a large scale first on Barbados, Guadeloupe, and Martinique in the 1640s. Through Dutch influence, they copied Brazilian methods, including plantation organization, black slave labor, and reliance on an overseas market. It was on Barbados that the planter class, composed of rich sugar barons, first took shape in the Caribbean (Dunn, 1972). The sugar estate gradually was introduced into other English and French islands, so that by the first decade of the eighteenth century the center of sugar production in the Americas had shifted from Brazil to the Caribbean, where it has remained to this day (Table 2-3).

As in Brazil, natural conditions in the West Indies favored sugar cultivation: lack of frost, plentiful rainfall with a dry period for harvest, and fertile soils. The volcanic and coral limestone soils of the Lesser Antilles and the alluvial plains of Jamaica and St. Domingue (Haiti) were highly productive. The paucity of arable land in the mountainous islands, however, limited the extent of sugar cultivation and, in most cases (flattish Barbados excepted), plantations occupied the narrow coastal rims close to the sea and the ports.

Table 2-3   Sugar Production in the Americas for Export, 1580–1875, in Tons

	1580	1650	1700	1770	1800	1825	1850	1875
Brazil	4,800[a]	28,500	22,000	20,400	21,000[b]	99,000[c]	138,000[d]	102,500
English & French West Indies	—	7,000	31,400	168,200	161,400	183,000	134,600	260,700
Guianas	—	—	4,100	9,200	6,900	47,700	38,900	91,100
Spanish West Indies	—	—	—	10,000[e]	28,400	54,700	273,200	790,100

Source. Compiled from Deerr, 1949, Vol. I.
[a]All figures rounded to nearest 100.
[b]1796.
[c]1823.
[d]1853.
[e]1770–1778 average.

The plantations, acquired through government grants or by purchase, although smaller than those in Brazil, were similarly organized. Cane fields occupied the best land; plots tilled for food, primarily manioc and sweet potatoes, were relegated to mountain slopes; the mill and workers' quarters formed the settlement center. Mills were powered by either water, wind, or animals. On the mountainous islands swift streams were often harnessed to turn the mill wheels; on Barbados and other flattish islands the steady trade winds turned huge, Dutch-type windmills for grinding cane. Oxen, however, formed the main power source, and these were raised on the plantations or imported from the North American colonies. Cattle and dried meat were also imported from Venezuela. Contrary to the Brazilian case, an extensive range cattle industry never developed on the islands to supply meat and other animal products to the plantations. Instead, most protein food, primarily in the form of dried fish, was imported from North America to feed slave labor. To this day, despite the decline of the plantation, West Indians prefer dried cod from maritime Canada or New England to local fish, and most of the smaller islands still rely partly on imported food and clothing (West and Augelli, 1976, Chapter 4).

The West Indian planters were even less successful than their Brazilian counterparts in enlisting native labor; the rebellious Caribs of the Lesser Antilles would not work, and the natives of larger islands had long since vanished. Thus the North Europeans imported many black slaves, whose descendants today comprise most of the West Indian population outside the Spanish-speaking islands. After freeing their black slaves in the nineteenth century, the English imported many contract workers from southern Asia (mainly India); their descendants presently complicate the ethnic composition of some West Indian islands (chiefly Trinidad and Jamaica) and of Guyana.

Using the plantation system and black slaves, the French and English West Indies became the world's leading sugar-producing area during the eighteenth century. The largest producers were St. Domingue (Haiti), settled by France during the last half of the seventeenth century, and Jamaica, ceded to England by Spain in 1655 (Table 2-4). Partly because of the black rebellion in Haiti (1793), the emancipation of slaves in 1834 (England) and 1848 (France),

Table 2-4 Sugar Production in the North European West Indies, 1770, in Tons

St. Domingue (French)	60,000[a]
Jamaica (English)	36,000
Martinique and Guadeloupe (French)	19,600
Barbados (English)	8,600
Leeward Islands (English)	28,800
Windward Islands (English)	12,370

Source. Compiled from Deerr, 1949, Vol. I.
[a]All figures rounded to nearest 100.

and the increasing competition from other cane and beet sugar producers, the colonial plantation system had disintegrated in the West Indies by the middle of the nineteenth century. Although sugarcane continued to be cultivated on the English and French islands, by 1850 major production had shifted to the Spanish islands of Cuba and Puerto Rico. By 1900, with the influx of U.S. capital and the development of the large mechanized sugar factories, the Spanish-speaking islands, including the Dominican Republic, had become the leading growers of sugarcane in the New World. Meanwhile, the economy of the North European islands had so deteriorated and population pressure had become so great that they were noted as the "poor houses of America," an opprobium that can be applied to many of the islands today.

TRANSPORT PATTERNS OF COLONIAL LATIN AMERICA

To effect the success of their various economic activities in the New World, Europeans introduced their own modes of travel and established a transport pattern that, in some places, has lasted until the present time. Spaniards, Portuguese, and North Europeans obviously all depended on the sailing ship to transport goods overseas. Land transport, however, with the use of pack animals and wheeled vehicles, was far more important to the Spaniards than to the Portuguese or North Europeans, mainly because of the former's interior orientation. Connection of colonies to mother countries. Spanish forbidden to trade w/ foreign powers

Sea Transport and Trade

Transatlantic sea routes and trade, connecting the colonies with the mother nations and the large markets of western Europe, were equally significant to all three groups. Like the trade policies of the Portuguese and North Europeans, the Spanish crown established rigid commercial controls, forbidding its colonies to trade with foreign powers. Moreover, early beset by piracy, Spanish ships for most of the colonial period were forced to sail in convoy, carrying manufactures, mercury, and various luxuries to the colonies and returning to Seville with precious metals, hides, and other New World products. Sailing southwest from Spain, the convoys picked up the trade winds, which carried them to the Caribbean and Mexico. To reach the Pacific ports of South America, goods were transshipped across the Panamanian isthmus by mule train and, at Panama City, were loaded on ships for the voyage southward along the coast. This crossing point was one of the most strategic spots of the Spanish Empire because most of the Peruvian silver was shipped to Spain through Panama. Largely for that reason the province of Panama fell under the political jurisdiction of the viceroyalty of Peru for most of the colonial period. On the return trip to Spain, ships from Mexico and the Caribbean ports assembled in

Havana to form a convoy. Controlling the Florida straits, the main exit for ships heading northward to catch the westerly wind, Havana was another highly strategic point for Spanish transatlantic shipping.

Far to the south of the normal Spanish American sea-lanes another transatlantic route linked the La Plata estuary with Europe, largely through illegal trade. After its refounding in 1580, Buenos Aires became notorious for its clandestine commerce with smugglers of various nationalities. Flemish cloth and other North European goods were exchanged for silver from Potosí, at least one-tenth of whose production was filtered illegally through Buenos Aires (Chaunu, 1955, Vol. 6). In terms of distance and ease of transport, Buenos Aires was the most logical port for Spanish trade into the Potosí mines, but royal edict required all overseas contact with upper Peru to pass through Panama for security reasons.

Rarely troubled by pirates, Portuguese and North European sugar ships never sailed in convoy (Mauro, 1961). Vessels plied directly between Lisbon and Brazil, taking Portuguese wine and other luxuries to Recife, Salvador, and Rio de Janeiro and returning with sugar and tobacco. In addition to carrying sugar directly to Europe, English shippers in the West Indies took molasses to New England in exchange for livestock and foodstuffs; New England rum, processed from the molasses, was shipped to West Africa, where it was traded for slaves, who were then carried to the West Indies.

Besides its dominant transatlantic commerce, Spain also developed a small but prosperous transpacific trade between the west coast ports of Mexico and the Far East. Begun in the 1580s, the famous Manila galleon plied annually between Acapulco, Mexico, and Manila in the Spanish-occupied Philippines, bringing oriental silks and spices in exchange for Mexican silver. With the decline of the Manila trade at the end of the colonial period, Acapulco lost its role as one of the leading Pacific ports of the Americas, a role it has never regained.

In most of colonial Latin America coastwise sea routes were probably more significant than trails on land in local trade. Maritime travel was more rapid, comfortable, and economical than transportation overland. This was particularly true in Brazil, where few roads existed between coastal settlements and local commerce was perforce by sea. Likewise, the island character of the West Indies required sea travel for local trade. In Spanish America maritime travel was especially important along the Pacific coast, where products from both the coast and the interior moved more by sea than by land, resulting in the development of several ports, large and small. Most of the Potosí silver, for example, was carried overland to Arica, the nearest Pacific port, which also was the main entry for imports into upper Peru. Again, instead of paying the high cost of overland transport, government officials sent mercury from Huancavelica destined for Potosí to the small port of Chincha, whence it was shipped by sea to Arica and thence over the short Andean trail to the mines (Vázquez de Espinosa, 1942, p. 472). Most of the agricultural products from the Peruvian coastal oases also went by sea to Lima, Panama, or Arica through small local ports, many of which are used today to ship out cotton and sugar. Callao, near Lima, where goods in coastwise trade were officially registered, was the largest South American Pacific port. In size and importance it was followed by Guayaquil, the main shipbuilding center within the viceroyalty of Peru.

In 1540 a sizable trade by sea was established between New Spain and Peru (Borah,1954). Textiles and luxury items were shipped to Peru from the Mexican port of Huatulco; from the port of Realejo in Central America came cacao for making chocolate and pine pitch for coating Peruvian wine jugs. In return, the merchants of Lima sent silver bullion, mercury, and wine. Because of the increasing restrictions on interviceregal commerce, this trade ceased in the 1630s.

Animals; la 2 wheeled carts to haul. pulled by oxen; llamas used.

Land Transport and Trade

The development of land transport in colonial Latin America was closely associated with mining and commercial agriculture, especially in Mexico, the central Andes, and the province of Minas Gerais in Brazil. Mule and donkey trains formed the most common type of transport over rough mountain trails, and in upper Peru the native llama was used extensively as a pack animal throughout the colonial period. In two areas of Spanish America—Mexico and Argentina—large two-wheeled carts pulled by oxen were employed to haul cargoes to and from mining centers and towns over roads constructed on level terrain. Land transport was arduous and costly. Colonial reports are replete with statements to the effect that to haul a unit of goods for a relatively short distance overland by pack train or cart cost several times more than to bring it by ship across the Atlantic. This large cost differential continued until the advent of the locomotive and automobile, and it persists in isolated areas of Latin America where colonial-type transport is still used.

In the New World, Spaniards early established land routes, many of which are followed today by railroads and highways. In Mexico three major routes led northward from the capital to the mining districts and the settlement frontier. One of these followed the main Silver Belt through Zacatecas to the upper Rio Grande in New Mexico; because of its level terrain it was traveled by cart trains. The most frequented routes in Mexico led from the ports of Acapulco and Veracruz to the capital. On these two trails at any given time during the dry season, thousands of mules were used to haul silver bullion and other products to the ports, returning with imported goods. Pack trails also led southeastward from the Valley of Mexico to Central America but, with the exception of the transisthmian route across Panama, Central American trails carried little traffic. Lack of frequent communication and trade between the isthmian provinces may have led to the political separatism that resulted in the formation of the Central American nations after independence. In the Andes the short mule trails that led from the highlands to the Pacific ports carried a large amount of traffic, such as silver bullion from the mines and luxury goods imported from Spain. Examples of highland-coast roads include those connecting Quito and Guayaquil, Cerro de Pasco and Lima, and Potosí and Arica. Although frequently made, the 1000-mile journey between Potosí and Lima through Cuzco required 4 months of arduous travel by mule over one of the most difficult land routes in Latin America (Coní, 1956, p. 38). Travel between Potosí and the plains of Argentina was much easier. By the end of the sixteenth century, a cart road had been built between Buenos Aires and the valley towns of Salta and Jujuy in northwestern Argentina, with branches to the vineyards of Mendoza and to Paraguay. Hugh two-wheeled carts, each pulled by six to eight yokes of oxen, hauled hides, wine, and smuggled imports to Salta and Jujuy, where the cargo was transferred to mule trains destined for the mines of Potosí (Vázquez de Espinosa, 1942, pp. 671, 691; Coní, 1956, p. 80).

In Brazil cattle trails between the *sertão* and the coast formed the only well-established land transport pattern until the discovery of gold in the interior at the close of the seventeenth century. Thereafter Portuguese merchants established a series of donkey trails among the mining camps of Minas Gerais, the port of Rio de Janeiro, and the food supply center of São Paulo (Webb, 1959). The main trail north from Rio de Janeiro up the plateau escarpment was later followed by both railroad and highway to Minas Gerais and is today one of Brazil's most heavily trafficked thoroughfares.

River Transport. During the colonial period, neither Spaniards nor Portuguese utilized rivers for transport and trade to any extent; there were few navigable streams within the main areas of economic activity, and river navigation was not an outstanding Iberic trait. Within the Spanish realm only the Magdalena River in northern South America became a major route of communication, connecting the interior of New Granada (Colombia) with the port of Cartagena on the Caribbean. The Magdalena retained the role of Colombia's main trade artery until the 1960s, when truck roads were completed to the coast. Other rivers that the Spaniards occasionally used for transport included the San Juan in Nicaragua, the Guayas in Ecuador, and the Paraná-Paraguay system in Argentina and Paraguay. The latter, however, did not become Paraguay's major commercial outlet until the independence period. Likewise, the Amazon River system in northern Brazil and eastern Peru was little used for commerce until the rise of rubber collecting in the Amazon rainforest during the late nineteenth century. These important themes concerning transportation are enlarged on in Chapter Three.

SUMMARY

Many aspects of modern Latin America, including population distribution, racial composition, and economic and social patterns, have roots in both the aboriginal and colonial eras. Colonial Spaniards occupied and developed mainly the parts of the New World that were densely settled by civilized natives and were rich in precious metals: Mexico and the Andean highlands. Today these two areas form the major centers of Spanish culture and of what is left of aboriginal life in the New World. In both areas miscegenation has created the dominant *mestizo* element, considered by some to be a new race. In both areas mining was the mainstay of the economy until recently. Lands that lay outside Mexico and the Andes held scant interest for the Spaniards; for example, southern South America and the northern borderlands of Mexico were settled late, more for political than economic reasons, and the development of both has been largely postcolonial by non-Spaniards.

In contrast to the Spaniards' inland orientation toward mineral deposits and concentrations of Indian population in the mountainous interior, the interests of the Portuguese in Brazil and the North Europeans in the Caribbean lay on the coastal fringes. There fertile soils could be exploited for the production of sugar, tobacco, and other agricultural products for export. In both Brazil and the Caribbean native peoples were uncivilized and were quickly diminished or destroyed by disease and maltreatment. Through the importation of African slave labor to work the plantations, the Portuguese and North Europeans rapidly changed the racial composition of their respective areas. This is reflected today in the dominant black and mulatto population of the Caribbean and coastal Brazil. Moreover, sugar is still king in the Caribbean economy, and plantation agriculture, although modified from its colonial form, is still dominant in Brazil and in some West Indian islands. In type, colonial Brazilian economy approached that of the Spanish areas only in the eighteenth century, when gold was mined in the immediate interior. Brazil now relies on both mining and agriculture, but its population is still concentrated near the coast, and most of its far interior is as undeveloped today as it was in colonial times.

In the effectively settled parts of colonial Latin America landholding was a dominant feature of the rural scene: the livestock-grain *hacienda* in Spanish America, the sugar and cattle *fazendas* in Brazil, and the North European sugar estate in the West Indies and the Guianas. The agricultural village in Latin America derived largely from Indian tradition. Today the enforcement of land reforms has nearly obliterated the large landholdings in many Latin American countries, but the agricultural village of peasant farmers is still a significant form of rural settlement. The pattern of dispersed rural homesteads, so familiar in the North American scene, rarely developed in Latin America.

The urban life of modern Latin America also has deep roots in the colonial past. Most of the Spaniards who migrated early to the New World were
town dwellers, and the main type of initial Spanish settlement in the Americas
was the *villa* (town) or *ciudad* (city), established as a political, military, and religious control point for given administrative units (Morse, 1962). Port towns,
of course, had the additional functions that attend overseas and coastwise
shipping. Some inland administrative towns later became trading and manufacturing centers for local markets, but only the mining towns processed goods
(bullion) in large quantities for overseas trade. Both Spaniards and Portuguese
attached social prestige and political advantage to urban living. For example,
the large landowner, in addition to his *hacienda* or *fazenda* mansion, usually
owned a townhouse in the nearest provincial seat or even in the viceregal capital, where he often spent much of his time close to royal officials. In Brazil
most urban centers were port towns; only in the eighteenth century did mining
and market centers develop inland from the coastal fringe. During the nineteenth and twentieth centuries, urbanism in Latin America greatly intensified
because of the migration of many rural people into the cities and larger towns.
The viceregal and many provincial capital cities of colonial days have maintained their primary character as the national capitals of the modern Latin
American countries.

BIBLIOGRAPHY

Armillas, P., "Gardens on Swamps," *Science*, Vol. 174, 1971, pp. 653–661.

Bakewell, P. J., *Silver Mining and Society in Colonial Mexico: Zacatecas, 1546–1700*,
London, Cambridge University Press, 1971.

———, "Technological Change in Potosí: The Silver Boom of the 1570s," *Jahrbuch
für Geschichte von Staat, Wirtschaft und Gesellschaft Lateinamerikas*, Vol. 14,
1977, pp. 57–77.

Borah, W., "New Spain's Century of Depression," *Ibero-Americana*, No. 35, Berkeley and Los Angeles, University of California Press, 1951.

———, "Early Colonial Trade and Navigation between Mexico and Peru," *Ibero-
Americana*, No. 38, Berkeley and Los Angeles, University of California Press,
1954.

Borah, W., and S. F. Cook, "The Aboriginal Population of Central Mexico on the Eve
of Spanish Conquest," *Ibero-Americana*, No. 45, Berkeley and Los Angeles, University of California Press, 1963.

Boxer, C. R., *The Golden Age of Brazil, 1695–1750*, Berkeley and Los Angeles, University of California Press, 1962.

Brading, D. A., and H. E. Cross, "Colonial Silver Mining: Mexico and Peru," *Hispanic American Historical Review*, Vol. 52, 1972, pp. 545–579.

Caraman, P., *The Lost Paradise, the Jesuit Republic in South America*, New York,
The Seabury Press, 1976.

Chaunu, H., and P. Chaunu, *Séville et l'Atlantique, 1504-1650*, 8 vols., Paris, Colin, 1955.

Chevalier, F., *Land and Society in Colonial Mexico: The Great Hacienda*, Berkeley and Los Angeles, University of California Press, 1963.

Cobb, G. B., "Potosí, A South American Mining Frontier," in *Greater America: Essays in Honor of Herbert E. Bolton*, Berkeley and Los Angeles, University of California Press, 1945, pp. 39-58.

———, "Supply and Transportation for the Potosí Mines, 1545-1640," *Hispanic American Historical Review*, Vol. 29, 1949, pp. 24-25.

Coní, E. A., *Historia de las Vaquerías del Río de la Plata, 1555-1750*, Buenos Aires, Editorial Devenir, 1956.

Cook, S. F., and W. Borah, *Essays in Population History, Mexico and the Caribbean*, Vols. 1 and 2, Berkeley and Los Angeles, University of California Press, 1971, 1974.

———, *Essays in Population History, Mexico and California*, Vol. 3, Berkeley and Los Angeles, University of California Press, 1979.

Cortesão, J., *Brasil, de los Comienzos a 1799*, Barcelona, Savat, 1956.

Crosby, A. W., "Conquistador y Pestilencia: The First New World Pandemic and the Fall of the Great Indian Empires," *Hispanic American Historical Review*, Vol. 47, 1967, pp. 322-337.

Curtin, P. D., *The Atlantic Slave Trade, A Census*, Madison, University of Wisconsin Press, 1969.

Deerr, N., *The History of Sugar*, 2 vols., London, Chapman & Hall, 1949.

Denevan, W. M., "A Cultural-Ecological View of the Former Aboriginal Settlement in the Amazon Basin," *Professional Geographer*, Vol. 18, 1966a, pp. 346-351.

———, "The Aboriginal Cultural Geography of the Llanos de Mojos of Bolivia," *Ibero-Americana*, No. 48, Berkeley and Los Angeles, University of California Press, 1966b.

———, "Aboriginal Drained-Field Cultivation in the Americas," *Science*, Vol. 69, 1970, pp. 647-654.

———, "The Aboriginal Population of Amazonia," in W. M. Denevan (ed.), *The Native Population of the Americas in 1492*, Madison, University of Wisconsin Press, 1976, pp. 205-234.

Dobyns, H. F., "Estimating American Population," *Current Anthropology*, Vol. 7, 1966, pp. 395-416.

Dunn, R. S., *Sugar and Slaves, The Rise of the Planter Class in the English West Indies, 1624-1713*, Chapel Hill, University of North Carolina Press, 1972.

Eidt, R. C., "Aboriginal Chibcha Settlement in Colombia," *Annals of the Association of American Geographers*, Vol. 49, 1959, pp. 374-392.

Fisher, J., "Silver Production in the Viceroyalty of Peru, 1778-1824," *Hispanic American Historical Review*, Vol. 55, 1975, pp. 25-43.

Freide, J., *Los Quimbaya bajo la Dominación Española*, Bogotá, Banco de la República, 1963.

Gade, D. W., and R. Rios, "Chaquitaclla, the Native Footplough and its Persistence in Central Andean Agriculture," *Tools and Tillage*, Vol. 2, 1972, pp. 3-15.

Gerhard, P., *A Guide to the Historical Geography of New Spain*, London, Cambridge University Press, 1972.

Gibson, C., *The Aztecs under Spanish Rule*, Stanford, Calif., Stanford University Press, 1964.

Greenleaf, R. E., "The Obraje in the Late Mexican Colony," *The Americas*, Vol. 22, 1967, pp. 227–250.

Greenlee, W. B., "The First Half Century of Brazilian History," *Mid-America*, Vol. 25, 1943, pp. 91–120.

Helmer, M., "Commerce et Industrie au Perou a la Fin du XVIIIᵉ Siècle," *Revista de Indias*, Vol. 10, 1950, pp. 519–526.

Jiménez de la Espada, M. (ed.), "Relaciones Geográficas de Indias: Peru," *Biblioteca de Autores Españoles*, Vols. 183–185, Madrid, Ediciones Atlas, 1965.

Lasserre, G., "Le Nord-Est du Brazil," *Les Cahiers d'Outre-Mer*, Vol. 1, 1948, pp. 40–67.

Lipschutz, A., "La Despoblación de las Indias después de la Conquista," *America Indígena*, Vol. 26, 1966, pp. 229–247.

MacLeod, M. J., *Spanish Central America: A Socioeconomic History, 1520–1720*, Berkeley and Los Angeles, University of California Press, 1973.

MacNeish, R. S., et al., Second Annual Report of the Ayacucho Archaeological-Botanical Project, Andover, Mass., Robert S. Peabody Foundation for Archaeology, Phillips Academy, 1970.

Mauro, F., *Le Portugal et l'Atlantique au XVIIᵉ Siècle (1570–1670)*, Paris, Études Economique, 1960.

——, "México y Brasil: Dos Economías Coloniales Comparadas," *Historia Mexicana*, Vol. 40, 1961, pp. 571–587.

Mellafe, R., *Negro Slavery in Latin America*, Berkeley and Los Angeles, University of California Press, 1975.

Mörner, M., "The Spanish American Hacienda: A Survey of Recent Research and Debate," *Hispanic American Historical Review*, Vol. 53, 1973, pp. 183–216.

Morse, R. M., "Some Characteristics of Latin American Urban History," *American Historical Review*, Vol. 67, 1962, pp. 317–338.

——, *The Bandeirantes: The Historical Role of the Brazilian Pathfinders*, New York, Knopf, 1965.

Palmer, C. A., *Slaves of the White God: Blacks in Mexico, 1570–1650*, Cambridge, Mass., Harvard University Press, 1976.

Patch, R., *Modern Indians and the Inca Empire*, American University Field Staff Reports, West Coast South America Series, Vol. 5, No. 8, 1958.

Phelan, J. L., *The Kingdom of Quito in the Seventeenth Century*, Madison, University of Wisconsin Press, 1967.

Poppino, R., "Cattle Industry in Colonial Brazil," *Mid America*, Vol. 31, 1949, pp. 219–247.

Rippy, J. F., and J. T. Nelson, *Crusaders of the Jungle*, Chapel Hill, University of North Carolina Press, 1936.

Robinson, David J., *Social Fabric and Spatial Structure in Colonial Latin America*, Ann Arbor, Mich., University Microfilms International, 1979.

Rosenblat, A., *La Población Indígena y el Mestizaje en América*, 2 vols., Buenos Aires, Editorial Nova, 1954.

Rowe, J. H., "Inca Culture at the Time of the Spanish Conquest," in J. H. Steward (ed.), *Handbook of South American Indians*, Vol. 2, Washington, D. C., Smithsonian Institution, Bureau of American Ethnology, Bulletin 143, 1946, pp. 183–330.

Sauer, C. O., *The Early Spanish Main*, Berkeley and Los Angeles, University of California Press, 1966.

Schmieder, O., "The Historic Geography of Tucuman," *University of California Publications in Geography*, Vol. 2, 1928, pp. 359–386.

_____, "The Brazilian Culture Hearth," *University of California Publications in Geography*, Vol. 3, 1929, pp. 159–198.

Simpson, L. B., *The Encomienda in New Spain*, Berkeley and Los Angeles, University of California Press, 1950.

Smith, C. T., "Depopulation of the Central Andes in the Sixteenth Century," *Current Anthropology*, Vol. 11, 1970, pp. 453–464.

Stanislawski, D., "Tarascan Political Geography," *American Anthropologist*, Vol. 49, 1947, pp. 46–55.

Super, J. C., "Querétaro Obrajes: Industry and Society in Provincial Mexico, 1600–1810," *Hispanic American Historical Review*, Vol. 56, 1976, pp. 197–216.

Vargas, J. M., *La Economía Política del Ecuador Durante la Colonia; Esquema Histórico*, Quito, Editorial Universitaria, 1957.

Vásquez de Espinosa, A., *Compendium and Description of the West Indies*, Miscellaneous Collection, No. 102, Washington, D. C., Smithsonian Institution, 1942.

Webb, K. E., "Origins and Development of a Food Economy in Central Minas Gerais," *Annals of the Association of American Geographers*, Vol. 49, 1959, pp. 409–419.

West, R. C., "The Mining Community in Northern New Spain: The Parral Mining District," *Ibero-Americana*, No. 30, Berkeley and Los Angeles, University of California Press, 1949.

_____, *Colonial Placer Mining in Colombia*, Baton Rouge, Louisiana State University Press, 1952.

_____, "Ridge or 'Era' Agriculture in the Colombian Andes," *Proceedings*, 33rd International Congress of Americanists, San Jose, Costa Rica, 1958, Vol. 1, 1959, pp. 279–282.

_____, "Population Densities and Agricultural Practices in Pre-Colombian Mexico, with Emphasis on Semi-terracing," *Proceedings*, 38th International Congress of Americanists, Stuttgart-Munich, 1968, Vol. 2, 1970, pp. 362–369.

West, R. C., and J. P. Augelli, *Middle America, its Land and Peoples*, 2nd ed., Englewood Cliffs, N.J., Prentice-Hall, 1976.

Wilken, G. C., "Drained-Field Agriculture: An Intensive Farming System in Tlaxcala, Mexico," *Geographical Review*, Vol. 59, 1969, pp. 215–241.

Wrigley, G. M., "Salta, An Early Commercial Center of Argentina," *Geographical Review*, Vol. 2, 1916, pp. 116–133.

Zavala, S., *The Spanish Colonization of America*, Philadelphia, University of Pennsylvania Press, 1943.

CHAPTER 3

Transportation

Peter W. Rees

Transportation, the physical movement of people and goods, makes possible the geographic organization of society. Without trail, road, rail, sea, and air transport, all human social and economic activities would have to be conducted in one place, obviously an impossibility. Thus the expressions of transportation, their orientation and intensity over time, are useful indicators of the forces in society that create geographic landscape patterns. Such expressions fall into two categories. First, there is the traffic carried, its nature, direction, and volume. Second, there is the transport form or structure composed of the artifacts of transportation technology: the routeways, visible on land as roads, railroads, and canals as well as the terminals of air and ocean commerce; and the mechanical means of transport, whether truck, train, aircraft, or boat.

In theory, it is possible to determine a specific cost for the transport structure, depending on the distance and nature of the physical environment to be overcome. In a region such as Latin America, these costs are often high, given barriers such as the Andean mountain chain, the steep climb to the Mexican plateau, or the great distances across the Amazon Basin. The theme of this chapter, therefore, is that the existence of a transport link and the intensity of traffic flow is evidence either of an existing level of demand for interaction between two linked points or of the *perception* on the part of transport developers that such interaction would be forthcoming once the link was forged. This latter distinction between actual and perceived interaction is particularly important in Latin America because of the frequency with which a transport project was seen as a heroic endeavor. Once transportation technology had accelerated in the nineteenth century with applications of the steam engine on land and water, grandiose schemes to connect diverse regions, which would sweep away ignorance and economic stagnation at a stroke, were common in the minds of both domestic and foreign investors. An explanation of the historical development of the Latin American transport pattern is thus concerned as much with dreams as with reality.

[handwritten annotation: Territory must be established enough to generate fixed transport networks]

PRE-HISPANIC TRANSPORTATION ON THE EVE OF THE CONQUEST

Only the Aztec, Mayan, and Incan cultural hearths had developed sufficient control over territory to generate a fixed transport network prior to the conquest. Although the nature and role of transportation varied in each area, there were some similarities. There was no use of wheeled vehicles, and only the Incas made limited use of animals. Roads and trails were therefore constructed primarily for human movement, a condition that gave considerable flexibility in overcoming topography. The routes were also internally oriented, fanning out from a focus on interior cities. Coastal trade was peripheral and seems only to have been important among the Mayas. Port locations did not rank highly in the settlement hierarchy, in marked contrast to the externally oriented colonial transport pattern that followed.

[handwritten annotation: Paths + roadways for travel + trade. Set up garrisons + inns established along the way to protect + sustain traveling merchants.]

The Aztecs

Although the Aztecs were not formal road builders, well-traveled pathways were kept open and bridges constructed where deep rivers or steep *barrancas* had to be crossed. Furthermore, garrisons and inns were established along the way to protect and sustain travelers, merchants, and couriers.

Two categories of goods, derived from tribute and long-distance commerce, moved over the roads. Tribute, a tax payable in products from conquered peoples, came from within the Aztec state and tended to be local in movement. Much of it was destined for provincial rulers and appeared in regional markets. Long-distance commerce, composed of luxury goods such as cotton, feathers, gold, and precious stones, came from beyond the limits of the Aztec Empire. It was quite separate from local tribute movements, being reserved for the elite and not the common people. A special class of traders, the *pochteca*, conducted the long-distance trade using *tamemes* (human carriers) to move the goods, but often they also acted as informers, probing the military weaknesses of tribal groups on the periphery of the Aztec Empire. Thus, in any one area, commerce preceded tribute; as the political and economic hegemony of the Aztec state was slowly pushed out to cover much of central and southern Mexico, so this was reflected in the proportion of tribute and long-distance trade moving over the roads.

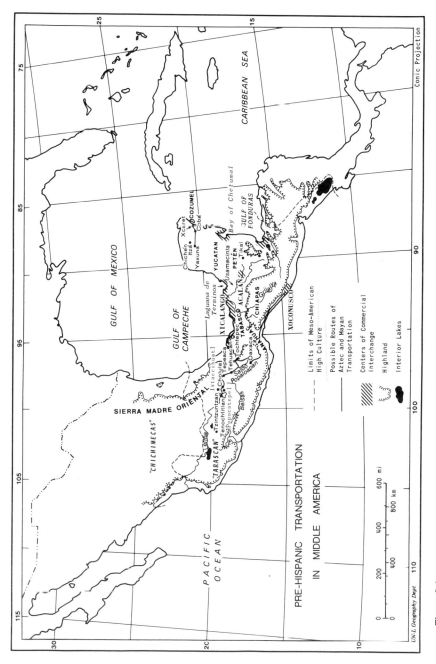

PRE-HISPANIC TRANSPORTATION
IN MIDDLE AMERICA

Figure 3.1

The pathways followed by the *pochteca* ran mostly south and east from their focal point in the Valley of Mexico (Figure 3-1). The Aztecs made no real commercial expeditions to the north, a land of nomadic and hostile *chichime-cas*, although there is some evidence they traded with Tarascans to the west who were then the finest metallurgists in Mesoamerica. Their principal goal, however, was what has been called, "ports of trade," ecological transition zones between highlands and lowlands occupied by politically weak peoples whose military control was poorly developed. In such locations strangers felt sufficiently confident to meet and trade.

Xicalango, an area between Laguna de Terminos and the town of Xica-lango itself, contained the main points of warehousing and trade on the Gulf of Mexico. Xoconusco was the Pacific coast counterpart, although it was less important in terms of trade volume. However, it was the only port of trade that continued in use after being absorbed within the Aztec Empire in 1486. Finally, a third region, Acalán, was located inland around the upper reaches of the Candelaria River. In all three areas the *pochteca* bartered with peoples from the Mayan culture, exchanging craft goods manufactured in the Valley of Mexico for raw materials unavailable in highland Mexico. Two other port-of-trade areas faced the Caribbean, one in the Bay of Chetumal and the other in the Gulf of Honduras. Although probably dominated by Mayan traders and acting as trading bridges between Mesoamerica and Central America to the south, they may also have been penetrated by Aztec influence. In general we have tended to underestimate, not overestimate, the distances Mesoamerican peoples were capable of traveling.

The precise orientation of the principal pathways remains obscure because no formal roads were constructed. Scraps of evidence, such as reports of attacks by local people against the *pochteca* or tribute lists that mention local provision of *tameme* labor, provide a few key locations from which we can hypothesize possible routes. Principal among these was a route that ran from Tenochtitlán by causeway and canoe across the lakes of the Valley of Mexico and then breached the barrier formed by the volcanic peaks of Popocatépetl and Ixtaccihuatl. Descending the eastern slopes of the range, the traders probably headed for Cholula. Since ceremony and myth acted as much more important determinants of trade organization than more modern influences of economic cost based on time and distance, this major ceremonial town was a logical stopping place. From Cholula, the route led east through the connecting basins of the Mexican plateau to Tepeaca and along the dry, scrub-covered longitudinal valley to Tehuacán. The merchants then picked up the trace of the Río Salado to its meeting with the Río Papaloapan, which at this point slices a narrow valley between the folds of the Sierra Madre Oriental to reach Tochtepec. This town was the gateway to the lowland ports of interchange, the axis from which pathways long since vanished in the humid tangle of forest and stream fanned out to tap the wide variety of tropical products.

Mayan · vast commercial empire - Trade exports for
exchange; Mayan porters have unpaid slaves to be sold
along w/ products they carried.

The Maya

The Yucatecan Mayas occupied a vast commercial empire that stretched from Tabasco to northern Honduras. Traders dealt with sources as far away as Nicaragua and with Chiapas and highland Guatemala, but the primary contacts were probably with representatives from highland Mexico at the ports of interchange already mentioned. Salt, cotton, cloth, slaves, and honey were the principal exports, exchanged for cacao from Tabasco and Honduras; bells, small axes, copper sheets and obsidian, rabbit hair for embroidery from Oaxaca; and yellow topaz nose beads from Chiapas.

As with the Aztecs, commerce was a lucrative occupation for the Mayan traders, or *ppolm*; they did not compose such a specific social class as the *pochteca*, but trade tended to be the province of noble families. Goods moved overland on men's backs, although Mayan porters differed from Aztec *tamemes* in being unpaid slaves to be sold along with the products they carried. Foot trails followed through the forest were often little more than tunnels of vegetation sufficient to permit the movement of one man and his load, which frustrated the mounted Spanish horsemen who attempted to follow such pathways in their exploration of the region. The Mayas also used dugout canoes, and water travel by traders was common in both the Gulf of Campeche and the Gulf of Honduras.

Reconstruction of the route pattern of Mayan trade would be as imprecise as that of the Aztecs were it not for the raised causeways or roads to be found in the Petén and Yucatan peninsula. Often running considerable distances in straight lines through the forest, with no detours to avoid swampy sections, these structures of partly dressed limestone blocks and tamped surface stood as much as 6 feet above the ground and measured up to 66 feet wide. In the absence of wheeled vehicles or animal transport, their use can only be surmised; however, the fact that they usually are axial *intraurban* linkages between the dispersed elements of major Mayan cities and change compass direction at religious sites suggests that their purpose may be as much symbolic and ritual as economic. On the other hand, the longest causeway yet uncovered is *interurban*, running 62 miles between Yaxuná, Cobá, a major commercial city, and Xcaret, a principal Mayan port on the Cozumel coast. In this instance, the causeway may well be reflective of Mayan transportation. Nevertheless, the present nature and density of causeways that have so far been uncovered is not of sufficient detail to suggest that they represent the visual, geographic expression of pre-Hispanic trade movement in this cultural region.

The Inca

If there is uncertainty about the role of Mayan road construction, there is no question about the geographic orientation and basic purpose of the Incan

[handwritten marginal notes at top of page] 2 main routes ran length of the Incan Empire; the 2 great roads connected at various points by shorter transverse roads than ran up the Andean escarpment from the Pacific. City of Incan description as the "navel of the Empire." Rapid communication + ease of transportation were central to the means by which Incan control over people + territory was achieved. Incas built a system of shelters stocked w/ supplies.

highways. The rapid political consolidation of separate culture groups scattered within the Andean realm between 1438 and 1525 was accompanied by an impressive system of highways, which colonial Spanish observers claimed exceeded in scale and technology the Roman roads of Europe.

Two main routes ran the length of the Incan Empire (Figure 3-2). From just north of Quito, a major highland road connected numerous Andean communities, extending as far south as Tucumán in present-day Argentina. There is some uncertainty about the southern terminus of the highway, where Incan political control was less established, and it has been suggested that at least a branch road extended beyond Tucumán into modern Chile, ending south of Santiago at Talca, or even as far as the Río Bio Bio. Nearly as long as the 3000-mile highland road was a parallel coastal highway that began in the north at Tumbez and reached as far south as Arequipa. These two great, continuous arteries were connected at various points by shorter transverse roads that ran up the Andean escarpment from the Pacific. Principal among these was a link between Nazca, on the coast, and Vilcas, on the highland route, a site anciently regarded as the geographical center of the Incan Empire. In addition to these primary highways, a denser network of secondary roads was developed, some of which pushed across the *cordillera* to penetrate the dense tropical forests on the eastern slopes. All roads ultimately arrived at the imperial capital of Cuzco, an orientation that earned that city its Incan description as the "navel of the Empire."

The construction of these roads required a combination of technical and organizational skills unmatched either in Europe or the rest of the New World at the time. Overcoming remarkable topographic obstacles, Incan engineers sometimes carved their mountain highways out of solid rock faces or spanned deep river gorges with suspension bridges made of aloe-fiber ropes. On the level plateaux and lowlands, the prepared, raised roadbeds, often up to 16 feet wide, were bordered by stone walls to prevent travelers and animals from trampling the planted fields. On the drier coast the highways were lined with trees to provide shade and fruit. At times markers were established to note distances and, in the deserts where shifting sands might obliterate the highway, alignments were marked with wooden posts that the Spaniards later used for firewood.

The enormous resources of time and human labor committed to the development of this transport network were justified because of the political, organizational, and economic purposes it fulfilled. Rapid communication and ease of transportation were central to the means by which Incan control over people and territory was achieved. Messages moving swiftly over considerable distances could be quickly followed by military forces to put down disruption or revolt. The Incas built a system of shelters, or *tambos*, along the highways; they were stocked with supplies for traveling officials or soldiers. Other less substantial shelters housed couriers (*chasquis*) who were prepared at all times

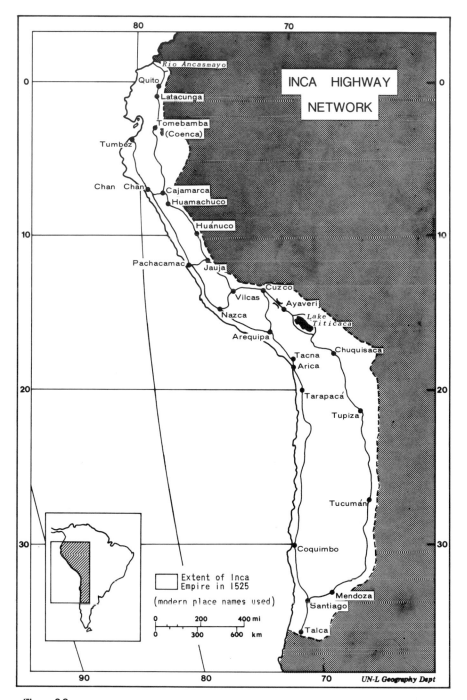

80 70

Rio Ancasmayo

Quito

INCA HIGHWAY
NETWORK

Latacunga

Tomebamba
(Coenca)

Tumbez

Chan Chan
Cajamarca
Huamachuco

Huánuco

10

Pachacamac
Jauja

Cuzco

Vilcas
Ayaveri

Nazca
Lake
Titicaca

Arequipa

Tacna
Chuquisaca
Arica

20
Tarapacá

Tupiza

Tucumán

30
Coquimbo

Extent of Inca
Empire in 1525

(modern place names used)

Mendoza
Santiago

0   200   400 mi
0   300   600 km

Talca

90 80 70   *UN-L Geography Dept*

Figure 3.2

to run messages in relay fashion. It was estimated that with this communication system a message could travel along the mountain chain 1500 miles between Cuzco and Quito in only 10 days. Highway maintenance, provisioning the *tambos*, and supplying the *chasquis* were the responsibility of local communities as part of their *mita* tax.

The highways also facilitated a substantial but controlled population displacement as well as the monopolization of trade and distribution of goods. Many people were moved over the roads, partly through the treatment of the whole Incan Empire as one labor pool with workers moved to points of construction necessary for the state, and partly under the *mita* system, in which the local elite of a recently conquered area were moved to "foreign" areas where they were required to control the population. The volume of trade and the extent of its contribution to highway traffic is more complex. Before the Incas, the movement of economic goods had been stimulated by the complementarity of coastal, highland, and Amazon forest zones. From the coast came cotton, fruit, fish, and shells; the highlands provided metals, wool, maize, potatoes, and agave fiber; and the forests east of the *cordillera* generated wood, feathers, and coca. As with the areas of Mesoamerica, long-distance commerce was a trade in luxuries: fine textiles, precious stones, metals (especially copper), and obsidian. These goods moved great distances up and down the *cordillera*, and even into Middle America, through markets in Darién. Under the Incas, where residence of the population was controlled, self-sufficiency within communities encouraged, and free movement over the roads forbidden for all but the elite, there was no trading class. Through local exchange, luxury articles reached the ruling class in places such as Cuzco, but goods probably moved much greater distances, through barter and exchange, than did the people and llama trains that carried them.

In contrast to the Aztecs, therefore, trade under the Incas was probably not a major stimulus for the development of their transport network. As Katz (1972) has observed, the Incan domain included areas of considerable ecological contrasts and contained a wide variety of raw materials, while the Aztecs occupied a highland environment relatively scarce in resource variety compared to the surrounding tropical lowlands. Thus, for the Inca, transportation was a question of redistribution of supplies. For the Aztecs, however, it involved an elaborate trading system in which manufactured products, primarily from the Valley of Mexico, were exchanged for the raw materials of the lowlands, often coming from areas outside Aztec political control.

In spite of these contrasts between cultural realms, it can still be said that pre-Hispanic transportation was marked by *internal* transport alignments serving regional or domestic stimuli. This geographical pattern was reversed by European colonization, with its *external* political and economic influences. For this reason there was only little accidental continuity between the routes of indigenous and colonial transportation in Latin America.

[Handwritten annotations in top margin: "Patterns of transportation reflect colonization / Spanish colonies 2 basic objectives ① estab. of Catholicism in New World (?) Organ of colonial economy producing raw materials & precious metals for shipment to Spain / People wanted to return to Spain a[fter] their fortunes."]

THE COLONIAL PERIOD

The patterns of transportation developed by Portuguese and Spaniards in Latin America, although quite different, reflected the conditions of colonization. Portuguese settlement began as a series of agriculturally based coastal enclaves, relatively isolated from one another in comparison with their transatlantic contacts with Portugal. Although the mining boom in the eighteenth century drew some population inland, 60 percent still remained within 30 miles of the coast by the end of the colonial period, and land transport was not geographically extensive. In the Spanish colonies, on the other hand, the attempt to control a vast area in Middle and South America resulted in the development of a widespread pattern of sea and land communications that was the basis for much of the contemporary transportation landscape of Latin America.

Spanish colonial policy early reflected two basic objectives—the establishment of Catholicism in the New World through instruction and conversion of the indigenous population, and the organization of a colonial economy producing raw materials and precious metals for shipment to Spain, while reserving for Iberian producers the limited American market for consumer goods. Furthermore, this policy was administered whenever possible through cities and towns, since reliance on settlements aided both the crown's desire for control over the affairs of its distant colonies and the Spanish belief in the civilizing influence of town life.

The religious objective, promoted especially by monastic orders and later by the Jesuits, focused primarily on areas of previously dense indigenous populations, frequently involving their further geographical concentration on certain communities under the system of *reducción* or *congregación*. Although this system was later used by *hacienda* owners to obtain Indian land and labor, the Indian settlements sustained by religious motives were often self-contained and isolated. While they usually yielded tribute and supported limited regional market exchange, they rarely generated the large volume of goods and supplies over substantial distances sufficient to sustain the principal features of the colonial transportation network. Indeed, if these had been the only settlements to appear in colonial Spanish America, they probably would have produced a pattern of internally oriented local roads reminiscent of the pre-Hispanic past. Instead, it was the second (economic) objective of colonial policy that gave rise to the extensive pattern of highways and sea traffic.

The economic policy of the government in Spain during the first two centuries of the colonial period viewed the New World as a dependent, if distant, part of the Iberian economy. Accumulated wealth was to accrue to the homeland, an objective supported by many of the early settlers who hoped to return to Spain with their fortunes. Thus, in theory, the silver and gold gained from mining towns and commodities such as hides, sugar, grain, dyewood, cochi-

most Spaniards didn't return to Spain - developed
more interest in [intra] + intercolonial trade in Americas
wealth as Spain drained by pirates against
trans-atlantic shipping - restricted, limited
+ even restricted at times forbidden

96   TRANSPORTATION

neal, indigo, and cacao from farming regions were to be concentrated in a few principal administrative and commercial urban centers, carried to ports, and shipped to Spain. Backhauled over these same routes were to come Spanish cloth, oil, wine, mercury for the mines, and all manner of manufactured goods from quill pens to nails to sustain colonial production and an Iberian way of life. Reality, of course, differed from theory. Mining towns and major urban commercial centers, often lacking a sufficient local food supply, took much of the colonial agricultural output. Since this was paid for by specie from the mines, a complex set of interchanges and transportation flows developed within the colonies among mining, agricultural, and administrative-commercial settlements. Furthermore, many settlers never returned to Spain, in spite of their intentions and, as generations of creoles strove to control more of the colonial commerce from which true fortunes could be made, they developed greater interest in both intra- and intercolonial trade within the Americas. Finally, colonial wealth destined for Spain was often drained off to other European nations as a result of piracy against transatlantic shipping, while the market for European goods in the colonies was frequently penetrated by contraband landed from British, Dutch, and French vessels.

The Spanish crown reacted to these incursions on its anticipated wealth throughout most of the colonial period with attempts to exert control over the movement of commerce and so bring it closer to the ideal pattern. Import-export traffic was limited to a small number of ports or collecting points in both Spain and the Americas, intercolonial trade was restricted and at times forbidden, transatlantic exchange was confined to two official fairs in Mexico and Panama, and ocean crossings were to be conducted in convoys. On both land and sea these edicts, along with many other more detailed rules on the conduct of commerce, restricted the paths of trade movement and the articulation of the transportation pattern.

Enforcement of these attempts by the crown to monopolize the benefits of commercial exchange were not always successful. "I obey but will not comply" was a common enough reaction by colonial settlers to the trade laws, while venality among crown officials was not unusual. However, by sharing some of the fruits of monopoly with powerful interests in Mexico City and Lima, the crown prevailed and a majority of the principal routes of commerce that developed reflected the external orientation of colonial economic policy. Thus it is convenient to identify a hierarchically structured pattern of Spanish colonial transportation. At the lowest intracolonial level, trails fanned out from major commercial centers such as Mexico City, Guatemala City, Cartagena, and Lima to connect with more remote mining and agricultural towns; where the commercial centers were not also ports, important arterials connected them with the coast, such as the highways that linked Mexico City and Veracruz. An intermediate, intercolonial level comprised a small number of

[Handwritten notes at top of page: "H2O trade routes developed. Transatlantic trade so did attacks against Spanish shipping by other Eur. nations. To send goods - need permit."]

coastal and sea routes linking the principal ports of each colony, such as the trade that developed between Mexico and Peru, Mexico and Venezuela, Peru and Chile, and the American colonies and the Philippines. At the highest level was the transatlantic artery of commerce between the American colonies and Spain, restricted for much of the colonial period to the convoy system, or *flotas*. In investigating the details of colonial transportation, it is convenient to begin at this level, which the Spaniards called the *Carrera de Indias*.

[Handwritten notes: "Attn. turned on mainland. Permits were needed to send goods. Trade fell in hands of wealthy. Legal constraints in trade imposed on movement of goods."]

The Carrera de Indias

The Spanish conquest in the Americas was substantially complete by 1540. At this time, trade with the Caribbean islands had diminished greatly as these earliest Spanish settlements had become, in Sauer's words, "a shabby fringe of empire," and attention was turning to the mainland. During the following 10 years, transatlantic traffic among Spain, Mexico, and Peru increased substantially, but so did the attacks against Spanish shipping by other European nations. As losses mounted at the same time that the scale of potential wealth to be yielded by the new colonies dawned on the crown, restrictions on trade were imposed. Non-Spanish Europeans were forbidden direct access to Spanish colonial trade and, within Spain itself, all trade with the American colonies was to be controlled by a *Casa de Contratación*, organized by the merchant guild, or *Consulado*, of Seville. Any merchant wishing to travel or send goods to America first had to obtain a permit from the *Casa* and, since minimum investments and minimum sizes of vessels crossing the Atlantic were also introduced, almost all American trade was soon in the hands of a few wealthy commercial houses in Seville, the city to which (with its subsidiary Cádiz) all legal exports to the colonies were confined.

This monopolistic position was shared in the colonies by the *Consulados* of Mexico City and Lima, who controlled much of the distribution of Iberian products and assembly of exports in the Americas. At first, the colonial merchant houses often included relatives of Seville merchant families but, as creoles became more numerous, rivalry developed between the *Consulados* of Seville and those of the colonies. The stakes were high; in spite of the wealth produced from some mines and haciendas in the New World, commerce was the principal means of sustaining a high income and, according to Brading (1971), by the eighteenth century merchants had emerged as dominant figures in society in both Mexico and Peru. The privileged position of the merchant groups could not be sustained, however, without the legal constraints on trade imposed by the crown and similar geographic limitations on the movement of goods. This occurred after 1552, with the introduction of the *flota system*, in which all vessels destined for the colonies were required to travel in two annual protected convoys, one to New Spain and the other to Tierra Firme (Panama).

Furthermore, after 1572, all goods of the *Carrera de Indias* were to be exchanged in a limited number of fairs (*ferias*).

The *flota* for New Spain was supposed to clear the bar of San Lucar, at the mouth of the Guadalquivir River, in May (Figure 3-3). After entering the Caribbean, some ships headed for various island ports, but most made for Veracruz, which was reached 6 weeks after leaving Spain. The harbor at Veracruz was a hazardous, poorly protected roadstead on the leeward side of the island of San Juan de Ulúa, where vessels were often subject to the ravages of fierce *nortes* and disease might kill off half of the ship's crews. Carried by lighters to the mouth of the Antigua River, the goods brought by the *flota* were then transferred to long trains of mules (*requas*) that wound up the steep inclines of the Sierra Madre Oriental to Mexico City on the plateau, where the *feria* would take place. The exchange was frequently subject to prices that had already been set in earlier secret negotiations between representatives of the *Consulados* of Mexico City and Seville. This tended to restrict the participation of smaller merchant houses located in other parts of New Spain. It also contributed to the focus of economic activity on the capital, which was already well-developed as the center of political administration of New Spain and the site of the colony's only mint. Thus, under the Spaniards, Mexico City maintained the same dominant role in the urban hierarchy as it had under the Aztecs; consequently it remained the focal point of the colonial route pattern. Goods brought from Spain, and ultimately destined for places as widely scattered as León, Guadalajara, and Oaxaca, and silver from the mines of Parral, Zacatecas, Pachuca, and Taxco to pay for the goods, were all assembled in Mexico City instead of following more direct alignments.

Attempts to reduce Mexico City's dominance were frequent. The Seville merchants in particular felt at a disadvantage; they had to bear the high cost of moving their goods up to the plateau from Veracruz. This was made even more difficult, since the timing of the *flota's* departure from Spain, designed to take advantage of the northerly position of the subtropical high-pressure zone over the Atlantic, often resulted in the arrival of the fleet at the height of the rainy season in Mexico. Delays, caused by the quagmires to which the roads were reduced in this season, could amount to 2 months or more before the goods reached Mexico City after arrival in the Gulf port. If the Spanish merchants were to complete their price negotiations and return in time to catch the departure of the *flota* for Spain the following February, they clearly placed themselves at a disadvantage in bargaining with the merchants of the capital, who had no such time limit. The many complaints to the crown by the *Consulado* of Seville in concert with other disaffected merchant groups in New Spain, such as those of Veracruz, were finally heeded in 1718, when the *feria* was moved to Jalapa, located halfway up the steep eastern escarpment of the Sierra Madre Oriental and only 75 miles from Veracruz. It was hoped that the change

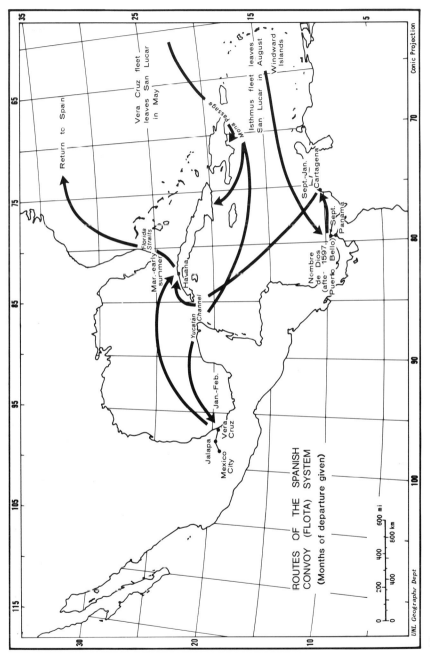

ROUTES OF THE SPANISH CONVOY (FLOTA) SYSTEM
(Months of departure given)

Figure 3.3

would achieve a greater balance among the economic interests that handled the Indies trade. However, by this time the power of Mexico City and the lines of transport that sustained it had acquired a degree of inertia and advantage that could not be overcome.

If Mexico City was the terminus of the *flota* in New Spain, Lima, not Panama, was the terminus of the *flota* in South America; the crown's desire to maintain control over commercial movement was so great that it determined that trade with Peru should be from the Pacific and not the Atlantic coast, following the direction of original colonization and avoiding conflict with the Portuguese. The more southerly *flota* departed Spain in August and reached Nombre de Díos in late September. After 1597, the Caribbean terminus was moved to Puerto Bello, a better and more protected port, and there the largest *feria* in the Spanish colonies developed, primarily because of the restriction that merchants from Spain could only trade on their own account as far as Panama while Peruvian merchants were likewise limited in the opposite direction. As with the *feria* in New Spain, trade was dominated by a few large merchant houses, members of the *Consulados* of Seville and Lima.

Typically, as in a case described by Lockhart (1972), a trading company participating in the Indies trade was created only for a limited number of shipments. One factor was stationed in Toledo and assembled goods for the Americas, paying with Peruvian gold and silver. The principal owner of the company was located in Seville and handled the consignments of goods to the *flota*. Another partner in Panama received the goods, and either sold them to Peruvian merchants at the *feria* or arranged for their transshipment by mule train across the isthmus and on by ship to Lima. There, relatives in Seville could dispose of them at once or ship them on to Arequipa, where another trading house was maintained. Prices fluctuated wildly, since the total volume of goods involved was small (the average flota might carry no more than 3000 tons of cargo), and there was a considerable time lapse between the appearance of demand in the colonies and response on the part of Iberian shippers. Meanwhile, depending on the level of warehouse hoarding or the sudden appearance of contraband goods, the regular *flota* could arrive to a barren or saturated market. Although returns to the participants in the Indies trade averaged 100 percent, enormous profits (and equal losses) as high as 500 percent were possible, and venality and theft by factors were common occurrences among trading companies, even when relatives controlled the major transfer points in the passage of goods.

In such an atmosphere, the fair at Puerto Bello thrived for 14 to 40 days, after which the *flota* sailed on to the strongly fortified harbor of Cartagena for supplies and overhaul. Many of the ships by this time had been in tropical waters long enough to suffer substantial damage to their hulls and were scrapped; the salvaged timbers were incorporated into the port architecture. Other ves-

The Carrera de Indias served its purpose permitting Spain to monopolize the commercial & resource benefits developed in Amer. colonies.

sels remained in the Americas as part of the coastal trade. For the rest, another smaller *feria* in Cartagena, stimulated by the gold production of Antioquia, furnished an additional source of commerce for the return voyage to Spain. In January the departing vessels first made for Havana, where they linked up with the returning fleet from Veracruz and then together headed out through the dangerous Florida straits to follow the westerlies across the Atlantic to Spain.

These generalized details of the *Carrera de Indias* were often subject to considerable variation. The dates of departure from Spain could differ by 3 or 4 months, and hurricanes, *nortes*, and buccaneers did at times make sharp inroads into the number of vessels that completed the round trip. Neither were the *flotas* always an annual event. Even at the height of the *flota* traffic in the late sixteenth and early seventeenth centuries, some years would pass without the arrival of any authorized galleons, and these intervals increased in the seventeenth century during the period of economic depression in Spain and its colonies. At such times, the colonies became totally dependent on foreign contraband goods to supply their imports. Foreigners also penetrated legal trade. According to Haring (1963), French goods comprised a majority of the cargoes in the *flotas* until the eighteenth century, when English goods gained the lead. By the end of the seventeenth century, Spanish goods already amounted to no more than one-sixth of the total, a figure that deteriorated to only one-twentieth in the following century. Spanish vessels were also in the minority by this time. Although it controlled the movement of the *flotas*, Spain now contributed little more than 10 percent of the ships engaged in the American trade. Indeed, the eighteenth century saw a progressive weakening of the whole monopolistic character of the *Carrera de Indias*. It began with the *asiento*, in which Spain was forced to grant England the right to limited but legal trading with the Indies, and continued with the Bourbon economic reforms, the most famous of which was the decree of *comercio libre* in 1778. This destroyed the Seville-Cádiz monopoly by opening up Iberian ports and selected ports in the colonies to the Indies trade and effectively ended the *flotas*, the restricted *ferias*, and the privileged position of Veracruz, Puerto Bello, and Cartagena.

The *Carrera de Indias* was a cumbersome system, enormously costly to operate, and subject to restrictive regulations and chronic fraud. Yet, as Parry (1966) has observed, it served its purpose throughout most of the colonial period in permitting Spain to monopolize the commercial and resource benefits developed in the American colonies. This was borne out by the volume and nature of the traffic. Bullion dominated eastbound cargoes and, during the late sixteenth and early seventeenth centuries at the height of the traffic, the proportion of gold and silver never amounted to less than 80 percent by value. Moreover, the balance of trade remained in Spain's favor; the value of exports shipped by the private sector from America was more than four times that of imports. This reduced the freight rates on westbound cargoes and encouraged the competitiveness of European products, particularly textiles.

Finally, the restrictive nature of the *Carrera* resulted in a well-articulated instead of diffuse pattern of colonial transportation at the transatlantic level, with a limited number of routes, ports, and centers of commercial interchange. Although this pattern was altered after 1778, its principal features remained intact; the ports and commercial centers that had previously been excluded from the *Carrera* still often found it difficult to attract sufficient traffic to support major new routes and thereby mount an effective challenge to the centers that had handled the Indies trade.

Intercolonial Movement

The attention usually devoted to the *Carrera de Indias* is justified since, prior to the Bourbon reforms, it represented the framework and limits within which the patterns of official trade and transportation developed in colonial Spanish America. Furthermore, much of the traffic movement within the colonies and some intercolonial transportation were in *direct* response to overseas trade, such as the Rio San Juan route in Nicaragua, which developed to supply the *flotas* at Nombre de Dios and Cartagena with foodstuffs assembled in Granada from Guatemala, Honduras, El Salvador, and Costa Rica. However, while it is often difficult to distinguish traffic generated by the *Carrera* from that resulting directly from intercolonial trade, there is no doubt that some transport routes did develop in response to movement independent of, or even in competition with, overseas commerce. One such example was the traffic between Mexico and Peru.

Mexico-Peru. Coastal shipping existed in the Pacific as early as the 1520s, when Indian slaves were transported from the Nicaraguan coast to Panama. The Nicaraguan hinterland also offered good shipbuilding materials that became the basis for a number of its Pacific seaports and, together with Panama, it provided many of the ships and sailors that ultimately participated in the Peruvian coastal trade. By the end of the 1530s, an annual fleet left Realejo for Peru with provisions and goods; the port of Acajutla later developed a trade in indigo with Peru and Chile. However, as early as 1537, Mexico had begun to supersede Central America as the northern destination of Pacific trade.

The Mexican terminus at Huatulco was a good port, relatively easily linked with Mexico City by a highway through Oaxaca, and to Guatemala by trails through Tehuantepec and the Xoconusco coast. The voyage south took at least 2 months, landfall first being made at Manta, the island of Puná, or Paita, where goods destined for Guayaquil and northern Peru were landed. The main Peruvian terminus was Callao, the port of Lima. Participating vessels in the trade were neither large in number or size; however, sailings were sufficiently regular, especially between 1550 and 1585, that they became an important part of the economies of both colonies.

The basis of the trade rested on Peru's much larger production of silver, especially after the discovery of the great Potosí mines in 1545, and the colony's high costs for the importation of Spanish goods by the official *flota* because of storage and transshipment losses in tropical Panama and the potential dangers of two longer ocean voyages. On the other hand Mexico, with a much larger Spanish population than Peru, achieved greater development in European agriculture and production of native textiles yet was perennially short of specie within its borders, since so much went to Spain as part of the crown tax (the royal fifth). Because the crown resisted all Mexican requests to keep more coins in the colony, the exchange of Peruvian specie for Mexican goods and supplies was an obvious basis for trade.

Once established, other items were added to the traffic. After specie, a second major commodity shipped by Peru to Mexico was mercury. The use of this metal as an amalgam in silver refining began in 1556 with the introduction of the *patio* process at the Real del Monte mines of Pachuca in Mexico; this process permitted the mining industry to use lower-grade ores. Since no mercury was found in Mexico, it was imported from the Almadén mine in Spain. However, after the opening of the Huancavélica mercury mine in Peru in 1563, the Mexican miners were offered a second, cheaper source. Such was the output of Huancavélica that even after the successful adaptation of the *patio* process to Peruvian ores 10 years later, the needs of Potosí did not absorb its total production and the metal continued to be shipped to Mexico. Finally, toward the end of the sixteenth century, the Peruvians found in their locally produced wine and brandy a third category of goods in demand in Mexico.

Resistance to this intercolonial trade was soon forthcoming, even at times in Mexico itself; in the years when the *flota* failed to sail, New Spain was sometimes drained of its stock of imported Spanish goods by Peruvian merchants whose greater availability of specie permitted them to outbid the merchants of Mexico City in their own territory. But opposition was greatest in Spain. Spanish merchants were unhappy at the development of an alternate route for Peruvian imports of Iberian goods over which they had less control, while the crown was nervous lest any development of economic independence from Spain by Peru lead to political independence. The crown also stood to lose financially, especially in mercury shipments, since the royal monopoly at Almadén, established in 1559, was threatened by Peruvian production. Thus one of the early attempts to curtail Mexican-Peruvian trade was the crown's insistence in the 1570s that exports of mercury from Spain be given preference over those from Peru in the Mexican market. The strongest reaction against the trade, however, came with the participation of Chinese goods from Spain's new colony in the Philippines.

The first of the Manila galleons following the North Pacific and California currents landed on the southern coast of Mexico in 1565. Sailings soon became annual occurrences and, in 1573, Acapulco was designated as the Pacific
terminus. Although it was a fine, natural harbor, the new port was connected
to Mexico City only by tortuous and difficult trail. Its choice may have been
due to a much closer proximity to the capital than other coastal sites, thus supporting the crown's expectation that the Orient trade would become an extension of the *Carrera de Indias*. However, Chinese goods were soon being
diverted to Peru. Throughout the 1580s, their quantity increased unimpeded
until they comprised enough of the total intercolonial traffic that the terminal
port of Huatulco was abandoned in favor of Acapulco in 1587.

The lure of these goods was, first, their variety, which ranged from iron
and copper to exotic Oriental luxuries, especially silk; the second attraction
was their cheapness. Chinese textiles sold for perhaps one-ninth of the price
Spanish cloth fetched in Lima, while Mexican textiles fell midway between the
two extremes. In addition, Peruvian merchants were attracted to this new Pacific trade because of its relative safety. Peruvian specie could earn Oriental
imports without incurring the risks of Atlantic travel or even impoundment, as
occurred in 1590 when the needs of Phillip II's treasury were met by a forced
loan on the entire returning Indies fleet.

The merchants of Seville were alarmed at the implications of the Oriental
trade. With their monopoly position, they had previously driven up the prices
of imported goods to whatever level necessary to acquire the available specie in
the New World. Now they saw their lucrative monopoly being ruined by competition with cheaper Chinese goods while they continued to bear the costs of
the now diminished transatlantic *flotas*. The crown was equally concerned,
particularly because the Oriental trade meant the diversion of American specie
beyond the borders of the Spanish Empire. Yet, at the same time, it was accepted that some degree of transpacific trade was necessary to benefit the
economy of the Philippine colony. Toward the end of the sixteenth century,
therefore, the crown continually tried to prevent Oriental goods from entering
the Mexican-Peruvian traffic and, after 1593, restricted the Manila trade to
two annual galleons of 300 tons each to be sailed to New Spain for the benefit
of the islands, with reshipment to Peru forbidden. This had little or no effect
on intercolonial trade, which shifted to smuggling instead. In one instance,
even the viceroy of Peru invested in an illegal consignment departing Peru for
the Philippines. Finally, in 1634, after numerous *cédulas*, or royal orders, in
the seventeenth century had failed to curb the diversion of Oriental goods, the
crown forbade all trade between Mexico and Peru, an order that remained in
force until colonial trade was liberalized under the Bourbons in the eighteenth
century. During the intervening period, the transportation route between the
two colonies was effectively ended except for occasional illegal shipments.

Mexico-Venezuela. The availability and distribution of specie, so important to the Pacific coastal trade, was also a major stimulus to another intercolonial transport route that developed between Mexico and Venezuela. The first shipments of cacao probably left Caracas for Veracruz in 1622 and were paid for in *pesos de plata* minted in Mexico City, or possibly in Lima. For the first 30 years prior to 1650 Caracas sent 35,512 *fanegas* of cacao to Mexico and only 289 directly to Spain. In the following 50 years the quantities increased tenfold, although at the end of the century Spain still accounted for less than one-quarter of the total. Shipments from Maracaibo seem to have followed similar trends. The attraction of the trade for Mexicans was the product itself; cacao had been highly prized since precolonial times, when the beans were a medium of exchange between traders besides being a privileged drink. For the Venezuelans, the trade offered fewer risks than shipment across the Atlantic but, most important, secured specie that could then be used for legitimate trade with the flotas and for obtaining contraband goods from Dutch, French, and English vessels along the Venezuelan coast. In addition, Mexico provided wheat flour at times when European hostilities interrupted shipments from Spain.

The direction of the cacao trade did not begin to alter until the eighteenth century, when the Bourbon monarchy sought to change the means of controlling the American trade from a strict reliance on the *flotas* to the additional creation of trading companies modeled after the East India companies, with power to monopolize the overseas trade of a particular part of the colonial empire. Thus the Honduras Company was founded in 1714, the Havana Company in 1740, and the Santo Domingo Company in 1757. However, the only profitable venture was the Caracas Company (Compañía Guipuzcano), established in 1728, which delivered cacao, cotton, tobacco, indigo, and dyewoods to Spain at reduced prices while lowering the costs on imported Spanish goods to Venezuela. This greatly reduced contraband traffic, while increasing the direct shipments of cacao to Spain that finally exceeded those to Mexico after 1740. The dent in Mexico-Venezuela commerce caused by the organization of the Caracas Company was enlarged after the free trade order of 1778, when Ecuadorian cacao was permitted to be exported to Mexico through Acapulco. Most Venezuelan cacao had been consumed in the Veracruz region; from 1774 to 1775, for instance, only one-quarter of the total imported had reached Mexico City, and this lack of distribution provided the justification for the opening of the Guayaquil-Acapulco trade.

Peru-Chile. A third intercolonial route developed between Lima and Valparaiso. In the early years of colonial rule, Chile suffered a dependent relationship with Peru, receiving European goods distributed by Lima merchants in exchange for agricultural produce. Although the Spaniards had known of the sea passage around Cape Horn by 1616, Chile continued to be tied to the colonial economy by the longer Pacific link because of the crown's policy of restricting the number of overseas routes. This left Spain's most distant South American colony highly susceptible to smuggling, and it has been estimated that in the first quarter of the eighteenth century 153 French ships rounded Cape Horn to saturate the Chilean market. Considerable protest from the *Consulado* of Lima failed to prevent the continued appearance of foreign goods in Chile, either through the southern sea passage or, more often, overland from Buenos Aires.

Other examples of intercolonial trade developed, especially in the last quarter of the eighteenth century when the number of ports able to trade overseas and with each other was substantially increased. But many of these ports had poorly developed hinterlands, and few of them that were not also part of the *Carrera de Indias* maintained their importance much beyond the colonial period. Along the Central American coast, for example, San Blas, Huatulco, and Realejo are all minor fishing villages today, as was Acapulco before the Mexican government decided to develop it as a major tourist center in the 1950s. Indeed, it is a feature of the routes of intercolonial commerce that, although they represented expressions of major forces in the colonial economy, they possessed almost no post-Hispanic continuity and contribute little today to the routes of inter-American transportation. The same, however, cannot be said about the pattern of *overland* colonial commerce.

Highways and Intracolonial Trade. The major highways (or *caminos reales*) of Spanish America frequently were subject to specific legislation designating which route should receive government funds or taxes for road construction; where forts might be established for the protection of traffic; where *ventas*, or hostelries, might be located as rest stops for travelers and animals; and what prices should be charged for their food and lodging. Even when groups of merchants or a *Consulado* invested in highway construction, it was usually with government consent. Since resources for road development were limited and costs excessive, major traffic flows did not proliferate, and the routes developed were often those that supported the crown's ideal concept of colonial commercial organization instead of the pattern commodity flows might actually have taken if no outside influences had been present. The "ideal" transport pattern thus became reality, which may account for the externally oriented focus of highways on the principal capitals and commercial distribution points linked to major ports. It may also explain why mining centers in particular were the objective of highways pushing into the colonial interior and why illegal commerce, although common enough, gave rise to no major route other than the highway connecting upper Peru with Buenos Aires. A brief review of the principal overland routes developed in the colonies illustrates these conclusions (Figures 3-4 and 3-5).

Gov. chose what highways were best + funded a limited few established protection, food, lodging + prices.

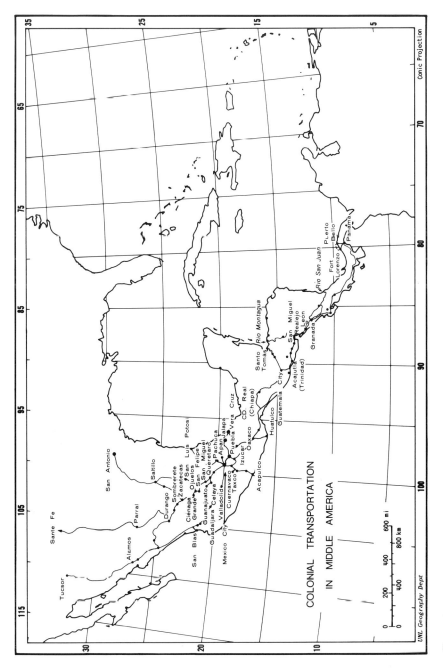

COLONIAL TRANSPORTATION IN MIDDLE AMERICA

Conic Projection

UNL Geography Dept

Figure 3.4

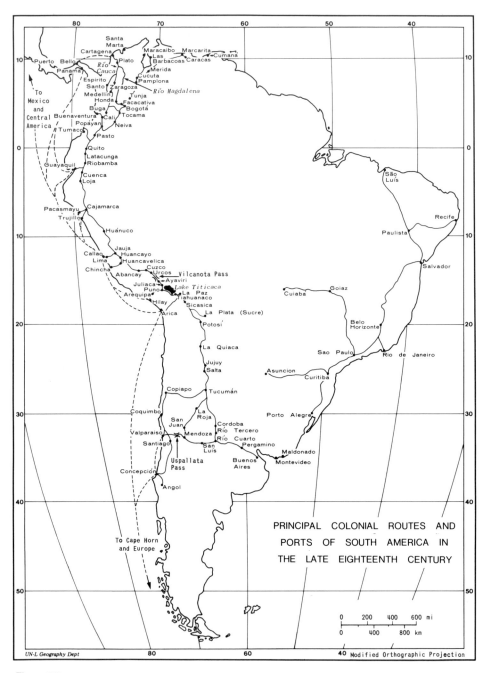

PRINCIPAL COLONIAL ROUTES AND
PORTS OF SOUTH AMERICA IN
THE LATE EIGHTEENTH CENTURY

Figure 3.5

In Mexico the earliest highway connected the ships at Veracruz on the Gulf coast with Mexico City, located in the midst of a strange and suspicious native population. At first, there was no specific path followed once the traffic had negotiated the Sierra Madre Oriental through the Jalapa pass, and travelers picked their own way across the flat-floored basins of the Mexican plateau to the capital. But, as colonial settlement was established and the highway became the western end of the *Carrera de Indias*, its route acquired a greater degree of permanence in the landscape. Hostelries (*ventas*) and rudimentary bridges over the more difficult *barrancas* fixed certain points of its path and, in 1530, the first documentary evidence is found of actual road construction along certain stretches to open the way for the movement of carts or wagons across the plateau. The highway, as it evolved, proved typical of subsequent colonial transportation routes with emphasis on the long-distance connection of terminal points over the shortest practical path instead of making deviations to pick up additional traffic. Thus, throughout the sixteenth century, the government refused to authorize the diversion of the official Mexico City-Veracruz highway to pass through the new Spanish city of Puebla, located only a short distance south of the *camino real*, in spite of vigorous pressure from its citizens. By the time the government finally relented and the Mexico City-Puebla segment became properly recognized, the original alignment north of the city through the plains of Apan had become sufficiently entrenched that it continued to be used as an alternate highway by direct cart traffic throughout the colonial period.

Among the major highways of New Spain, a similar duplication of routes was only found on the link between Mexico City and Oaxaca, which could be reached either from Puebla or through Cuernavaca and Izúcar. Other highways were single arteries of commerce, but all fanned out from a focus on the capital. Across the southern border of the Valley of Mexico and down the escarpment of the east-west volcanic axis a major route ran to Cuernavaca early in the life of the colony, since the sugar *haciendas* surrounding the town included the vast estate of Hernan Cortés. From Cuernavaca, the highway was continued due south to Acapulco, with a branch trail to the highly productive silver mines of Taxco. To the west, another sixteenth-century road linked together the agricultural basins of Toluca and Valladolid (Morelia) and finally reached Guadalajara, the colony's second major city. From this western outpost of Spanish settlement, expeditions seeking mineral prospects and clergy seeking converts explored the northwestern coastal strip of Mexico. Their paths led to the opening of a highway that ran along the base of the Sierra Madre Occidental and, by the middle of the eighteenth century, connected a series of frontier forts, missions, and silver mining communities such as Alamos, leading ultimately to Baja and Alta California.

The growth of the great highway penetrating the arid vastness of northern

Mexico beyond Querétaro depended on pushing back the frontier between Spanish settlement and the wandering, ferocious Chichimec Indian tribes inhabiting much of the plateau. The incentive for expansion was the discovery of silver in Zacatecas in 1546. By 1551, the main Zacatecas-Mexico City highway, or *Camino Real de la Tierra Adentro*, was a well-traveled route passing through a series of interconnected, flat-floored basins that allowed the use of two-wheeled carts (*carretas*). However, the Zacatecan mines were still beyond the settlement frontier at this time. The growth of the mining economy required a protected means of communication through hostile territory to carry silver ore to Mexico City and move agricultural supplies north from more productive, irrigable lands than the barren areas found around the mining camps. In the latter half of the sixteenth century, therefore, the highway became lined with a series of military *presidios* at San Miguel, San Felipe, Ojuelos, and Ciénega Grande. The discovery of silver in Guanajuato added to the importance of the highway, and Celaya was similarly founded as a *presidio* town, protecting shipments from these new mines as well as the interests of Basque ranchers who populated the surrounding fertile lands of the upper Río Lerma, or Bajío.

In subsequent centuries this great highway was pushed north along the western edge of the plateau as silver was discovered near Sombrerete, Durango, Parral, and Chihuahua, while branches of the highway to Saltillo from Zacatecas and San Luis Potosí opened up additional mines on the eastern side. The formation of settlements established to protect the traffic and serve the interests of ranchers attracted to supply the mines was repeated. By the end of the eighteenth century, however, mining had finally given way to religion as the major force extending the frontier, and the northern highways now reached over 900 miles to the missions of Santa Fe, New Mexico, and San Antonio, Texas.

Interior communications in Central America were not as developed as in Mexico, reflecting the more limited interest of the Spaniards in a colonial area that produced little mineral wealth. The area was important at various times as a source of indigo, dyewood, tobacco, cacao, and cotton, but settlement often was scattered, and only the administrative capital at Guatemala City in the center of the most populous part of Central America attracted an interior focus of highways. From this city, merchants extended control over the import and export trade throughout the region until only Chiapas and Costa Rica stood outside their sphere of influence by the end of the eighteenth century. Roads ran from the capital to both coasts, although the highway to Santo Tomás on the Caribbean coast was the more important trade arterial. Occasionally, when the Central American ports were subjected to attack from English corsairs, merchandise was shipped overland to Veracruz by a road that left Guatemala City, thereby further strengthening this city's focal role. One other major highway in Central America followed a sinuous route linking settlements on the Pacific slopes of the isthmus. Although the English Catholic priest, Thomas Gage, traversed its entire length in the 1640s, most regular traffic probably moved only short segments, using the coastal sea route for longer distances.

The transportation pattern that developed in New Granada (Colombia) was among the most complex and unusual in Spanish America; it was one of the few cases where rivers as well as roads were used extensively. The three great *cordilleras*—Occidental, Central, and Oriental—separated by the deep, narrow valleys of the Cauca and Magdalena rivers, gave the colony a strong north-south alignment, but so separated it into distinct parts that the administrative center at Bogotá was not the dominant focus of the transportation pattern. Instead, the city (and its surrounding highland agricultural basin) was only one of a number of traffic objectives that included the neighboring productive basin of Tunja, the mining camps of Antioquia and Popayán, and the main port of Cartagena, through which passed all goods from Spain, slaves from Africa and the West Indies, and gold from the interior mines in exchange.

Both the two principal rivers allowed trade from Cartagena to penetrate deeply into the Colombian interior. The Cauca was navigable 250 miles upstream from its confluence with the Magdalena, which itself was navigable 530 miles from its mouth. River traffic conducted by heavy dugout canoes (*chamoanes*), requiring 12 to 14 boatmen each, was seasonal; during the two rainy seasons poling against the strong currents was difficult. Although there were a number of river ports, Espíritu Santo and Zaragoza on the Cauca system were mostly used for the Antioqueño mines, while Honda was most important on the Magdalena, serving the highland basins of Tunja and Bogotá as well as the mines of Popayán.

Among the roads in the colony one of the most important formed a part of the great *camino real* that ran over 1800 miles from Lima, through Quito and Bogotá to Caracas (Figure 3–5). This highway entered New Granada from the south through Pasto and Popayán, where it split into two alternate routes leading to Bogotá. One branch continued due north down the upper Cauca Valley through Cali, and the other crossed the Cordillera Central to the upper Magdalena, following its path downstream as far as Tocama, where the road then climbed the steep forested escarpment to Bogotá. The highway carried textiles from Quito for the mines, while cattle were driven over the northern branch from the Cauca Valley into Antioquia.

Important though the north–south highway was, it was the shorter but much more difficult transverse trails across the *cordillera* that were most significant to the various mining centers. The Nare-Zaragoza road that linked the two major river systems, and carried goods imported from Spain as well as wheat flour from the Tunja Basin was the "life-line" of the Antioqueño mining districts in the seventeenth and eighteenth centuries, even though the trip of only 145 miles required 16 days of travel. The short link between Bogotá and Honda, on the Magdalena, was equally important for the economy of the capital, although parts of the escarpment trail were so steep and slippery in the rainy season that they were at times impassable even to mules. The worst of these important transverse trails, however, were those that led from the Cauca Valley across the Cordillera Occidental to the Pacific lowlands and to the placer mines of the Chocó. The Chocó could have received needed supplies much more easily from the Atrato River route but, throughout most of the eighteenth century, the river was closed to commerce in an attempt by the government to prevent the illegal flow of gold to English, French, and Dutch traders. Once again, the crown's pursuit of a controlled, monopolistic, commercial policy had influenced the pattern of colonial transportation.

The most extensive routes of overland travel in colonial South America developed in Peru, and it is tempting to compare the patterns of transportation designed to sustain the Spanish Empire with those established to weld together the empire of the Incas. In both cases, a major arterial traversed the spine of the Andes, and examination of Figures 3-2 and 3-5 shows a similarity in some sections of each route. But such duplication is illusory, once the functions of transportation are taken into account. The Inca highways, serving an essentially political purpose, were internally focused on Cuzco in the highlands; Spanish roads, reflecting economic considerations, were externally oriented to the coast and the center of commercial exchange in Lima. The Inca system was dominated by two parallel longitudinal arteries, whereas the Spaniards laid particular emphasis on the several transverse highways, such as Arica-Potosí, Puno-Hilay, Jauja-Lima, and Cajamarca-Trujillo, that ran down the Pacific escarpment and provided interior mining centers with access to the sea. Reliance on these lateral roads encouraged the independence of the interior hinterland each highway served. This reduced the dependence of the Spaniards on the ancient Sierra highway, which became more important as a series of separate sections instead of as a continuous route. At the same time, the Spaniard's use of oceangoing vessels to link the coastal ports with each other and to Lima caused the abandonment of many sections of the Inca coastal route.

Differences in transportation technology also limited the usefulness of the Inca highways that were incorporated into the colonial transportation system and, as Diffie (1967) points out, the very features of Inca road construction so admired by later observers were those that gave the most difficulty to the Spaniards. Steps cut into the sheer faces of mountain walls and elaborate suspension bridges over deep chasms each revealed the principal defect: an inability to solve the problem of bridging canyons and constructing graded winding roads up the mountain sides. While the pre-Hispanic highways were adequate for the relatively light foot and llama traffic of an empire whose population movement was strictly controlled, they were less useful for iron-shod animals, loaded carts, and the much heavier traffic of the colonial period, a traffic consisting of commercial goods and also of people in large numbers. One six-teenth-century observer estimated that with release from the Inca interdict on travel, about one-third of the Indian population had entered vagrancy. Roads were filled with Indians bearing tribute in kind from the *repartimiento* where it was produced to the town dwellings of their masters. Kubler (1962) estimated that these journeys sometimes took months, given the distances involved. A constant flux of Indians moving in large companies to the scene of draft labor swelled the volume of travelers, while a further cause was the movement of In-dians wandering back and forth between their *repartimiento* and the seat of their *audiencia* to secure legal papers which, for the Indian, held a fascination, like a talisman.

Under the press of all this traffic the old Inca highways rapidly deterio-rated, hastened by colonial ignorance of the carefully maintained pre-Hispanic road surfaces. The Spaniards also ignored the Inca highway support system, sacking the *tambos* (shelters) and killing or enslaving the *chasquis* (couriers). Although the system was later revived to carry colonial mail and local Indians were organized to maintain the highways, the continuity between the two sys-tems of transportation was limited, and the Inca roads had little influence in determining the routes of colonial commerce.

A major objective of colonial routes was upper Peru (part of present-day Bolivia), especially following discovery of the mountain of silver at Potosí. Within 2 years of its foundation in 1545, the Potosí market was among the most lavish in America; with a city population that sometimes reached 120,000, it was a major consumer of imported European goods. By 1601, there were more than 200 merchants residing in Potosí and dealing with every type of merchandise. Supplies came officially from Lima by sea to Hilay and then to warehouses in Arequipa. From there, they moved over the mountains to the heavily settled Lake Titicaca Basin, where a well-traveled road led to Potosí. Another route to the mining city was later developed through the port of Arica to carry mercury from Huancavélica, after the introduction of the *patio* refin-ing process.

The lure of the Potosí market was so great and its production of silver so prodigious that at times it exhausted the supply of official goods in Peru and stimulated a substantial contraband traffic. Some illegal commerce came through Lima itself, particularly Oriental goods, as we have seen, and it was not unknown for lines of mules loaded with fraudulently imported merchan-dise to pass beneath the balcony of the viceroy. But the mines also attracted a variety of contraband that entered Buenos Aires, crossed the *pampas* to Córdoba, and reached upper Peru through the "back-door" route of Tucu-mán and Salta.

Buenos Aires, at the mouth of the Rio de la Plata, had been permanently established by 1580 and, although much closer to Spain than the Pacific coast colonies, its participation in legitimate trade was forbidden, since it would

have jeopardized the monopoly of the *Carrera* system. The port and hinterland of the La Plata region therefore occupied a backwater in the colonial empire, even though after 1616 Buenos Aires was grudgingly granted permission
to trade with two annual vessels of less than 100 tons, when the crown perceived the settlement to be a check against Portuguese expansion over disputed
land in what is now Uruguay. Yet this limited official role did not prevent the
city from developing a trade of such size and variety that it rivaled Lima for
the market of upper Peru and Charcas. By the beginning of the eighteenth century, gold and silver were being exchanged freely at Buenos Aires for any
European merchandise, while ships from England, France, Portugal, Turkey,
Prussia, Sweden, and the North American colonies could be found in its harbor. English merchants controlled the La Plata trade in black African slaves,
who were often sent as far as Chile and even Peru, while merchants of Buenos
Aires had firm if illegal trade agreements with merchant houses in Rio de
Janeiro and London. So open, extensive, and regular was this smuggling that
toward the end of the century, English textile manufacturers even offered
products especially designed for the South American market, such as distinctive rustic *ponchos* for the *campesinos* of the Río de la Plata and Chile. Contraband, therefore, was a major element of the traffic that pioneered the highways across the *pampas*; it joined the supplies destined for the mines of the
Andean high country, yet it was never sufficient to achieve the economic capture of the region. The journey from Buenos Aires was long and difficult and,
in crossing the lowland interior, was subject to attack from Indians in much
the same fashion as the early traffic on the highway to Zacatecas. Thus, even
when the Bourbon reforms legalized much that had previously been illegal and
permitted unminted gold and silver to be exported through Buenos Aires, the
cost of transport was not reduced. By the end of the colonial period, freight
rates still favored the west coast suppliers, and upper Peru remained oriented
to the Pacific, an outlook that continued after independence.

The availability of contraband from La Plata in the Chilean market was
more successful in weakening the hold of Peruvian merchants in this southern
colony. Chile, with little mineral production during the colonial period, was
primarily agricultural and somewhat more self-contained. Its remoteness and
lesser economic status in Spanish eyes offered considerable opportunities for
smuggling, as we have seen. The major overland route passed through Mendoza and linked Chile and La Plata over the Uspallata Pass across the Andes.
Robinson (1964) estimates that by the 1790s 20,000 mules were involved annually in the traffic between Santiago de Chile and Mendoza, even though the
mountain pass could be blocked by snow for 2 to 4 months of the year. In
Chile itself evidence of regular and distant trade over established routes is
abundant, although the volume of goods was small and moved slowly. Carriage travel was rare; in 1792 a trip from Santiago to Concepción was viewed

as an adventure, and it was 3 years more before a carriage road was opened from Santiago to Valparaíso.

Technology and Costs of Colonial Transportation

The extensive geography of colonial transportation that has been identified, the great distances covered, and the major topographic obstacles overcome are all the more remarkable given the level of technology and cost of transportation. While the simple, two-wheeled cart of medieval Castile, with either solid or spoked wheels and pulled by two oxen, was in use in the more easily traversed sections of most colonies, large-scale carting, according to Ringrose (1970), was confined to the flat Mexican plateau and Argentine *pampas*. Furthermore, he argues that the state of cart transport in these two areas reflected the state of those region's economy.

Carting on the Mexican plateau was conducted with the *carro*, a huge, spoked-wheel vehicle pulled by 16 or more mules and sometimes described as a "juggernaut" or "rolling blockhouse." In the sixteenth century some trains might comprise 30 to 80 *carros*, all owned by one individual, a level of capital availability derived from mining that was unknown elsewhere in the Spanish kingdom. Grazing for such a large number of animals was always important. On the plateau it was usually available; where it was lacking, some towns were required to provide feed. Mules were preferred to haul the huge carts because of advantages of speed over oxen, and certain areas such as tropical Veracruz and Tabasco became important areas for mule breeding. With the decline in silver production in the middle of the seventeenth century, less funds were available to maintain the roads in Mexico, and large-scale carting disappeared.

In Argentina the growing prosperity of Buenos Aires and its hinterland caused carting to become common in the late eighteenth century. Most took place in a roughly triangular area bounded by Buenos Aires, Mendoza, and Jujuy. As in Mexico, grazing was available, the terrain suitable, and a sufficient supply of animals existed; however, oxen were more likely to be used because of the high demand for mules in Peru. The trade itself involved three types of movement: wine, brandy, olive oil, wheat, flour, and hides destined for Buenos Aires from the foothills of Mendoza, San Juan, and Tucumán; imports from Buenos Aires for consumption in the interior and in Chile and Peru; and local movements of goods between Mendoza and Tucuman. Carting continued in Argentina well into the middle of the nineteenth century, stimulated especially by a growing trans-Andean trade with now-independent Chile; throughout the period the use of the great carts allowed overland transport along this route to remain competitive with sea transport around Cape Horn.

On most of the roads of colonial America, however, long lines of mules, winding across the countryside, were the most ubiquitous form of transporta-

Llamas used, mules preferred. carry more — adjust
better to altitude, needed less water. Llama do not [?]
higher. Beginning ever had human labor carry
freight. Road conditions were
sometimes bad.

TRANSPORTATION

tion, and the numbers of animals involved was enormous. In 1803 Humboldt estimated that almost 70,000 mules were employed on the roads to Veracruz. An equally large number were in use in upper Peru, having been raised in northwestern Argentina and sold at the famous mule fair at Salta. The traditional llama was also used in the Andean highlands, although the mule was preferred because it could carry a heavier load, adjusted better to the extremes of altitude, and needed less water to survive. When llamas were used, the mortality was extremely high. On the Arica-Potosí highway, where the first part of the journey was without water, it was normal to increase the llama teams by one-half in order to replace the animals that died along the way.

The use of human labor to carry freight (*tamemes* in Mexico, *apires* in Peru) had been common in pre-Hispanic times and was continued in the early years of colonization because of the insufficient number of serviceable draft animals. By the middle of the sixteenth century, however, Indian numbers were declining dramatically, and increasing controls were placed on the use of the survivors as beasts of burden, especially in permitting them to move between highland and lowland. This had always been avoided under the Aztecs and Incas, but the Spaniards were slower to realize the destruction of health that came from too swift a movement from extremes of barometric pressure and temperature. Human carriers of Spanish freight had greatly declined by the end of the century, although in many rural areas Indians carried their own goods in this fashion, as they still do today. However, Indians continued to be used as carriers of litters, by means of which the colonial elite traveled within the colonies; some *tamemes* were employed as late as the eighteenth century on certain extremely difficult trails, such as those in Colombia that crossed the Cordillera Occidental between Pasto-Barbacoas and Cali-Buenaventura, which were so treacherous that even mules were useless.

With such means of transport in Spanish America, the rate of travel was often extremely slow. On the Mexican plateau, the average mule carried 300 pounds and might move no more than 12 or 13 miles a day. This rate was roughly comparable in other parts of the empire. Mule teams took 4 days to cover the 40 miles between oceans across the isthmus of Panama, 24 days to carry bags of mercury from the port of Arica 435 miles to Potosí, and 16 days to move goods the 125 miles between Nare and Zaragoza in Colombia. Highway conditions further contributed to this slow movement. Most road construction amounted to some rough grading, occasional infilling of the worst potholes, and the bridging of deep *barrancas*. Prepared surfaces were occasionally undertaken on the most important highways, such as the cobblestoned section completed almost at the end of the colonial period on the Veracruz road, where it crossed the mountains through the Jalapa pass. But this was a rare case; most road conditions were poor and worsened throughout the colonial period so that travelers vied with each other to condemn the wretched conditions they encountered. The Spanish priest, Vázquez de Espinosa, who traveled through the empire in the 1620s over so many difficult highways, elected the Guayaquil-Quito road as the worst. Indeed, he claimed that "it is the worst road anywhere in the world; it is very steep and it rains all the time, the mules keep getting stuck in the mud and on the ridges which hit them in the belly, so that it seems impossible for them to move; in fact, many of them die on this road."

Transport was therefore very expensive, which added greatly to the cost of goods. Wheat in Mexico City, for instance, was more than double its price at the point of production only 175 miles away, while wine, unloaded at Veracruz, had increased in price by 70 percent by the time it reached the capital. In Colombia, the cost of transportation was sometimes so great that the resulting high prices of imports in the camps forced some miners into bankruptcy.

The fact that overland transportation existed at all in the face of such conditions reflects the strength of demand for interaction among the points connected by the highways. As we have seen, this demand was externally imposed in support of Spain's colonial economic policy, but it was initiated by the productivity of major mining centers. Such centers, while they stimulated the traffic that flowed over a hierarchially ordered transportation network that led ultimately to Spain, also acted as genuine economic growth poles within the boundaries of the colonies.

Most mining regions were located in areas of insufficient agricultural productivity to be locally self-supporting. Their production of precious metals and their need for food, rough textiles, Indian labor, and draft animals initiated an exchange with important multiplier effects in the supply areas, which often became satellite economies of the mines. Moreover, this chain of economic interrelations initiated by the mines covered a much wider area of colonial territory than is often recognized, and stimulated a corresponding subsidiary pattern of intracolonial traffic that used both the main highways already described as well as other intracolonial routes that were not directly the consequence of externally oriented demand. Some impression of the extent to which mining centers thus contributed to the geography of transportation within colonial America as regional growth poles can be gained from examples of Zacatecas and Potosí. In each case, these major centers of silver production in New Spain and Peru stimulated a far-flung set of supply linkages and determined many of the transportation alignments in their respective colonies.

Although extensive and pervasive, the social and economic influence of such mining centers was not permanent. By the middle of the seventeenth century, the silver boom in upper Peru was over as the Potosí veins were exhausted. In Mexico the focus of mining shifted from Zacatecas north to Parral. As the mining populations moved away, there remained a lower-density, more isolated pattern of remote communities focused on huge, largely self-suf-

The outward focus of economic activity shifted back toward the principal settlements in the colonial periphery.

ficient estates. However, unlike the mines, this agricultural base did not sustain additional transportation demand. To link the widespread centers of each estate together, and to the major transportation arteries, would have required a pattern of local transport whose expense could not be justified by the level of agricultural productivity. Yet, without such transport development, productivity was discouraged. Thus isolation became a self-perpetuating problem on the large estates, which did not achieve anything approaching the stimulus to transportation of the mines. Instead, the focus of economic activity and trade with the outside world shifted back to the principal settlements located toward the colonial periphery. *Development — product of conditions / external commercial patterns most enforced & prod. of metals by interior mining centers. Settlements grew*

Inertia in the Geography of Colonial Transportation

along paths - property lines show local on generation the

The development of colonial transportation in Spanish America was essentially a product of conditions in the sixteenth century, when an externally oriented commercial pattern was most successfully enforced and the production of metals by interior mining centers was increasing. The routes established in this period acquired an inertia in which their very existence tended to deter locational obsolescence. Settlements grew up along their paths, property lines became oriented to their location, and additional on-line economic support beyond that originally generated between terminals often developed when the additional traffic could not by itself justify the substantial cost of an alternative route. The economic decline of the middle of the seventeenth century, which brought contraction of traffic volume, only accentuated reliance on the existing highways.

The original settlements responsible for the traffic growth of the sixteenth century, being relatively well served by the transport network they initiated, gained an economic advantage in competition with later potential, but less well-served, settlements. Furthermore, the power of such early centers frequently received additional stimulus with their designation as administrative points in the political network of the colony. This, of course, tended to keep any new traffic generated flowing over the old, original sections of the highway network and thereby encouraged a further degree of route inertia. This self-reinforcing relationship, which perpetuated the sixteenth-century pattern of settlement and transport linkages, was finally challenged with the economic revival of the eighteenth century, when the Bourbon reforms offered opportunities for new traffic movements. In many cases, however, the power of economic and political advantage wielded by existing major transport terminals and the strength of route inertia were sustained. The following case is representative of the method by which this was achieved.

During the colonial period, the major artery of commerce between Mexico City and Veracruz had stimulated two duplicatory routes across the extremely difficult country over the Sierra Madre Oriental, where one would certainly have sufficed. Given the cost of transportation, the principal highway through Jalapa might have been expected to eclipse its southern rival using the Orizaba Valley, especially when the site of the *feria* was changed in the eighteenth century. However, the complex character of commercial competition associated with each alternative route was such that when, toward the end of the century, the government was urged to reconstruct one of the routes, the choice was continually delayed. Ever since the Jalapa fair which, as we have seen, was an act by Spanish merchants against the interests of Mexico City, the merchants of the capital had allied their cause with the southern route. Veracruz merchants, for whom Jalapa was a semitropical refuge and extension of the disease-ridden port, were allied with the *Consulado* of Cadiz. The formation of the *Consulado* of Veracruz in 1795, another feature of the Bourbon reforms, formalized their choice of the northern route.

Consecutive viceroys delayed the decision on new road construction, believing that the result would be the disappearance of the excluded route and the ruin of the mercantile interests with which it was associated. Finally, in 1803, a compromise was made. The *Consulado* of Veracruz won the right to collect tolls in order to finance reconstruction of the Jalapa route, yet such was the power and influence of the *Consulado* of Mexico City and the state of route competition that it, too, was granted the same privilege to repair the Orizaba highway. Although much greater improvement was achieved on the Jalapa highway because its traditionally higher volume of traffic yielded more funds from the tolls collected, the inertia and costly duplication of routes in this part of New Spain were perpetuated. Furthermore, the contemporary expectation that Veracruz would rise as an independent mercantile center at the expense of Mexico City never materialized, and the port continued its role as a maritime appendage to the capital.

Colonial Transportation in Brazil

The patterns of transportation that developed in the Portuguese colony exhibited many of the same features as those in Spanish America, but on a much less extensive scale and in a sequence that was the reverse of the Spanish experience. Settlement began more slowly and with less attention from the home country than the colonial enterprises of other nations. By the end of the sixteenth century, colonization comprised a series of isolated agricultural enclaves, primarily in northeast Brazil between São Luis, in Maranhão and Salvador, and in Bahia. Each produced a similar mixture of products, primarily sugar and dyewoods, although cotton and tobacco were also important. These items stimulated some overseas trade, not only with Portugal but also with the ships of other European nations that traveled the long, unprotected Brazilian coastline. Unable to prevent effectively the contact of English, Dutch, French, and even Spanish traders with their colony, and with more important economic interests in the Old World, the Portuguese never attempted to monopolize the transatlantic traffic in the same way as Spain. Compared to external trade, intracolonial exchange in Brazil was virtually nonexistent, since the economic similarity of the colonial enclaves offered no basis for interaction. Equally undeveloped at this time was any commercial relationship between the coastal periphery and forested interior.

The following century brought a contraction of the overseas trade that had evolved; sugar production suffered from competition with the more efficient English, French, and Dutch producers in the Caribbean. The economic focus remained in the northeast; Rio de Janeiro on the southern coast was little more than a defensive outpost, while the São Paulo highlands behind São Vicente were sparsely settled and penetrations of the interior were left to the slave-hunting expeditions of the *bandeirantes*.

Economic conditions in the colony finally improved in the eighteenth century when gold and diamonds were discovered in the interior province of what became Minas Gerais. At a time when parts of the Spanish Empire were undergoing geographic contraction of traffic and trade toward strictly local areas of economic interest, the new Brazilian mines were becoming regional multipliers in the same way as Potosí and Zacatecas in the sixteenth century. The basis for a pattern of internal interchange now existed because the mining centers could not begin to supply their own agricultural demands. Consequently, old ranching areas of the northeast *sertão* were revived to some extent but, more important, agriculture and ranching spread into the south, even to Rio Grande do Sul. Here, mule and cattle breeding developed on a large scale as the basis for the first settlement in the area. The stock was driven north from Porto Alegre along the eastern edge of the highlands to the great livestock fair at Sorocaba, near São Paulo, where it was traded and herded to the mines. At the same time, the mining centers were diffusing the earnings of mining on a wider basis to supply the means for financing foreign imports both to the mining districts themselves as well as to the other interacting regions of the country. Not the least important were the effects of the mining boom on Rio de Janeiro, where the natural harbor became a major distribution point handling a large volume of mineral exports and imported goods. Moreover, this role led to Rio's designation as the capital of the colony in 1763 and an enhanced position of influence in political administration.

Although the pattern of transportation in colonial Brazil was a more recent phenomenon than the trade routes of Spanish America and was still undergoing active development at the time of independence, similar characteristics of route inertia were making their appearance, stimulated by the overriding economic objective of highways to facilitate raw material exports and bring in manufactured goods. It is interesting to note the striking persistence in the alignment of routes from one historical period to another in Brazil. For example, the present-day Padre Anchieta superhighway from Santos to São Paulo is separated from the first colonial trail over the Serra do Cubatào by a single spur.

Perhaps the most important example from the colonial period, however, was the rapid growth of Rio de Janeiro relative to São Paulo. Both were potential entrepôt sites for an expanding hinterland, but Rio, on the coast, possessed an early advantage in the ease with which it could develop a network of transport routes into the interior. São Paulo, with its highland location and single connecting route to the port of Santos, required inland traffic to pay an extra set of transfer costs in order to reach the coast. As long as the basic transport orientation was external, Rio maintained its prominence over São Paulo. Only a reorientation of the purpose of transportation could vitalize the role of the highland city, a change that had occurred by the end of the nineteenth century when coffeelands in the Paraíba Valley hinterland of Rio de Janeiro had been exhausted and production had shifted to the São Paulo interior. The stimulus this gave to São Paulo ultimately resulted in its growth as a manufacturing center, redistributing its own goods to the interior instead of funneling important goods across the escarpment with the extra transfer charges this entailed. By this time, however, general route inertia in the transport system perpetuated the advantage gained by Rio de Janeiro. Moreover, Rio's political role remained undiminished. Consequently, it is only in modern times that São Paulo has drawn even with its rival.

Summary of Transportation in the Colonial Period

Considerable attention in this chapter has been given to the factors that underlay the establishment of transportation in colonial Latin America because of the persistence, or inertia, that has perpetuated many of the routes developed to the present day. However, the later development of São Paulo raises an important point about route inertia. We have already seen that a transport route, together with the terminal points that originated the interaction, operated in a self-reinforcing fashion so as to attract additional traffic over an existing route instead of a costly new route. Moreover, every new traffic movement attracted to an existing path increased the competitiveness of the terminal points over centers not so well connected. This chain of compounded attractiveness and consequent inertia can be broken, however, whenever the overall function or purpose of the transport network is changed or whenever a substantial innovation in transport technology is introduced that requires a radical change in the physical requirements of the route. In the nineteenth century in Latin America, both conditions existed: independence from Spain and Portugal might have eliminated the economic function that had bound the colony's productive capacity and markets to outside economic stimuli, while the introduction of the railroad certainly represented a considerable change in transport technology. In fact, neither political independence nor the railroad made basic changes to the geography of transportation developed during the colonial period.

THE RAILROAD ERA

Political, and not economic, independence marked the changes that occurred in Latin American countries in the early nineteenth century. The colonial elite, especially the merchants, generally supported the break with Spain and Portugal as a means of increasing their share of the wealth derived from overseas trade. Most had no incentive to dismantle the externally oriented colonial economic structure from which they had benefited in the past. Moreover, their reliance on imported goods was a habit of consumption not easily rejected. It was much simpler to acquire such goods in exchange for raw material exports than through the creation of domestic production. This internal Latin American inclination toward continued overseas economic dependency was complemented by attitudes of the industrializing countries of northern Europe, whose need for an increased quantity and variety of raw materials, as well as additional markets for their factory production, stimulated a search for new foreign investments. Newly independent Latin America, rid of Spain's exclusionary policy, was an attractive objective. Translation of Humboldt's widely read account of the wealth still to be won from the mines of New Spain, together with more ancient and shadowy myths of the riches of the New World, had excited the imagination of investors. The English in particular, with capital born of their early industrial revolution, were eager to enjoy the anticipated natural wealth of the continent, and German, French, and U.S. citizens were not far behind. With such pressures both within and without, it is hardly surprising that a neocolonial economy prevailed in Latin America for much of the nineteenth and early twentieth centuries.

There were occasional exceptions to the dominance of foreign economic interests in the continent. Some domestic industry was attempted when governments could be persuaded to erect high tariff walls, protecting local products from foreign manufacturers who could normally deliver much cheaper goods because of their economies of large-scale production. One such instance was the emergence of a fledgling textile industry during the 1830s in Mexico City, Guadalajara, Orizaba, Jalapa, and especially Puebla, which had a long tradition of craft production. At first, the industry achieved modest success; by the 1840s, the earliest factory built in Puebla was returning a net profit of

[handwritten marginal notes at top of page, partially legible:]

...deterioration of highways...time + cost of transportation...foreign investment had same limitations cont. to deteriorate...econ. activity in the interior awaited the elimination of the transportation barrier. It was against background of [agitation] for improvement [improved] communication + railroads develops.

20 percent. Yet there were soon immense difficulties, many associated with the rapid deterioration of the highways following independence, which raised the time and cost of transportation even above colonial levels. The mills at Jalapa and Orizaba suffered particularly. They had been located at sites that offered inexpensive waterpower and good supplies of cotton from lowland Veracruz. But their growth was severely hampered by the cost of transport, which limited their access to the populous market on the plateau. The advantage to manufacturers on the plateau was offset by the greater costs they incurred on the movement of machinery and parts by cart and mule over the tortuous roads from Veracruz, since all plant materials were imported and any repair or expansion in response to increased demand encountered inordinate expense plus a long wait before the hardware could be delivered.

Additional problems existed in securing sufficient raw materials. Most domestic raw cotton came from Veracruz and Oaxaca but accounted for only one-half the necessary supply demanded by the textile industry. The result was a heavy reliance on imported cotton, making the underlying cost structure of the domestic Mexican industry dependent on the price fluctuations of the world market. Finally, manufacturers faced consistent opposition to the tariff protection from merchants, who stood to gain from importing and selling the low-cost, high-quality foreign textiles. Ultimately, the forces for free trade prevailed and, after 1846, the Mexican government closed the primary source of domestic capital it had established earlier to support the textile industry. Thereafter Mexican textiles followed the experience of most domestic Latin American industrial ventures in the nineteenth century—absorption by foreign capital.

Foreign investment, however, encountered the same limitations of inland transport as the roads continued to deteriorate throughout the first half of the nineteenth century. The English company that tried to run the Real del Monte silver mine at Pachuca between 1824 and 1849, for instance, needed 6 to 8 months on the average between the time its commissioner at the mine requested supplies and their delivery from England. Furthermore, one-sixth of the delivered price of its chief import, mercury, was the cost of its transport from Veracruz. Conditions were no better in other countries. In Argentina it was estimated in the 1820s that the cost per ton-league of land travel across the *pampas* from Buenos Aires to Mendoza and Salta was 100 times the rate across the Atlantic from Buenos Aires to the European ports. Most of the early nineteenth-century foreign ventures, therefore, were along the Latin American coasts. British merchant houses were already established by the 1830s in Buenos Aires, Rio de Janeiro, Santiago, Lima, and Mexico City, and other lesser ports, thereby contributing to the importance of peripheral locations that had ranked high in the colonial settlement hierarchy. Economic activity in the inte-

All [lines] built by British + Amer. relied on foreign imports + capital. Took a long time for railroads to penetrate interior due to engineering problems. due to topography.

rior, however, awaited the elimination of the transportation barrier, and it was against a background of growing agitation for improved communications that the railroad was introduced to Latin America.

Within a decade of the Rainhill trials in England in 1829, where the viability of the railroad was first convincingly demonstrated, this new transport form was operating in Latin America. Its first major application was in Cuba, where American and British interest in sugar and coffee cultivation resulted in the building of the Havana Railroad in 1837 and the construction of almost 300 miles of track before a single mile was built elsewhere in Latin America. But it was not until the 1850s that serious construction began on the mainland (Figures 3-6 and 3-7). In 1851 a line was laid down between Lima and its port of Callao; a year later the Chilean port of Caldera was connected to Copiapó; across the continent, in 1855, a rail line from Rio de Janeiro appropriately reached to the foot of the royal palace at Petrópolis; the traditional colonial route from Arica to the Tacna oasis was joined in 1857, in the same year that a line opened to carry the devout from Mexico City a few miles north to the shrine of Guadalupe; finally, in 1859, Argentina's first rail link was completed for 15 miles from Buenos Aires to Morón. All these lines were built by British or American engineers and relied on imported equipment and, frequently, on foreign capital. With the exception of the Cuban railroads and a vital but poorly built line across the isthmus between Panama and Colón, completed in 1855, the lines established in the 1850s were significant for their short length and concentration on traditionally important peripheral cities and ports.

It was not until the 1860s that the extensive penetration of the interior by the railroads occurred because time was needed before the enormous engineering problems posed by Latin American topography could be solved. When the Mexican Railway was finally opened in 1873 between Mexico City and Veracruz, it reached a height of 8250 feet, and the climb out of the Orizaba Valley up the escarpment of the Sierra Madre Oriental averaged a gradient of 1 in 20 over 25 miles. Even more dramatic were the railroads constructed by American engineer Henry Meiggs in Peru between 1868 and 1877; the most impressive was the Mollendo-Arequipa-Puno railroad, which climbed over 14,850 feet from the coast to the Andean *altiplano*. Nothing on this scale was ever encountered in Europe or the United States.

In the subsequent decades of the century the railroads spread the fingers of their networks farther into the interior and more densely near the periphery. Their rate of growth was not distributed evenly across the continent, however. The 1870s and 1880s saw the railroads of Mexico, Central America, Brazil, Uruguay, Argentina, Chile, and Peru relatively well developed. The 1880s also saw the beginnings of railroad penetration in Bolivia, Ecuador, and Colombia, although it was another two decades before these railroads were well established, perhaps reflecting the even more severe engineering problems set

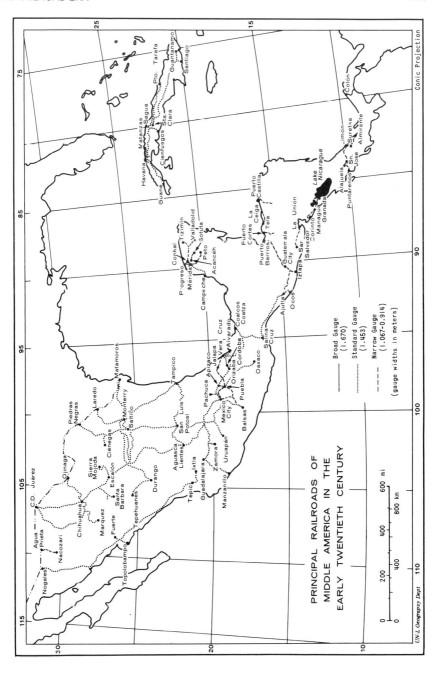

PRINCIPAL RAILROADS OF
MIDDLE AMERICA IN THE
EARLY TWENTIETH CENTURY

Broad Gauge
(1.670)

Standard Gauge
(1.453)

Narrow Gauge
(1.067-0.914)

(gauge widths in meters)

Conic Projection

UN-L Geography Dept

Figure 3.6

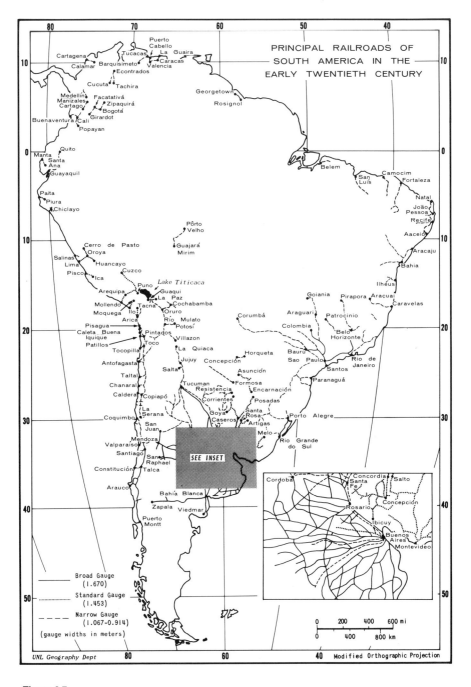

Figure 3.7

against the slower development of an incentive for communications. Finally, some countries, such as Venezuela, Paraguay, and the Guiana colonies, experienced very little railroad construction at all.

It is impossible (and, indeed, unnecessary) to detail the geographic growth of every major railroad line that developed in the nineteenth and early twentieth centuries in Latin America, but it is possible to provide a general classification of the different types of line, both in terms of the reasons for construction and choice of route and in terms of their economic consequences.

Types of Latin American Railroad

Three types of railroad may be identified, although the definitions are not necessarily mutually exclusive and any railroad or network may fall into more than one category. Nevertheless, the attempted classification does provide a means of emphasizing the major influences that initiated the different rail routes in Latin America.

The first and most representative type was the railroad established to facilitate the extraction of a known raw material or to strengthen a preexisting line of interaction. Traffic *from* the interior dominated, since centers of consumption were usually located along the coastal periphery and the backhaulage of imported goods to the interior was less significant except for the carriage of mining, manufacturing, and agricultural supplies in order to sustain or expand raw material extraction. Only when the major market center of consumption was located in the interior, such as in Mexico City, La Paz, or Bogotá, was the traffic flow more balanced. On the railroads that connected the Mexican capital with Veracruz, for instance, quantities of freight carried were relatively even in each direction, even though a large number of rails and equipment to be used to build additional, and competing, railroads were among the imported goods.

With some exceptions to be noted later, most railroads in Mexico can be included within the first general type. The rail alignments followed routes established in the colonial era. Between Mexico City and Veracruz, two competing railroads built with British capital imitated the earlier highway duplication along this important artery and thereby reinforced both the economic position of the capital and the role of Veracruz as Mexico's primary port. To the north, American companies built three railroads that approximated the three principal colonial highways and, with connections to the expanding U.S. railroad network, provided an additional and competing route to the industrialized markets of North America and Europe. However, with the ownership of each railroad in foreign hands, the Mexican domestic economy gained little from such competition, since the American and English companies frequently established pools in which profits were shared and freight rates mutually agreed on.

In Brazil the earliest railroads were clearly geared to the improvement of raw material extraction. Those of the northeast ran inland a few miles from the principal coastal settlements, such as Salvador, Aracaju, Maceió, and Recife, and only much later, in 1949, were tied together in a long, winding line that linked them to the south. More important, however, were the lines built in the central region of the country to which the economic focus had shifted by the 1850s with the development of coffee production in the Paraíba Valley. The Central Railway, built by the British and begun in 1858, followed the expansion of coffee along the valley to São Paulo, at first just a minor terminus. But, as the world demand increased and the land along the Paraíba was exhausted, coffee growing expanded into the interland of São Paulo state. The highland city became the focus of an expanding network of interior lines, built and operated mainly by foreign companies and with no concern for the coordination of gauge or rolling stock. At the same time, service declined on the Central Railroad, and several merchant houses in Rio began to open branches in São Paulo. As Brazil captured an increasing share of the world coffee market, from 50 percent in the 1870s to more than 75 percent by 1900, the railroads continued to push out into the interior toward Paraná in the south, the Minas "triangle," and the southern Mato Grosso. With lines all converging on São Paulo, this growing interior region became a single market for the city. Some merchants then began to transfer all their business from Rio de Janeiro to São Paulo, providing the city with a capital base for its significant growth as a manufacturing center at the turn of the century.

A similar pattern of individually developed railroads focusing on a primary city occurred in Argentina. Fanning out across the *pampas* from Buenos Aires, the lines built between 1880 and 1910 formed the densest rail network in Latin America. Many of the Brazilian features were repeated. The investment was British, and the objective of most companies was to facilitate the commercial agricultural development of the *pampas* for the production of export goods. A strong encouragement to externally oriented traffic did not require the railroad companies to be concerned with interior, cross-country interconnections; consequently, it was often necessary to pass through Buenos Aires in order to travel across the grain of the railroad pattern. Concern for common gauges was equally ignored, and the choice could sometimes be cavalier. It is reputed that the broad gauge (5 feet, 6 inches) was used in the construction of Argentina's first railroad because the owners had purchased secondhand locomotives and rolling stock of that gauge seized by the British during the siege of Sebastopol in the Crimea. Although the gauge was unsuited to the treeless *pampas*, requiring larger ties and more ballast than narrower gauges, it was nevertheless adopted by other railroads in the central and eastern parts of the country. In 1872, however, the first line to Entre Ríos used the standard gauge (4 feet, 8 1/2 inches), which was then adopted by other lines built in the Mesopotamian provinces. A third group of railroads in the Andean region used the narrower gauge, first adopted by the Cordoba-Tucumán line. No less than five other gauges were also in use by the end of the nineteenth century.

The consequences of the spread of the Argentine railroads were to encourage over many decades the production and export of grain, livestock, citrus fruits, olives, tobacco, cotton, and lumber products from the interior, and especially sugar from Tucumán and grapes from Mendoza. The railroads also encouraged the settlement of many European immigrants, who cleared the land for agriculture, often under short tenancy, after which their fields reverted to large landowners who thereby acquired extensive improved properties. But the rigidity of a system of lines that ran to a single, dominant port, slicing up the hinterland into thin wedges, effectively crushed most local manufacturing concerns that might have developed to serve the domestic market. They could in no way compete with the superior access to the interior market at the disposal of imported goods, or those manufactured in Buenos Aires. The result was a continued economic depression for the population of the interior and a much greater incentive to settle in the capital.

One of the earliest opportunities for the exploitation of new raw materials after the colonial period was in northern Chile. After 1810, the mining of gold, which had been produced in meager quantities, was replaced by larger deposits of silver and copper. At first, Valparaíso and Coquimbo, well to the south of some of the mines, were the only ports through which the minerals could be legally exported. An early shift from traditional burros to more sturdy mules raised transport costs to the point where some of the more distant mines were uneconomical to operate. This led, in the 1840s, to the development of a number of ports farther north along the coast that were connected by short transverse trails to two principal, longitudinal roads, one near the coast and the other more inland, linking the departmental capitals. However, wheeled vehicles could still be used only in the vicinity of the major towns; in spite of attempts to develop cart trails and improve the efficiency of animal energy, the roads were often badly constructed and quickly reduced to a sorry state. In this regard, the condition of transportation in its relationship to mining was very similar to the early experience in Mexico.

The construction of railroads in the 1860s and 1870s were thus largely inspired by the needs of a growing mining industry. Primarily funded with U.S. capital, the rail lines were once more expressions of raw material exportation, being discrete systems focusing on the small northern ports, which had been established in the 1840s and were almost entirely dependent on their mining hinterlands. As in Argentina and Brazil, there was little concern for potential interconnection, even though the railroads were ultimately linked by the expansion of the early Caldera-Coquimbo line. Throughout the nineteenth century, equipment was highly variable between railroads, and no less than seven different gauges were in use.

Nevertheless, within the context of the mining export economy, the railroads brought great changes. All manner of supplies could now be imported, and the mining camps attracted coal, coke, machinery, salt, food, and even Yankee ice. Production was intensified, and formerly worthless copper ores became valuable while inaccessible deposits were made accessible. Caldera was an example of the boom town conditions that the railroads brought to the coastal transfer points. Within 3 years of the railroad's construction to the port, this desolate section of the Chilean coast boasted smelters, water distillation plants, coal storage facilities, docks, warehouses, and housing for more than 2000.

The location of the smelters along the coast at this time may also have been stimulated by the railroad because freight rates were higher uphill than downhill. In the later years of the century, after the best ores had been worked out, the railroads with their fixed costs could not continue to lower freight rates in order to generate the same amount of traffic from lower-grade ores. The inertia of the railroads, fixed in their tracks, thus came to be "the industry's cross and deterrent." Furthermore, although they had served the mining industry well and, indeed, facilitated a more modern revival based on technological innovations in the mining of very low-grade copper deposits, the railroads also compartmentalized the region of Norte Chico.

In the far north of Chile a similar set of rail lines developed, based on *guano* and then nitrate deposits. Export of *guano* for fertilizer had begun in the 1840s from sites just south of Cobija (Antofagasta), drawing Chilean settlement to the Atacama Desert. Thirty years later, rich deposits of sodium nitrate salts were uncovered in the region in a wider, 30-mile band of lowland. At first Argentine mules were used for shipping the nitrate the relatively short distance to the coast for export. However, lack of feed and water in the arid environment quickly led to a substitution of narrow gauge railways and tramways, again constructed with outside capital. These lines have not made a major contribution to the modern Chilean network, but they facilitated greater Chilean interest in this remote region, ultimately resulting in its acquisition from Bolivia after the War of the Pacific (1879–1882).

The complex details of Bolivia's border disputes need not be discussed here except as they relate to transportation. We have already seen that, as upper Peru, Bolivia's main concentration of population had always been economically oriented to the Pacific. Its colonial outlet to the sea had been through Arica, although routes through Arequipa and Cobija had also been used. After independence, Arica and Arequipa both lay within the area claimed by Peru, while Cobija had the advantage of being within the coastal enclave claimed by Bolivia. Neither Chile nor Peru were receptive to Bolivia's desire for a coastal route and port under her own control; as Fifer (1972) has described in great detail, Bolivian politics subsequently became mesmerized by its "Pacific question." The pursuit of this issue has been very much within the context of transportation routes, and it is noteworthy that the conflict has centered on the three colonial routes whose inertia has been sustained by competition among the interests associated with each route to serve the Bolivian interior.

Before the railroads, traffic from the *altiplano* continued to use the Arica route, even though it was in Peruvian hands, instead of the trail through Cobija, which Bolivia then controlled. The principal reason was distance. Arica could be reached from La Paz in 7 or 8 days; in spite of the high customs charges imposed by Peru, it was a cheaper route to follow than that from La Paz to Cobija, which could take over three weeks. The traffic pattern switched after Meiggs extended his Mollendo-Arequipa railroad to Puno in 1874. Goods now moved through Mollendo on the railroad and from Puno by steamer across Lake Titicaca to Chililaya (Puerto Pérez). There they followed a 40 mile journey by U.S.-imported wagons to La Paz. Although twice as long as the overland route and with numerous transfer points, it was still a cheaper route, especially after 1905 when the wagon road was replaced with a railroad and Mollendo became Bolivia's most important outlet for a few years.

Meanwhile, to the south, a railroad from Antofagasta (Cobija), now a part of Chilean territory, had been constructed to Uyuni. Three years later it had reached Oruro and, by 1917, it connected with La Paz. Although two and one-half times as long as the Mollendo route, it soon captured the great majority of Bolivia's trade, particularly the export of large quantities of ore, which were now forming the basis for an enlarged traffic. The major advantages of the new route were its avoidance of serious gradients and tortuous curves and the elimination of all but the terminal transfer points.

In the face of such competition from Mollendo and then Antofagasta, the traditional Arica route might have been expected to disappear but for Bolivia's continued belief in its importance. Thus one result of the War of the Pacific was an agreement that Chile would construct a railroad over the old route. With some changes to account for alterations in what was now the boundary between Chile and Peru, a railroad, including a 25-mile rack section, was finished to La Paz by 1913, and Arica once more became an important port for Bolivia, second only to Antofagasta.

Fifer(1972) observes that the three ports continue to compete for Bolivia's trade to the present day (with Matarani now substituted for Mollendo). Antofagasta's predominance in the traffic flow is being challenged by Arica's attempt to revive its fortunes with electrification of the line to La Paz and elimination of the rack section. This route is challenged in turn by new highway construction being proposed to parallel the existing railroads as well as the possible opening of a fourth, duplicatory route between La Paz, Moquegua, and the Pacific port of Ilo, located between Mollendo and Arica.

As an example of the persistence of duplicatory routes over a long period of time, the connections between Bolivia and the Pacific parallel the example of the two routes that cross the Sierra Madre Oriental between Mexico City and Veracruz. In both cases competitive interests became associated with the different routes. Each crossed extraordinarily difficult terrain, which precluded route capture, and new stages of transportation technology failed to dislodge the route inertia that developed.

A second type of Latin American railroad was the interoceanic connection between Atlantic and Pacific, completion of which would fulfill the recurring nineteenth-century dream of a cheap and shorter passage west between Europe and Asia. It was always assumed by foreign investors that completion of such a link across the western hemispheric land barrier would automatically grant the operators of the route a sudden surge of traffic; to Latin American champions of the idea, the route would spin off great economic rewards for the agents who handled the commerce. Furthermore, the grand concept of such a project matched the common image of the railroad as a worker of commercial miracles. It was behind the promotion of a surprising number of railroad lines in Latin America, some of which were built, a few even reaching transcontinental status. Those that did not achieve this role were usually incorporated into the existing, export-oriented network. It is therefore important to emphasize where possible the *intentions* as well as the actions of railroad companies in Latin America, especially if we are to understand the reasons behind the routes chosen.

In Mexico the transcontinental idea surfaced 20 years before the first rail had been laid in the country. Most of the early concessions, including the agreement for the Mexican Railway, envisaged a rail link between Veracruz, Mexico City, and Acapulco, thus revitalizing the old colonial transport axis across Mexico. In any event, no rail link was ever forged across the mountains from Mexico City to Acapulco. The failure of the Mexican Railway to build beyond the capital did not deter investors from supporting the parallel Inter-oceanic Railway, whose name alone announced its professed intentions. Strung together from previously built segments on the plateau, with a long, winding route, the Inter-oceanic was completed 18 years after its rival in 1891, but it also terminated at Mexico City.

By this time, the outlook of foreign investors was more realistic in terms of traffic. The Suez Canal (1869) had already brought Asia closer to Europe, while the California gold rush offered more immediate prospects of serving transcontinental traffic in the United States. Even after the first U.S. transcontinental railroad was completed in 1869, a shorter land crossing, with the rest of the journey by ship, was thought to be competitive. Thus attention was turned south to a rail link across Mexico's isthmus; in 1894 the Tehuantepec Railroad was completed between Salina Cruz and Coatzacoalcos. Although constructed with considerable cost to human life in the tropical heat (the burden being borne mostly by imported Jamaican workers), the railroad was a great success until World War I, when worldwide trade was cut, and a disastrous slump in traffic began from which the line never recovered. The opening of the Panama Canal in 1914 sealed the fate of the Tehuantepec Railroad, a project whose only purpose was transcontinental connection, after which it could acquire no other function and so earned its title as Mexico's "White Elephant."

In Central America nineteenth-century transportation was also initially developed to further interoceanic interests; here, however, adaptation to more traditional traffic flows was possible. The earliest attempt to connect with two Central American coasts involved the steampship, not the railroad. The route, stimulated by the California gold rush, followed the traditional path of the San Juan River to Lake Nicaragua, where steamships established by Commodore Vanderbilt ferried prospectors across the lake to a short trail that ran down the Pacific slopes to the coast. Attempts to supplant this with an all-rail link through Honduras were begun in 1853, again with American capital, but efforts lasted only until the U.S. transcontinental line was completed. At this time, in 1869, the project was abandoned, leaving a partially completed railroad from the Atlantic coast running 57 miles inland to a point a little beyond San Pedro Sula.

Visions of a sea-to-sea link were revived once more in Costa Rica when, in 1879, a concession for such a route was granted to Minor C. Keith. The railroad was built in sections from the Caribbean port of Limón toward San José, but there were numerous delays, often because of a lack of capital. The substantial costs encountered were partly the result of the difficult terrain and tropical environment; they were also caused by the decision to build both from the coast and from points inland. Thus the first locomotive was hauled up the coastal escarpment from the Pacific coast at Puntarenas to the western terminal of Alajuela by a train of ox carts. Keith resolved to solve part of the problem of financing the railroad by raising bananas in plantations established alongside the tracks and shipping them by his own steamship line to the U.S. market. His banana empire became the United Fruit Company in 1899, and the symbiotic relationship of railroad construction and banana production became the basis for subsequent transportation development in Central America. The Costa Rican railroad was completed through San José to Alajuela in 1890 and was extended to Puntarenas in 1910 to complete the transoceanic link. In Guatemala in 1884 Keith opened another railroad from Escuintla on the Pacific to Guatemala and connected it to the Caribbean along the Motagua Valley by 1908. Again, bananas were to provide the freight; the United Fruit Company agreed to plant over 1 million trees along the railroad. The result was an immense plantation beside the Motagua and the company's ownership of the

[handwritten margin notes at top:] most impo. interoceanic connection — Panama Canal w/ its locks.
3rd Speculative R.R. construction is initiated over a route w/ no existing pattern of interaction — but is expected to generate movement w/ presence of completed line. less likely to succeed —

docks at Guatemala's only Caribbean port of Puerto Barrios. When, in the twentieth century, sigatoka and leaf-spot disease afflicted the bulk of the banana production in the Caribbean valleys of Central America, bananas spread to the Pacific coast area, where they had been less intensively planted in the nineteenth century. Here some railroad communication already existed, and these lines were adapted to the familiar role of facilitating raw material exports. Nevertheless, in Central America we have a case in which the original motivation for transportation routes had been interoceanic communication, and adaptation to the more usual function occurred later.

The goal of transcontinental connection also stimulated railroad construction in South America. As early as 1857, shouts of "on to Chile" greeted completion of the first mile of track on the Western Railroad in Argentina. Yet it was not until the twentieth century that a railroad from Buenos Aires to Valparaíso was finally completed. By that time, however, the transcontinental stimulus was not as strong, and the railroad was in reality formed from a patchwork of rail sections that had not been evolved with the specific intention to link the oceans. This was even more the case with the second transcontinental link, finally achieved in 1925 when the Bolivian section between Atocha and La Quiaca joined a meandering route across the continent between Buenos Aires and Antofagasta, a route that probably carried no traffic across its entire length besides the occasional hardy and persistent tourist.

The most important interoceanic connection, and one that overshadowed all others in Latin America was, of course, the Panama Canal which, by means of locks, allowed oceangoing vessels to cross the Panamanian isthmus after its completion in 1914. Its effect in Latin America was at least twofold. First, it virtually ended the development of any new routes established specifically for ocean-to-ocean transit until after World War II, when discussion stimulated by political uncertainties in Panama and growing obsolescence of the canal itself resulted in evaluation of new Central American routes. Second, the canal brought numerous benefits to the many bulk producers of exports for the U.S. and European markets in the Pacific countries. Expansion occurred in the production of sugar in Peru, ores in Chile and Bolivia, coffee in Colombia, and later, in the 1950s, bananas in Ecuador.

The third type of railroad that may be identified in Latin America is probably the hardest to determine since, once again, it involves the intention as much as the actual outcome of the promoter's activities. It might best be called the speculative railroad, where construction is initiated over a route that possesses no existing pattern of interaction but is expected to generate such movement by the very presence of the completed line. It is much more the pioneer railroad than the other two types, much more subject to hyperbole in its promotion, and much less likely to succeed, since it seeks to create instead of to respond to traffic demand. Many examples never extended beyond the issue of

[handwritten margin note, left side, vertical:] Panama Canal

[handwritten notes at bottom:] Seeks to create instead of respond to traffic demand
Best ex — Madeira Mamoré R.R.

stock or granting of a government concession, but a few did reach the stage of construction, contributing to the railroad map of the continent. One of the best examples was the Madeira-Mamoré railroad.

The Madeira and Mamoré rivers offered a means of penetrating the Amazon rainforest and interior Bolivia. The Amazon had long been a mysterious attraction for foreigners, from the early myths to the extravagant claims of nineteenth-century travelers such as Maury. Brazil's closure of the Amazon River to steamships until after 1867 only served to heighten curiosity. The Madeira-Mamoré route seemed a logical line of access to develop a major section of the basin and to redirect the economy of highland Bolivia toward the east. However, a 40-mile stretch of rapids and falls between Pôrto Velho on the Madeira and its confluence with the Mamoré was impassable to river traffic and required a difficult portage. Removal of this bottleneck with a railroad thus became a favorite suggestion of foreign observers. In 1868, for instance, an American, George Earl Church, claimed that by overcoming the Madeira-Mamoré barrier and routing traffic northeastward from the principal centers of Pacific trade, a reduction from 180 days by clipper ship to 30 days by rail and ship could be achieved in reaching U.S. and European markets. Freight rates would also be cut by one-quarter. Others claimed that such a route would boost the Amazonian production of cotton, tobacco, sugar, timber, and rubber. This lure of instant economic success finally attracted an English company to attempt construction of a railroad around the rapids in 1871, but without success. Five years later, a Philadelphia company began a new attempt. Rippy (1968) describes the enormous difficulties of railroad construction in the tropical lowlands:

> Every inch of the line had to be cut through almost impenetrable vegetation. Quite frequently immense trees, after being severed at the base, would continue to stand . . . held firmly in place by a network of vines. . . . Surveying through these forests was like surveying by the light of a lantern at midnight. The humid heat was relentless; millions of stinging and biting insects made life miserable day and night; swarms of crickets and roaches ate the men's clothing and gnawed their shoes; termite ants destroyed everything except concrete and steel. Dreadful diseases attacked . . . malaria, dysentery, yellow fever. . . .

After 18 months, the effort was abandoned. Finally, in 1906, with the Amazon now yielding the world's largest supplies of rubber, a third attempt was successful. Another American company overcame the hazards and completed a railroad between Pôrto Velho and Guajará-Mirim, cutting the overland journey around the rapids by 2 weeks. Ironically for this essentially speculative railroad, the last spike was driven, in 1912, the year the Amazonian rubber boom ended.

In the 1980s, a fourth, tentative category might be added in which governments undertake new rail construction to stimulate economic or political unity. As we will see, such modern railroad building is rare.

Relationship of the Railroads to Other Transport Technology

Railroads were not the only transport innovation to be found in postcolonial Latin America. Road transport, steamships, port improvements, and aviation have played a significant part.

Generally, roads took second place to railroads in the nineteenth century and, where they existed, served the needs of local traffic. However, in some cases, new highway construction that competed with the railroad was undertaken in support of long-distance traffic. For instance, toward the end of the century in the Mexico City-Veracruz corridor, it was not unusual to see highway traffic composed of heavily loaded animal teams following a route parallel to the railroads, since it was often cheaper to send goods by road instead of rail.

Steamboats were important on several rivers in South America in the nineteenth century. The earliest were working the Magdalena River in 1828. There was steam navigation on the Orinocco to Ciudad Bolivar in the 1860s and, after 1867, when government restrictions were lifted, steamboats helped open up the Amazon Basin. During the rubber boom, oceangoing vessels traveled 1000 miles upstream to Manaus, the center of the trade.

In the second half of the nineteenth century steamboats became the common form of river travel on the Magdalena in Colombia. The steamers reduced freighter rates by a factor of four or five over the previous forms of river transport, although the rates charged were still high and movement slow. The variability of the river level was a great hazard for the larger boats; moreover, they were constantly forced to tie up beside the bank while replenishing their supply of wood. Thus the trip from Cartagena to Bogotá could still take as long as 6 weeks. The effect of the steamboats, therefore, was to bring the river country closer to the international market, enlarging the shipments of cotton textiles, tobacco, and cacao. In this regard, the steamboats conformed to the externally oriented pattern adopted by so many of Latin America's railroads.

The traditional reliance on the river arteries, the high cost of transportation, the relative remoteness of the highlands, and the small pockets of dispersed population and settlement all combined to retard the introduction of the railroad to Colombia. Not until the 1920s was there a boom in railroad construction, and then it was highly correlated with coffee exports, suggesting a strong mutual interdependence. Indeed, it has been suggested that if railroad construction had come in the 1880s, coffee might have reached its export levels four decades sooner and the country might be that much farther along the road to economic development.

River steamers have also been important on the lower courses of the Rio de la Plata system, and there is an important ferry system linking Buenos Aires, Colonia, and Montevideo. A vessel carries passengers and cargo across Lake Titicaca, high in the Andes. Nevertheless, navigation on the inland waterways of the region has made less economic impact than might have been anticipated. There are two major reasons for this: the technologically primitive hinterlands served by the river steamers, and difficult navigation conditions on many rivers. On the Apuré River, for example, in August the river could carry the greatest liner afloat; in March it would barely support a 40-ton steamer.

Overseas shipping companies had begun to include Latin American ports in their regular services as early as 1840. By the 1880s, many of the major harbors were lagging far behind the technological advances in shipping, and some were in danger of losing their predominant position in spite of the focus of railroads and the intertia this imparted to their location. Buenos Aires, for instance, was an open roadstead until late in the nineteenth century, and it was so shallow that steamers of any size had to lie 10 miles out to obtain sufficient depth; Montevideo lacked any breakwater and was open to the strong *pampero* winds that could severely damage shipping; at Valparaíso in 1900, shipping still anchored in the open bay, with cargo unloaded by lighters at a rate of 60 to 70 tons a day; and at Rio de Janeiro, the lack of proper docks also required lighters and four separate transfers: from ship to lighter, lighter to trollies on the customs quay, trollies to elevators, and elevators to the warehouse. The substantial port improvement schemes undertaken in the early part of this century were, therefore, indicative of the need of primary centers to maintain actively their position of dominance in the face of changing transport technology.

The most drastic change in technology came with the introduction of the aircraft. A modern map of Latin America will show a considerable number of airstrips in the continent's less accessible parts; this, combined with an overlying layer of regular flights between major cities, suggests a pattern of transport much more oriented toward the interior. In fact, in the early days of aviation the routes followed were remarkably similar to the major lines of surface transport and concentrated on the country's principal settlements. Moreover, the early investment in aviation was made once again by foreign interests, after World War I had provided the expertise and capacity for aircraft production.

Perhaps as a reflection of the difficulties of communication, the earliest development of air service was in Colombia, with German initiative. German interests also started the service in Ecuador in 1925, while North Americans began the first lines in Peru. Germans and French together were important in the development of the Brazilian network after 1926 and in Argentina in 1928.

R.R. penetrate new areas · response to discovery
of new materials to be exported to overseas markets
R.R. helped to enlarge & intensify the externally
oriented route pattern J reinforce the dominance
138 of traditional settlement.   TRANSPORTATION

Mexico, Central America, and the islands of the Greater Antilles came under U.S. carrier influence. This foreign interest almost guaranteed the ultimate focus of routes on overseas connections with the primary cities. In this respect the early development of aviation very much followed the same pattern as the railroads.

Continuity, not change, characterized the introduction of new forms of transportation to Latin America. Frequently, they followed the same routes pioneered by colonial highways and concentrated traffic on the same settlements that had achieved prominence in the colonial urban hierarchy. When the railroads did penetrate new areas, it was usually in response to the discovery of new raw materials to be exported to overseas markets and not as a stimulus to the development of an internal market. Railroads particularly helped to enlarge and intensify the externally oriented route pattern and reinforce the dominance of traditional settlements instead of creating a totally new geography of transportation in Latin America. This persistence or inertia in route alignment and traffic flow was not surprising, given the almost complete control of railroad construction by foreign interests. Even where the companies were nominally Latin American, many investors were overseas; the engineers were always foreign, usually from the United States or Britain; the equipment and rolling stock were imported, even railroad ties were sometimes brought from California; frequently the laborers included gangs of Irish or Chinese; and, once in operation, the lines often burned coal from Britain or Australia. The builders of nineteenth-century railroads and colonial highways thus had a similarity of purpose: to facilitate the development of Latin America as an appendage of a Euro-American economy. Consequently the railroads were a response to the demands of a neocolonial economy and mirrored the forces that had stimulated the original, externally oriented patterns of colonial transportation. This in turn further reinforced the attractive force of the peripheral urban centers and so made more difficult any trend toward a more balanced, internal domestic market, which became a Latin American objective with the rise of twentieth-century economic nationalism. Due to depression Lat. Am. forced to turn inward -development moved internally oriented linking clusters of populations in the interior w/ centers of manufacturing

THE MODERN PERIOD OF TRANSPORTATION IN LATIN AMERICA

The mood for greater indigenous instead of foreign control of Latin American economies began to take hold during the Depression, when demand for raw materials overseas decreased and export prices declined. In order to save foreign exchange, Latin Americans were forced to turn inward and substitute domestic manufactures protected by high tariff walls for their traditional reliance on imported goods. The need of local industry to decrease its own high costs and increase its viability required an expanded domestic market, which could only be achieved through the development of an internally oriented and integrated transportation network, linking together clusters of population in the interior with centers of manufacturing. The beginnings of such a reorientation away from the traditional externally oriented and poorly integrated network of the colonial past marks the emergence of the modern period in Latin American transportation.

One of the earliest examples of this change was the proposal for a Pan-American railway, which would string together a series of existing and future lines extending from Buenos Aires through South and Middle America to connect with the U.S. railroad network. Although suggested as early as 1872, it was not seriously contemplated until the 1890s, when several potential routes linking the various Latin American capitals were surveyed. By 1923, lines ran from the United States to Mexico City and on to Guatemala and from Buenos Aires to Lake Titicaca. Several other countries had also built sections of the route, although it is not possible to determine to what extent the proposed Pan-American railway was the principal motivation for such construction. Arguments in the 1920s over the route to be followed in Central America held up further work long enough that the project was ultimately abandoned in favor of a Pan-American highway that would stretch from Alaska to Patagonia.

Since the first Highway Congress met in Buenos Aires in 1925, the slow and sometimes erratic development of a series of highway links, most of them constructed after World War II, has almost achieved its objective. Only the section between southern Panama and northern Colombia, the so-called Darién Gap, remains to be completed. Work began in 1972 on the 185-mile Panamanian section between Tocumén and the Colombian border, and the Colombians have finished the road from Medellín to Guapá as part of the Medellín-Turbo highway. The section still left crosses the Atrato River Valley, and the problems of spanning it involve engineering and ecology. The area itself is a region of low-lying, swampy, tropical rainforest separated by numerous water channels, where the indigenous inhabitants live from canoes and firm soil is only found 130 feet below the surface. This traditional land barrier between the two continents can now be overcome with modern techniques of highway construction, yet its disappearance could have serious ecological consequences, since it presently prevents the spread of foot and mouth disease, endemic to Colombia but unknown in Panama at this time. In late 1974 the United States, which is contributing two-thirds of the cost of the highway, held up funds until Colombia agreed to a 25-mile cattle-free zone as part of a program to erradicate the disease near the border.

It might be said that the U.S. sponsorship of the Pan-American Highway project, to which it has been a major financial contributor, places the scheme in the category of a traditional, foreign-initiated series of transport lines. However, regardless of the original motivation for the highway, the actual impact of construction has been significant in increasing the degree of internal economic interaction in Latin America. For example, in a local study of the Mexican *municipio* of Villa Las Rosas, it was found that a short spur road to the village from the Pan-American Highway, as it pushed through this previously isolated section of Chiapas, brought substantial economic changes. Now that beef could be moved by truck to the capital, the effective market accessibility of the town was extended to Mexico City, resulting in a much greater local specialization in cattle production. Equally significant was the return flow of commercial, mass-produced goods that competed with local products (e.g., *Nescafé* versus local coffee). The spur road from the main highway was built not so much to aid the *municipio* as to provide market access for a new sugar refinery in nearby Pujílitic, yet such was the economic multiplier effect of the highway that its influence extended considerably beyond the specific purpose of its construction to produce a profound impact on the *municipio* and a powerful influence on its inhabitants.

A further example of this effect followed the decision of the Central American governments in 1963 to complete a central network of highways through the spine of the region as part of the foundation for the Central American Common Market. The Inter-American Highway (part of the Pan-American system), connecting all six capitals with a paved, all-weather road, was the prime artery of the network; it brought significant economic changes to the landscape and stimulated numerous feeder roads. Prior to its completion, the bulk of land transport in the region followed the traditional pattern of short spurs to the coast, serving the export of bananas and coffee. Before 1958, most trade between the countries had been by sea, since the average freight charge was only 8 percent of the cost of the product, compared with 20 to 30 percent by road. After highway integration and improvement, the percentage of the total cost incurred by road transport dropped to an average of 3.4 percent. The result was a substantial reversal of the proportion of total Central American trade traveling by road—up to 78 percent compared to only 22 percent by sea. Moreover, the volume of freight movements was greatly increased through the initial success of the Common Market. Cattle production, for instance, was dramatically expanded on the Pacific lowlands, with the meat shipped in refrigerated trucks to Caribbean ports and then by ship to Miami and the U.S. market. The recent political tension within the region, especially friction between Honduras and El Salvador after the "Soccer War" of 1971, together with the general decline of world trade have reduced the traffic flow over the main highway from its level in the late 1960s but, by this time, the impact of the road had already been substantial.

Another early stimulus to the growth of internally oriented transportation in Latin America was the profusion of ungraded and dirt roads that, beginning in the 1940s, permitted the new transport innovations of truck and bus to

Each village provides labor - gov. provides the machinery.

reach deep into hitherto isolated sections of the countryside, bringing regional market centers into contact with their surrounding hinterlands. The overloaded third-class bus, top heavy with bundles of goods, chickens, and bicycles on the roof, crammed with passengers, some hanging off the outside, groaning and belching black diesel fumes as it winds up a steep, stony, track miles from the nearest paved road, represents an innovation of enormous proportions to the development of Latin American communications. More recently, local interaction has been further improved in certain countries through the concept of the *camino vecinal*, a local road, often only of graded stone, that is built cooperatively by the villages that benefit from its completion. Each village provides substantial donated labor, while the central government provides the necessary machinery. Under such a program, begun in Mexico and Colombia in the 1960s, the cost per mile of the road was estimated in 1975 to be about U.S. $15,500, considerably below conventional costs using regular machinery.

esp. overseas investment. The action required was reliance on raw material to pay for imports of capital + equip. to find expansion.

Constraints of the Traditional Transport Pattern

The modern growth of Latin American domestic economies, begun in the Depression, expanded during World War II when ocean shipping was threatened and the traditional overseas suppliers in Europe and America were engaged in military production. After the war, foreign competition became common again, not only in imported finished goods, but also in terms of overseas investment in domestic Latin American production. Even though this competition could be countered by increasing the scale of the domestic economic base, such action required continued reliance on raw material exports to pay for imports of capital and equipment to fund the necessary expansion. An alternative, although not a substitute approach, in order to retain as much benefit as possible from the new scale of economic activity within Latin America was to expand the internal domestic market from a national to an international level within the region. The result was the creation of the Latin American Free Trade Association (LAFTA).

Since then, proponents of continentwide economic integration have stressed the need to create an integrated Latin American transport system as a major prerequisite to the development of LAFTA. Yet, at the same time, there is recognition of the extent to which this requirement has been constrained by the existing postcolonial railroad network; it is the railroad that has been the traditional overland bulk carrier of long-distance cargo. The problem lies not only in the orientation of the rail network developed to serve an earlier era, but also in its obsolescent condition and lack of integration.

In Bolivia, for instance, the railroad between Santa Cruz in the eastern foothills of the Andes and Corumbá on the Bolivian-Brazilian frontier represents a link in a transcontinental railroad between Brazil and Chile. Corumbá

In order to retain as much benefit as..., from new scale of econ. activity - Lat Am is to expand the internal domestic market from a national to an international level (in the region.

is connected with São Paulo by a 48-hour journey, and by this route come mostly Brazilian manufactured goods for the Bolivian market. However, the Bolivian stretch of the railroad, built in 1924, is a major bottleneck to increased interchange because of its decayed condition. Fifer (1972) has written that:

> The track is slow and worn, with thousands of its sleepers burned by cinders dropped from the wood-burning locomotives. . . . Operating costs are so high that in the case of *autocarril* passenger fares, the railway barely competes with the aircraft flying overhead, conveniently following the rail track's narrow red gash through the almost continous jungle lying below.

Furthermore, she notes that customs delays of 2 weeks to move goods are usual and, on occasion, may be two or three times as long.

The condition of the old railroad in eastern Bolivia is not an isolated example. The Argentine government pledged in 1974 that it would bring nearly 60 percent of its 25,800 miles of track up to a "good condition" classification. It was acknowledged that 50 percent of the track was below standard and 40 percent of all rolling stock was in various stages of dilapidation because of old age or poor maintenance. But perhaps it is in Brazil where the worst railroad conditions are to be found. The country's 20,000 miles of track, built principally in the first three decades of the century, suffer from maintenance problems and old equipment that frequently produces bridge collapses, snapped tracks, and breakdowns. Switching and interchange have been inadequate solutions because of the different gauges in use and because there are almost 40 different kinds of steam locomotives in service built to burn a variety of fuels, including wood on some interior lines. Finally, much of the track is circuitous, having been constructed to serve rural properties and not as direct connections between urban centers. Thus the distance by rail between the Monlevade steel plant and São Paulo is 680 miles compared to 430 miles by road.

Even if the problems of track, equipment, and maintenance could be solved, the lack of integration would still exist. At present, only 9 out of 25 frontiers in South America possess a rail crossing, and three of these (Brazil-Argentina, Brazil-Uruguay, and Bolivia-Peru) require a change of gauge at the border. Moreover, full integration would involve an organizational revolution. There are still no direct international tariffs; goods cannot be paid for at the station of origin but must have charges collected after crossing each border. There are few direct through trains across borders, little sharing of railroad cars, and no coordination of national schedules to facilitate international traffic. Recently, however, there has been some growth in the use of bulk intermodal units such as containers and piggyback truck sections on the railroads linking Argentina, Uruguay, and Brazil. Nevertheless, a major increase in the use of railroads for interregional trade would require substantial investments that have so far been resisted by many Latin American governments. Most countries possess ambitious railroad plans, but new construction is rare and its value frequently unproven. This is the case with the Chihuahua- Pacific line, completed in 1961 across the Sierra Madre Occidental of Mexico through the famed Cooper Canyon and designed to connect the rich mining district on the plateau with the presently undeveloped port of Topolobampo. So far, only a trickle of tourist traffic, not the expected flow of ore shipments, have materialized. A more certain basis for traffic generation exists on the new line between mineral-rich Ciudad Guyana and San Juan de los Morros, south of densely populated Caracas. Bids for this rail link were let in 1977 as part of Venezuela's plan to build 2500 miles of track by 1990. However, even when potential demand can be demonstrated, the enormous costs of construction can overwhelm a project. Thus, in Brazil, the so-called "Steel Line" between the iron ore deposits of Minas Gerais and the steelworks at Volta Redonda has been so costly that a decision on its completion was deferred in 1978.

Where demand for interaction has remained unfulfilled by the aging rail system, there has been a shift to other transport forms, particularly highways. In Brazil trucks instead of rail are often used to ship supplies to and from steel plants, despite higher costs. Indeed, 65 percent of Brazil's traffic moves by road; 18 percent uses rail. Trucks are also supplanting river transport, the other traditional large-bulk medium. Shipments from Santos to Belém, at the mouth of the Amazon, take 10 times as long by boat as by road. In Argentina and Uruguay competition from the highways reduced by one-half the amount of freight carried on the railroads between 1945 and 1963.

Pipeline construction also has been substituted for new railroads, particularly in the carriage of oil from the new interior fields east of the Andes. In Bolivia, for instance, 68 percent of the country's trade moved by rail in the first half of the 1960s; however, once the pipelines were finished from the Santa Cruz field to Arica and Yacuiba, Argentina, in 1967, this figure dropped dramatically to only 12 percent. Construction on an additional crude oil pipeline from Santa Cruz to Puerto Suárez and a new parallel natural gas line, both financed by Brazil, are likely to reduce further the effectiveness of the transcontinental railroad between the two countries. This will be particularly so if, as seems likely, Brazil extends the two pipelines across its territory to São Paulo.

Nevertheless, new highways and pipelines spanning parts of interior Latin America have certainly not been on a scale and density sufficient to support even the modest amount of international trade that has developed among LAFTA countries. Instead, the constraints of the old transport pattern and its orientation toward peripheral centers and major ports has insured that 90 percent of such trade is still conducted by coastal shipping. Basically, these flows can be broken down into three types: first, traditional trade in raw materials between pairs of countries, such as lumber from Brazil to Argentina, iron

(2) sporadic or occasional flow in response to a temp. breakdown in a country's supply capacity.
(3) Industrial Products -

from Chile, Brazil, and Peru to Argentina, meat from Argentina to Chile (also by rail), wheat and fruit from Argenetina to Brazil, bananas from Ecuador to Chile, and petroleum from Venezuela to Brazil; second, sporadic or occasional flows in response to a temporary breakdown in a country's supply capacity, such as the shipment of pipe to Bolivia from Argentina for construction of the Santa Cruz-Yacuiba pipeline; and third, industrial products, primarily from Mexico, Brazil, and Argentina to the rest of Latin America.

Transportation and the Contemporary Space-economy of Latin America

The present movements of inter-American trade are one contribution to the persistence of an externally oriented transport pattern. But this trade accounts for only 11 percent of the continent's total international business, and the continued importance of overseas exports following colonial patterns is even more influential. Of similar significance is the disproportionate economic growth centered on the major urban centers that have long been linked to the traditional transport network. The mutually reinforcing relationship between primary cities and a restricted route pattern was intensified with the development of domestic manufacturing. The privileged cities, with their access to larger markets provided by superior transportation, offered firms greater opportunities for more efficient production than potential rival centers. It is therefore no accident that, with the possible exceptions of Brasilia and Ciudad Guyana, every major urban center of Latin American economic growth has a colonial foundation. Moreover, the commercial power of these economic centers is such that they have been the focus of investments in transportation during the last two decades. This geographical bias in transportation, far from diffusing the economic benefits of domestic production over a greater area of the continent to those interior regions not originally associated with the traditional transport network, has accentuated the attractiveness and agglomerative power of the principal urban centers. The result has been the emergence of a limited number of core cities, loosely linked into zones of intensified demographic and manufacturing activity. These have become magnets for rural population.

In Mexico the traditional economic concentration on Mexico City has been expanded to include the nearby cities of Toluca, Querétaro, Puebla, and Cuernavaca, each connected to the capital during the last 15 years by a series of fast, modern highways, or *autopistas*. Highway construction continues to concentrate on the needs of this region. The Mexico-Puebla *autopista* has already been pushed eastward over an old sixteenth-century route alignment to connect with the industrial complex in the Orizaba Valley, and it is expected to be continued to Veracruz, bringing the major gulf port within 3½ hours of the capital. An additional *autopista* is under construction from Mexico City to the mining center of Pachuca. The more distant economic foci, however, such as the country's second city, Guadalajara, and the heavy industrial complex of Monterrey, Saltillo, and Monclova in the far north, are at present relatively independent of the regional complex around the capital; exchange between the centers, although considerable, is conducted over inefficient rail connections.

For Venezuela, the traditional focus of economic concentration has been on Caracas; however, the need for space has forced industrialists to seek additional sites in the formerly important colonial towns of Maracay and Valencia. This axis has attracted the majority of transport investment. As early as 1958, a second *autopista* was completed between Caracas and Valencia to handle the expansion of traffic, which had exceeded the capacity of the Central Railroad and the old Pan-American Highway, whose routes the *autopista* paralleled. More recent extensions of the modern highway to the coastal ports of Puerto Cabello and La Guaira have aided the region's general accessibility to overseas trade.

The major zone of economic activity in Brazil focuses on the so-called economic triangle of Rio de Janeiro, São Paulo, and Belo Horizonte. This area also has attracted much of the recent development of transportation. For instance, as part of the country's proposed railroad electrification scheme, a new 515-mile high-speed rail line will link São Paulo with Belo Horizonte, a major improvement over the present circuitous route. Again, as part of the "Export Corridors" transportation plan of 1974, the government expects to rid the major bottleneck between São Paulo and its port of Santos caused by the existence of only two rail lines, one a standard gauge, indirect line, and the other a narrow gauge, cable-assisted railroad. Both lines are to be extensively modernized and their carrying capacity doubled. The Corridor plan involves other Brazilian ports and extends from the Rio Grande to Belém. Three new rail lines are to be built, and capacity over existing tracks is to be trebled; all of this is designed to stimulate agricultural exports such as coffee, soybeans, corn and vegetable oils from each port's hinterlands. The improvement of loading and storage facilities at each port is also anticipated, an important feature in a continent where the cost of port transfer averages 50 percent of the value of the merchandise compared with a worldwide average of 12 to 15 percent.

In Argentina the economic primacy of Buenos Aires has long been maintained, at first by the railroads and more recently, since the 1950s, by the highways that have paralleled them. Two new transportation proposals, even though they concentrate on traffic within the general South Atlantic zone of economic development, may well divert some movement away from the extreme orientation on Buenos Aires. The first involves replacing the ferries across the Paraná and Uruguay rivers. A series of bridges carrying both rail lines and roads over branches of the Paraná River, from Zárate in the densely populated province of Buenos Aires to the isolated tip of Entre Rios Province, is expected to be completed shortly. When the second of two new bridges over the Uruguay River between Puerto Unzue-Fray Bentos and Colón-Paysandú is also finished, a fast, free flow of motor traffic between the major urban centers in Argentina, Uruguay, and southern Brazil will be a reality. However, if this facility is combined with a second scheme involving port improvement, some of the products from Argentina's export hinterland may be diverted from Buenos Aires to Uruguayan ports. The present size limit for vessels on the River Plate is only 30,000 tons. The Argentine government thus proposed to build a new deepwater port at Cabo San Antonio. However, the cost forced the plan to be shelved in 1975, an act that strengthens Uruguay's proposal to construct a deepwater port on the Rocha coast, probably at La Paloma, where studies suggest facilities could be developed to handle vessels of 100,000 tons at one-tenth the cost of the Cabo San Antonio project.

Along the western coast of South America, the reach of the zones of economic activity is more restricted and stresses core cities. The Valparaíso-Santiago region in Chile and the Lima-Callao urban core in Peru are the primary zones of importance; while Quito, in Ecuador, and the regional centers of Colombia have not yet achieved the same degree of dominance over their respective national markets. Since terrain often limits the profusion of surface routes in the region, air transport in the modern period has acquired greater significance in this part of Latin America. Yet aviation is possibly an extreme case of the way developments in transportation have been oriented to the principal cities; it has become almost impossible to fly directly between two neighboring cities separated by a national frontier without first traveling to the two respective capitals. Thus a journey between, say Loja, Ecuador, and Cajamarca, Peru, would require a journey of three flights instead of one, thereby discouraging direct interaction between minor cities.

Modern aviation has made major changes in some parts of Latin America, particularly the Caribbean. Airfield lengthening in small islands such as Antigua and Barbados allowed larger jets to bring tropical environments within 4 or 5 hours of wintry North America. A transformation of the island's economies to tourism followed swiftly. But such air transport remains international in form and therefore stresses the major cities and towns. Inter-island travel by the common folk is generally restricted to small sailing schooners.

The continued concentration of economic activity on a few metropolitan regions has been supported therefore by many of the historic elements of the transportation network evolved during colonial and neocolonial eras and by many more recent national and international transport innovations. The result has been to facilitate an excessive emigration from the impoverished countryside to primary centers, a volume of rural-urban migration that has placed immense stress on the urban fabric of the major cities. It has in turn led to a new appraisal of transportation investment, and recent suggestions have argued for improved communications with secondary cities and agricultural lands in the hinterland as a means of reversing the flow and achieving a more evenly balanced spatial distribution of the national economy. However, in view of the processes we have so far observed regarding the growth of transportation in Latin America, it is fair to ask whether improved communications between primary and secondary or tertiary centers will not simply increase instead of decrease the flow of population and economic wealth toward the primary centers. A few final examples may illuminate this situation.

Quito has been the traditional economic focal point in Ecuador; however, in recent decades the port city of Guayaquil has risen to challenge the capital. Although political as much as economic reasons are behind the rise of this secondary city, the relative isolation between the two centers may have fostered the independent growth of the coastal city. A railroad and road connect both locations, but the terrain is a major hurdle and the routes of the two transport arteries are narrow, congested, and subject to frequent landslides as they traverse the damp Pacific slopes of the Andes. Traffic is therefore limited presently; over the existing road pass only about 5000 vehicles a day, two-thirds of them trucks. A proposal has been made, however, to construct a new 250-mile motorway between Quito and Guayaquil that would be expected to quintuple the capacity of the old highway. If this construction is ultimately completed, Quito's slim economic lead may widen as its market area is extended.

Some evidence of such a trend is available in Colombia, a country that, as we have seen, developed a considerable degree of regional separateness, partly because of the immense difficulties of communication and the slowness with which transport links have been established. Medellín, a manufacturing center, currently rivals Bogotá, the capital, although the agricultural processing center of Cali and the cities of Báranquilla on the coast and Bucaramanga in the highlands are also important focal points of economic growth, each having evolved with some independence from the others. Railroad modernization has proceeded, but much of the network still retains its early twentieth-century lack of interconnection. Considerable attention has therefore been devoted recently to the main north-south highway arteries. Primary roads from Bogotá reach Bucaramanga and Cúcuta on the Venezuelan border and extend south to Cali. Bogotá can even be reached now by a good highway from Medellín, although the routing is circuitous. As a result of these modern improvements in interregional transportation between the capital and the other major urban nodes, Bogotá is now receiving a growing share of national industrialization. The lesson seems to be that once isolation breaks down, so also does a regional balance of secondary centers as the reach of the largest center makes itself felt over a greater distance. In Colombia this process is far from complete. The terrain still mitigates against an effective integration of the transport system, and the country's traditional regionalism may still restrict the extent of Bogotá's dominance.

The potential lesson of Colombia, and one well known in the economically advanced countries of Europe and North America, concerns the capture of smaller peripheral markets by larger dominant centers favored with improved transportation. The removal of customs barriers would increase the accessibility of small nations such as Uruguay and Paraguay to the major markets of Buenos Aires and Brazil (São Paulo-Rio de Janeiro). It would also enlarge the Santiago-Buenos Aires transcontinental axis. Improvements in the roads would gain greater access for other peripheral regions such as the Bolivian-Brazil border, eastern Paraguay, and the Argentine Misiones area. But the short-run effect of improvements in transportation costs and conditions would be to intensify geographic concentration of economic activities on existing centers, not create new ones in peripheral regions.

If this conclusion about the role of transportation improvements is correct, it has important implications for the most recent and most dramatic transportation projects in Latin America—the highways being constructed across the Amazon Basin by Brazil. These roads are designed to stimulate pioneer settlement in the interior, to open up productive lands, and to relieve the pressures of population in the major cities and in the poor and arid northeast. They fall into the category of the nineteenth-century speculative railroad; they are projects that it is hoped will uncover and generate economic growth by their very presence, instead of responding to an existing basis for interaction. And as with railroads such as the Madeira-Mamoré, they have generated extravagant expectations.

Reality is somewhat different. Brazil has made considerable headway in the construction of two major highways, one east-west from João Pessoa on the coast just north of Recife to Cruizeiro do Sul, near the Brazilian-Peruvian border, and the other a north-south route from Arinos, north of Cuiabá in Mato Grosso, to Santarém on the Amazon. A number of sections—broad, red gashes through the forest—have been opened, including the Santarém-Cuiabá stretch in late 1976, but in conditions of high rainfall and humidity the permanency of such roads is questionable. Moreover, early observations about the effects of the highways suggest considerable ecological damage results followed by a low intensity of economic activity. The following sequence of events will possibly occur after completion of the Amazon roads. First, a band of agricultural colonization 10 to 15 miles wide will be developed beside the road in which the forest is effectively cleared. There follows 2 or 3 years before the soil ceases to yield a reasonable return, so the land is abandoned by the colonists in favor of cattle ranches. By this time, the forest has been converted to scrubland, a consequence of the highways, which many believe may result in the disappearance of the Amazon Basin tropical rainforest by the end of the century if the current practice of exploitation continues. As far as economic stimulus from the new highways is concerned, there is little indication of a major urban exodus from the eastern cities in Brazil or of the development of any

improvements in transportation, representing
extension + intensification of the
traditional pattern / have encouraged
further concentration on established
BIBLIOGRAPHY *centers*   **149**

interior, counterbalancing settlement other than Brasilia which, as the national capital, was an enforced political decision and not the result of economic processes.

Present evidence therefore suggests that investment in transportation in Latin America, which has invariably commanded the largest capital outlay in the public sector, has not achieved a more even spatial distribution of economic activity. Instead, the opposite has occurred. Improvements in transportation, representing an extension and intensification of the traditional pattern, have encouraged further concentration on established centers. The question that follows from this analysis but goes beyond the scope of this chapter is whether such economic concentration must necessarily have negative consequences, whether economic concentration is not perhaps the most rapid method of achieving a fairer distribution of economic benefits to the population.

BIBLIOGRAPHY

Altman, I., and J. Lockhart (eds.), *Provinces of Early Mexico: Varients of Spanish American Regional Evolution*, Los Angeles, UCLA Latin American Center, 1976.

Brading, D. A., *Miners and Merchants in Bourbon Mexico 1763–1810*, Cambridge, Cambridge University Press, 1971.

Diffie, B. W., *Latin American Civilization, Colonial Period*, New York, Octagon Books, 1967.

Diffie, B. W., amd G. D. Winius, *Foundations of the Portuguese Empire 1415–1580*, Minneapolis, University of Minnesota Press, 1977.

Fifer, J. V., *Bolivia, Land, Location, and Politics since 1825*, Cambridge, Cambridge University Press, 1972.

Haring, C. H., *The Spanish Empire in America*, New York, Harcourt, 1963.

Katz, F., *The Ancient American Civilizations*, translated by K. M. L. Simpson, New York, Praeger, 1972.

Kubler, G., *The Art and Architecture of America; the Mexican, Maya, and Andean Peoples*, Baltimore, Penguin Books, 1962.

Lockhart, J. M., *The Men of Cajamarca; a Social and Biographical Study of the First Conquerors of Peru*, Austin, University of Texas Press, 1972.

Meyer, M., and W. L. Sherman, *The Course of Mexican History*, New York, Oxford University Press, 1979.

Parry, J. H., *The Spanish Theory of Empire in the Sixteenth Century*, Cambridge, Cambridge University Press, 1940.

———, *The Spanish Seaborne Empire*, New York, Knopf, 1966.

———, *The Discovery of South America*, London, Elek, 1979.

Ringrose, D. R., *Transportation and Economic Stagnation in Spain, 1750–1850*, Durham, N.C., Duke University Press, 1970.

Rippy, J. F., *Latin America: a Modern History*, Ann Arbor, University of Michigan Press, 1968.

Robinson, D. A., *Peru in Four Dimensions*, Lima, American Studies Press, 1964.

Sherman, W. L., *Forced Native Labor in Sixteenth Century Central America*, Lincoln, University of Nebraska Press, 1978.

CHAPTER 4

Agriculture

C. Gary Lobb

In spite of rapid urbanization and the growth of new types of employment, agriculture provides the largest single form of employment throughout Latin America. Agriculturalists live in diverse physical and cultural environments. Some farmers engage in production for subsistence, and others produce commercial crops for market. There is no *one* type, or model, of Latin American agriculture.

The agricultural systems in Latin America can be analyzed from environmental and human perspectives. Environmental factors may have influenced the selection of certain plants and animals and certainly influence the seasonality and intensity of agricultural work. The structure of agricultural systems and the timing of agricultural labor are often related to solar energy, moisture availability, and nutrient resources in the soil. But there is also the human or cultural dimension to be considered in relation to Latin America. In many traditional societies farming and other productive activities are seen as a part of the social fabric. Some aspects of agriculture may only be explained in terms of cultural traditions instead of the type of input-output accounting procedures used in relation to most U.S. farming operations, where agriculture is viewed as predominantly an economic activity.

In Latin America, as in other parts of the world, traditional modes of cultivation are being transformed into more commercial types of agriculture as new technologies become available. This is not to suggest that technical innovation has not previously been practiced in the region, as the pre-Colombian use of irrigation, terracing, fertilizing, and specialized adaptations such as the *chinampa*, or floating garden, of central Mexico illustrate. However, during the last four decades the pace of technological innovation has accelerated as commercial fertilizers, genetically improved crops, and tractors have become available throughout Latin America. Transformation in the agricultural sector of the region has been significant. This has been particularly true of countries such as Mexico and Brazil, where commercial agriculture is export oriented. Now most states are pursuing policies aimed at applying modern technology to help increase gross agricultural production.

The earliest forms of agriculture in the region employed a very basic technology and were tied closely to locally available environmental resources. Traditional methods, ecologically similar to the earliest forms of cultivation in the New World, are still in use in many parts of Latin America. Although it is not certain that the earliest agriculture in the New World emerged in the tropics, the traditional systems in use today have a wide distribution within the tropical portions of the Western Hemisphere. The impediments to productivity of the humid tropical environment—plant and animal pests and low levels of soil fertility—are managed in much the same way as they were 3000 years ago.

THE ECOLOGY OF TROPICAL AGRICULTURAL PRODUCTION

Much of Latin America, almost 5.5 million square miles (8.8 million square kilometers), or 82 percent of the region, is tropical (Figure 4-1). In this area the traditional systems that use a limited technology have persisted.

The fertility of soils in tropical areas can quickly diminish if the existing vegetation cover is removed for cultivation. Strategies to cope with this problem have been in use for thousands of years in what is now Latin America. Basically, a variety of "swidden cultivation" methods are employed by which vegetation is cleared and the ground cultivated for a few years; when yields begin to decline, the cultivators move on and clear another plot.

In Latin America there is a lexicon of terms identifying swidden agriculture. The term *roza* is widely used in Spanish-speaking areas from Mexico to Paraguay. In Brazil the Portuguese equivalent is *roça*. There are other more localized terms such as *conuco*, used in Venezuela and the Spanish-speaking area of the Caribbean, and *chaúa*, used in the Amazonian region of Peru. *Milpa*, a term used to identify traditional agriculture in many parts of Mexico and Central America, is sufficiently specialized and productive to be thought of as ecologically different from swidden.

Roza cultivation is small in scale: cleared plots seldom exceeding 2.47 acres (1 hectare) (Harris, 1972). The plots may be planted in one regionally preferred staple such as maize or manioc (a starchy, vegetatively reproduced

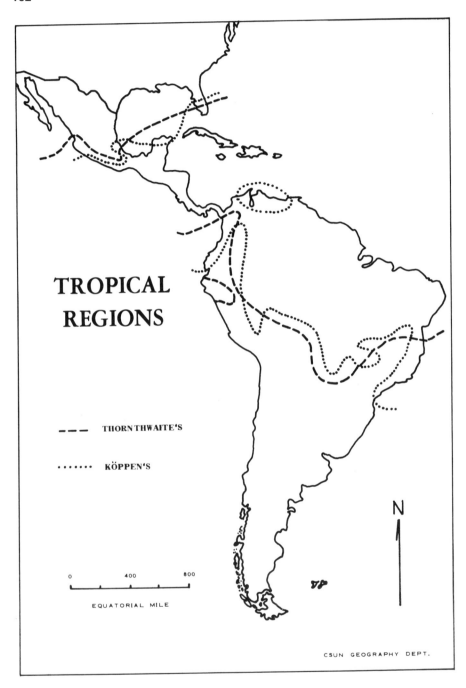

TROPICAL
REGIONS

- - -   THORNTHWAITE'S

· · · · · · ·   KÖPPEN'S

0   400   800

EQUATORIAL MILE

N

CSUN GEOGRAPHY DEPT.

Figure 4.1

root crop), or it may be planted with a variety of useful crops, all grown together in the plot.

Another characteristic of *roza* is that it is necessarily land-extensive. For ecological reasons the plots are only cultivated for short periods of time—1 to 3 years on average—before being abandoned for longer periods. These periods of abandonment are fallows, when natural vegetation is allowed to regenerate on the vacated *rozas*. This long fallow feature provides the most convenient definition of swidden: an agricultural system in which the periods of fallow exceed the periods of cultivation.

To many North Americans the large areas of fallow may seem wasteful. Indeed, if the fallow land is considered a part of the total agricultural land, the long-run yields per unit area are incredibly low (Lobb, 1974). On the other hand, the system can be highly productive in terms of yields per unit of labor expended and has been known, when measured in kilocalories, to give returns in excess of 16 to 1 on the energy invested in agriculture (Rappaport, 1971).

The length of fallow periods varies from 2 to 6 years, as among the modern Kekchí- and Quiché-speaking Indians of Guatemala (Carter, 1969) to 25 years or more, as among the Kuikuru and Akanaio of Brazil and Guyana, respectively (Carneiro, 1961; Butt, 1970).

Abandoning one cultivation plot and moving to another involves the additional effort of clearing and burning the natural vegetation. But the move is made necessary by the decline of yields and the increasing difficulty of keeping weeds under control. In fact, the problem of weed invasion may be equally as important as that of soil nutrient rundown in influencing the time of abandonment. During the fallow, the perennial weeds tend to be shaded out by taller vegetation (Seavoy, 1973).

THE SPATIAL AND CULTURAL PARAMETERS OF SWIDDEN

An example of *roza* agriculture in tropical Guatemala may help to illustrate the human inputs and their timing associated with the manipulation of the environmental factors. *Roza* cultivation is widespread on the north slopes of the Cuchumatanes Mountains in northwest Guatemala around the community of Todos Santos Cuchumatán (elevation 7600 feet). The limestone soils of the Cuchumatanes foothills are of better than average fertility considering the tropical nature of the environment. Under such conditions, in addition to the nutrients stored in the living vegetation, the soils too are able to provide some nutrient support for cultivated crops. Temperatures are warm throughout the year, and the seasonality of production is regulated by the availability of moisture. There is a pronounced dry season from late November to late January. The timing of most of the major human activities associated with crop production is related to this period of dryness.

Even though the soils are not altogether leached of their nutrients, the Todos Santos cultivator depends on the availability of nutrients contained in the living vegetation and released through burning to achieve expected yields. Fully developed forest vegetation is therefore very much cherished as an ideal environment in which to practice *roza* cultivation. But well-developed forest ecosystems are becoming rare in this part of Guatemala, and such a situation is a microcosm of the dilemma of swidden cultivators throughout Latin America. Thousand of years of *roza* cultivation in this region have resulted in the destruction of most of the primary, fully developed rainforests because they have been systematically converted into *roza* plots. The forestland that presently exists is considered secondary forest, which means that it is a forest ecosystem that has reestablished itself on abandoned *roza* plots. Unless such reestablished, secondary forests are quite old (more than 50 year), they most likely will not contain the variety of forest species or the volume of biomass typical of the original forest and, therefore, they are not as important a source of nutrient support for agriculture. Secondary forest lands and primary forests, where they exist, are referred locally as *montaña* lands. *Montaña* lands are considered a valuable resource by the Todos Santeros because they are potentially the most valuable lands for successful *roza* cultivation.

In 1976 only half of the villages in the Cuchumatanes foothills had access to *montaña* lands. Increases in population in the last 20 years have greatly increased the pressure on available agricultural lands, and the result has been that the forests have been cut for *roza* plots at a faster rate than they have been able to regenerate themselves. The lands most commonly being used now for *roza* cultivation are second-growth ecosystems in an early stage of regeneration. These bushlands, called *hautál* lands by the native population, are now the most widespread. They are poor in species composition and biomass content compared with the *montaña* ecosystems and are therefore less valuable as potential agricultural lands. It is now common to use this land for cultivation but, ideally, it should be allowed to undergo succession to a mature forest system.

If the peasant cultivator has *montaña* land to utilize for *roza* plots, he will begin to clear the wild vegetation from a selected plot in the middle of November at the onset of the dry season. First, the underbush is cut with a large machete, and the large trees are then felled with an axe or power chain saw. Branches are chopped off the trees, and the mass of cut vegetation is allowed to dry. The debris is collected into piles with clearings surrounding them so that the fire will not spread out of control. The dry forest debris is then burned. The amount of work required for this phase of the agricultural cycle varies with the size of the trees and their numbers, but it usually ranges from 15 to 30 days per worker per acre. After a successful burn, the ashes are scattered over the plot to be cultivated and the *roza* may be planted within a few days, "after the ground has cooled," it is said.

The *huatál* land (bushland), which is now the kind of land most available for the new *roza* plots, is cut later in the dry season than is the case with the *montaña* because it dries in less time. It is cut in the middle of December with a machete only and is planted a few days after a successful burn. A serious problem confronting *roza* cultivators in this part of Guatemala is the invasion of coarse perennial grasses into the environments where *huatál* lands are cut. These grasses become more and more common in bushlands that are cut for a *roza* cycle before many tall, shade-producing bushes or trees have had time to reestablish themselves. In such a situation the open, shadeless areas are ideal habitats, or "ecological niches," for the successful growth and reproduction of perennial tropical grasses. After repeated burns and intermittent *roza* croppings, the environment may become largely a grassland, at which time it is no longer valuable as a potential *roza* plot. There is not sufficient biomass to provide adequate nutrients for the cultivated plants and, perhaps more importantly, the growth of the grass is never retarded sufficiently to eliminate it as an aggressive weed that smothers out the domesticated plants. Many square miles of once forested countryside in the Cuchamatanes foothills have been converted into *pajonales*, or tropical grasslands, as a result of the management practice just described.

The land actually under cultivation is called the *rastrojo*, or cornstalk land. If the *roza* plots are cultivated for more than 1 year in succession, which is the case in this part of Guatemala, last year's *rastrojo* land is prepared for another year of cultivation by breaking down the remaining cornstalks, collecting them in piles, and burning them, thereby releasing any nutrients tied up in the remains of last year's cultivated crop.

The planting of the seeds is undertaken in February, at the onset of the rainy season. Seeds are carried into the cleared fields in a *henequen* shoulder sack; with a simple digging stick called a *pachán*, a hole is opened to a depth of about 3 inches and five grains are tossed into the hole. This is done at intervals of 16 to 20 inches and loose soil is mounded over the opening, creating a little hill called a *montón*. If the rains begin on schedule and conditions are average, the maize starts to sprout within 3 weeks, and the *roza* field may be replanted in areas where the seeds were destroyed or did not germinate.

The removal of weeds, both annual and perennial, becomes more of a problem each successive year of cultivation. The first year after a *montaña* plot has been converted into a *roza* field, competition from weeds is not a serious threat; however, after the second year, weed invasion seriously threatens productivity. During the years the *roza* plot is in use (usually 3 years in Guatemala), the number of cultivations to remove weeds varies from one to four per growing season. Four cultivations a year would be typical of a *roza* plot in its final stages of use before abandonment. The usual number of cultivations is two, the first in the middle of April and the second in June or July. The hoe is the only agricultural tool used in the weeding operation. At the time of the first cultivation, or *limpiada*, leaves are selectively removed from the corn plants to prevent shading of the lower leaves, thereby enhancing productivity. Most of the leaves are simply hoed into the soil along with the weeds, where they decompose and contribute to soil fertility.

In September most of the green leaves are stripped from the corn plants and the tassels are removed. This act greatly reduces the photosynthetic activity of the plants; the sugar in the grains begins to convert to starch, and the kernels harden. In October the stalks are all bent over below the lowest dried ear, a process known as doubling (*doblando*), which seems to prevent water from entering the ear and reduces damage from predatory birds, particularly parrots. The harvest then takes place in November as the dry season approaches once more.

Such a tropical system of cropping can, when practiced on recently cleared *montaña* lands, be employed for as long as 5 years before a decision is made to abandon the plot and allow it to return to forest fallow. The average maize yields are about 446 pounds per acre during the 5 years of cropping. However, if the *roza* plot is established on recently cleared bushlands, now the most common practice, the plots can be cropped for only 2 or 3 years, and the yields average from 134 to 223 pounds per acre, after which the plots must be fallowed for 5 years to allow *hautál* lands to regenerate. If the *roza* plots are cultivated for more than 3 years after the clearing of *huatál* lands, production per unit area becomes lower and the plots become clogged with annual and perennial grasses. When the field is finally abandoned, it becomes a grassland ecosystem (*pajonal*). If left unburned these *pajonal* lands may again return to bushland within 15 to 20 years.

The tropical cropping system described here, which is widely practiced with some variations throughout Central America and southern Mexico, should be thought of as an example of traditional agriculture involving the cultivation of seed plants such as maize and beans. Traditional systems of tropical cultivation share many ecological characteristics, but there is a wide range of specific applications. In the Caribbean and the Amazon lowlands and in other localized areas, root crops such as manioc, sweet potato, arrowroot, and a New World yam are the essential components of the agricultural systems.

Many scholars who have analyzed swidden agriculture in Latin America and elsewhere have determined that an extensive system of food production such as *roza* is seldom the only means of supporting tropical subsistence cultivators. It is common for *roza* to be used in conjunction with more permanent and intensive small-scale plots that are kept in perpetual tillage and that yield a wide variety of supplemental food products. They usually will contain yams, climbing beans (habas), sweet potatoes, chili peppers, bananas and plantains, coffee bushes, and tree crops such as citrus, avocado, papaya, and mango. These small "dooryard gardens" are usually adjacent to the houses and are fertilized by organic wastes from the household.

Roza Plots; Cuchumatanes Foothills — Guatemala

While representing similar strategies regarding the problems of agricultural production in the tropics, the *roza* systems of the seed cultivators of Mexico, Central America, and the sub-Andean regions of South America are distinct from the root cultivators of tropical South America and the circum-Caribbean region.

The two traditions of cultivation, seed culture and vegeculture, exhibit contrasting demands on soil fertility. The protein-rich seed crops require larger supplies of nutrients in the ash, litter, and soils than is true of the starch-rich food crops of vegeculture. This difference is accentuated during harvest, when the seed-crop cultivator removes highly concentrated nutrients from the *roza* for consumption in the form of beans and grains (maize). The vegeculturalist removes a much smaller fraction of available fertility in the harvest of tubers and roots. Seed-culture systems are therefore often associated with ecosystems in which there is a higher degree of initial soil fertility. Such systems often correspond to areas of geologically recent volcanic activity, areas of limestone parent material, or areas where the soils are not excessively leached of nutrients because of heavy amounts of precipitation.

Just as maize is the mainstay of the seed-culture areas of tropical Latin America, manioc is the staple of traditional vegeculture societies. Many varieties of manioc are grown; most of them are poisonous and require special preparation before they can be made edible. In one form or another manioc makes up as much as 85 percent of the diet of many cultivators in the Amazon

Basin. The timing of the agricultural work being done in a cycle of vegeculture (referred to as *roça* cultivation in Brazil) is closely related to that of a seed-culture *roza* cycle. Shortly after the end of the rainy season, the forest vegetation is cut and left to dry for several weeks. Just before the next rainy season it is piled up and burned, and planting begins about the time of the first rains. Manioc is always grown from cuttings planted in low mounds made by hoeing up the loose soil. A hole is opened with a dibble, and 4 to 10 cuttings are dropped in. Plots are weeded one or more times a season, depending on the age of the cultivated field. Manioc tubers develop to a harvestable size 5 or 6 months after the cuttings are planted; if they are allowed to remain in the soil for a longer period, say 18 to 20 months, the tubers are considerably larger and attain their highest starch content of about 30 percent (Schery, 1963). Among the vegeculturalists, too, the roza plots are often accompanied by a more permanent "dooryard garden" supplying some variety to the diets of subsistence cultivators.

Although closely related in many ways to *roza* cultivation, the short-fallowing of permanent fields is common in some areas of Mesoamerica and the sub-Andean region of South America. This system, called *milpa* cultivation in Mexico and Central America, involves the initial clearing and burning of the vegetative cover, but 3 or 4 years of successive cropping is ordinarily followed

House Site and Typical Dooryard Garden in Petén Region of Guatemala

Roza Cultivation Featuring Manioc in the Brazilian Mato Grosso

by a short fallow of equal or less duration. Such relatively short-fallow agriculture is made possible by a combination of the following environmental and cultural factors: (1) relatively high levels of soil nutrients common in the cool highlands, particularly around the fertile volcanic and lacustrine basins on the Mesa Central of Mexico, in southwestern Guatemala and Chiapas, and in sub-Andean Colombia; (2) no severe competition with perennial weeds, which are also characteristic of the cooler highlands; and (3) the introduction of the European plow and draft animals, such as the ox, resulting in a permanent short-fallow system that has changed little among traditional cultivators since colonial times. The aboriginal crops of maize, beans, and squash, together with chili, are the principal food plants of the *milpa* and are the predominant subsistence foods of most Mexicans and Central Americans. Average maize yields from *milpas* are less than 350 pounds per acre but, in certain locations, the

Manioc Tubers in Market at Concepción, Paraguay

yields are impressive. For example, the average long-term yields for the Quezaltenango Basin in Guatemala are 625 pounds per acre, with only 2 years of
cropping being common followed by a one-year fallow. *ecolog, adapt. to high*
high alt → tropical lowlands.
terraces + irrigation

AGRICULTURAL SYSTEMS OF HIGH-ALTITUDE ENVIRONMENTS

The agricultural systems of the high-altitude environments of Latin America,
particularly in the Andean region of South America, represent ecological
adaptations suited to a set of environmental variables that are different from
those of the tropical lowlands. It is probable that some important species of
plants, which were not indigenous to the area, reached the Andean highlands
at an early date. The highlands became one of the greatest centers of intensive
short-fallow agriculture in pre-Columbian America. The agricultural practices
went beyond the exploitive stage and reached the point where soils were protected from erosion and systematically built up with fertilizers for maximum
utilization.

    Current traditional agricultural practices in the Andean area continue to
be intensive and include the use of terraces and irrigation. These methods are
characteristic of the valleys between 7000 and 12,500 feet in elevation and are
also found in the cultivated areas of the cool desert coast of Peru. Andean valleys are characteristically deep and narrow. There is little flat land, and runoff
after rains is rapid. The chief agricultural solution for these problems has been

Milpa Plots and Commercial Wheat Fields in Quezaltenango Basin, Guatemala

the construction of terraces, and most valley sides have been extensively terraced and equipped with elaborate stone channels to distribute irrigation
water. A long dry season makes irrigation desirable almost everywhere. Plows
pulled by oxen are common on the flat surfaces. On steeper cultivated slopes
the Inca foot plow (*taclla*) is used along with a hoe. A variety of specialized
food plants are cultivated presently, over 40 species of which were cultivated
during Inca times along with Old World domesticates such as wheat and barley. Even in basins at over 13,000 feet in elevation eight species of domesticated plants can be raised. The potato is the staple, but other root crops such
as the tubers oca (*Oxalis tuberosa*), ulluco (*Ullucus tuberosus*), and ysaño
(*Tropaeolum tuberosum*) are cultivated. An important crop in the high valleys
is quinoa (*Chenopodium quinoa*), which is sometimes referred to as a grain
but is, in fact, a small annual herb that produces many small seeds that can be
boiled like rice or ground up to make meal. The leaves of the herb can be
cooked in a manner similar to spinach. Cañihua (*Chenopodium pallidicaule*) is
a related plant cultivated at high levels along with hardy varieties of introduced
wheat.

In valleys of lower and intermediate elevation wheat and maize replace
quinoa and cañihua, but potatoes, chili peppers (*aji*), and squash remain important.

Potatoes are in widespread use throughout the Andean region. At least 13
cultivated species are known. Potatoes are often stored in a dehydrated form

known as chuñu, and oca is also dehydrated for preservation. In the lower valleys, which approach conditions of humid tropicality in some cases, and along the desert Pacific coast, cotton, beans, chili peppers, sweet potatoes, tomatoes, and manioc (yuca) are cultivated. Since the time of the Incas, the products of the hotter valleys and the coast have been important to the economy of the highlands. A narcotic plant called coca (*Erythroxylum coca*) is cultivated in the warm lower valleys of the interior and transported to the highlands. The leaves contain cocaine and related substances and are chewed as a stimulant.

The dry season in central Andean South America runs from April until November, and the rainy season is from November to the end of March. Potatoes are planted early in the rainy season, in December, and are harvested the following June. Maize and quinoa are sown in September and October and harvested in May. The chief agricultural work during the rainy season is the weeding of the fields, bird scaring, and control of pests.

THE HISTORICAL GEOGRAPHY OF LATIN AMERICAN AGRICULTURE

Agricultural Origins

The earliest systems of agriculture that developed in what is now Latin America must have been ecologically similar to the modern forms of *roza* cultivation already discussed. The place, or places, of origin have been identified as the

Pre-Columbian Agricultural Terraces still in use in Ucumbamba Valley of Peru

Chuñu in La Paz Market, Bolivia

areas in which domestication of wild plants took place. The archeological evidence for early agriculture in Mesoamerica is relatively substantial and is becoming more convincing. In Mesoamerica we have the suggestion of a true center definable in time and space, where agriculture originated, and out of which it may have dispersed. Mesoamerica has all the characteristics of a center of agricultural origin, including an impressive list of domesticated plants.

List of Plants First Domesticated in Mesoamerica

Seed Crops

Maize (*Zea mays*)
Chia (*Salvia hispanica*)
Amaranth (*Amaranthus cruentus*)
Huauhtli (*Amaranthus leucocarpus*)
Chiagrande (*Hyptis suaveolens*)

Vegetables

Squash (*Cucurbita moschata*)
Pumpkin (*Cucurbita pepo*)
Chilcayote (*Cucurbita ficifolia*)
Chayote (*Sechium edule*)

Legumes

Common bean (*Phaseolus sps.*)

Tubers

Yautia (*Xanthosoma sp.*)
Arrowroot (*Maranta arundinacea*)[1]
Sweet potato (*Ipomoea batatas*)[1]
Jícama (*Pachyrrhizus erosus*)
Manioc (*Manihot esculenta*)[1]

Fruits	*Others*
Chili peppers (*Capsicum annuum*)	Agave (*Agavaceae sp.*)
Pejibaye palm (*Guilielma utilis*)[1]	Cotton (*Gossypium sp.*)[1]
Avocado (*Persea americana*)	Cacao (*Theobroma cacao*)
Capulín (*Prunus serotina*)	Indigo (*Indigofera suffruticosa*)
Guava (*Psidium quajava*)[1]	
Sapodilla (*Achras sapota*)	
Zapote (*Calocarpum mammosum*)	

[1]Possible domestication in both Mesoamerica and South America.

Mesoamerica is widely recognized as a center of agricultural origin; however, other centers have been identified as possible independent areas of origin. The Russian ethnobotanist, N. L. Vavilov, writing in the 1920s, suggested a South American center with two subcenters in addition to the Mesoamerican hearth (see Figure 4-2).

The South American locations were considered centers of root crop domestication. Within the Andean center (Center B) certain species of tetraploid potatoes were first cultivated along with other tubers such as oca, ulluco, and ysaño and the herb quinoa. It seems apparent that early civilizations in the Andean highlands owed their basic agriculture to plants that reproduced vegetatively by division of the plant parts and not by seeds. In commenting on early Andean agriculture Sauer (1956, pp. 518–519) noted:

> It is possible to assign to the potatoes the leading role in the agricultural colonization of the Andes, except for the one fact of the existence, side by side with the potatoes, of the lesser tuberous crops. . . . It seems to me therefore, that we have in these minor tuber crops the remnants of the oldest Highland agriculture; that long before potatoes were bred to grow on the bleak reaches of *altiplano* and *paramo*, these microthermal native tubers had made sedentary life possible by supplying starch food and had been made into domesticated plants. Also, the storage problem had been solved by inventing *chuñu* making and this was transferred later to potatoes, when these became developed for *puna* climate cultivation.

Vavilov identified two subcenters of domestication activity. In addition to a central Andean site, he suggested another subcenter of potato domestication in south-central Chile, particularly on the island of Chiloe (Center B₁), and another subcenter for the domestication of tropical root crops in sub-Amazon Brazil (Center B₂).

Figure 4.2

List of Plants First Domesticated in South America

Seed Crops

Quinoa (*Chenopodium quinoa*)
Cañihua (*Chenopodium pallidicaule*)
Mango grass (*Bromus mango*)
Madí (*Madia sativa*)
Jataco (*Amaranthus caudatus*)

Legumes

Common bean (*Phaseolus sp.*)
Peanut (*Arachis hypogaea*)
Chocho (*Lupinus mutabilis*)

Vegetables

Zapallo (*Cocurbita maxima*)
Sicana (*Sicana oderiferal*)
Achoccha (*Cyclanthera pedata*)
Bottle gourd (*Langenaria sp.*)

Tubers

Manioc (*Manihot esculenta*)
Arrowroot (*Maranta arundinacea*)[2]
Sweet potato (*Ipomoea batatas*)[2]
Yampee (*Dioscorea sp.*)
Jícama (*Pachyrrhizus ahipa*)
Achira (*Canna edulis*)
Yacón (*Polymnia sonchifolia*)
Potato (*Solanum sp.*)
Oca (*Oxalis tuberosa*)
Ulluco (*Ullucus tuberosus*)
Ysaño (*Tropaeolum tuberosum*)
Maca (*Lepidium meyenii*)
Arracacha (*Arracacia xanthorrhiza*)

Fruits

Pepino (*Solanum muricatum*)
Tomato (*Lycopersicon esculentum*)
Chili peppers *aji* (*Capsicum sp.*)
Pejibaye palm (*Guilielma utilis*)[2]
Guava (*Psidium guajava*)[2]
Pineapple (*Ananas comosus*)
Soursop (*Anona muricata*)
Cashew (*Anacardium occidentale*)
Papaya (*Carica papaya*)
Cherimoya (*Anona cherimolia*)

Others

Cotton (*Gossypium sp.*)[2]
Coca (*Erythroxylon coca*)
Tobacco (*Nicotiana tabacum*)

[2]Possible domestication in both Mesoamerica and South America.

Recent studies by botanists and plant geneticists imply that domestication may have taken place in many locations throughout South America and that no one center (or even centers) emerges as an appropriate site of early domestication. South America tends to resemble a general center, not a complex of specific centers. As Harlan (1971, p. 472) has stated:

> Wild peanut and wild *ulluco* are found in Jujuy (Argentina) and the adjacent mountainous portion of Bolivia. Wild beans stretch for 5000 kilometers, from Argentina to Venezuela, and (it has been demonstrated that) different races of beans were domesticated at different times along this distribution. . . . Bean domestication seems to have taken place along a band 7000 kilometers long. How can one speak of "a center of origin" for *phaseolus vulgaris* (the common bean)? Its domestication was not even confined to one continent. Sometimes centers exist, sometimes they do not.

Most of the activity in South America, however, seems to have been along or near the Andes. But the South American Indians were domesticating plants over almost all of the continent and, if centers do exist, they have not been convincingly defined. An important characteristic of Western Hemisphere plant domestication is the parallel between Mesoamerica and South America. Domesticated representatives of no fewer than 11 genera of plants are shared between the two areas.

Wherever the places of domestication may have been, the Amerinds must be credited with significant contributions to modern agriculture. Of the 15 principal food crops utilized in the world today, 6 are of American origin: maize, potato, manioc, sweet potato, common bean, and peanut (Harlan, 1975).

Pre-Columbian systems of agriculture, some of which were highly productive and supported high-level civilizations, closely resembled traditional subsistence methods such as *milpa* and *roza*, which are still widely used in Latin America. More intensive forms associated with terracing and irrigation contributed greatly to the support of many societies. Some intensive methods used in preconquest times to achieve relatively high levels of production have become extinct. The use of the *chinampa* is no longer as widely practiced in the Valley of Mexico, nor are raised fields utilized in the tropical lowlands of South America and the Caribbean, although this agricultural strategy may have contributed to high yields in the areas where it was used. Abandoned raised fields have been found in the Beni and Mojos lowlands of northeastern Bolivia, the lowlands of northern Colombia, the Caribbean lowlands of Yucatan, and other places. Most of these are relic fields associated with poorly drained tropical lowland savannas, suggesting populations that were once dense and productivity that was once high, in areas where agriculture is now regarded as marginal or impossible. There are no technical descriptions of these fields in use, so one can only speculate on their construction, function, and use for cropping (Denevan, 1970).

most impo. event in land use — intro. of European crops + farming
practices. Criollo + Mestizo represent blend of native
Amer. cropping practices.

168   AGRICULTURE

Wherever agriculture originated in the Western Hemisphere, it had spread widely over both North and South America by the time of European contacts, occurring even into the high-altitude environments of Mesoamerica and South America. Much tropical lowland was settled by agriculturalists practicing *roza* cultivation. Groups of nonagricultural hunting and gathering people inhabited the Amazon Basin, and major areas of nonagricultural peoples occurred at the northern and southern limits of what is today Latin America. Except in the Casas Grandes Valley, agriculture was not practiced in the dry, intermontane basin of northern Mexico, the temperate grasslands of the *pampa* and Patagonia, and the humid, southwest coast of Chile and Tierra del Fuego. In between these areas the vast majority of the aboriginal inhabitants of what is now Latin America engaged in agriculture to one degree or another.

Colonial Agricultural Land Use

The most important event in the history of land use in the Americas, apart from the initial development of agriculture, must have been the introduction of European crops and farming practices beginning in the early sixteenth century. A *criollo* peasant agriculture emerged in the hands of Iberian and *mestizo* populations; it represented a blend of native American cropping practices with certain plants, animals, and implements associated with European agriculture. Wheat and barley were spread into the upland environments, and wheat was being grown, for example, by Spanish and *mestizo* cultivators in the Quezaltenango Basin of Guatemala by 1571. Other crops such as onions, garlic, turnips, carrots, radishes, and peas also diffused widely and contributed to the development of *criollo* agriculture. Of even greater importance were the tropical plants of Asian and African origin introduced into the New World by the Spanish and Portuguese. Chief among these were bananas and plantains, sugarcane, yams, mangos, citrus fruits, and rice. These plants were spread widely into tropical and subtropical environments and, in many instances, were incorporated into the *roza* systems of Indian cultivators.

The dooryard gardens associated with indigenous *roza* agriculture were greatly enriched by the addition of bananas, plantains, mangos, and citrus fruits. Maize remained the staple grain crop, however, among most Indian peoples of Mesoamerica and, in fact, became even more widespread as a result of Spanish and Portuguese colonial activity. Maize cultivation diffused throughout what is today Brazil as a result of Portuguese and Spanish contacts with native peoples such as the Tupí and the Guaraní.

The widespread distribution of exotic crops and practices among the native Indian population was largely made possible by the Catholic church. Around every mission settlement in Latin America European priests, frequently Jesuits, cultivated fruit and vegetable gardens and introduced Indian farmers to new crops and methods of husbandry.

Commercial Farming During Colonial Times

Production of crops for the use of townspeople was important among pre-Columbian societies such as the Aztecs, Mayas, and Incas. However, it remained for the Spanish and the Portuguese, with their money-based economies, to develop commercial agriculture in Latin America. Not all colonial agricultural institutions were commercial. Large landholdings (*latifundios*) became the basis of a system of social domination of the masses by an ethnically differentiated minority. The landowner was usually motivated by a desire to acquire large properties and live a life-style characteristic of an Iberian *caballero* (Furtado, 1970). Indians often came to occupy the role of laborers or sharecroppers; a class of tenant farmers known variously as *inquilinos, colonos,* or *huasipunqueros,* formed the small-scale (*minifundio*) stratum of the colonial hierarchy. Throughout colonial times and during most of the nineteenth century the prevailing agricultural system was the *latifundio-minifundio* complex, characterized by large estates, with off-farm satellite small holdings, or estates that had within their borders many small units worked by tenant farmers.

Commercial production was developed in response to the demands of mining settlements and urban centers. Generally, agricultural production for export was not encouraged in the Spanish territories. For example, sheep-rearing interests in Spain were successful in limiting wool exports from the New World to the Old World. Some products for which there was excess demand in Spain, such as hides and tallow, were exported to the mother country from areas such as northern Mexico, Argentina, and Uruguay.

Gold was found in impressive amounts in interior Brazil in the seventeenth century, but agriculture was the mainstay of the earliest phase of colonization in the Portuguese territories. Brazilian commercial agriculture was based on the *fazenda de açucar* (sugar plantation), an institution established along the coast of tropical Brazil from the beginning of the sixteenth century.

Throughout most of the colonial period subsistence agriculture was mainly in the hands of Indians and *mestizos* or *ladinos*. Traditional methods of production such as *roza* and *milpa* were employed. Some European crops and techniques were incorporated into the indigenous systems. Commercial farming was controlled by the Spanish and the Portuguese. The regions producing precious metals and the imperial administrative centers were the chief markets during the colonial period. The demand for food, rough textiles, and draught animals generated by these centers, and transportation between them, resulted in the organization of tributary economies. For example, in Peru the coastal regions were organized into *latifundios* to supply produce to the urban markets of Lima, Guayaquil, and the interior mines.

Cattle ranching proved to be particularly lucrative as a commercial enterprise in parts of Mexico, Argentina, Uruguay, and southern Brazil. Grassland environments within these countries were especially suitable to provide the basis for a successful export economy involving hides, tallow, and dried or jerked beef (*charque*). Of course, all these products were used in mines: hides in the form of ropes, tallow for candles, and jerked beef as a dietary element. Jerked beef was also in demand as a foodstuff on sugar plantations in Brazil and the Caribbean. Sugar, tobacco, and indigo remained the most important commercial crops in Brazil and the Caribbean rimland throughout the colonial period.

Postcolonial Agriculture

As the colonial period came to a close, political and economic power in the new republics passed mostly into the hands of the substantial landowners and the proprietors of mines. Both groups, together with the merchant class, were in a position to benefit from freer trade by acquiring wider markets for traditional products and by developing new forms of agricultural activity and mineral exploitation. In fact, the impetus for development frequently came from Western Europeans and North Americans seeking new outlets for their technology, capital, and entrepreneurial skills. The colonial period had linked Latin America with a region that became, by the late eighteenth century, one of the most traditional and economically backward of Europe. Trade between the Iberian peninsula and Latin America tended to be concerned with higher-value commodities: precious metals, sugar, tobacco, and indigo.

During the nineteenth century, the Latin American republics were connected economically with the industrializing areas of Europe and North America, and demands emerged for bulk commodities: wheat, meat, and cheap fruits to feed industrial workers, guano to fertilize fields, nitrates to make gunpowder for modern armies, rubber to provide tires for transportation, and a host of nonferrous items needed as raw materials in industrializing countries.

None of this was immediately apparent. The conclusion of the Napoleonic wars (1815), which had created the political conditions in which it was possible for the emerging republics to sever, or weaken, links with the Iberian peninsula, resulted in a sustained slump in world trade. Nevertheless, the British established a network of consuls in Latin American centers in the 1820s, and the groundwork was laid for the strong trade links that came to exist, in the second half of the nineteenth century, between Britain and South America, in particular.

The Opening of the Pampas

British commercial interests took particular notice of the temperate lands of Argentina, Chile, and Uruguay. In 1824 Woodbine Parish (1796–1882)) was sent to negotiate a treaty of friendship and commerce with Argentina. He did this successfully and, in 1825, Britain formally recognized the independent existence of Argentina. Thus Argentina became the first of the newly independent South American republics to be recognized by an external power.

Parish was also a geographical writer of some importance who was responsible for making much material relating to Argentina generally available (Parish, 1839). Shortly after his return to Britain in 1832, he became very active in the affairs of the Royal Geographical Society and steadily promoted academic and commercial interest in South America.

Parish and others saw the potential of the *pampas* temperate grasslands, with herds of feral cattle and horses. Before the potential could be exploited, much had to be done to improve stock and bring land into cultivation, to say nothing of establishing reliable and regular ocean transport with market areas. Parish thought the cattle were lean, scrubby beasts and, as for the local sheep, doubted if the wild dogs would touch the meat. The wool was so coarse it was hardly worth the expense of cleaning it.

However, it was the export potential of wool that was first developed, since this commodity was not easily perishable and would stand transportation to Europe and North America. Improved breeds of sheep were introduced in the 1830s; wool exports built up until the flocks were diminished in the latter part of the century and pushed onto poorer lands to the west and south, and the more profitable beef production took over the better lands of the humid *pampas*.

In the first half of the nineteenth century cattle remained sources of hides, tallow, and *tasajo*. This last product was made at *saladeros* where the meat was preserved in strips by salting and drying in the sun. *Tasajo* was very much a low-quality meat product that could not be sold in quantity to European consumers. If export markets were to be gained a means had to be found to process meat into more palatable forms. In 1847 Liebig, the agricultural chemist, published a method of producing a meat extract; in 1865 a large plant was set up at Frey Bentos, in Uruguay, to utilize the process. Although profitable, the market for extract was relatively small, and attempts were made to can and preserve meat. None of these experiments were wholly satisfactory.

Although the principles of refrigeration and chilling were understood, it took a considerable time to develop systems that would allow meat to be transported from North America, Argentina, Australia, and New Zealand to European markets. In 1875 chilled meat was successfully shipped from the United States to Liverpool, but this did not involve crossing the tropics, and the journey was short when compared with the voyage from Argentina or Australia. Chilled beef has a maximum life of about 40 days. In 1876 as an experiment a French vessel, the *Frigorífique*, sailed from Rouen to Buenos Aires with a cargo of chilled meat, but the quality was poor because the journey time was too long. In 1877 the *Paraguay* sailed from Marseilles to Buenos Aires with frozen meat in a refrigerated chamber. This voyage was a success, and the Rio de la Plata frozen meat trade to Europe dates from this time, although more efficient systems of refrigeration were to be brought into commercial operation.

A system of refrigeration was not enough to insure the success of the trade. As had been pointed out from the beginning, it was no use exporting low-quality beef and hoping that it would sell in European markets. British shorthorn cattle had been introduced in small numbers since the 1820s, but their use had been limited partly because the *saladeros* preferred a thick-hided animal that was not fully fleshed. In 1876 the first Aberdeen Angus beasts were imported, and the process of stock improvement gathered pace. While this was going on the *saladeros* continued to produce *tasajo* for traditional markets. Many of the improved animals were shipped live to British markets, and it was not until after 1900, when the United Kingdom banned the import of live animals in an effort to control hoof and mouth disease, that frozen products came to dominate the La Plata meat trade.

These technical, marketing, and legislative changes, many of them made far away from South America, had a dramatic impact on the landscape of the *pampas*. Until the middle decades of the nineteenth century the area still had a colonial look. In 1850 Buenos Aires was a city of less than 100,000 inhabitants. Overland transportation was mainly by slow-moving ox carts that used tracks leading to the smaller towns such as Bahia Blanca, Rosario, Santa Fé, and Cordoba. Around the urban centers were farms and gardens, but a great part of the *pampas* was roughly divided into *estancias*. Herds of cattle, horses, and sheep were extensively grazed on the properties. The animals looked after themselves to a large extent, and there was no attempt at selective breeding. The flocks and herds were lightly culled for meat and other products.

During the second half of the nineteenth century, however, the *pampas* was extensively developed, with resultant changes in land use and settlement. Incidentally, there are many parallels between the development of the *pampas* in the second half of the nineteenth century and the settlement of parts of the U.S. Midwest. Both regions are temperate grasslands marked by increasing uncertainty of rainfall toward the west. Drought can be a problem. For example, between 1827 and 1832 there was an extensive drought in Santa Fé and Buenos Aires provinces, huge dust storms developed, and there was heavy loss of livestock. Both areas were occupied by indigenous inhabitants with whom wars were fought for possession of the land. For both regions railroads and European immigrants played a major role in the settlement and agricultural exploitation of the land.

The motives for opening up the *pampas* for settlement were various and included: the need to populate territory in order to confirm sovereignty; the desire to push up land values by bringing estates into cultivation; the need of railroads to build up traffic; the demand for locally grown foodstuffs; the need to provide feeds such as alfalfa and grain for livestock being prepared for the meat trade; and the desire of external financial interests to profit from the opening up of a new area of commodity production.

Railroads played a significant role in opening up the region. In 1862 the Argentine government granted a concession to the Buenos Aires and Great Southern Railway, and this company eventually built lines to Bahia Blanca. In 1865 the Central Argentine Railway was given a concession and, in 1870, completed a line from Rosario to Cordoba.

The major source of immigrants to the *pampas* was Italy, although many other ethnic groups were represented. Immigration was slow between 1850 and 1879, but the 1880s saw a rapid buildup in numbers; in 1889 over 200,000 migrants entered Argentina. Migration collapsed dramatically during the worldwide financial crisis of the early 1890s but recovered to average around 250,000 per annum in the years prior to the 1914–1918 war.

In Santa Fé province many colonies were set up for migrants. The first such colony was established at Esperanza in 1856 (Jefferson, 1926). These colonies were settled farming communities; the migrants were either tenants or were able to purchase the land from the entrepreneurs who organized the settlements. Such colonies were particularly common in central Santa Fé, where cereals were the dominant crop. In southern Santa Fé sheep rearing on more extensive holdings was important, and there were few migrants and agricultural towns in the region. In recognition of these agricultural and ethnic distinctions, the central region was known as the *pampa gringa* and the south as the *pampa criolla*. The immigrant farmers of the *pampa gringa* were politically active and given to populist activity, as in the rural protest movements of 1893 (Gallo,1977). On the *pampa criolla* the traditional rural *caudillos* continued to dominate political processes.

The pattern of agricultural development in Buenos Aires province was different and did not result in the establishment of as many independent farmers as in the *pampa gringa*. If stockmen in the province of Buenos Aires were to increase production and the quality of animals, the traditional pattern of extensive grazing had to be modified and fodder crops grown. The system employed initially was to offer land to migrants for a few years (usually 3 to 6 years), with the stipulation that alfalfa would be planted before the farmers moved on. The advantage of this scheme to the landowner was that it got ground into a fodder crop without the expense of cultivation. When migrant demand for this type of arrangement built up, the landowners eventually asked for a share of the migrant farmers' crops in the years prior to the planting of the alfalfa.

Although some attempts were made to establish the legal equivalents of the U.S. Homestead Act (1862) and the Kinkaid Act (1904), the efforts did not succeed in placing many independent farmers on the land. In 1876 a land law was passed in Argentina that was intended to provide free land for immigrants and promote settlement. Abuses of this law by speculators were great, and the legislation never performed its function. In 1884 a homestead act became law but this was limited to grazing lands south of the Rio Negro, and abuse was again common (Scobie, 1971).

By the end of the first decade of the twentieth century, the *pampas* had been transformed. Buenos Aires was no longer a colonial, provincial city but the first city with 1 million inhabitants, more akin to Chicago than to other Latin American cities (Sargent, 1974). Much cultivable grassland on the *pampas* had been ploughed, and the area of tilled land, in the republic as a whole, had increased from 373 square miles in 1865 to around 150,000 square miles in 1910 (Jefferson, 1926). In 1850 Argentina was a net importer of grains; by 1900 it was one of the world's leading exporters of wheat. Traditional activities had disappeared or had been pushed outward from the La Plata area. Sheep raising was found in the semiarid lands of the west and south. The production of *tasajo* and extract had moved to less central locations as a result of competition for land from profitable forms of meat processing such as freezing and chilling (Crossley, 1976). If the traditional landowning classes had retained a hold on the wealth and political power during the development process, they had to take notice of the needs of large corporations, frequently capitalized from Britain, that owned railroads, shipping, banks, meat-processing plants, and land. At the other end of the scale, at least some of the immigrant Italian farmers had succeeded in making their political aspirations understood.

Agricultural Exports

As has been illustrated with reference to Argentina, agricultural exports from the temperate lands of Latin America were mainly wheat and animal products. But within the tropical regions of Latin America sugar and tobacco were the most important commercial products until the last quarter of the nineteenth century, when the demand for coffee, cacao, cotton, bananas, and rubber in the European and U.S. markets increased the involvement of Latin America in world trade. In some areas, notably the coffee region of the states of São Paulo and Paraná in Brazil, tropical export agriculture played an important role in general economic development. But in relation to other commodities, for example, rubber in Amazonia, although fortunes were made by individuals, the export economy did little to improve technology, transportation, and general living conditions in the region of production.

In some cases the area of commodity production was owned, organized, and operated by a large international corporation. The United Fruit Company started in a small way in the late nineteenth century as a shipper of bananas from Jamaica. Eventually it came to hold banana plantations in Jamaica, Guatemala, Honduras, Panama, Costa Rica, and Columbia. The budget of the company exceeded that of several of the states in which it operated and, not unnaturally, its size and dominance of economic life came to be resented. At the opposite end of the scale, relatively small farmers opened up banana cultivation in the Ecuadorian *oriente* (Parsons, 1957) and made that country into the world's largest exporter of the crop (Preston, 1965).

By the beginning of the twentieth century, Latin American export agriculture was well integrated into world markets, and some regions had become very dependent on the sale of particular products—Brazil on coffee, Central America on coffee and bananas, Colombia on coffee, Cuba on sugar, and Argentina on meat, wool, and grain.

The highly successful agricultural export economy that developed through integration into world markets came to an abrupt end with the Great Depression of the 1930s. Demands for all kinds of raw materials fell drastically, bringing down the price of most of the region's agricultural exports. The most important exports—coffee, cacao, sugar, and bananas—suffered an average decline in real price of about 60 percent between the peak years of the late 1920s and the low point of the Depression in the 1930s. During a time of diminishing incomes in the industrial societies, Latin America found itself the producer of the world's "desserts," and the demand for such luxury imports declined sharply. Many economists attribute the present economic difficulties in Latin America to the catastrophic decline in agricultural exports during the 1930s. The crisis of 1930–1945 produced a variety of responses in Latin America. In the short run there were attempts to diversify agricultural exports as prices of the various commodities fluctuated wildly. In Brazil, for example, there was a considerable transfer from coffee to cotton as the price of coffee fell drastically and remained low and cotton prices were maintained (Furtado, 1965).

International efforts were made to control the marketing of particular commodities. International agreements covering the production of sugar, tea, wheat, and rubber were signed between February 1931 and January 1936. Schemes were devised to maintain the prices of agricultural exports. A major compensatory scheme was that of the accumulation and destruction of coffee stocks in Brazil. The government bought up and destroyed 4 to 5 million tons of coffee, about one-third of world production during the 1930s. Between the late 1930s and the end of World War II, 550 million coffee trees were destroyed. These measures finally restored some balance in the coffee market, but they were not followed by other producing countries, with the result that Brazil lost a large share of the world market. Brazilian production of coffee increased after World War II, and vast acreages in western São Paulo and Paraná were brought under cultivation.

The crisis of the 1930s stimulated efforts to substitute domestic manufactured goods for imported goods. This process of import substitution became a major stimulus to industrial development; in the years since 1930, the most dynamic sector of the Latin American economy has been manufacturing industry. While the growth of the industrial sector has been impressive, approximately one-third of the income derived from exports was earned by agricultural products. The traditional products of coffee, sugar, bananas, and cotton remain leading generators of foreign exchange earnings, although soybeans have been of increasing importance in the last decade. Four traditional export crops (coffee, sugar, bananas, and cotton) occupy approximately 15 percent of the arable land in Latin America. The rapid and sustained growth of world prices of most of the region's exportable commodities in recent years has contributed greatly to the overall value of agricultural exports.

Only in the last two decades has the importance of agricultural products as a percentage of total exports diminished, and then only slightly and only in a few countries. Even though manufactured exports are more and more important, agricultural exports will remain significant for most countries in the region. As a generator of domestic capital, however, the agricultural sector has been diminishing steadily. The contributions of agriculture to the overall gross domestic product (GDP) has fallen significantly in most Latin American countries since 1960. In 1960 agriculture contributed more than 30 percent of the GDP in eight countries; by 1976 there were only two countries, Haiti and Paraguay, in this category. In six countries—Brazil, Chile, Venezuela, Mexico, Trinidad-Tobago, and Jamaica—the agricultural sector contributes less than 10 percent to the national GDP.

The production and marketing situation in the commercial sector of agriculture has changed considerably in recent decades. New techniques have altered production prospects considerably. In some countries, such as Mexico and Venezuela, government intervention in the agricultural economy has substantially raised the average yields by providing irrigation infrastructure and technical assistance in plant breeding and fertilizer application. Over one-half the value of Mexican crop production presently comes from irrigated land but, to accomplish this, 10 percent of the federal budget has been spent on irrigation development each year since 1941. There is some question as to whether irrigation has been overextended, particularly in the dry Mexican northwest. Problems with water cost and water quality have been plaguing farmers there recently, but it should be noted that the average wheat yield obtained on the irrigated land in the Tres Rios and Colorado Delta regions of northwest Mexico (24 pounds per acre) is higher than in the United States or Canada, where the crop is dry farmed. Average cotton yields are very high in Mexico and Peru when they are grown on irrigated land, and maize yields increased from 14.5 pounds per acre to 22 pounds per acre in Argentina and from an impressive 12.6 pounds per acre to 30 pounds per acre in Chile during the two decades from 1951 to 1971. Manioc yields more than doubled in El Salvador, Cuba, Ecuador, and Venezuela over the same 20-year period. During the same two decades, maize yields in the United States increased from 22.2 pounds per acre in 1951 to 48.6 pounds per acre in 1972, and wheat yields increased from 10 to 20.3 pounds per acre (Ruddle, 1972).

Contemporary Food Production

With the exception of the temperate agricultural regions of the Argentina humid *pampas*, the central valley of Chile, and the irrigated oases of northwest Mexico, Latin American agriculture has not been noted for its productivity. Although the traditional farming systems, such as *roza* and *milpa*, proved ecologically stable and attractive from the point of view of yield per unit of labor, they have proven to be inadequate in supplying a rapidly increasing human population with nutritious food. It is significant that even in countries such as Mexico, where impressive yields are obtained in the commercial sector, traditional subsistence farming is the predominant form of agriculture. For example, all commercial acreage combined does not equal the acreage in beans, a traditional subsistence or semicommercial crop.

In the past few decades there has been an expansion of the internal demand for agricultural products. Population growth, rapid urbanization, and the rise in the purchasing power of a part of the population have increased domestic demand. The agrarian sector has not responded with increased production. Only in exceptional cases has agricultural production exceeded population growth, and demand has grown much more rapidly than the population. The realities are that most Latin American countries have to cope with food supply deficiencies.

Population growth rates have been especially high in the rural areas of Latin America, exerting considerable pressure on the tenure and production systems in these areas. Rising agricultural populations in the areas where traditional slash-and-burn methods are used result in shorter fallows or prolonged periods of cropping, both of which may be ecologically disastrous and usually result in a malfunction of the entire swidden cycle. In areas of more intensive *milpa* cultivation the pressure results in untenable partitioning of landholdings into tiny parcels called *minifundios*. Many underemployed rural residents are leaving the farms and hoping for a better life in the city. In some countries, such as Argentina, Chile, and Mexico, over one-quarter of the rural population migrated to urban areas between 1950 and 1960 (Barraclough, 1973). Such rural refugees usually end up in slums and squatter settlements within the large cities and greatly tax the ability of the urban system to absorb them.

Although Brazil is riding a wave of expanding industrial development, and for many years optimistic writers on world food prospects have alluded to the potential of Brazil (and particularly the Amazon Basin) as an important source of food for the world, it is doubtful whether Brazil can keep pace with its own food needs (Brown, 1975).

The problem is not so much that Brazil has not been able to expand its food production; it has, and at a fairly impressive rate. But Brazil is faced with an unprecedented growth in the demand for food, because the population of Brazil grows at nearly 3 percent per year. In addition, its economy has been growing at an impressive 8 to 10 percent yearly over the last decade. Together these two sources of growth in demand are increasing food needs by some 4 percent per year.

This means that to be self-sufficient Brazil needs to increase agricultural output far more rapidly than any major country has succeeded in doing.

Gains in the value of agricultural products in the export of Latin America's economy have averaged over 20 percent per year since 1975, and gains have been even stronger in Brazil and Argentina. The importance of coffee in Brazil and meat products in Argentina are shown when one considers that these two countries accounted for almost 60 percent of Latin America's agricultural exports throughout the 1970s. But when coffee is excluded and only food products are considered, quite a different picture emerges.

Since 1960, increases in total food production have occurred in every Latin American country except Haiti, Jamaica, Guyana, Trinidad and Tobago Honduras, Bolivia, Ecuador, and Peru. However, increases in production were offset by population increases in most countries. Considering Latin America as a whole, food production has been able to keep pace with population increases, mostly because of strong performances by Brazil, Argentina, and Venezuela. The other eight countries just mentioned all have a downward trend in per capita production since 1960, and Mexico has barely maintained the 1961 per capita levels throughout the 1970s.

Modernizing Agriculture

Virtually no country in the world has succeeded in fully modernizing its agricultural system. This is not to say, however, that there are no modern agricultural systems in the world. Agriculture in the United States is mostly conducted on large, mechanized units, and farming activity is linked, by efficient communication systems, with the economic life of the country. However, the U.S. system was born relatively modern. When the Midwest and the West were opened up their economies were extensions of the modern industrial system that existed in the East and in Western Europe. "Pioneer farming" was developed on the basis of substantial landholdings, cash crops, commodity markets, railroads, and agricultural machinery. The pattern of events was somewhat similar on the Argentine *pampas*. But the *pampas* and the Great Plains are exceptional cases in the history of world agriculture and should not be used as models for other regions.

Most modern farming has evolved from some form of peasant agriculture. In Britain, France, and West Germany there are still many small farms of

Some families struggle w/ agric. other
things...but little evidence of the suffering
due to food shortages because of agricultu
many appear well adjusted.

Table 4-1 Latin America: Indices of Per Capita Food Production, by Country, 1970–1977

Country	1970	1971	1972	1973	1974	1975	1976	1977
Mexico	107	109	104	108	102	112	105	106
Dominican Republic	99	105	105	104	107	95	105	99
Haiti	90	93	104	92	87	83	80	79
Jamaica	76	78	77	73	75	69	71	66
Trinidad and Tobago	82	79	81	70	74	63	75	72
Caribbean	94	98	99	96	98	89	95	91
Costa Rica	128	119	129	130	123	139	135	126
El Salvador	107	109	97	111	105	115	106	108
Guatemala	116	124	121	127	124	135	138	134
Honduras	100	111	98	98	88	72	83	85
Nicaragua	108	116	104	111	111	115	110	116
Panama	121	124	112	100	105	108	103	107
Central America and Panama	114	117	111	114	110	113	113	112
Argentina	106	103	95	105	109	108	116	114
Bolivia	97	92	92	95	97	104	108	95
Brazil	112	109	110	116	120	119	129	129
Chile	109	110	91	81	97	103	95	110
Colombia	102	103	106	106	111	116	112	111
Ecuador	95	91	91	91	92	89	90	85
Guyana	83	87	74	65	86	85	75	97
Paraguay	104	85	88	84	95	93	101	114
Peru	94	95	86	83	83	79	79	77
Uruguay	108	94	86	97	109	108	120	96
Venezuela	115	115	110	109	114	119	110	120
South America	106	104	100	105	109	109	114	113
Latin America (22 countries)	107	106	102	105	108	109	111	112

Source. Inter-American Development Bank, *Economic and Social Progress in Latin America, Annual Report 1977*, p. 13.

less than 100 acres, where families struggle to make a living from a variety of activities, including producing much of their own food. Cash incomes are low, and it can be difficult to keep the farm going. Of course, there are excellent modern farms in Western Europe as well, just as there are in parts of Latin America, but in France especially farming has not yet moved completely away from eighteenth-century patterns.

Overall in the last 400 to 500 years there is little evidence that Latin America has suffered severe regional food shortages on the basis of traditional agricultural systems, which seem so inefficient to North American eyes. In fact, many of the local productive systems appear to be well adjusted to environmental conditions and the needs of the communities they serve.

However, as Latin America has urbanized, the population has left rural communities, and the traditional farming system is not well adapted to supplying large quantities of cash crops to distant markets. Much of Latin American agriculture is small scale and not capable of absorbing the type of inputs that have improved the efficiency of farming in the United States. If agriculture is to meet the needs of the growing urban communities, traditional, rural lifestyles and value systems will undergo considerable alteration. If farming is to modernize, so must the communities in which traditional farmers live. This type of change is not achieved in a generation.

A major problem is the structure of landholdings. At least until relatively recently, landownership was concentrated in few hands. The problem of the concentration of landownership is, as West suggests in Chapter 2, a heritage of the colonial period, when large estates emerged. Many peasants held land from the *hacienda* and paid rent with produce or labor services.

But, during the present century, there have been more and more effective cries for land reform policies, involving the breakup of large estates. The land question was a major issue that fueled the Mexican Revolution and, under the constitution of 1918, the peasantry was eventually given access to land under the *ejido* system. Other countries, including Venezuela and Bolivia, have broken up large landholdings and given small farmers title to land. Such policies may be a move toward social justice, but they do not necessarily promote more efficient agriculture or better rural living standards. A Spanish minister of agriculture commented on policies involving the redistribution of land titles in Spain that such efforts merely parceled out rural misery unless there was an accompanying, sustained effort to improve agriculture generally. Such a remark could equally apply to Latin America.

Modernizing agriculture will involve employing the techniques of "green revolutions" such as crop breeding to provide higher-yielding varieties of crops, as in Mexico. Above all, a more productive agricultural sector will require additional educational and informational institutions in rural areas, together with storage and communication systems, that will allow surpluses to be marketed when they are available. *# of landless peasant cont. to grow.*

Agricultural Settlement and Colonization

Despite attempts at land reform, the number of landless peasants continues to grow, and the subdivision of already small agricultural units is creating more *minifundios*. In many parts of Latin America the settlement of essentially unoccupied terrain, particularly in the humid tropical lowlands or disputed border regions, has been used as an escape from tenure and modernization problems by many governments. In the same category are the less directed and more spontaneous settlement activities brought about by opening new roads or new irrigation projects. Newly settled tropical lands have added significantly to agricultural output in the past 30 to 40 years. Expansion of agricultural production continues to depend more on the extension of areas under cultivation than on increased yields.

In most tropical countries the flow of agricultural settlement has been from traditional highland centers of population to the lowlands, which remained sparsely settled during historic times. Important areas of settlement activity have been on the plains and valleys of Mexico's Gulf coast, the tropical interior and coastal lowlands of Central America and interior Venezuela, the Santa Cruz de la Sierra area of Bolivia, and the Guayas River Basin of Ecuador. The vertical movement is well represented by the general eastern extension into the Amazon lowlands from the Andean foothills by nationals of Colombia, Ecuador, Peru, and Bolivia. The Brazilians, too, are promoting agricultural developments in the Amazon Basin. These developments are dependent on ambitious highway projects such as the *Carretera Marginal de la Selva* in Peru, Ecuador and Colombia, and the *Cuiabá-Acre, Cuiabá-Santarém*, and Trans Amazonia Highway in Brazil. In the dry lands of northwest Mexico wealthy agricultural interests, some with U. S. backing and peasant farmers working through cooperatives (*ejidos*), have developed lands for agriculture.

The results of settlement projects have been generally disappointing. There have been problems in processing land titles and protecting property rights. Remoteness from markets has resulted in the persistence of subsistence patterns of agriculture. Frequently mentioned are problems with agricultural credit and extension assistance, and sometimes complete ecological malfunction occurs, particularly in tropical lowland areas. Nelson (1973, p. 5) states that:

It is evident that experience in the development of new lands in the humid tropics has been very mixed. There is no clear understanding of why some areas seem to have prospered and others have stagnated. Only in Brazil has any attempt been made to assess how new land in the humid tropics contributes to the overall development process. There is no record of what has happened as a result of previous land development investments and policies nor of their economic, social, and political objectives and the extent to which these objectives have been achieved. We have only fragmented knowledge about the requirements for capital, managerial talent, and foreign exchange and about how the agrarian structure affects the results of investments.

Perhaps more emphasis should be placed on improving production in humid temperate zones, many in areas above 5000 feet, instead of new agricultural endeavors on the soils of the humid tropics. For all their dramatic ring, the scttlcment schemes have not been effective in modifying the traditional land tenure structure, and the *latifundio-minifundio* disparity remains one of the striking characteristics of agrarian life in modern Latin America.

BIBLIOGRAPHY

Austin, J. P., *Agribusiness in Latin America*, New York, Praeger, 1974.

Barraclough, S., and J. C. Collarte, *Agrarian Structure in Latin America*, Lexington, Mass., D.C. Heath, 1973.

Brown, J. C., *A Socioeconomic History of Argentina 1776–1860*, Cambridge, Cambridge University Press, 1979.

Butt, A. J., "Land-use and Social Organization of Tropical Forest Peoples of the Guianas," in J. P. Garlick and R. W. Keay (eds.), *Human Ecology in the Tropics*, Oxford, New York, Pergamon, 1970, pp. 26–42.

Carneiro, R. L., "Slash and Burn Cultivation among the Kuikuru and its Implications for Cultural Development in the Amazon Basin," in J. Wilbert (ed.), *The Evolution of Horticultural Systems in Native South America: Causes and Consequences, A Symposium*, Caracas, Editorial Sucre, 1961.

Carter, W. E., *New Lands and Old Traditions: Ketchi Cultivators in the Guatemala Lowlands*, Gainesville, University of Florida Press, 1969.

Chang, J. H., "The Agricultural Potential of the Humid Tropics," *Geographical Review*, Vol. 58, 1968, pp. 333–361.

Chapman, A. M., *Puertos de Intercambio en Mesoamerica Pre-Hispanica*, Mexico City, Mexico, Instituto Nacional de Antropologia e Historia, 1959.

Crossley, J. C. "The Location of Beef Processing," *Annals of the Association of American Geographers*, Vol. 66, 1976, pp. 60–75.

Denevan, W. M., "Aboriginal Drained-Field Cultivation in the Americas," *Science*, Vol. 169, 1970, pp. 647–654.

Duncan, K., and I. Rutledge, *Land and Labour in Latin America: Essays on the Development of Agrarian Capitalism in the Nineteenth and Twentieth Centuries*, Cambridge, Cambridge University Press, 1977.

Freyre, G., *The Masters and the Slaves*, New York, Knopf, 1946.

Furtado, C., *The Economic Growth of Brazil*, Berkeley, University of California Press, 1965.

———, *Economic Development of Latin America*, Cambridge, Cambridge University Press, 1970.

Gallo, E., "The Cereal Boom and Changes in the Social and Political Structure of Santa Fé, Argentina, 1870-95," in K. Duncan and I. Rutledge (eds.), *Land and Labor in Latin America: Essays on the Development of Agrarian Capitalism in the Nineteenth and Twentieth Centuries*, Cambridge, Cambridge University Press, 1977.

Grunwald, J. and P. Musgrove, *Natural Resources in Latin American Development*, Baltimore, Johns Hopkins University Press, 1970.

Gudeman, S., *The Demise of a Rural Economy: From Subsistence to Capitalism in a Latin American Village*, London, Routledge and Kegan Paul, 1978.

Harlan, J. R., "Agricultural Origins: Centers and Noncenters," *Science*, Vol. 174, 1971.

_____, *Crops and Man*, Madison, Wis., American Society of Agronomy, 1975.

Harris, D. R., "Swidden Systems and Settlement," in P. J. Ucko, R. Tringham, and G. W. Dimbleby (eds.), *Man, Settlement and Urbanism*, London, Gerald Duckworth, 1972.

Harrison, P. D., and B. L. Turner (eds.), *Pre-Hispanic Maya Agriculture*, Albuquerque, University of New Mexico Press, 1978.

Inter-American Development Bank, *Economic and Social Progress in Latin America, Annual Report*, Washington, D.C., 1977.

Jefferson, M., *Peopling of the Argentine Pampa*, New York, American Geographical Society, 1926.

Lobb, C. G., "The Viability and Ecological Stability of Re-settlement in the Interior Lowlands of Guatemala," in Richard P. Momsen, Jr. (ed.), *Geographical Analysis for Development in Latin America and the Caribbean*, Chapel Hill, N.C., CLAG Publications, 1975, pp. 140–153.

MacArthur, R. H., *Geographical Ecology, Patterns in the Distribution of Species*, New York, Harper & Row, 1972.

Nelson, M., *The Development of Tropical Lands*, Baltimore, The John Hopkins University Press, 1973.

Parish, W., *Buenos Ayres and the Provinces of the Rio de la Plata*, London, John Murray, 1839.

Rappaport, R. A., "The Flow of Energy in an Agricultural Society," *Scientific American*, Vol. 225, 1971, pp. 117–132.

Ruddle, K., and D. Odermann (eds.), *Statistical Abstract of Latin America*, Los Angeles, Latin American Center, UCLA, 1972.

Sargent, C. S., *The Spatial Evolution of Greater Buenos Aires, Argentina, 1870–1930*, Tempe, Arizona State University, 1974.

Sauer, C. O., "Cultivated Plants of South and Central America," in *Handbook of South American Indians*, Washington, D.C., Smithsonian Institution Bureau of American Ethnology, Bulletin 143.

_____, *The Early Spanish Main*, Berkeley and Los Angeles, University of California Press, 1966.

Schery, R. W., *Plants for Man*, Englewood Cliffs, N.J., Prentice-Hall, 1963.

Scobie, J. R., *Argentina: A City and a Nation*, 2nd ed., New York, Oxford University Press, 1971.

Seavoy, R. E., "The Shading Cycle in Shifting Cultivation," *Annals of the Association of American Geographers*, Vol. 63, No. 4, 1973, pp. 522–528.

Staff of the Land Tenure Center Library, *Agrarian Reform in Latin America: An Annotated Bibliography*, 2 vols., University of Wisconsin-Madison, Land Tenure Center, 1974.

Wolf, E. R. (ed.), *The Valley of Mexico: Studies in Pre-Hispanic Ecology and Society*, Albuquerque, University of New Mexico Press, 1976.

CHAPTER 5

Population: Distribution, Growth, and Migration

Brian W. Blouet

Rapid growth

A characteristic widely shared by the countries of the less developed world is a rapid rate of increase in population. This feature is well displayed in Latin America where population increase is currently proceeding at approximately 3 percent per annum. At this rate, a population will double its numbers in 20 to 25 years. The overall average for world population increase is approximately 2 percent per annum, while in the economically developed countries population growth rates tend to be under 1 percent each year.

The rapid rate of population growth is of relatively recent origin in Latin America. The marked increase of population in the region during the past century is basically the result of the application of modern control techniques, which has led to the eradication of many diseases that formerly enjoyed a widespread lethality. The growing ability of Latin American governments to limit food shortages and to establish some basic sanitation and health services over wide areas of their countries has also played an important part. Although epidemics, famines, and high infant mortality still control population increase in more remote areas, the range of these problems has been progressively limited by the action of government and international organizations. Within the space of a few decades the techniques of death control have markedly reduced mortality rates in Latin America, and there is still opportunity for the curtailment of the activities of the agencies of death.

Because birthrates reflect complex social patterns they are less susceptible to alteration, even where birth control techniques are available. Societies that have maintained high birthrates to insure the continuation of family units do not rapidly adjust their behavior once death rates fall. Usually the factors that have given rise historically to high birthrates are no longer recognized by a society. The causes have been forgotten, but the response is perpetuated in communal patterns of behavior that include beliefs and prejudices that are not susceptible to speedy adjustment. It is unlikely that birthrates will decline prior to the development of higher educational standards, but it does seem that a degree of knowledge about many matters, including birth control, can be relatively rapidly acquired by Latin American communities. When we talk of developing societies, we are talking not only of economic development but also of rapid social evolution. Traditional patterns of life, and the values these embody, are altering at a great pace; birthrates are likely to reflect these changes. Already, for example, population growth rates in Mexico and Brazil have begun to slow from the very rapid increase experienced in the 1950s and early 1960s. Dickensen (1972), in an analysis of the Brazilian census taken in 1970, has shown that while the population growth rate of the 1950s was 36.6 per 1000 inhabitants, in the decade ending in September 1970 the rate of increase had declined to 29.9 per 1000 inhabitants. Dickensen attributes the decline to ''the impact of urbanization, increasing birth control, and changing social values which show greater concern for the level of well-being of the family.''

The most striking example of decreasing birthrates in Latin America is provided by Costa Rica, a country that in the recent past was cited as an area with a birthrate approaching the biological maximum. In 1960 the birthrate was 48.0 per 1000 inhabitants; by 1970 the figure had dropped to 35.0 per 1000 inhabitants.

In the short run we are liable to see the maintenance of high rates of population increase for the region as a whole. It has been suggested that an increase in the rate of economic development tends to push up the birthrate; the reason is that as the level of the economy rises there is an increase in optimism, which is reflected in earlier marriages and an increased number of births. As Benjamin Franklin noted more than two centuries ago: ''Where families can be easily supported, more persons marry, and earlier in life.'' The optimism factor, in the earlier stages of economic development, perhaps partly explains why certain countries, such as Venezuela and Mexico, experienced rapid population growth at a time when they started to undergo marked economic growth. However, it is true that the relationships between economic development and population growth are not well understood.

PROBLEMS ARISING FROM A RAPID RATE OF POPULATION GROWTH

The high rates of population increase presently displayed in the region give rise to a number of problems. Quite simply, if the population of a country grows at the rate of 3 percent per annum, the gross national product of the country must grow at a rate in excess of 3 percent per annum if living standards are to be maintained. This is a considerable burden and, even in countries that attain rates of economic growth well above 3 percent per annum, rapid increase in population numbers frequently slows down the pace at which living standards improve.

It is an economic given that to maximize investment, a group must minimize consumption. Clearly, in societies with rapid rates of increase, a large percentage of the population will be found in the lower, predominately consuming age groups. In Peru and Mexico over 40 percent of the population is under 15 years of age. Attempting to provide health, social, and educational facilities for this section of the population can consume a large part of the capital that a nation has available for investment. At a family level, large numbers of children limit savings and investment, whatever form these may take.

There is an alternative view that suggests that communities will not easily allow their living standards to decline and, when faced with increasing numbers, will search for mechanisms to increase productivity. Thus an increased population may well stimulate innovations and additional activity.

REGIONAL VARIATIONS

Important as the general economic considerations discussed in the previous section are, it must be remembered that there are very large geographical variations within countries. States with high rates of population increase do achieve economic growth, even if this growth is confined to a few regions of the country. The available capital may be, and frequently is, concentrated into relatively small areas, the remainder of the country encountering static or declining living standards. The fact that overall population increase seems to indicate that little rise in living standards is taking place on a per capita basis does not mean that economic growth is not taking place in all regions. For instance, in Peru (annual rate of population increase approximately 3 percent) there is no doubt that economic development is proceeding rapidly in much of the *costa*, while the traditional societies in the *sierra* develop at a much slower pace. In this sense average figures for the whole country can be extremely misleading.

In summary, one of the major economic problems in Latin America today is how to develop the very considerable physical resource base of the continent rapidly enough to raise living standards. If lower birthrates can be achieved the task should become easier and the rise in living standards more rapid.

THE DISTRIBUTION OF POPULATION

It is apparent from Figure 5–1 that the population of Latin America is unevenly distributed. In the present state of our knowledge it is not possible to offer satisfactory explanations as to why certain areas have been more successful in

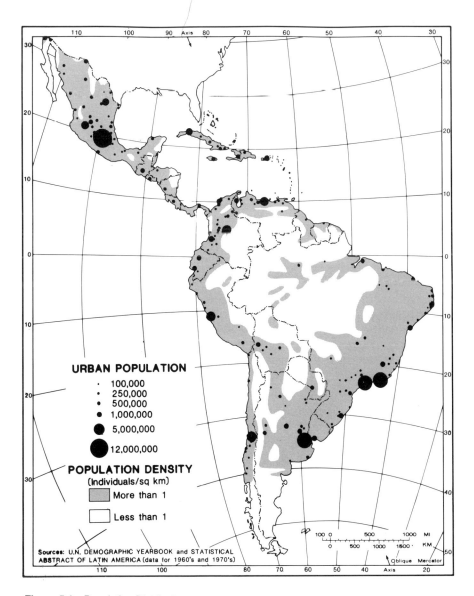

Figure 5.1 Population Distribution

supporting population than others. It is tempting to seek easy explanations: deserts are uninhabited because they are deserts, the Amazon Basin is "vast and impenetrable" and therefore sparsely populated. Environmental determinist explanations no longer stand up (if they ever did). The west coast desert of the continent contains large concentrations of population, and tropical rainforest regions in Latin America, and elsewhere, do support relatively dense populations. It is clear, states Zelinsky (1966, p. 34), that "the economic characteristics of an area exert a much more direct effect upon its population patterns than do its physical characteristics." Such a view may not fit all historical circumstances but, at present, an economic explanation, regarding the physical environment as a variable cost factor, is a more rational way of attacking the explanation of population distribution than starting from a concept of physical environmental determinants.

When the Europeans made contact with Middle and South America, there were a number of densely populated areas supported by intense agricultural activity. Several Caribbean islands were heavily populated. The Maya, although in decline, had considerable concentrations of people in Yucatan and, in the Central Valley of Mexico there were massive settlements, such as Tenochtitlán, the Aztec capital on the shores of Lake Texcoco. In South America the major contrast was between the well-peopled upland basins of what is now Bolivia, Peru, Ecuador, and Colombia and the remainder of the landmass, which was occupied largely by shifting cultivators or hunters or gatherers. There were exceptions to this in the western deserts where irrigation was practiced in places and in some eastern coastal regions where more advanced agricultural techniques had been developed but, overall, away from the upland basins, there were many regions that were lightly populated.

The Iberians came from traditional agrarian societies that still retained some feudal elements. In such societies land is the fundamental resource that determines status, influence, and wealth within groups. But land without people was of lesser value; in Western Europe high status was linked to the control of land and its inhabitants and not to the direct working of a farm by the landowner. The desire to acquire cultivable inhabited land was certainly not the sole motive for Iberian New World settlement: churchmen were anxious to make converts to Christianity, and there was a desire to find substantial sources of precious materials. But all these factors reinforced each other and created a situation in which Iberian settlement tended to be attracted to areas where there were already substantial indigenous populations. The thinly populated *pampas*, which might have been attractive in the sense that there were physical similarities to the Spanish *meseta*, was not settled heavily until after the close of the colonial period. There is an interesting contrast between the European settlement of the eastern seaboard of North America by families anxious to acquire farms and the settlement of Middle and South America by men who wanted estates. Whether this distinction would have prevailed if there had been what West, in Chapter 2, calls "a great mass of organized and subservient labor" on the eastern seaboard of North America is a subject for debate. The overall effect of the Iberian conquest was to reinforce the existing pattern of population distribution·even if the immediate result, in many areas, was to lower population numbers.

For strategic reasons it was necessary to attach the acquired territories and their inhabitants to the imperial structures of Spain. New towns and cities were founded at points where they could act as nodes in the administrative and communication network that the Spanish were constructing to link their New World territories with Europe. Many of the coastal cities of Spanish America were founded as links in an expanding imperial system, and they became administrative and trade centers in which population concentrated. Vera Cruz, Panama City, Cartagena, Guayaquil, Lima-Callao, and Valparaiso are among these "points of attachment" that Sargent describes more fully in Chapter 6.

In the Portuguese zone of penetration along the east coast of South America, a different pattern of events emerged. In the coastal areas of what are now northeast and southern Brazil native population densities did not compare with those of the Caribbean or upland basins. There were, as a result, few zones of concentrated indigenous population that might have acted as an attraction to Europeans by virtue of their value as a labor force. The early pattern of colonial settlement was coastal, with inland towns eventually emerging along navigable water or in mining areas like Minas Gerais.

Several east coast regions of Latin America offered the possibility of growing agricultural products for sale in European markets. These possibilities were not generally available in the Andean region because of a group of transportation problems resulting from terrain and the juxtaposition of land and sea. In the east coast regions, close to seaborne communication, it was possible to grow agricultural commodities such as sugar, cotton, and coffee (after 1727) and export them competitively to European markets. However, the subtropical and tropical lowlands where the crops could be grown either did not have available populations to act as a work force or, as in the case of several Caribbean islands, the indigenous populations had succumbed in contact with Europeans. The labor deficit was met by a vast forced migration of Africans brought to the New World as slaves. The influx eventually altered aspects of the distribution, density, and composition of the population of Latin America. The heaviest concentrations of populations of African origin were found in the areas suitable for plantation agriculture and closest to the potential markets. To this day the Caribbean islands and northeast Brazil have large black populations, as do parts of the *costa* regions of Colombia, Ecuador, and Peru. In the case of Caribbean islands, the black population is frequently preponderant; for example, in Barbados over 90 percent of the population is of African origin. Although the British outlawed the slave trade in 1807 and abolished slavery itself in 1834, other countries continued the trade well into the nineteenth century, and the existing slave populations on Cuba were not fully released until the 1880s.

When we examine the broad outlines of population distribution in Latin America, many of the features are explicable in terms of the distribution of pre-Colombian populations and the modifications made to the pattern in the early decades of Iberian intervention. As parts of Latin America were linked with the industrializing world in the nineteenth century, some new areas, like the Argentinian *pampas* and the Caribbean shore of Central America, were opened up. But, at least as far as South America is concerned, many areas of the region are still sparsely populated.

In crude terms the further one has to go into the continent the greater the costs of transportation and the less competitive any crops or mineral resources produced there are likely to be. To date, very few commodities have been produced in the central areas of South America cheaply enough to absorb the transportation costs. Population densities in the heart of South America remain low, although the opening up of the *oriente*, Amazonia and Guyana regions to agricultural colonization and mineral resource exploitation is beginning to modify this pattern.

POPULATION MIGRATION

At least one aspect of population distribution is not fully explained by the interaction of indigenous people with Iberians in the sixteenth century. The origins of most major cities in Latin America can be traced to colonial times, but their present size and importance, in the overall distribution of population, is a phenomenon of relatively recent origin. As Latin American countries have begun to industrialize and modernize, the cities have drawn migrants from small urban places and rural areas. In short, Latin America, in the second half of the twentieth century, is undergoing the process of urbanization of population that characterized much of Western Europe in the nineteenth century. Although a fundamental change in population distribution seems to be a part of economic transformation in the Western world, analogies between Europe and Latin America or the United States and South America should not be pushed too closely. There are important differences in the *pace* of development and the *type* of development between Western Europe and Latin America, whether we are speaking of social or economic matters.

Zelinsky (1971) has suggested a cross-cultural scheme to describe migratory processes at different stages of development. Phase I is represented by a premodern traditional society in which there is little internal migration. During phase II, the onset of modernization is experienced, bringing with it "a great shaking loose of migrants from the countryside." In phase III the modernization process is well advanced and, although there is still significant migration from the countryside, the rate of flow begins to decrease. Zelinsky saw phase IV as fitting an advanced society, roughly equivalent to the presently economically developed countries. In this phase movement from the countryside continues at a much reduced rate and is replaced by inter- and intraurban migration. Phase V outlines some possible characteristics of a future superadvanced society.

Many Latin American countries displayed the characteristics of phase I in the early decades of this century. For the Latin American countries that are modernizing, the "great shaking loose of migrants" came in the 1950s and 1960s. Many countries now have an urban majority, and thus the relative rate of rural to urban migration is beginning to decline, as in phase III of Zelinsky's system.

Two important questions that should concern us about population migration are as follows. When the inhabitants of a developing country or region begin to migrate, where do they go? And what are their motivations? The initial statement on this problem was made in 1885 by the pioneer geographer E. G. Ravenstein. Ravenstein's "laws of migration" are still the starting point for discussion on migration, and they are paraphrased here.

1. The great body of migrants only proceed a short distance.
2. The inhabitants of the country immediately surrounding a town of rapid growth, flock into it; the gaps thus left in the rural population are filled by migrants from more remote districts.
3. Each current of migration produces a countercurrent of lesser strength.
4. Migrants proceeding long distances generally go to a major center of commerce or industry.
5. The natives of towns are less migratory than those of rural areas.
6. Females are more migratory than males over short distances, but males more frequently are a part of international migration.
7. Most migrants are adults: families rarely migrate out of their county of birth.
8. Large towns grow more by migration than by natural increase.
9. Migration increases in volume as industries and commerce develop and transport improves.
10. The major direction of migration is from the agricultural areas to the centers of industry and commerce.
11. The major causes of migration are economic.

Before proceeding further, it is important to recognize the context in which Ravenstein was writing and the source of his data. His initial analysis was primarily based on the 1871 and 1881 censuses of Britain. By that time Britain had, or was close to possessing, a mature industrial economy; therefore the "laws" may not be wholly applicable to the currently advanced industrial nations or to regions in the earliest phases of economic development. For example, as a country becomes urbanized, the natives of towns become mobile. In the United States today there is very considerable migration from one city to another. Similarly, the statement on female migration may well be related to a stage in the migratory process. When populations at first became highly mobile, the male members of society tend to make the initial migrations. As they

establish themselves in new locations, women from the source communities ·
follow, either by request or to overcome the disparity between the sexes that
strong migratory flows may induce. Furthermore, around cities in the early
phases of the development process, when unskilled labor is both plentiful and
cheap, there seems to be a considerable demand for female domestic workers.

Of course, many of Ravenstein's suggestions have been further developed, and frequently the terminology has been revised. We now speak of direct migration when a migrant moves without interruption from one location
to another. The term stepwise migration is used to cover the situations where a
man or woman stops at an intervening point, or points, on the way to a final
destination: for example, moving from a village to a small town and then on
to a city. The term fill-in migration describes patterns where, as one group of
migrants moves out, another enters to take its place.

We now understand more clearly the relative attraction of destinations
based on their population size. It has been possible to construct gravity models
that will predict migratory flows on the basis of the relative size of the population centers involved and the distance between them. Several studies of migration patterns in Latin American countries have reinforced the idea that the reasons for moving are primarily economic. In a study of migration in Costa
Rica, Carvajal and Geithman (1974–1975) state that "people migrate because
they have reasons to expect that by doing so they can better their conditions."
And Sahota (1968), in a study of internal migration in Brazil, found it to be
"highly responsive to earnings differentials." In general, economic cycles affect migration flows, and Lee (1969) has shown that "the volume of migration
varies with fluctuations in the economy." Thus we should expect increasing
migratory flows when the economy of a region is expanding and a decrease of
population movement in times of recession. Peach (1968), in a study of outmigration from West Indian islands to Britain, found that the volume of people
leaving the Caribbean was strongly influenced by whether or not the British
economy was in a phase of growth. If Lee's conclusions are as applicable to
Latin America as they are to the economically developed lands, it would seem
that it is the pull factors that are the dynamic element in the migratory process
and not the negative, or push, factors. However, the economic mechanisms
that influence the rate of migration seem to work very imperfectly in many
areas of the Third World. Most large Latin American cities have high unemployment rates, this would indicate that migrants, in aggregate, are not responding well to changes in economic forces. Some authorities believe that this
is because even in times of recession the wage differentials between rural and
urban areas are so great that migratory flows are not much influenced.

Population migration in Latin America has been predominately from rural to urban areas. Although, as Lobb described in Chapter 4, there are movements from highland centers of population to agricultural frontiers in tropical

lowlands, the numbers of people involved are relatively small. The overall effect of migration is to cause the more rapid growth of population in urban areas when compared with the countryside. In rural areas population numbers tend to grow at rates of 1 to 2 percent per annum. In the urban areas the rate of growth is 4 to 5 percent per annum (Figures 5-2 and 5-3).

During the 1950s and early 1960s, the larger cities were growing at a faster pace than the average for all urban places. These primate cities often displayed annual population growth rates of 7 to 8 percent per annum, and it seemed that an increasing proportion of the population of many countries was concentrating in fewer and fewer places. In the last decade the trend has been for many of the secondary cities and regional centers to assume an increased importance in terms of economic activity and population growth. Overall, the growth rate of the primate cities seems to be slowing, although it is still too

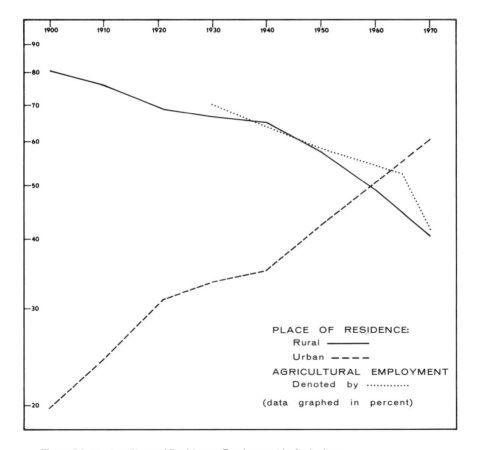

Figure 5.2 Mexico: Place of Residence, Employment in Agriculture

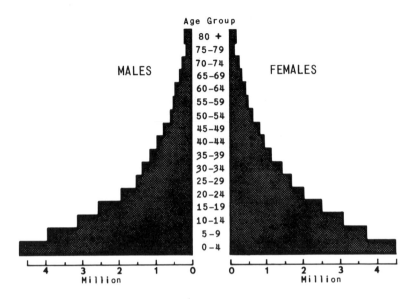

Figure 5.3 Mexico: Population Pyramid

soon to predict that the expansion of the second-order places will result in a condition where the "rank size rule" will be approached. The major cities, such as Lima, Santiago, and Buenos Aires, still remain very attractive to entre-preneurs and industrialists setting up enterprises. Writing of Lima, Smith (1968) has outlined its advantages in terms that apply to virtually all major centers.

> There are many reasons why industry should prefer Lima: an expanding and resil-
> ient market; the presence of associated industries and marketing structures; reli-
> able power and water supplies; the availability of a professional and managerial
> class; proximity to government and its highly centralized bureaucracy; easy inter-
> nal and external communications; and international middleclass standards of
> housing, shopping, recreation and education.

WHAT MOTIVATES MIGRATION?

Most authorities, including Ravenstein (1885, 1889), Lee (1969), and Zelinsky (1971), assume that economic matters are the major driving force in the migra-tion process, at least as it applies to developed and developing countries. The work of Ravenstein and Zelinsky is empirical, which means they have exam-ined the evidence, described the pattern of events, and attempted to ascribe causes for the movements they can document. It should be possible to gain an increased measure of understanding of the processes involved by adopting a behavioral approach to the problem. This approach is extremely time consuming; if it is done properly it involves determining the attributes and attitudes of residents of rural communities and then, over a period of years, studying the behavior of persons who migrate to another place. Many of the studies done in Latin America have not been as thorough as this and have only involved interviewing migrants after they have arrived at their destination. There is a problem with this; people are great rationalizers and, when asked about motives for migrating, are capable of manufacturing arguments to justify their behavior. Frequently these arguments were not uppermost in the mind when the decision to migrate was made. Questionnaires administered to migrants after they have lived at their point of destination for some time tend to confirm that economic motives were the main decision to migrate.

Concern solely with economic motivation tends to obscure other important aspects of the migration process. Migrants do not set off blindly for the nearest large urban center. A large amount of evidence is now being accumulated that shows that people only move after they have acquired information about conditions at the point of destination and that this information is transmitted through a chain of contacts from city to source area. The result of these information flows frequently is to establish migration chains that tend to perpetuate themselves, so that, once a member of a village has moved to a city successfully, it is highly likely that some relatives and associates will follow. Information fields are subject to distance decay factors, so that what Ravenstein said about the attraction of large centers and the length of migratory journeys still applies. But when a migrant arrives in a city, he is likely to join a neighborhood of which he already has some knowledge and may well know at least some of his neighbors. The fabric of the migratory process is social as well as economic.

The study of the attributes of migrants has been rewarding, and it has been shown that the average migrant is "better educated and better informed and from a higher occupational background than many of his fellows in the rural areas" (Gilbert, 1974, p. 103). Migratory flows may be in some ways a disadvantage to the countryside, since the persons who leave tend to be the younger and more innovation-receptive members of society. The rural area loss is the urban area gain, but absorption into the economic life of the city may be slow. The problem is similar to that perceived by some European statesmen in the nineteenth century as they watched with mixed emotions the migrations of their countrymen to the world's new areas of settlement. In 1855 William Gladstone, a future prime minister of Britain, wrote that the migrant was not "needy and necessitous, but it is the most adventurous, the most enterprising, and most intelligent . . . who goes to seek his fortune in those distant lands."

Like rural areas, small provincial towns also tend to lose inhabitants to the metropolitan areas. In this case it is not a question primarily of the *number* of people moving but the *type* of people migrating. The lesser urban places lose a significant proportion of their trained manpower to larger urban centers. The reason for this is simple and applies to some degree all over the world. In the cities and metropolitan areas the opportunities to undertake many careers are much greater and, from the point of view of the professions, such centers are often the only areas in which it is possible to obtain the full range of employment opportunities. In Latin America the tendency is much stronger than it is in Western Europe or North America since, in the former, very few countries have more than one or two large urban centers. For example, the town of Popayán (population 80,000) in southern Colombia is a pleasant Spanish colonial creation, graciously laid out around spacious squares and architectural features. The town possesses a university founded in 1640, but it is clear that graduates of this institution can expect few local forms of employment other than as doctors, teachers, lawyers, and priests. It is hardly surprising that persons with other skills find they have to migrate to Bogotá, Cali, or Medellin to seek other employment opportunities. Comparatively, Colombia is better provided with large urban centers than many countries. In the case of Uruguay there is only one major city, Montevideo, which, with a population of approximately 1.25 million persons, contains over 40 percent of the population of the country. The second-ranked towns by number of inhabitants, Paysandu and Salto, each have less than 100,000 inhabitants, and the range of employment opportunities, compared with those at the capital, is limited.

INTERNATIONAL MIGRATION

Necessarily, international migration has played an important part in the emergence of Latin America as a distinctive region. Western Europeans, from the time of Columbus' second voyage, have settled in the region. At first, settlers were drawn predominantly from Spain and Portugal, but Italians, Germans, and Frenchmen later migrated into the region. The cultural impact of the Europeans was much greater than their numbers might suggest, and they became the dominant elements in *criollo* society, even though the greatest part of the population was made up of indigenous elements.

The Europeans were responsible for moving populations into their new world. By 1520 there are records of black slaves having been imported, through Spain, into Caribbean islands to be used as agricultural laborers. When plantation crops began to be raised on a large scale for export to European markets, the English, French, Dutch, and Portuguese made the slave trade a big business. The slave trade resulted in direct, forced migrations of Africans across the Atlantic to the Caribbean region and the sugar-growing areas of northeast Brazil.

During the nineteenth century, the slave trade and slavery were progressively suppressed, and plantation interests made searches for ethnic groups that could serve as alternative sources of cheap agricultural labor. For example, in the British West Indies slaves began to leave the plantations after the abolition of slavery in the 1830s. Large numbers of indentured laborers from India and China were persuaded to enter into contracts that obliged them to work on plantations at low wages for 5 years. Many indentured laborers never returned home and formed the basis of the Indian and Chinese populations in countries like Trinidad (44 percent Indian) and Guyana (52 percent Indian).

The history of the Caribbean region contains a long record of migrations. When the Europeans entered the region, they came upon a situation in which the Caribs were progressively invading many islands formerly settled by Arawaks. The Europeans dispossessed both groups over time and replaced them as a labor force with Africans, Indians, Chinese, and those of their own countrymen who would enter into indentured labor contracts. Population flows have not ceased in modern times. Jamaicans and other West Indians migrated to Panama to help build the canal. Barbadians have gone to Curaçao to work in the oil industry. Between 1909 and the end of World War I over 1 million migrants settled in Cuba; the majority of them came from Spain, but Caribbean islanders were well represented.

The flows of people have not been confined to the circum-Caribbean region. West Indians and Puerto Ricans have moved to New York and other eastern cities of the United States. Mexicans form large communities in Texas and the West. Many Barbadians and Jamaicans have settled in the central areas of cities in Britain. Recently outflows of migrants have been emanating from Haiti and Cuba and landing in the United States. The Cuban outflow is seen as having all manner of political implications. The fact is that the human outflow, which is a characteristic of virtually all Caribbean islands, had been held in check by the Castro regime. When the regime changed the rules, a backlog of migrants was released. Early in 1980 they arrived in the United States by the thousands each day.

The Caribbean has been described as a region of institutionalized outmigration. The causes of outmigration are relatively straightforward. Most of the islands are relatively small (Antigua and Monserrat are tiny) and have a limited economic base. The historical commitment to the production of a few crops, like sugar and coffee, has contributed to the making of a narrow economy. Without diversified economies the range of employment opportunities is limited, the chances for advancement are few, and unemployment is high. Not surprisingly, those with ambition, education, and skills are drawn to countries with better job opportunities. The result is that the region is deprived of the trained human resources needed to create more viable economies.

The Caribbean has drawn widely on the world for its populations. Although Europeans were the dominant political and economic force in the region, the percentage of population drawn from Europe was always small. This statement is generally true for much of Latin America: the Portuguese and the

Spanish controlled and organized the territory, but their numbers were relatively small. There are several important exceptions to this statement. Between 1870 and 1914 the population of Argentina increased from 1.7 to 7.9 million persons. The greatest part of the increase was accounted for by migration from Europe and, in 1914, 30 percent of the population of the country was foreign born. These figures for the peak migration phase are comparable to those for the Dakotas and Nebraska at the time of their most rapid inflow of Europeans. However, in the case of the northern plains region, the majority of the settlers came from Scandinavia, Germany, and Central Europe. In 1914 Argentina had drawn 40 percent of its foreign-born population from Italy and 35 percent from Spain; Germany contributed just over 1 percent of the total foreign-born population. The Germans were, however, an important element in the settlement of southern Brazil.

In the decades before World War I 30,000 Italian and Spanish workers would arrive annually to help with the harvest on the *pampas*. These *golondrinas* (or swallows) then returned home, presumably to work on the northern hemisphere harvest in their country of origin. Seasonal migration of labor used to be common in the Caribbean, and many workers would move to other islands or even the United States at harvest time.

There is a long tradition in Latin America of international migration and even settling across borders without legal entry. Many El Salvadorians have settled on farms in Honduras. Many Peruvians settled in the Ecuadorian *oriente* in the first decades of this century. In both cases the illegal settlement was a factor in starting a war between the countries concerned. Now international movement is more carefully administered so that both permanent and seasonal migratory flows within Latin America have been curtailed. The Caribbean remains an area of continued migration.

PROGNOSIS

If we were asked to speculate on future trends in the population geography of Latin America, what points should be made? First, the rate of population growth will tend to slow down as an increasing proportion of the inhabitants come to live in urban areas. With increased urbanization should come lower rates of migration from rural to urban areas. However, if agriculture were to be modernized, many more people would be shaken out of the countryside. If the trend toward the growth of secondary economic centers continues, this should enhance the importance of many provincial cities in the region and lead to increased interurban migration of population. If the world economy continues to expand at something approaching the rates of the last three decades, we can predict that the trend toward opening new agricultural and resource frontiers in Latin America will continue. This means more farming communities in the *oriente* of Bolivia, Peru, Ecuador, and Colombia and the opening up (or is it destruction?) of Brazilian Amazonia. Rising prices for many industrial raw materials would reinforce the trend of going deeper into South America for resources such as oil, again in the *oriente*, and metals, as in the case of the Guyana region of Venezuela. If, however, there is a general slowing of world economic growth, commodity prices would decline, and it might no longer be feasible to penetrate into the heart of Latin America.

BIBLIOGRAPHY

Carvajal, M.J. (ed.), *Population Growth and Human Productivity*, Gainsville, Center for Latin American Studies, University of Florida, 1976.

Carvajal, M.J., and D. T. Geithman, "An Economic Analysis of Migration in Costa Rica," *Economic Development and Cultural Change*, Vol. 23, 1974-1975, pp. 105-122.

Dickenson, J.P., "Brazil's Census Surprises," *Geographical Magazine*, Vol. XLIV, No. 1, 1972, p. 60.

Gilbert, A., *Latin American Development: A Geographical Perspective*, Baltimore, Penguin, 1974.

Gonzalez, A., "Population Growth and Socio-Economic Development: The Latin American Experience," *Journal of Geography*, Vol. LXX, 1971, pp. 36-46.

Grigg, D.B., "E.G. Ravenstein and the 'Laws of Migration'," *Journal of Historical Geography*, Vol. 3, No. 1, 1977, pp. 41-54.

Heer, D.M., and E.S. Turner, "Areal Differences in Latin American Fertility," *Population Studies*, Vol. 18, 1965, pp. 279-292.

Lee, S.E., "A Theory of Migration," in J.A. Jackson (ed.), *Migration*, Cambridge, Cambridge University Press, 1969.

McCoy, T.L. (ed.), *The Dynamics of Population Policy in Latin America*, Cambridge, Mass., Ballinger, 1974.

McNeill, W.H., and R. S. Adams (eds.), *Human Migration: Patterns and Policies*, Bloomington, Indiana University Press, 1978.

Merrick, T.W., and D.H. Graham, *Population and Economic Development in Brazil: 1800 to the Present*, Baltimore and London, Johns Hopkins University Press, 1979.

Norris, R.E., "Migration as Spatial Interaction," *Journal of Geography*, Vol. LXXI, 1972, pp. 294-301.

Peach, C., *West Indian Migration to Britain: A Social Geography*, New York, Oxford University Press, 1968.

Ravenstein, E.G., "The Laws of Migration," *Journal of the Statistical Society of London*, Vol. XLVIII, 1885, pp. 167-227, and "The Laws of Migration," *Journal of the Statistical Society of London*, Vol. LII, 1889, pp. 214-301.

Sahota, G.S., "An Economic Analysis of Internal Migration in Brazil," *Journal of Political Economy*, Vol. 76, 1968, pp. 218-245.

Smith, C.T., "Problems of Regional Development in Peru," *Geography*, Vol. 58, 1968, pp. 260-281.

Smith, T.L., *The Race between Population and Food Supply in Latin America*, Albuquerque, University of New Mexico Press, 1976.

Viel Vicuña, B., *The Demographic Explosion: the Latin American Experience*, translated by J. Walls, New York, Halstead Press, 1976.

White, P., and R. Woods, *The Geographical Impact of Migration*, New York, Longman, 1980.

Zelinsky, W., *A Prologue to Population Geography*, Englewood Cliffs, N.J., Prentice-Hall, 1966.

_____, "The Hypothesis of the Mobility Transition," *Geographical Review*, Vol. LXI, 1971, pp. 219-249.

CHAPTER 6

The Latin American City

Charles S. Sargent

Towns and cities have always been at the heart of Latin America's economic, political, social, and cultural development. From the start of the Iberic conquests in the sixteenth century, the towns have provided the foothold for the political occupance of the land and for the development and distribution of its natural wealth. Towns, in short, were stepping-stones toward the political and economic control of the new lands; they were the symbol and the mechanism of the colonization process.

By promoting the settlement and development of rural lands, Latin America's urban centers have had a strong impact on the pattern of rural land occupance and development. This *centrifugal* effect of giving order to the rural landscape has been common to most of Latin America's history; more recently even stronger *centripetal* forces are drawing people from the countryside into small towns and from small towns into the larger urban centers or, by migration, directly from the rural to the major urban areas.

The harshness of rural life, the exploitation of both landed and landless peasants, the economically marginal nature of much of Latin America's agriculture, and the limited amenities of the smaller towns increasingly enhance the perception of the larger city as an attractive alternative in which to work and reside. Unfortunately, the inward flow of migrants has not been balanced by available jobs, housing, or services, and the migrant's perceptions are often not matched by realities. Still, for many the city does offer a release from a de-

pressing cycle of rural poverty and lack of opportunity, and the result is a bur-
geoning, social, economic, and political urban crisis that is already at a
"critical mass" in many parts of Latin America.

Because one can only understand the present in terms of the past, it is essential to examine the evolution of the colonial and nineteenth-century urban
system. Equally, the present-day pattern of land use *within* the city reflects
both its colonial heritage and the later impact of nineteenth- and twentieth-
century influences, such as changing transportation systems, rapid population
growth, large-scale speculation in urban land, and other forces that affect urban change. The network of cities and their internal structure is the subject of
this chapter.

Stages of Urban Growth

Three major stages of town foundings and urban growth have attended the
European arrival and occupation of what became Latin America. The first was
the creation of a colonial urban framework. This initial period of town foundings lasted until about 1600 in Spanish America and about 1700 in Brazil. It
was followed by a late colonial and early "republican" stage of network adjustment that lasted until about the middle of the nineteenth century in both
Spanish and Portuguese America. The third major stage is the "modern" period, since about 1850 a time of network maturity characterized by some new
town foundings and particularly by the selective urban growth that has resulted in the present-day urban hierarchy, or ranking of cities by importance
and size. The latter portion of this last stage, since about 1950, has been typi-
fied by large-scale rural to urban migrations and the creation of very large metropolitan areas.

A Model of City Network Development

The history of Latin American urbanism shows that most of the earliest towns
were ports meant to *attach* the New World with the Iberian peninsula. In the
interior other towns quickly developed as mining towns that supplied gold, silver, and precious stones exported to Spain and Portugal through the ports.
Still other towns were established as agricultural settlements to supply food to
the ports and the mining areas or, indeed, even to provide an export crop such
as sugar. A significant number of towns developed as the way stations needed
for the movement of local agricultural products and European manufactured
goods to the mining districts and for the shipping of New World products to
the ports, the *points of attachment* to Europe. In time some of the interior
towns became even more important than some of the early ports. They came to
combine political roles with growing importance as internal production and

trade centers while also benefiting from their role as collection points in the chain of towns engaged in long-distance overseas trade.

A simple four-stage model, or abstraction drawn from the real world, clarifies this "mercantile" or trading motivation that lies behind the pattern of urban network development (Figure 6-1). The mercantile model indicates that long distance, international trading, and political ties and not the development of local or regional markets are the initial and major impulses behind the creation and growth of an urban network. The urban system, in other words, was linked to Iberian mercantile policies more than to local factors. The key to interpreting the urban system of the New World lies in understanding its ties with Europe and the political, religious, and mercantilistic policies of the European countries involved in the development of Latin America.

Cities also were important to their own developing regions and the growth of local markets. In time, these local ties became more and more important vis-à-vis ties to Iberia (i.e., a number of *endogenic* relationships came to be of increasing significance as towns came to be "central places" for local and regional trade). As the mercantile model demonstrates (stage 1), this central place aspect of a town's development is an addition to the outward-looking, *exogenic* ties to Iberia developed earlier. The present hierarchy of cities is a result of the early *exogenic* ties and the later development of regional economies within the Latin American countries, based on local and regional trade. The mercantile model accommodates the early trading networks with the nineteenth and twentieth century "in-filling" of a colonial frontier.

Because of Latin America's size, physical and cultural diversity, and different political regimes, it is understandable that the four stages of the mercantile model did not occur everywhere at the same time. Clearly, the stages of urban development varied widely in the forests of Amazonia, the *pampas* of Argentina, and the islands of the Caribbean. The mercantile model should therefore be viewed and utilized within a regional context that takes the chronology of development into account. For instance, the initial search phase, stage 1, encompassed the four voyages of Columbus (1492–1504) and the exploration of inland Brazil in the 1600s and of California in the 1700s. The second stage includes the harvesting of brasilwood after 1500 and also Caribbean mahogany production in the 1700s and the gathering of latex for rubber in the Amazon in the latter nineteenth century. Yet another example of the time variation is the stage 3 development of towns and the sugar economy of coastal Brazil after about 1530 in contrast to the development of agriculture and towns in interior Brazil only after 1700. The settling of southern Brazil's interior took place only in the late nineteenth century.

With few exceptions, the major cities of Latin America today were also the major cities in the colonial period. That these cities were bound to Spain and Portugal becomes clear after examining the evolution of the colonial urban framework of Latin America.

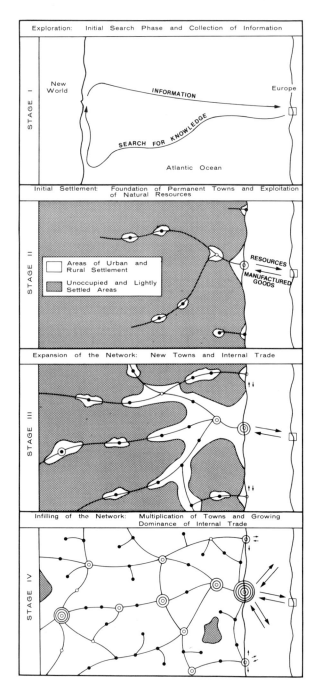

Figure 6.1   A Mercantile Model of Urban Settlement (after Vance)

The Colonial Urban Framework

Much of the Latin American urban system that one perceives today took root in the 100 years that followed the European discovery of the New World in 1492. It largely represents the introduction of Spanish towns into areas of relatively dense native populations or into mineralized areas. Throughout Spanish America, towns were founded with one or more objectives in mind—to exercise authority over a subjugated area and people, to facilitate the generation of trade and revenues (derived principally from the exploitation of gold, silver, and a few crops), and to bring the Holy Faith, the *Santa Fe,* to the Indians.

There were two distinct phases to the initial century of town foundings. The first, a brief interval of some 25 years, was characterized by exploration of the Caribbean islands and the laying out of towns meant to serve as ports and bases for inland exploration. This phase took place in the circum-Caribbean area between about 1496 and 1521 and along the northeastern coast of Brazil from about 1500 to 1550.

In Spanish America this was followed by a longer penetrative phase until about 1600 as explorers and conquerors moved into the interior. Probably most famous were the town foundings in conjunction with the 1519–1521 conquest of Mexico by Cortez and the later Andean conquests of Pizarro who, like others, sought fame and fortune without much regard for methodology. In Portuguese America, the longer penetrative phase that lasted until about 1700 was carried out principally by expeditions of *bandeirantes*, or quasi-military expeditions, who wandered the interior in search of slaves and minerals.

It is desirable to distinguish between various regions of Latin America in terms of the evolution of the colonial urban system, since there were significant regional differences in the timing, pace, and purpose of town foundings. In particular, it is useful to distinguish among (1) the Caribbean, Mexico, and Central America, (2) the Andean lands and Chilean frontier, (3) Argentina and Paraguay, and (4) Portuguese America (Brazil).

Zone 1. The Caribbean, Mexico, and Central America

The Caribbean. The islands and the continental shores of the Caribbean were the initial areas of Spanish contact with the New World, with many small towns quickly founded throughout the area as the Spanish searched for gold (Figure 6–2). Where little or no gold was found, a geological reality for many of the islands, there was little or no permanent settlement, leaving a vacuum that was filled more than 100 years later by the precursors of the modern North European countries. Where gold was found, as on the islands of Hispaniola and Cuba, towns developed and the local Indians were exploited both for mining and for agricultural production. When no local Indians were available, distant ones were forcibly brought to the mining sites. On some islands justifiably hostile Indians made settlement difficult and slow.

Figure 6.2

Major among the early towns was Santo Domingo, first founded in 1496. While not the first town, or *villa*, on Hispaniola, it is the oldest to survive and, consequently, the oldest city of the Americas. Fifteen *villas* were established on Hispaniola by 1505 and another seven in Cuba by 1515, including Trinidad (1512), Havana (1514), and Santiago (1515). On the island now known as

Jamaica, the *villa* of Sevilla La Nueva was established in 1509, but it no longer exists.

The resiting and abandonment of these early towns was common. Disasters such as hurricanes, volcanic eruptions, earthquakes, and fires took their toll. Some towns were rebuilt, but many others were abandoned when anticipated riches did not materialize or were quickly depleted, when the fragile tropical soil was exhausted, or when exploration routes changed. Many towns disappeared as the native labor force was decimated by disease. The Indian population of the island of Hispaniola, for example, was greatly reduced, mostly as a result of overwork, poor living conditions, and the virulence of European diseases against which the natives had no immunity. Additionally, mining settlements based on placer, or streambed, deposits were particularly short lived, while those related to the exploitation of veins of ore had longer lives. By and large, the major towns were the small ports that tied the new lands to Spain, and a number of these survived because of this long-term role and consequent investment in the port defenses, elaborate churches, public buildings, and residences.

Central Mexico. The Spaniards encountered a wealth of golden artifacts, millions of sedentary Indians, and a well-established network of Indian towns when they entered the Aztec Empire of central Mexico in 1519. The Aztecs had settled in the fertile Valley of Mexico in the ninth century and about 1325 had begun to develop their capital city of Tenochtitlán on the islands of Lake Texcoco. By 1519 it had a population in excess of 100,000, with many striking temples and an impressive separation of land uses within the city. Cortez described it as a magnificent city, divided into four districts by major streets, with a great plaza, temples, pyramids, and mansions. The city of Texcoco, across the broad lake, possibly had a population of over 100,000. Yet another large city, Tlaxcala, whose residents came to support Cortez against the Aztecs, lay between Tenochtitlán and Veracruz, the Spanish supply base established in 1519. There were numerous smaller cities. Not surprisingly, the Spaniards were impressed by this urban world inasmuch as only a handful of cities in Europe—Paris, Naples, Venice, and Milan, in that order—could claim more than 100,000 population at that time. Seville, just prior to the departure of the *conquistadores,* was a city of perhaps 50,000. Impressive also were the remains of Teotihuacan, a religious, market, and trade center 8 square miles in extent that lay 30 miles northeast of Tenochtitlán. Active between about 300 and 900 A.D., it had a peak population in excess of 125,000 that left behind impressive pyramids, temples, and extensive ruins.

Accessible only by causeways or boat, the superior defensive position of Tenochtitlán and its recognized dominance as a trade and tribute center largely explains why Cortez founded Mexico City on the embattled site after the final defeat of the Indians in 1521. Additionally, the temples and other buildings could be razed to provide a ready supply of building materials for the new city. What is today the largest cathedral in Latin America thus rose on the site of an Aztec temple.

Other town foundings took place quickly after the conquest, but all focused on Mexico City. Among the more important were silver centers such as the Indian towns of Taxco and Pachuca. Others, such as Guadelajara (1531), Puebla (1532), and Oaxaca (1536), were agricultural towns established in already densely settled and fertile areas. These and many of the smaller new towns were administrative centers and religious *congregaciones* into which Indians were herded for religious proselytization, instruction in Spanish trades, and to provide pools of agricultural or mine workers. The result was the rapid development of an extensive yet integrated nuclear pattern of towns and cities that focused on Mexico City.

Beyond this core, towns such as Tepic (1531) and Culiacan (1532) were established as way stations along lowland Pacific exploration and slaving routes. Acapulco was sited as a port for silver shipments to Spanish-held Manila in the Philippines and as a receiving port for Asian silks and other goods that made their way to Spain through Mexico City. Manila itself came into the administrative control of Mexico City in 1583. To the north of the nuclear core, additional town foundings occurred after the defeat of hostile nomadic Indians in the early 1540s and the discovery of silver at Zacatecas in 1546. In time Zacatecas, central to numerous rich silver veins, became the second-largest city of New Spain, or Mexico. A number of other silver camps, or *reales de minas*, such as San Miguel (1542), Guanajuato (1548), and San Luis Potosi (1592) became important towns as well. New agricultural settlements such as Leon and Celaya supplied food and animals to the mines. Additionally, the continued presence of hostile Indians meant that a number of fortified towns had to be established on the route between Zacatecas and Mexico City. To the northwest of Zacatecas, mining towns such as Fresnillo, Sombrerete, and Durango (1563) developed along the silver-rich foothills of the Sierra Madre Occidental as far north as Santa Barbara (1570). Town development farther to the north beyond the Silver Belt was delayed until about 1600, but the silver towns, agricultural settlements, and Franciscan missions represented the foundation of the linear pattern of cities characteristic of northern Mexico, a pattern in contrast with the more nuclear grouping of towns in central Mexico.

Central America. The Spaniards quickly converged from both Mexico and Panama on the advanced Indian culture area of Central America. As before, the penetrations were motivated by the search for mineral wealth and the extension of the empire.

The overland entry from the north was through Indian settlements such as Chichicastenango, Huehuetenango, and Quetzaltenango in the Guatemalan highlands and was further marked by the new towns of San Salvador (1524) and Antigua (1526), the establishment of the ports of Trujillo and Puerto Caballos (Puerto Cortez), and towns such as San Pedro Sula (1536) inland along the more densely settled and fertile river valleys. The Yucatan peninsula, the rainforests of Peten in lowland Guatemala, and the Caribbean coast of what is today Belize were all quickly seen to be physically difficult areas without gold and only sparsely settled since the disappearance of the Mayans. Merida and Valladolid, in Mexico, were consequently founded only in the early 1540s, and the area was relatively deficient in town development.

Explorers from Panama City, the base for explorations to both north and south, sailed to Nicaragua and established the agricultural colony and slaving base of Granada (1524) in fertile, densely settled lowlands. At the same time, another administrative and slave center was founded at Leon. The Nicaraguan highlands of Nueva Segovia became a major gold area after 1527, to which were later added the Honduran gold and silver districts around Comayagua (1537) and Tegucigalpa (1578), the latter becoming a mining and smelting center, focus of a number of smaller mining camps.

Movement south from Nicaragua led to the Costa Rican agricultural colony at Cartago (1562). But here there were few Indians because of the earlier arrival of European diseases, and Costa Rica quickly became an almost totally European district following planned immigration of European settlers. It remains so today. By 1650, in fact, the Indian population of Central America had declined from an estimated 11 million (1620) to only about 2.5 million. Depopulation was especially widespread in the warmer, more disease-prone lowlands, a fact that also helps explain why most of the major cities in Mexico and Central America today are highland cities.

After the 1521 conquest of Mexico and the following exploration of Central and South America, most of the Caribbean quickly became a support area, and a number of towns turned strongly to port, supply, and defense roles. Many others simply disappeared. Among the most important to develop were Havana, Cartegena, Nombre de Dios, and Veracruz. Havana, founded in 1514, became the chief fortress of the Spanish Main, guarding the approaches to the Gulf of Mexico. Veracruz, Nombre de Dios [later replaced by Portobello (1502)], and Cartagena (1533) were the only continental ports initially authorized to trade with Spain, and they underwent considerable development as a result of their being keystones in the Caribbean defense and trade system. These repositories of treasure were the terminals of the convoys that linked the New World to Spain between 1561 and 1748 (Figure 6-2). The fortification after the middle 1520s of these and other cities such as San Juan (1511), Santa Marta (1525), and St. Augustine (1565) was designed to fend off pirates and the navies of foreign powers that sailed this transportation corridor, the famous Spanish Main. Cartagena, for instance, was fortified between 1558 and 1735 with a 40-foot-high wall and a series of outlying forts that protected the approach from the sea.

Zone 2. Andean America

In their almost frantic search for mineral wealth and in order to expand the limits of empire, the Spaniards were quick to penetrate the interior of South America from bases earlier established along the Caribbean coast as well as newer settlements on the Pacific coast. As in Mexico and Central America, permanent and large-scale settlement was dependent on finding minerals or fertile land and on the availability of indigenous labor for the mines and the fields.

In the Andean region the Spaniards superimposed their economic system over the earlier Indian urban network and reoriented it to suit their interests. Unlike central Mexico, however, where large basins and high plains facilitated movement, the isolation of the high Andean mountain basins from one another and the mountain barrier between the Pacific lowlands and upland zones precluded the growth of a closely knit nuclear urban network. Instead, the strongly linear pattern of towns was favored. But the north-south linkages that had been established in the Inca period with the construction of a well-developed pedestrian road system were replaced by shorter, east-west trade routes between inland towns and Pacific ports. There was relatively little economic interaction between highland towns except as way stations on the bullion routes or centers of agricultural surplus.

Venezuela. As with Central America, not all of Andean South America proved attractive to the Spaniards. In Venezuela, for instance, early town development was primarily the result of the interests of a German commercial house, the Welsers of Augsburg. Some towns, including Cumaná (1516), Coro (1527), and Maracaibo (1529), grew up along the coast, but they were impeded by native hostility earlier engendered by Spanish slaving expeditions sent out to procure labor for the Caribbean islands. Even when Venezuela was back in Spanish hands after the Welser contract was revoked in 1556, growth was limited, since inland Venezuela was largely devoid of mineral wealth, if of considerable agricultural potential. This goes far in explaining the slower development of colonial towns there. By 1600 what is today the small town of El Tocuyo (1545) was the largest town of Venezuela, while Barquisimeto (1552), Valencia (1556), Trujillo (1557), Merida (1558), and Caracas (1567) were only small farm towns in isolated Andean valleys.

Colombia. A paucity of mineral wealth was also characteristic of the Colombia segment of the Andean range that sweeps northward from Ecuador into Venezuela. As a result, new towns in eastern Colombia also had a predominantly agricultural and peripheral function. The small village of Bogotá (1538) was, for instance, in the midst of a densely settled and fertile area, the *sabana*, but was initially of little importance to the Spaniards. Nearby was the Indian town of Zipaquira, already famous for its salt mines.

In sharp contrast to these marginal areas, portions of Colombia were rich in gold and major mining areas developed by the middle 1530s in the Cauca Valley, on the Antioquian highlands and along the Pacific coast. Central Colombia was soon a landscape of impermanent gold camps, although a few, as exemplified by the town of Antioquia (1546), became important mining and trade centers. Other towns, including Pasto (1539), Popayan (1536), and Cali (1536), were founded in the same period as the Spaniards moved north into the area from the Pacific coast.

Ecuador. What is now Ecuador had little mineral wealth; after about 1575, mining played no notable role in the regional economy. A land of isolated mountain basins, the major settlement was the northern Inca capital of Quito, just to the south of which a Spanish town was laid out in 1534. But since Quito was far from both the sea and from the mines of Colombia, it grew only slowly. A string of towns including Cuenca and Ambato was founded in the populated basins to both the north and south of Quito to serve as way stations.

Peru. Farther south, the coastal lowlands of Peru, except where crossed by exotic Andean streams, were characteristically inhospitable desert without notable mineralization or native population. European diseases, moreover, had preceded the Spaniards to both lowland Ecuador and Peru, and the first chroniclers already noted the sparsity of Indians and widespread settlement abandonment.

It was the highlands of Peru and Bolivia (upper Peru) that quickly came to be a major focus of Spanish interests. Like Quito, the Inca capital of Cuzco was occupied and made over into a Spanish town after 1534. Indeed, Spanish Cuzco was built directly on the highly earthquake-proof Inca walls and foundations, so that today the heart of the city is still one of narrow streets faced with the famous Incan masonry. There was also the occupance of other Indian towns, including Arequipa and Arica. Farther south, on the *altiplano* of Bolivia, its valleys and eastern lowlands, a number of towns were founded, including Sucre (1538).

In 1545 the attention of the Western world was drawn to a rich hill of silver, the *Cerro Rico*, at the base of which the mining town of Potosí was quickly established. Despite its location and the harsh climate associated with an elevation of nearly 14,000 feet that limited local agriculture, Potosí became a city of about 120,000 by 1570. It reached its zenith of 160,000 inhabitants by about 1600 and was the largest city in Latin America and one of the largest in the Western world. The city was the locale of over 100 silver mills and, despite some fine churches, expensive homes, and theaters, it was really a mining camp, and its population predominantly forced Indian labor. It is estimated that in 1570 the city's Spanish population did not exceed 4000. As a result, it was scarcely on a par with London or Venice in terms of being a true city.

Although Potosí was much larger, Lima was the capital of most of the Andean region. A coastal base for the conquest of the interior, Lima (1535) soon became the administrative capital of the viceroyalty of Peru, with districts as distant as Bogotá and Buenos Aires nominally under its control. It was also a major religious and educational as well as commercial center for trade with Spain. Situated on the coastal desert, Lima was dependent on the waters of the exotic Rimac River and local Indian labor for its agricultural supplies. By 1600 the city's population was about 14,000, with the small port at El Callao only recently founded directly on the coast 8 miles to the west.

While Potosí may have been more a large mining camp than a city like Lima, its impact on Andean America was nevertheless enormous, affecting the entire urban network between Lima and Buenos Aires. Its silver was the principal commodity that sustained Lima as administrative center and port, and it was an enormous market for agricultural and mining products from a vast area. A number of towns, including La Paz (1548), now Bolivia's largest city, developed as way stations on the bullion route from Potosí to Lima; lowland settlements such as Ica became food sources. Huancavelica was quickly settled after mercury was discovered there in 1563, obviating shipments from Spain for use in the processing of silver ore. Arica was selected as the principal port serving Potosí, and the mercury from Huancavelica and much merchandise for the mining town passed through here, as did the silver en route to Lima.

Also directly influenced by Potosí was the founding and growth of a number of towns in lowland Bolivia and northeastern Argentina that were the result of movement south of the Bolivian *altiplano*. In Bolivia these included Santa Cruz (1557) and Tarija (1574). In Argentina Santiago del Estero (1553) was the older of these towns, but quickly more important were to be Tucumán (1565) and Salta (1582), towns founded from the Santiago base in response to silver exploitation in Bolivia. Salta, for instance, rose to some importance as a trading center that specialized in providing the mines with mules and horses from eastern Argentina; up to 60,000 mules a year moved through the annual Salta animal fair. Cordoba (1573) was equally an economic link between the mining districts and the mule and cattle grazing lands to the east.

A number of the towns founded from the Santiago del Estero base no longer exist. One was Londres (London, 1558), founded in a region known briefly as New England (Nueva Inglaterra) to commemorate the marriage of Philip II of Spain with Mary Tudor. But Londres, like so many other settlements, was soon destroyed by Indians, and the regional name likewise disappeared after 1563. As elsewhere in the Andes, a number of small isolated Indian settlements, effectively beyond the Spanish commercial orbit, were spread throughout the Argentine northwest. Ultimately, the effect of Potosí's silver was felt as far south as Buenos Aires (1580), which remained a minor port in this period with little direct trade with the mining districts. Nonetheless, the naming of the Rio de la Plata estuary and of Argentina itself both reflect a hopeful tie with Bolivian silver.

Chile. The initial settlement pattern in Chile was strongly linear and, as elsewhere, related to the search for gold and silver and the extension of the empire. The mineral search proved considerably less successful than in the Mexican Silver Belt, but the search was paramount and it was only after 1600 that Chile became more an agricultural area than a linear frontier of military outposts. Even earlier, however, the fertility of the soil and the Mediterranean climate of the Central Valley combined with the presence of hostile Araucanian Indians in the south and deserts to the north to favor the development of central Chile. Particularly important came to be the port of Valparaiso (1544) and Santiago (1541).

As the Spaniards advanced south of Santiago, they ran into the hostile Araucanian Indians and were obliged to build fortified outposts, one of which, Concepción (1550), was designated as the early administrative capital of the Chilean district. Farther south, walled towns were established in Angol, Imperial, Temuco, Villa Rica, Valdivia (1552), and Osorno (1558). Finally, on Chiloe island, the town of Castro was founded 26 years after the founding of Santiago. But the Indians proved resistant, especially south of Concepción, where the forts were abandoned by 1598 to be reestablished off and on during the colonial period. Araucanian resistance in the southern forests ended only in the 1860s.

Argentina and Paraguay. Until 1776 the Cuyo district of western Argentina was administered from Chile, and a number of towns were founded there by expeditions that crossed the Andes from Santiago and the fertile Vale of Chile. The piedmont oasis of Mendoza (1562) became particularly important as a trade and agricultural station, with traffic over the Andes using the Uspallata Pass, a direct route with relatively easy access and crossing. San Luis (1596) was also on the trade route. But a number of other oasis towns such as San Juan (1562) proved to be off the trade routes to Chile or Bolivia and either grew little or disappeared. As late as the middle of the nineteenth century there were no towns south of Mendoza because of hostile Indians.

Farther to the east, the nomadic and hostile nature of the Pampean and Chaco Indians, the peripheral location of this portion of South America from the political base at Lima, and the absence of mineral wealth on the *pampa* or in the Chaco precluded such settlement before the late eighteenth century.

The exceptions of note were Asunción and the small port of Nuestra Señora Santa Maria del Buen Aire, a name quickly shortened to Buenos Aires. First founded in 1536, Buenos Aires was sited as far north on the Atlantic coast and as far inland as possible, in order both possibly to establish an Atlantic route between Spain and Peru and to serve as a barrier to southern ad-

captaincies -eg. estate that stretched from coast to far inland, also development lead to production + markets, sources of cargo, for

214

THE LATIN AMERICAN CITY

vances by the Portuguese. As a consequence of Indian raids and food short-ages, however, most of the colony moved upstream to found Asunción in 1537. The site of Buenos Aires was abandoned by 1541 and not resettled until 1580, when colonists moved south from Asunción, founding Santa Fé en route in 1573.

Until very late in the colonial period, Buenos Aires had little economic im-portance because the Spaniards used the port of Lima-Callao for silver exports to Spain. The merchants of Seville, Lima, and Panama indeed objected to Buenos Aires as a port at all and managed to have its use severely restricted so that as late as 1753 the city had a population of only 15,000 and dealt to a great extent in contraband. Asunción, by then a minor and isolated point of depar-ture for expeditions to the north and west, was considerably smaller. Even more than in the case of Chile, the towns along the Parana were an indicator of Spanish claims to southern lands instead of a part of the highly exploited Spanish realm.

Zone 4. Portuguese America

The tripartite goals of colonization—the extension and protection of empire, the exploitation of colonial wealth, and religious conversion—were roughly the same for Portugal as for Spain, but the Portuguese found no mineral riches along the northeast coast of Brazil, the nearest landfall from Portugal. Moreover, colonization and trade in Africa and Asia diverted Portugal's inter-est from Brazil, and it was only the threat of encroachment by the French and Spaniards that finally whetted Lisbon's interest in the American colony. As late as the 1530s there were only small, ephemeral trading posts along the coast where the Portuguese bartered with the Indians and exported *pau-brasil*, a dyewood after which the country was named.

One of the initial responses to foreign encroachment was for the Portu-guese crown to grant large estates, or *captaincies,* that stretched from the coast far inland. This established claim to the land and fostered the development of coastal plantations to produce lucrative crops, particularly sugar, for the Eu-ropean market. The *captaincies* were also markets for Portuguese goods and sources of cargoes for Portuguese vessels, important considerations under the mercantilist economic policies then in currency throughout Europe. Each grantee was responsible for the colonization, development, and defense of his *captaincy*, a system in force until royal control was later reasserted. The coast-al towns of the different *captaincies* thus functioned as administrative centers, *entrepôts* for European products, collecting points for exports, and a safe ur-ban milieu. As new lands were opened to agriculture, new towns were often founded a short distance inland.

Both a port and agricultural center, São Vicente (1532) was the first such town in Brazil, soon followed by others that stretched along the coast as far north as the hump of South America. By 1550 there were 15 small towns along the coast, among them the short-lived Ilheus (1532), Salvador (1534), Recife (Pernambuco, 1536), and nearby Olinda (1537). A number of other towns were founded by plantation owners, ostensibly as acts of piety, but equally as acts of land speculation and labor exploitation. In these instances, land was given to the church, a town plan drawn up, and the town established in order to enhance surrounding land values and assure a labor supply for agriculture. One of the first of these so-called *patrimonios* (1545) was the coastal town of Santos, near São Vicente. Particularly after 1550 there were also a number of Jesuit missions, most of them on the lowlands adjacent to the towns. A few were in the interior, the most notable being the one that became São Paulo (1554). The fortified military settlement of São Sebastião do Rio de Janeiro was laid out on its present site in 1567, supplanting the destroyed French colony of Antarctic France (1555); the site had been occupied and fought over since 1531. Its excellent harbor and strategic location led it to become an important port and administrative center for southern Brazil.

By 1600 the major towns were the capital at Salvador, Recife-Olinda, Rio de Janeiro, and São Paulo. With few exceptions the other towns were only small ports or insignificant collections of dwellings adjacent to a church or fort. Nonetheless, the littoral was occupied and an urban network established that was to remain essentially unchanged until the discovery of gold late in the seventeenth century led to new town foundings and restructured the Brazilian urban hierarchy.

THE LATER COLONIAL PATTERN: 1600–1800

Urban development after 1600 in Spanish America was typically a process of urban "in-filling" and adjustment of the original settlement pattern. The rise and decline of towns and cities was common as mines opened and closed down, agricultural areas were developed, and political decisions led to a shuffling of administrative centers. The focus of Spanish attention was the intensification of the search for minerals in proven mining districts and the expansion of existing agricultural areas. With few exceptions, significant new town development took place within already occupied areas. Of secondary interest was the expansion into areas that were both distant from the already productive areas and probably graced with little development potential in terms of the economics, technology, and transportation of the time. In fact, the Spaniards had by 1600 already pretty well delineated the major areas of mineral wealth, high-yield agriculture, and tractable Indian populations.

If the opening of new lands was relatively insignificant in Spanish America, just the opposite is true of Brazil, where the settlement of the interior highlands led to a fundamental restructuring of the entire Brazilian urban hierarchy and the creation of many new towns. The impetus for this fundamental change was the discovery of gold and diamonds in the interior. To a lesser extent, the occupation of northeast Brazil by the Dutch also played a part in the urban transformation.

Throughout Latin America the rising fortunes of some towns offset the declining fortunes of others, but most towns were fairly static in growth and small in size. These were limits imposed primarily by slow and small-scale modes of transportation, restrictions on trade both within and beyond the colonies, a declining or only slowly increasing Indian population base, a relatively small number of Europeans, and the dominance of a local agricultural economic base. Few towns had a population in excess of 5000; most were considerably smaller.

The exceptions were the ports, political centers, and mining towns. Given the lower cost and greater ease of water transportation vis-à-vis overland movement, ports were important as links between the mines and Europe and regionally as well. Over time, a number of cities such as Buenos Aires, Bogotá, and Caracas came to share the political and economic roles earlier guarded so jealously by Lima. In Brazil Rio de Janeiro finally came to dominate as both a port and capital.

Even the largest cities of colonial Latin America were small in comparison with today's urban areas. And of the smaller towns of that time, most could scarcely be called "urban" by today's standards, either in terms of population, functions performed, transportation systems, or architecture. At the beginning of the nineteenth century, the largest city of Spanish America was Mexico City, but its population of 128,000 was only comparable to that of its predecessor, Tenochtitlán, at the time of Cortez's arrival in 1519. As late as 1800 Lima was a city of only 64,000, Buenos Aires, 45,000, and Caracas, 38,000. Rio de Janeiro was Brazil's largest city, with 100,000 inhabitants, followed by Salvador, 50,000, and Recife, 25,000. Most of the major inland regional centers and *entrepôts* throughout Latin America in 1800 ranged from 10,000 to 30,000, depending on the wealth of the region.

The population levels of mining towns were volatile, and even major centers like Potosí experienced declining numbers by 1800. Important ports such as Veracruz, Santos, and Callao were small towns of 11,000, 7000, and 2000, respectively, in 1800; even smaller were the port towns of the Caribbean. Most of the towns in the interior of Latin America were mere agricultural villages of modest dwellings and few commercial activities. In short, while many towns had been founded in the colonial centuries since about 1500, few of them were very large.

Mexico, Central America, and the Caribbean

Mexico after 1600 remained a key Spanish realm and, by 1790, was still producing more than one-half of the world's silver. Mexico and Brazil together accounted for approximately 90 percent of the world's output of all precious metals in about 1800. In both countries, as elsewhere, the strong mining base created demand for a host of goods and services. The manufacture or trading in mining equipment, leather goods, pottery, woollen and cotton goods, furniture, silver artisanry, and the like, were urban pursuits, as was the exchange of foodstuffs and livestock. The port of Veracruz, in particular, but also Acapulco, Tampico, and Campeche filled important roles as an increasing number of ships traded in the Caribbean and Pacific. The inland centers established in the earlier period were more and more important regional, political, and commercial centers, a level of activity roughly corresponding to stage 4 of the mercantile model (Figure 6-1).

The Mexican frontier after 1600 lay beyond the silver mining districts of Durango and Santa Barbara. Here, in an extensive area that included present-day California, Arizona, New Mexico and Texas, there came into existence a linear network of forts (*presidios*) and missions that were outposts of Spanish political interests and centers for the conversion of the Indians to Catholicism. Both *presidio* and mission represented the interests of the state and acted as a buffer to the expansive policies of other nations.

The earliest move into the north took place after 1598 into what is now New Mexico, 700 miles north of the Santa Barbara mining district. An administrative center was founded in Santa Fé (1608) that encompassed the Indian *pueblos* that stretched 200 miles along the Rio Grande, both to the north of Santa Fé (*rio arriba*) and to the south (*rio abajo*). Initially, there had probably been 40,000 Indians in 50 or 60 villages, but this total was reduced to perhaps 8000 by the beginning of the nineteenth century. The settlement void between the Rio Grande and Santa Barbara was later bridged by missions, including the one at El Paso del Norte (Juarez, 1659) and the mining town of Chihuahua (1703). Far to the east, the mission at San Antonio, Texas (1718), was to gain later fame as the Alamo. The mission at Laredo dates from 1769, and the Spanish held faraway New Orleans from 1762 until 1800.

To the west of the Rio Grande Valley, the Spaniards moved steadily northward with both *presidios* and missions into present-day California and Arizona, founding *presidios* at places such as San Diego (1769) and San Francisco (1776). Among the more numerous missions were those of Tucson (1776) and Los Angeles (1781). Northernmost of a long chain of missions was that at Sonoma, California, where the Spanish sphere of influence contacted the Russian fur trading realm, operating out of Fort Ross (1812). Numerous missions were the core of subsequent urbanization, as the string of towns and missions along the *camino real* (royal road) in California indicates.

In contrast with Mexican expansion and as in earlier years, relatively few Spaniards were attracted by Central America. Towns like Antigua, León, Granada, and Cartago failed to become important centers. The fate of Antigua was finally sealed by a severe earthquake in 1773 that led to its abandonment and the creation of Guatemala City (1776) as the new capital. Equally disruptive to development were the challenges to Spanish hegemony by the English, French, and Dutch after about 1625. Vying with the Spaniards and among themselves, parts of the Caribbean shoreline fell into their hands, as did undeveloped islands of the Caribbean and the marshy coastal lowlands of the Guianas. With a few exceptions, these economically marginal and peripheral lands were relatively unimportant to the Spaniards and Portuguese: there was an apparent absence of mineral wealth and a clear shortage of Indian labor. The towns of Belize (1630) and Greytown (San Juan del Norte) were among the settlements along Central America's coast. But they functioned as much as pirate bases as anything else. It was from Greytown, for instance, that Sir Francis Drake ascended the San Juan River and sacked Granada, Nicaragua.

The economic base for a long-lasting occupance of the land by other Europeans was not piracy, however, but the growing of sugar. Both small-scale landowners and larger plantations imported slave labor from Africa and competed in Europe with the slave-grown sugar of northeastern Brazil. The French colony of Sainte Dominique (Haiti), acquired in 1697, became the most productive of the sugar islands, leading to the founding of a number of port towns, including Cap Haitien and Port-au-Prince (1729), and the growth of some older places such as Jacmel.

South America

In Colombia settlement as late as 1700 was largely restricted to the Caribbean coast and the Magdalena and Cauca valleys, the areas of initial colonial development. Cartagena, the storehouse of wealth awaiting export to Spain, came to be the most frequently besieged city on the Spanish Main, a reality that, combined with hostile Indians and the difficult terrain of Colombia, diverted official attention from interior development. The exceptional case was the highland region of Antioquia, where gold continued to be mined and where Medellin (1650) developed as a regional service center.

After 1700 the accession of the French Bourbons to the Spanish throne brought significant changes in colonial administration and policy, which affected the relative importance of cities. Bogotá, for instance, was made the seat of a viceroyalty in 1717, an act that focused attention on an area that had been more or less ignored by the authorities and merchants of distant Lima. Caracas was designated a Bourbon political center in 1742, equally favoring urban development there. Combining this with the firm hand of a trading company created in 1728, Venezuela began to develop its agricultural potential, exporting coffee, cotton, and indigo as well as expanding cattle production on the *llanos* of the Orinoco.

At the other extreme of the continent, another instance of the power of political decision making was the 1776 creation of the viceroyalty of the Rio de la Plata, with Buenos Aires as the capital. The intent was to offset Portuguese influences in Uruguay, and the "free trade" regulations of 1777 and 1778 considerably enhanced the port town, earlier suppressed by interests in Lima. Despite these early restrictions, Buenos Aires was nonetheless already the largest town along the navigable Paraná River. With a population of 20,000 in 1776, its new administrative and military role simply reinforced its dominance in the region. On the north side of the La Plata estuary, the fortress settlement of Montevideo (1724) had only recently been established to stop Portuguese advances to the south. Development was favored by its becoming an official port of call on the Cape Horn route, which was more and more popular. In time, this cape route led to a decline in the importance of towns in Panama and a rise of Pacific ports, particularly Valparaiso.

Lima, as a consequence of these and other political, transportation, and commercial realignments, gradually lost its preeminence. Although Peruvian and Bolivian mineral products remained important as a result of new finds at Cerro del Pasco (1630) and elsewhere, Lima's boom days were numbered. The city's decline was compounded in 1746 by the severest earthquake ever recorded there, one that took an estimated 16,000 lives; the port of Callao was swept away by the resultant tidal wave. If a more attractive Lima was subsequently created, it was nonetheless downgraded both commercially and politically.

Portuguese America

In contrast to both Spanish America and the Caribbean area, there had been only little urban development in the interior of Brazil as late as 1650. Indeed, there were few towns of note even within the initial coastal zone, mostly because that region's development was essentially rural and plantation oriented. In addition, Brazil's growth was adversely affected both by Spanish control of Portugal after 1580 and by the occupance of northeastern Brazil, including Recife and Bahia (Salvador), by the Dutch West India Company after 1630. Before its return to Portugal in 1654 the Dutch controlled the coast from the São Francisco River to São Luis. Even after their departure the Dutch left a strong cultural, racial, and architectural heritage behind.

Gold Towns. The large-scale development of towns in the interior came in the eighteenth century following important gold finds by *bandeirantes*, or quasi-military expeditions, who had long wandered the interior in search of such minerals and of Indians to enslave. Finally, in 1693, they found gold in stream gravels throughout the Minas Gerais, but notably in the Serra do Espinhaço; 20 years later deposits were located to the west in Mato Grosso. In both areas, the larger mining camps evolved into the principal settlements, particularly after about 1720 when long-lasting vein mining replaced the peripatetic panning of streams.

The most famous of the gold towns came to be Vila Rica do Ouro Prêto, the Rich Town of Black Gold, so called because the gold matrix was black quartz. Founded in 1712, the gold mined there financed fine churches and townhouses that make the town, now a national monument, a gem of Latin American baroque architecture. At the height of the gold rush, between 1725 and 1750, the town had a population of 60,000 but, by 1800, with the rush terminated, it had declined to 8000, and scores of more ephemeral mining camps disappeared. Small gold towns such as Sabará, Marianna, São João del Rei, and Congonhas do Campo became mere villages.

The story was similar to the west in the Mato Grosso, where deposits of gold were found at Cuiabá in 1718 and Goiás in 1725. By the middle 1720s, Cuibá had a population of 7000, but it, Goiás, and other towns declined well before 1800, becoming small service centers in an area of quasi-subsistence agriculture. Elsewhere, diamond fields found after 1729 led to the development of mining towns in the modern states of Minas Gerais and Bahia. One of the largest towns, Diamantina, was founded in 1730. Unlike gold, however, diamonds were declared a crown monopoly, thereby restricting their trading and the number of mining towns that came into existence.

Not surprisingly, thousands arrived from Portugal for the mining fields and thousands more left the coastal settlement zone, thereby contributing to its decline in both population and economic significance. One consequence was a restructuring of the urban hierarchy (the ranking of towns by size and importance) in favor of the interior and in favor of the port of Rio de Janeiro, then the sole official port for the exportation of gold bullion. Mostly because of its central location vis-à-vis the mining interior and its expanded trading role, Rio replaced now poorly located Salvador as the capital in 1763. Decades later, in 1808, Rio de Janeiro also became the residence of the Portuguese royal family who fled Napoleon and set up court there until 1822, at which time Brazil declared its independence and was to be ruled by an emperor until 1889, when the republic was established.

As with the older silver district of Potosí in upper Peru, the Brazilian mining districts were incapable of providing enough food or pack animals to the suddenly booming interior. This encouraged the expansion of agriculture elsewhere in Brazil and also led to the formation of many new towns. Many overnight stopping places, or *pousos*, and stations for collecting taxes on gold shipments quickly came into existence and became small towns whose names, such as Pouso Alegre and Registro, reflect their initial function. Most of the mules destined for mine work and for goods transport came from the south, and the town of Sorocaba came to play the same role that Salta had performed in relation to the mines of upper Peru. Still other towns and overnight stops developed on the trail northward from Sorocaba to the mining districts. Many cattle destined to feed the mining districts of Minas Gerais came from the *sertào* of the northeast, where an expansion of earlier ranching was encouraged by the new markets in the mines to the south.

Already by the late seventeenth century a line of military posts adjacent to the São Francisco River had been established to fight banditry along the pregold trade routes; some of these posts also became small highland towns. In short, many preexisting settlements in the interior flourished for the first time, and many new towns were founded on the basis of the mining and exportation of gold.

In the highlands south of São Paulo gold had been discovered in the Curitiba district in 1654, with that town evolving as a mining center. A second zone of exploration was established along the coast south from São Vicente. Even farther to the south, forts and garrison towns were founded at São Francisco do Sul, Florianopolis, and Porto Alegre (1743) to protect against both Spanish and French encroachments. What was to be the southernmost extension of Portuguese influence had earlier been staked out at La Colonia del Sacramento (1680) on the broad estuary of the Rio de la Plata, opposite Spanish Buenos Aires.

Far to the north similar political considerations led to the siting of towns along the coast and deep into the Amazon Basin. The intent of the settlement at Fortaleza (1609) is evident in its name, but other towns, such as São Luis (1594) (the French town of St. Louis taken in 1615), had the same role—to secure the north from Dutch, English, and further French occupation. A fort and, soon thereafter, a mission station were founded in 1616 at Belem (Bethlehem), followed by similar foundings at Santarem, Obidos, and Manaus (1674) and elsewhere along the navigable Amazon.

MORPHOLOGY OF THE COLONIAL CITY IN LATIN AMERICA

The morphology, or form, of any city reflects its past, and the clearest reflections are found in the street pattern, the size of city blocks, the dimensions of urban lots, and the surviving colonial architecture. In the typical Spanish American city, this colonial past is today on view in what is now the city core, commonly laid out in a gridiron of square or rectangular blocks subdivided into long, narrow lots along equally narrow streets. In Spanish America the pattern is a response to royal regulations that set out instructions for the siting of towns and for their layout, or platting, in a fairly precise manner. This included guidelines on the location and proportions of the main plaza, the disposition of public buildings around it, the cardinal directions of the streets, and other urban elements.

Initially, the royal instructions on town foundings that were given to the *conquistadores* and other early town founders were so broad and undefined as to preclude a uniform application, and it was only in 1514 that royal orders were coherently formulated. The postulates were more formally structured in 1523, but it was as late as 1573 before the so-called *Laws of the Indies* definitively outlined 28 rules and regulations for town siting and layout. By that time, of course, many colonial towns and cities were already in existence, sited and platted according to the more informal orders. Nonetheless, a regularity of layout was evident despite personal interpretations of the orders by individual town founders (Figure 6–3).

Most mining towns were exceptions to the royal mandates because waterpower was essential to the operation of milling equipment and because most mineral finds were in mountainous locations. For these reasons the town was usually located at the bottom of a long, narrow valley or on a hillside that offered little level land for large plazas and a gridiron pattern of streets. Instead, there were an elongated and irregular pattern of winding streets, irregularly sized and shaped blocks and plazas, and other informal features that today give towns such as Guanajuato and Taxco much of their charm.

Dating back at least to Vitrivius, a Roman planner of Greek background, the gridiron as it was imposed onto Latin America probably reflected multiple influences—those of the Italian Renaissance, the planned thirteenth-century *bastide* towns of southern France, and the military towns established during the *Reconquista*, when Spain was slowly recaptured from the Moors by Christian forces in the centuries just prior to the discovery of the Americas. But the pre-Columbian Indian cities in America also exhibited an essentially gridiron layout. In Mexico, both Teotihuacan and Tenochtitlán had gridiron layouts, as did the pre-Incan cities along the Peruvian coast. The largest of these, Chan-Chan, was essentially rectangular, with a symmetrical pattern of streets and irrigation canals.

The Incan town was characterized by two principal axes that met at a central square that was both a commercial and religious center. The placement of religious edifices and the homes of the noble class was similar to the Spanish practice. The later layout of a number of Andean colonial towns thus easily fits into the general lines of the Inca city, utilizing existing street patterns and the firm Incan stone foundations for the construction of new buildings. The Incan capital at Cuzco is a notable example of this blending. In the final analysis, the simple grid of blocks seems to have been independently "invented" in various parts of the world, including pre-Columbian America, as a way to subdivide land and provide for extensions as the town grew.

In contrast to the towns of Spanish America, those of Brazil were more clearly laid out with reference to function than to either formal or informal royal orders. In some places houses clustered around forts, forming a tight nucleus. Elsewhere towns tended to stretch out along a road and become more linear than nuclear in shape. Mining towns, as in Spanish America, were more influenced by terrain and mining considerations than by some plan. Most

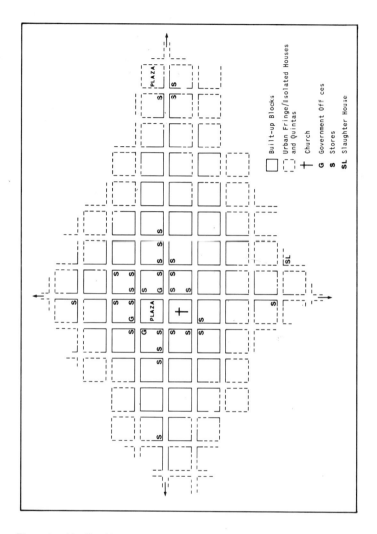

Figure 6.3 Idealized Layout and Land Uses in a Colonial Spanish Town

towns, nonetheless, did have some sort of a "natural" gridiron pattern, especially the early mission settlements that centered on the church, which itself faced a large rectangular *praça*, or plaza.

Land Uses

In any city there is both a segregation and a congregation dynamic in operation. Some land uses are incompatible—slaughterhouses and fine residences—and therefore ideally separated. On the other hand, it is often advantageous

for similar activities to cluster together, to congregate. Public buildings or people of like ethnic backgrounds or income congregate. These dynamics are ultimately expressed in downtown business districts, residential areas, and other
types of land use and are forms of land use clustering as old as the city itself.
At Teotihuacan, the pre-Aztec center, there was occupational specialization by
neighborhood, well-defined market areas, and a definite religious district. In
later Tenochtitlán as well, merchandise was sold in streets and quarters exclusively assigned to those goods, and the Inca capital of Cuzco had a similar segregation and congregation of functions.

There was a clear separation of land uses in both the Spanish and Portuguese colonial city. The heart of the city was its principal plaza, along whose
sides were located a church, government buildings, and some businesses. Nearby were the homes of many of the wealthy who sought a central location in order to enjoy easy access to the commercial outlets, government, and religious
offices. Some of the poor were intermixed with the more affluent, but most of
the middle- and lower-income group lived in *barrios* farther from the center.
Some of the wealthy, of course, chose not to live in the center, but more on the
periphery. Usually, however, the edge of town was reserved for the poor, the
Indians, and the municipal cemetery and slaughterhouse.

Such sharp economic, social, and political class distinctions were at the
heart of colonial society. At the apex of the social pyramid was the *peninsular*,
or immigrant, from Spain; next came the *criollo*, born in Latin America of
Spanish parents; the next level encompassed the *mestizos*; and at the bottom of
the social pyramid were the *mulattos, zambos,* and blacks. Income closely followed social rank, and the Indians were a separate class altogether, essentially
a slave class under the system of the *encomienda* that distributed both Indian
lands and the Indians to Spanish aristocrats. Brazilian towns were quite different in this respect; many of the elite lived not in town but on the coastal plantations. It was essentially a rural society.

Given the small size of a colonial town, it was only a short walk from the
fields, gardens, and hovels of the periphery to the heart of the town with its
jobs, shops, and amenities (Figure 6-4). The center of the city slowly became
the location of whatever public services—paved streets, municipal water, garbage collection, street lighting—that did exist, and this further enhanced its
appeal. There were few of these services before the end of the eighteenth century, however; for the colonial period all but the largest towns of Latin America have been characterized as somewhat "miserable" settlements with few
buildings beyond the core that had an appearance of elegance or permanence.
Most houses were crude thatch huts or more durable adobe shacks, and streets
were unpaved, filled with swirling dust and refuse in dry periods, a quagmire
in rainy times. Hogs ran loose to collect garbage, and dead animals lay in the
streets for days or even weeks. Outdoor toilets and private wells were close together and attracted infection and disease.

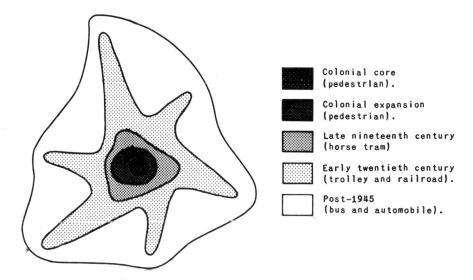

Colonial core
(pedestrian).

Colonial expansion
(pedestrian).

Late nineteenth century
(horse tram)

Early twentieth century
(trolley and railroad).

Post-1945
(bus and automobile).

Figure 6.4   Evolution of the Latin American City-Morphology

As a town slowly grew despite periodic epidemics, new *barrios*, which were marginal in more than just location, formed on the edge of town, as did new plazas, which often became business subcenters. The significant commercial, political, religious, and industrial activities remained firmly entrenched in the central city, however. Thus the cities of the colonial period can be fairly described as mononuclear, with slow growth taking place in a more or less concentric pattern out from that center. As the town grew, the *barrios* like the older ones, gained a strong neighborhood identity and, as in any city, a person's residence became a part of the personal identification of the individual.

The Evolution of the Modern Latin American City

For most of Latin America the early decades of the nineteenth century brought political emancipation. The latter decades brought forth its entry into world markets and a diffusion into Latin America of the fruits of Europe's earlier and ongoing agricultural and industrial revolutions. With these fundamental changes came a restructuring of the old colonial urban systems and major alterations in the internal morphology of the cities. The timing and intensity of these shifts varied widely, but all cities ultimately were influenced by the way in which they combined or resisted modern industrial technology, new modes of transportation, population changes, agricultural technology, and a host of other factors.

Mineral resource exploitation expanded from precious metals into the extraction of industrial minerals such as copper, tin, and iron ore. Agricultural areas were opened or restructured as newly introduced railroads tied them to European markets by extending the hinterlands of the ports. Technological advances such as the marine steam engine, the steel hull, the screw propeller, and refrigeration all effectively reduced the time, costs, and perishability distance between Latin American fields and major world markets.

The earlier colonial ports and political-commercial capitals continued to be especially favored in this enlarged commercial era, because the introduction of modern world trade and industrialization centered on the larger cities, and logically so. These cities were the source of an available and relatively skilled labor supply and the core of transportation networks that collected raw materials and shipped finished goods. Additionally, the cities were sources of investment capital and major markets in their own right. Urban growth thus became even more selective and intense than in the colonial period, because some cities were favored by being major administrative centers, transportation nodes, manufacturing centers, and major sources of capital and information.

The new economic system imposed by modern world trade patterns meant that hundreds of settlements became more peripheral to the commercial-industrial order that was evolving. The urban stagnation that followed for such towns was particularly acute in parts of Central and Andean America where poor access, physical limitations, economic restraints, and the lure of the larger cities precluded growth. Many towns grew little if at all. They were effectively bypassed by modern technology and even robbed of their traditional economic base as the development of the national economy and the growth of other regions worked to their disadvantage.

It is useful to look at some of the recurrent processes behind urban change by examining the continuing evolution of the urban network in areas already outlined in the colonial period.

Mexico, Central America, and the Caribbean

Mexico. Mexico City has persisted as Mexico's major urban area. Aided by the development of trade and industry, tourism, and politics, it is today the largest of Latin America's cities, while regional centers such as Guadalajara, Puebla, and Monterrey have also grown rapidly.

The growth of tourism has added significantly to the economic base of many Mexican cities, such as the colonial port of Acapulco and Puerto Vallarta, Mazatlan, and Veracruz. Inland cities such as Gunajuato, now preserved in part as a national monument, Taxco, Oaxaca, and Merida, the latter in the fast-developing Yucatan, also benefit significantly from international tourism.

On the Gulf coast the old towns of Tampico and Tuxpan grew in the early twentieth century as oil fields were exploited. The expansion of irrigated agriculture has particularly impelled the growth of towns in northern Mexico, towns such as Torreon in the highlands, Mexicali in the Colorado River delta, and numerous towns along the Rio Grande. Along the Gulf of California, agricultural centers such as Ciudad Obregon, Los Mochis, and Culiacan have also been favored by an expansion of irrigated agriculture as dams have been constructed to hold the waters off the Sierra Madre Occidental.

Perhaps the most spectacular example of rapid urban growth in the twentieth century is along the U.S.-Mexican border where, from Tijuana on the Pacific to Matamoros on the Gulf of Mexico, formerly insignificant towns (particularly Tijuana, Mexicali, Nogales, Ciudad Juarez, Nuevo Laredo, and Matamoros) have become sizable cities (Table 6-1). The origins of these and smaller border towns is uncommonly diverse: El Paso del Norte (Ciudad Juarez after 1888) began as a mission town in 1659, while Matamoros developed after 1824 as a refugee community for blacks escaping Texas. Nuevo Laredo was founded about 1850 by Mexican nationals who moved south after lands north of the river became part of the United States. Nogales evolved as a market town about 1860 on a cattle trail, while Mexicali was founded about 1902 as a consequence of irrigation development in the Colorado River delta. Tijuana, a ranch settlement as early as 1840, was only established as a town about 1903.

Characteristic of all the Mexican border towns and cities is a strong symbiotic relationship with the United States, a function of dependence on U.S. markets, tourism, and employment on the U.S. side for many Mexican nationals. The distance of these towns from the economic heart of Mexico and the arid character of the intervening space reinforces the close relationship with the United States. Particularly in the last decade, duty-free zones have been established to attract U.S. industry to the Mexican side of the border. In part this is a response to tightening entry requirements for Mexican workers into the United States; it also occurred in order to take advantage of inexpensive Mexican labor and lower operating costs. Electronics firms, garment manufacturers, and furniture makers are among the most common enterprises that have moved into the duty-free zones.

Table 6-1 Population of Border Towns

City (west to east)	1900	1920	1940	1950	1960	1968	1977
Tijuana		3,500	16,500	60,000	151,900	297,000	438,000
Mexicali	2,600	7,000	18,800	65,000	172,600	347,000	360,500
Nogales	2,700	13,400	13,900	24,500	37,700	62,000	
Ciudad Juarez	8,200	20,000	48,900	123,000	262,200	477,000	570,400
Nuevo Laredo	8,000	15,000	28,900	57,700	92,700	141,000	214,000
Matamoros	8,300	18,000	28,200	45,700	92,300	158,000	187,000

Source. Statesman's Yearbook.

Note: Some figures are estimates.

Once resident in a border town, relatively few Mexicans return to the interior, and the combination of high in-migration from the interior and natural population increase is reflected in the population growth of these border towns. Rapid growth came especially after about 1940 as a result of expanded irrigation projects, the employment of Mexican *braceros* in U.S. agriculture (either legally or illegally), increased American tourism, and the development of local manufacturing. In 1900 the six major towns had a combined population of approximately 30,000 persons; by 1980 the same cities had a combined population of over 2 million.

Central America. It is characteristic of the smaller Central American republics and the Caribbean islands that one city is dominant. Guatemala City, San Salvador, Tegucigalpa, Managua, San José, and Panama each are the capital, principal commercial center, industrial node, and cultural hub of their respective country. The desirability of this concentration in one city will be examined shortly. While these cities dominate, they are in many instances coming to represent a lesser proportion of the total urban population of their countries than formerly, because smaller regional centers are developing rapidly. Small but growing port towns on both the Caribbean and Pacific coasts route goods in and out of the major cities and act as export points for local agricultural and mineral products. Tourism is also more and more important in the urban economy. In Guatemala, for instance, the old Indian towns such as Chichicastenango and Huehuetenango and the colonial capital of Antigua are tourist favorites.

Unlike much of Latin America, however, the present hierarchy of cities in Central America does not represent the simple continuation of the colonial pattern inasmuch as some political centers shifted in the nineteenth century. For example, San José became the capital of Costa Rica only in 1823, replacing nearby Cartago. With the independence of Nicaragua came a strong rivalry for dominance between liberals based in Leon and conservatives based in Granada; this was resolved in 1858 by making the old Indian town of Managua a compromise capital. The capital of Honduras moved from Comayagua to Tegucigalpa in 1880.

The development in the twentieth century of large banana plantations in the lowlands of Central America led to the appearance of company towns, some new ports, and the growth of existing places. Among these were the company towns of La Lima and Aguan in Honduras and the growth of the Costa Rican ports of Puntarenas and Puerto Limon. Coffee production has played a role in enhancing some ports of Central America. The cutting of hardwoods has led to the growth of other small towns and ports. The impact of the Panama Canal on the economy of that country needs little comment, and its existence is a major factor in the growth of towns and cities along its route.

Caribbean. In the Caribbean the major towns of the colonial period remain the magnets for the wealth and population of each country. In Jamaica, for instance, Kingston remains the dominant center, although resort clusters around Montego Bay and Ocho Rios generate tourist revenues if not many jobs. In Haiti the capital of Port-au-Prince increasingly dominates the earlier center of Cap Haitien and the smaller cities, while to the east Santo Domingo continues to be the primary city of the Dominican Republic. San Juan remains the prime attraction in Puerto Rico. The smaller islands of the Lesser Antilles have little potential for the development of important secondary cities, given their small physical size and limited economic potential. In the Netherlands Antilles, Willemstad stands virtually alone, favored both by a large refinery and considerable tourist trade.

In common with the other islands, virtually all of Cuba's major colonial towns had been sited on the coast, with contact between them principally by water. The expansion of that network came with the concurrent development of sugar plantations and the first railroad in Latin America (1836) that took sugar to coastal ports. As plantations developed, so did small towns. Havana nevertheless maintained its position as the principal metropolitan area, center of manufacturing and shipping, tourism, and gambling. Until the Cuban Revolution of 1959, the latter two activities were important sources of income, given the short distance to Florida and the entire eastern seaboard of the United States.

Andean America

Here, as elsewhere in Latin America, the older major cities have remained the economic, social, and cultural centers of regional and national development. Caracas, Bogotá, Lima, La Paz, and Santiago now are all important national manufacturing and commercial centers as well as political capitals. But there has also been rapid growth of secondary centers such as Medellin and Cali in Colombia, the port city of Guayaquil in Ecuador, and the ports of Valparaiso and Concepción in Chile.

Commercial agriculture and mineral resource exploitation have persisted as the major base on which the urban system has grown beyond the major cities. The extraction of industrial raw materials, especially oil, tin, copper, and iron ore, has led to the creation of new mining towns and new ports since the middle of the nineteenth century. In a number of countries there has been the development of at least one city as a steelmaking town but, in some cases, these cities are more nationalistic symbols of "economic development" than rational economic operations in a worldwide context.

Among the first resource towns to develop in the nineteenth century were the nitrate ports of Iquique and Taltal. In Peru the silver and copper town of

Cerro de Pasco (1630) declined in the nineteenth century but has since re-bounded as advances in mining technology and rising prices have made mining profitable again. In 1966 the old townsite was abandoned because it sat atop now valuable ores that could be extracted by open-pit mining. In Bolivia Po-tosí has never regained its colonial rank as a silver city, but it is now an impor-tant tin center, as is the nearby colonial town of Oruro. Very few towns gained importance for coal mining. Peruvian iron ore has been important in the devel-opment of Marcona and the port of San Juan.

In Venezuela the exploitation of iron ore deposits south of the Orinoco has promoted urban growth at El Pao and Cerro Bolivar and has encouraged a planned center of heavy industry. In addition to iron and steel production, Ciudad Guayana is developing metal fabricating industries, an aluminum plant, and other enterprises in order to promote national industrial diversifica-tion and provide a viable alternative to the major cities as "migration targets" and "growth poles." Upstream, Ciudad Bolivar (earlier Angostura, 1764) was transformed in the late nineteenth century into a small port for the Venezuelan interior. The oil-rich Maracaibo Basin saw extensive development beginning in the late 1920s and, with it, the growth of the colonial town of Maracaibo into a city of over one-half million inhabitants.

The areas of greatest potential for oil are now along the eastern flank of the Andes, where there are already a number of oil towns. Although there were some settlements east of the Andes in the colonial period, this remote portion of Latin America is only now really being incorporated into national econo-mies. As roads are constructed over the Andes and along the flanks of the mountains, the older, isolated colonial towns all the way from Venezuela to Bolivia are slowly growing, and new oil towns are developing.

On the Pacific side of the Andes irrigated areas have particularly ex-panded in the coastal oases of Peru, leading to the growth of towns such as Chiclayo and Trujillo. Offshore, the enormous if sporadic harvest of ancho-vies has led to the development of fish meal factories at Chimbote and other coastal towns. Chimbote additionally benefits from being Peru's center of iron and steel production.

As early as the 1850s, German colonization was significant in the develop-ment of southern Chile, particularly in and to the south of colonial Concep-ción, a city of some importance today partly because of the iron and steel plant at nearby Huachipato. German immigration led to the growth of the colonial towns of Valdivia and Osorno and the establishment of the German towns of Puerto Montt (1853) and Puerto Varas (1854). The area today remains strong-ly agricultural, with local industry related primarily to agricultural processing and softwood production, although Puerto Montt also enjoys the benefits of a sizable fishing fleet. Situated in the spectacular lake and volcanic district of Chile, these small towns also enjoy some tourism, disadvantaged only by their distance from the major urban areas of central Chile.

Valparaiso remains one of Chile's most important ports, serving Santiago and the agricultural towns of the rich Central Valley. One of its suburbs, Viña del Mar, is Chile's major beach resort, but the cold Pacific waters here make Viña less attractive for tourists than the warmer-water resorts on the Atlantic coasts of Argentina, Uruguay, and Brazil.

The La Plata Countries

Argentina. Urban Argentina is one of the world's outstanding examples of the impact on regional and urban development of industrial technology, agricultural advances, improved access to markets, and large-scale immigration. Much like Potosí in colonial Peru, it demonstrates how the prevailing market system distributes people and their towns in a way that serves the goals of the system.

The transformation of the sparsely settled and unfarmed *pampas* into an intensive network of towns and fields was initiated by a 100-year campaign of frontier expansion and Indian extermination that began in 1779 and terminated with the so-called "Conquest of the Desert" between 1879 and 1883. The expansion of the frontier resulted in a network of forts and adjacent small settlements. The earliest of these garrison towns was less than 100 miles south of Buenos Aires, along a line that lay to the north of the Rio Salado. As late as 1815 it was estimated that only 600 persons of European stock lived south of the Salado. In contrast, by 1870 there were 100,000 Europeans living south of the river, most of them in the expanded network of fort towns. In all, about 50 settlements were established on the *pampas* in the 100 years after 1779.

Railroad construction, agricultural development, and European immigration onto the *pampas* turned many of these small, crude garrison settlements into farm towns late in the nineteenth century. Political decisions made some of them county seats. A number of new settlements were laid out along the railroads, as the intent was to establish stations every 12 miles along the rail lines. All of the towns depended on the railroad to move the wheat and cattle from the *pampas* to the ports, especially Buenos Aires, but also Rosario and Bahia Blanca.

The focus of the entire rail network was Buenos Aires, and that city grew accordingly, from 178,000 in 1869 to 1,561,000 in 1914. The population of its suburbs, reached by suburban service over the same rail lines that went onto the *pampas*, totaled 450,000 in 1914, giving the metropolitan area a population of 2 million. Not far away, the city of La Plata was laid out after 1882 as the capital of the province of Buenos Aires, for Buenos Aires, the former provincial capital, became the national capital at that time.

Today, the expansive city of Buenos Aires and its suburbs continue to dominate Argentina economically, socially, culturally, and politically, but cities like Cordoba, Rosario, Tucuman, Mendoza, Bahia Blanca, and the beach resort of Mar del Plata are important regional centers.

Uruguay. Across the broad, shallow estuary of the Paraná River, the capital city of Montevideo has functioned much like Buenos Aires, but on a smaller scale. As Uruguay's major port, capital, and business and industrial center, it has come to dominate the urban network completely. Towns such as Fray Bentos (meat processing), Paysandu and Salto along the Uruguay River, and Durazno on the plains are outlying centers in a settlement pattern that has always focused on Montevideo. Along the Atlantic coast some small settlements, notably Piriapolis and Punta del Este, have evolved into important beach resorts, as popular with Argentines as with Uruguayans.

Paraguay. The old colonial city of Asunción is the center of the very limited industrial and commercial growth of Paraguay. To the east of Asunción lie the country's more prosperous agricultural lands and farm towns; to the north are a number of small lumber towns.

Brazil

In Brazil two cities have risen to a position of dominance—Rio de Janeiro, the traditional center, port and capital, and São Paulo, the interior city of commerce and industry. Several other cities have evolved into regional centers.

The sugar and gold booms of colonial Brazil were followed in the late nineteenth century by a coffee boom. First grown in quantity in the Paraiba Valley near Rio de Janeiro, coffee expanded into the highlands north and west of São Paulo in the 1880s, especially to zones where the rich *terra roxa* (purple soils) were found. With the expanding coffee frontier came new towns that filled with European immigrants. As in Argentina, the expansion of the railroad went hand in hand with this movement. Lines radiated from São Paulo, a transportation node itself connected with the port of Santos by the single easy rail route off the Great Escarpment first opened in 1867. The rail network in time became second only to that of the Argentine *pampas*, and many coffee towns of all sizes, such as Ribeirao Prêto, Rio Claro, São Carlos, and Botucatu, prospered throughout the region. Campinas, as a transportation node, grew especially rapidly. Santos became the world's principal coffee port.

As in Argentina, dissatisfaction with the poor rural living conditions and low financial rewards encouraged many of the area's European immigrants to move back into the towns. They moved especially into São Paulo, which grew from about 30,000 in 1870 to 240,000 in 1900 and 1 million in 1930. Already by 1900, as coffee profits were locally invested in industry and commerce, São Paulo was becoming an industrial and financial center. It remains so today and ranks ahead of Rio de Janeiro, despite the fact that there has been considerable economic decentralization to nearby cities such as Sorocaba, Jundiai, and Campinas.

Between São Paulo and Rio de Janeiro is one of the earliest of Latin America's steel centers. Volta Redonda was planned by the national government after 1941 as a "model city," and its location and good access by rail for both raw materials and the movement of finished products to the major cities help explain its success as a steel town. Rio de Janeiro, of course, remains a major industrial and commercial center, port and, until 1960, national capital. Rio is also world famous for tourism, with its spectacular setting of mountains and sea and the fine beaches of suburbs such as Copacabana and Ipanema.

During the nineteenth century, as before, it was Brazilian policy to encourage settlement wherever there was a zone of contact with the Spanish. One such area was the south of Brazil, where agricultural colonization became common. The German settlement at São Leopoldo (1824) was the first of the government-sponsored colonies and the nucleus of a settlement region into which more than 20,000 Germans moved by 1869. A second, more northerly concentration of German colonies occurred in the settlements of Joinville (1849) and Blumenau (1850). Small Italian settlements in the south developed in the 1870s and 1880s concurrent with the large-scale Italian immigration into the more northerly states of Minas Gerais and São Paulo.

Without question, the most famous city to develop in the Brazilian interior has been the new capital of Brasilia. The search for an internal capital location dates back to independence in 1889, but the project was initiated only in 1956. The new city was meant to serve two principal purposes: first, to remove political activities to a neutral location away from the dominant Rio de Janeiro-São Paulo axis; and second, to provide a "growth pole" or area of attraction for the economic development of the interior. Inaugurated in 1960, Brasilia that year already had a population of about 13,000; by 1970 the population was 550,000 well above the population limit of 500,000 initially planned. By 1980, it will reach over 1 million!

The miscalculation of projected population aside, complaints about Brasilia range from distress over its distance from Rio de Janeiro (about 600 miles) to problems of inadequate water supply, a critical housing shortage, and a somewhat sterile urban and rural environment. On the positive side, it has drawn attention and investment capital to the largely undeveloped interior, but it is still too early to assess the effect of Brasilia on interior development.

Famous as it is, the creation of an entirely new capital like Brasilia is nothing new to Brazil. Teresina was founded in 1852 as an inland administrative and commercial center for northeastern Brazil, and Belo Horizonte was laid out in 1896 as a new capital for the state of Minas Gerais, replacing the colonial mining town of Ouro Prêto. Here as in another planned capital, Washington, D.C., the layout is characterized by the wide, diagonal streets, boulevards, and "round points" that are the heritage of baroque city planning. The city of Goiânia was occupied in 1937 as a new state capital, planned as an alternative to the lower, warmer, and unhealthier old gold town of Goiás 70 miles away.

The distribution of population in Latin America suggests that much of Latin America's population today is urban. In 1978, 60 percent of the population lived in urban areas, although many such areas would lack the urban facilities expected in North America. The twentieth century has essentially seen the intensification of a preexisting urban network. As this chapter has shown, much of that network was created in the colonial period, but there were important new areas of urban growth in the nineteenth century as Latin America became more involved in trade.

The Modern Latin American City

The typical Latin American city was small at the close of the colonial period and remained so toward the end of the nineteenth century. The median population of the 40 largest cities in 1880 was about 35,000, and there were only 8 cities in Latin America with a population in excess of 100,000. By 1970, in contrast, there were about 150 such cities, a number of which were within large metropolitan areas composed of a major city and outlying towns. In 1880 the largest city was Rio de Janeiro, with a population of about 350,000; by 1980 the largest metropolitan area will be Mexico City, with an estimated population in excess of 13,600,000, followed by São Paulo, Buenos Aires, and Rio de Janeiro (Table 6-2).

This transition to the large metropolis clearly has not occurred at the same time throughout Latin America. For some of the largest cities the transition began in the late nineteenth century as they began to profit from the expansion of commercial agriculture tied to foreign markets, federal expenditures, increasing trade, and the development of industry. Initially, large-scale immigration from abroad was a more important factor to growth than the movement of native-born from rural areas to the cities. This pattern is probably best exemplified by Buenos Aires, Rio de Janeiro, and São Paulo. Most of today's large cities, however, grew rapidly only after 1900, with notable population gains registered by 1950. But even this increase proved to be modest compared with that during the last 30 years. In this century urban growth has been tied to movement from rural areas and small towns instead of to large-scale immigration from overseas. In addition, the birthrate has soared and the death rate has declined.

Until after the 1930s, the large cities were predominantly commercial and administrative centers with limited industrial production. The bulk of the major manufactured items consumed came from Europe and the United States through the same ports that exported agricultural and mineral products. Local industry was mainly restricted to items that were protected from larger-scale foreign manufacturers by distance, transportation costs, and duties. Preeminent among these local urban industries were food processing, textiles, and household goods, such as mattresses and other bulky, low-value products.

The orientation of the Latin American city to manufacturing perceptibly changed with the worldwide economic depression of the 1930s and World War II. Both events stimulated government policy to encourage manufacturing in order to replace products previously imported from industrial countries. The rise of a broader spectrum of large-scale manufacturing throughout Latin America can generally be dated from this period. Consequently, the major metropolitan areas are industrial as well as commercial centers today.

There are, of course, sound reasons why industries are most closely related to larger cities. These include the *external economies* created by direct linkages between industries, as when the finished output of one factory becomes the "raw material" of a second. There are also *urbanization economies* such as the existence of local capital, a large labor pool, and an existing supply of workers' housing, however inadequate it might be. In addition, the cities are the centers of innovation, invention, and information—valuable prerequisites for industrial expansion. Finally, the large city is also a major market itself because of its large resident population and because of the customarily higher purchasing power of urban residents compared to rural populations.

The number of cities sharing these advantages has expanded considerably in the last 30 years so that there has been considerable commercial and industrial growth in regional centers outside the major metropolitan area. Cities such as Cordoba, Concepción, Chimbote, Cali, Medellin, Ciudad Guayana, Guadalajara, and Monterrey and a number of cities in the Rio de Janeiro-São Paulo regions have become more important industrial centers. Some of these growth poles are protected by distance from the competition of the major cities, but others represent important centers for the production of goods for national and international markets and intentionally benefit from transportation and communications improvements that draw the regional industrial cities closer together and facilitate the interchange of products and ideas.

The lure of the major cities in terms of both employment and the *demonstration effect*, a heightened awareness that urban dwellers generally live better than their rural counterparts, has attracted vast numbers of the rural population to the city. This attraction, moreover, is reinforced by negative factors such as the harshness, poverty, and hopelessness of much of rural life. Together, these so-called "push-pull" forces have led millions to the cities, whether or not employment and housing existed. As noted in Chapter 5, this migration often occurs as a *step migration*, the first step being a move from the countryside into a smaller city and subsequently the move from the smaller to the larger city. Others come directly from rural areas into the larger cities. Either way, this rural-to-urban flow accounts for a large portion of the rapid population growth of Latin American cities in the last decades. High birthrates in the city are also a significant factor of growth. The process of *urbanization* leads to the growth of cities of all sizes and, in several cases, reduces the former dominance of one single city in a country. In Central America, for instance, the share of urban population is rising, but the share of that urban population found in the single major city is declining and should continue to do so.

Internal Structure of the Postcolonial City

Even today many of Latin America's towns and small cities are not significantly different in *form* or *function* from what they were in the colonial period. They do not look exactly the same because there have been cosmetic, superficial changes—electric street lights, automobiles, high-rise apartments—as the result of modern technology. The picture is starkly different for the regional and national centers, however, where nineteenth- and twentieth-century population increases are combined with technology, new forms of transportation, and the development of speculation in urban land on a large scale. Here the overall *form* and the *internal structure* have been strongly affected, and the cosmetic effect of modern architecture has given them a new face.

Typically, the colonial city had been mononuclear, with the focus on the commercial and governmental areas of the central city. Residential *barrios* lay at the edge of this center and access between the two was generally by foot. As the larger cities grew, other means of access were devised. The first of such innovation, introduced about 1870, was the horse-drawn tram on rails, but its inherent limitations precluded any real effect on either the nuclear shape or the pedestrian-oriented structure of the cities. Its service was usually too infrequent, too slow, and too expensive to allow workers living in the central city to move into newer suburbs on the edge. In any case, most workers could easily walk to work from their crowded inner-city apartments or lodgings. None could afford land on the periphery.

The electric trolley had a much greater impact. First introduced into Latin American cities in about 1900 and widespread by the 1920s, it was faster and more dependable than the horse tram and allowed middle-income city dwellers to live farther from the city center. In Lima, for instance, outlying beach towns became upper- and middle-income suburbs after the adoption of the trolley shortly after 1900. In Rio de Janeiro the development of the beach areas at Copacabana and Ipanema was equally tied to trolley access. The extensive trolley network of Buenos Aires, begun in 1898, opened large areas of the adjacent *pampas* to settlement. Similarly, Mexico City and Caracas saw suburban development with the trolley, and even smaller cities, such as Quito, were markedly affected in their form by the trolley extensions.

Suburban rail service became significant only in a very few of the larger cities, especially Buenos Aires, but the bus was widely adopted in the Latin American city in the middle 1920s. Its widespread use, especially in the past three decades, has helped in the large-scale development of residential areas that formerly were too far from the city core or too distant from trolley lines to be settled. Increasing use of the automobile, still not widely used because of its high cost for most urban dwellers, also favors some suburban developments.

All these transportation modes usually concentrated on the central business district (CBD), making it the point of maximum accessibility for the entire urban area, just as it was in the colonial period. Today, the CBD of the typical Latin American city is strong and growing, although a number of outlying shopping streets or districts siphon off some of the trade. In some of the larger cities the partial *replication* of the CBD in terms of more elegant goods is taking place in prosperous neighborhoods, but this does not challenge most central-city stores.

As industry developed in the city, certain districts came to have a strong industrial character. Noxious industries and those requiring much space, such as stockyards, were located on the edge of the city, even in the colonial period, and had to be relocated as the city expanded. Recently, planned industrial areas have been developed on the periphery of some cities. Port districts evolved as important industrial zones as well, since imported raw materials and coal for power generation were often essential to large-scale production. Rio de Janeiro, Lima (Callao), and Buenos Aires, for example, all have important water-oriented industrial districts. Except for large-scale, noxious, or port industries, however, there is still little segregation of small-scale industry in the city. It is common today to find numerous and important manufacturing operations in middle- and upper-income residential areas as well as in working-class districts. As elsewhere in the world, city planning and restrictive measures such as zoning are relatively recent (post-1930 at the earliest) and have but limited effectiveness in truly controlling land use. As elsewhere, including the United States, private interests hold the upper hand in influencing the direction and form of urban growth.

Buenos Aires: A Case Study

An outstanding example of the way in which all these influences affect the outward form and internal functioning of a large city is the metropolitan area of greater Buenos Aires, which has been transformed in the past 100 years from a collection of isolated small villages and the port city of Buenos Aires itself to an enormous metropolitan area that today has a population of 10 million. As

Greater Buenos Aires (Platted area shown in black)

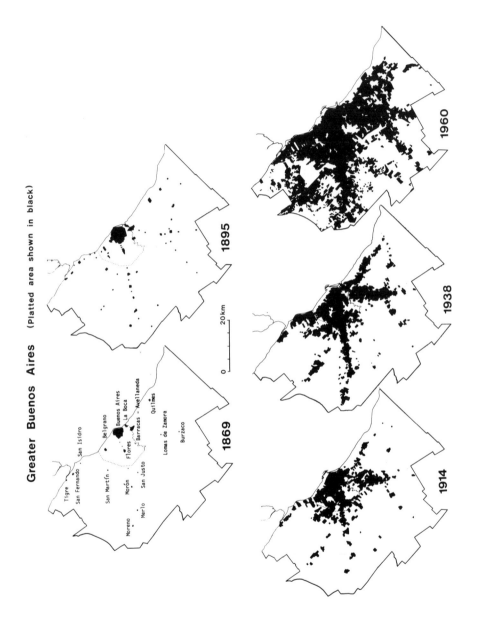

such, the metropolitan region, known as Gran Buenos Aires, clearly demonstrates how population and economic growth, transportation innovations, and the real estate market interacted to create a modern, multinucleated urban area (Figure 6–5).

As late as the 1850s Buenos Aires was a city of 90,000, despite a colonial past that, in the 1770s, made it a political and economic center of some importance. At the edge of the city, along the roads that led onto the *pampas*, were a number of small colonial towns and farming districts that had a total population no greater than 30,000. By 1870 there were 170,000 people in Buenos Aires plus another 50,000 in the outlying areas that were in part connected by rail to the port at Buenos Aires. Some of the outlying towns became the locale of summer homes for wealthy *porteños*, as the residents of the port city of Buenos Aires are called. These outlying areas and Buenos Aires itself constitute what is today Gran Buenos Aires.

With Buenos Aires itself, there was a single important commercial and political core, oriented north-south in response to the port and east-west along the major road out into the countryside. Several small subcenters evolved at the principal plazas on the edge of town. Until late in the nineteenth century the city's population was highly concentrated in this nucleus. And the population grew rapidly, mostly a consequence of European immigration, to 656,000 in 1895. Italians and Spaniards, in a ratio of 5 to 3, accounted for much of this growth.

With this population gain came the growth of the small, compact, urban core of 1870 to the more extensive, but still mononuclear city of 1895. Access to the expanding fringe before about 1900 was facilitated by some suburban trains and an extensive system of horse-drawn trams (Figure 6–6), but *porteños* were still clustered in the heart of the city. Relatively few had the money to buy land on the suburban fringe, and the slow speed of the horse tram precluded a long distance journey to work. The horse tram most effectively served the dense core, not the far reaches of the city.

The population of Buenos Aires rose from 656,000 in 1895 to 2,287,000 in 1930. With that growth came increased crowding in the central city but also the development of the periphery on a large scale. *Porteños* could use the faster trolley, introduced in 1898, to get free of the crowded core (Figure 6–7). And there was credit available for the purchase of a suburban lot after landowners and auctioneers began to utilize the *venta por mensualidades*, the sale at auction of small lots paid for in monthly payments. The combination of *porteño* demand for land, the trolley, and the new credit device resulted in the familiar ''checkerboard'' or ''leapfrog'' pattern of extensive urban land development along the trolley lines. After the introduction of the bus in the 1920s, other areas came under development.

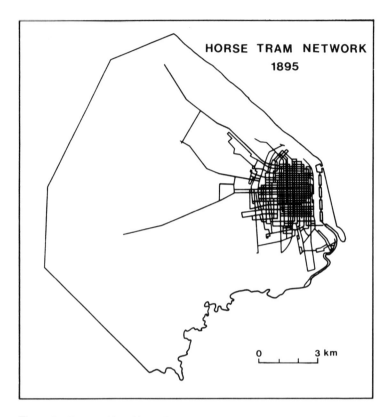

Figure 6.6 Buenos Aires: Horse Tram Network, 1895

Access to the countryside beyond the Buenos Aires trolley lines also improved as the frequency and speed of suburban trains encouraged many to move into the railroad corridors, thereby creating new towns and turning earlier summer towns and speculative subdivisions into year-round commuter towns. Population in the districts outside the boundaries of Buenos Aires, but still within greater Buenos Aires, rose from 118,000 in 1895 to an estimated 770,000 in 1930. The population of greater Buenos Aires in 1930 was thus over 3 million.

Many could not make the move to the periphery, however. Most of the poor could not afford to move, and most of the wealthy did not care to leave the amenities of the more affluent inner-city *barrios*. The middle-income office worker and the skilled industrial worker built up most of the peripheral *barrios* that only slowly acquired urban amenities. Initially, entire *barrios* were subdivided without regard to sanitation standards, and rarely did the seller put in a paved street or other facilities. In the absence of zoning, any piece of land

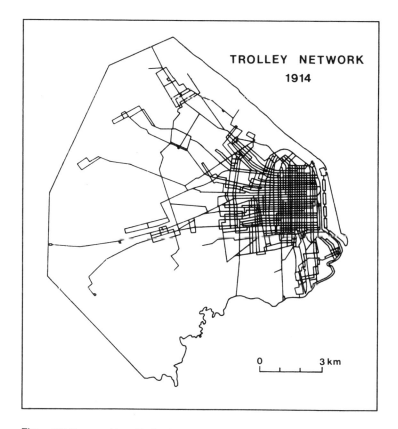

Figure 6.7 Buenos Aires: Trolley Network, 1914

might be used for a residence, a store, or an industrial facility. The result by 1930 was a sprawling metropolitan area with a crowded core composed of the poor in slums, the wealthy in mansions and apartments, and the middle class interspersed among these two extremes in the central city and on the periphery.

From 1930 to 1970 the population of greater Buenos Aires rose, mostly because of internal migration and general population increase instead of immigration from abroad, from 3,057,000 to 8,350,000. By 1980 it exceeded 10 million. A large percentage of that population went to the periphery, first to towns and lands along the railroads and trolley lines, but more and more also to the interstices of the rail lines in the *alrededores* as bus transportation improved. By 1960 more were living outside the federal district than within it, an increasing share of them in squalid *villas miserias*, or squatters' settlements.

Growth within the bounds of Buenos Aires has exhibited several distinctive patterns after 1930: (1) a filling-in of the peripheral area; (2) relatively steady and high central-city population densities; (3) increasing population density in the upper-income sectors as high-rise apartment blocks in great number were built, in part replacing older mansions; (4) population stagnation in the older industrial lowlands; and (5) the large-scale development of the shantytown, or *villa miseria*, as immigration from the provinces to Buenos Aires added to the traditional housing shortage. The central city continued to grow in importance after 1930 as subway lines built in the 1930s and early 1940s sharpened the focus already established on the CBD by the trolley, train, and an earlier 1913 subway line. The core began to share the commercial fruits of metropolitan growth with outlying commercial centers only in the 1950s and 1960s, but it is still dominant in commerce and virtually the sole cultural and entertainment focus for the entire metropolitan area.

With a population today of about 10 million, greater Buenos Aires ranks as one of the largest metropolitan areas in Latin America. It dominates Argentina and indications are that the city, although it may be experiencing diminishing returns in terms of the economies of urbanization, will continue to grow.

Contemporary Urban Problems in Latin America

The evolution of cities such as Buenos Aires, Rio de Janeiro, São Paulo, and Mexico City differs from that of other contemporary Latin Amerian cities only in timing and scale, not in the urban forces at work. As late as 1930 most Latin American cities were still relatively small in population and compact in form, with poorly developed intraurban transportation, little modern large-scale factory production, or other conditions recognized as prerequisites to the development of a modern metropolis. It was only after 1930 that the large rural-to-urban movements, now so characteristic of Latin America and other parts of the developing world, began on a large scale and that a number of cities grew rapidly. Today, these cities have come to share the problems of rapid urban expansion. Principal among these problems are housing, transportation, environmental deterioration, and limited employment opportunities for the growing population.

At least since the end of the colonial period, both the inadequacy and the shortage of housing have been major problems in the Latin American city. The magnitude of the problem is suggested by an estimate that in order simply to have *maintained* the same housing deficit in 1975 that existed in 1960 (when there was a need for 7 million urban housing units), almost 19 million urban dwellings would have had to be constructed. Unfortunately, the obstacles to such housing goals are numerous. The rapid urbanization of a country's growing population, the gap between the income of most workers and the rising cost of dwellings, the rising cost of land, the limitations of national financing agencies, the absence of housing policy in most countries, bureaucratic obstacles to construction, and the backwardness of the building industry all point to continued housing deficits.

Paradoxically, the major Latin American cities are visually striking because of the many modern high-rise office buildings and apartment houses. These buildings, however, serve what are really increasingly minority groups in the city: the stronger commercial elements and the more affluent city dwellers. In few cities, if any, does a housing shortage affect the wealthy or comfortable. The problem is in housing the ever-growing lower-income masses that flow in from smaller cities and directly from the countryside. The result has been proliferation of the central-city slum with its high population densities and poor living conditions and, especially in the last 20 years, the development of many squatter settlements in and about all the larger cities of Latin America. The squatters are either new in-migrants to the city or come from inner-city slums that are more crowded and more expensive than the squatter settlements. It is estimated that about 60 percent of the population of Bogotá and close to 50 percent of the population of Mexico City lives in either slums or squatter settlements. Caracas, Brasilia, Lima, Rio de Janeiro, Buenos Aires, and Santiago all have 25 to 40 percent of their population living in squatter settlements.

The generic name of these squatter settlements varies by country, being known as *favelas* in parts of Brazil, *poblaciones callampas* (mushroom towns) in Chile, *villas miserias* in Argentina, *ranchos* in Venezuela, *barriadas* in Peru and Panama, and *poblaciones tugurios* in Mexico. By whatever name, a common characteristic of these *barrios populares* is their location on marginal lands, either on the periphery of the built-up zone, along railroad tracks, on vacant pieces of public property, or on lands unsuitable for conventional land uses. Some of the *favelas* of Rio de Janeiro are good examples of the latter; they are in an inner-city location, but on steep slopes unsuitable for conventional commercial or residential usage.

Public ownership of the land is most common in areas of squatter settlement but, in many cases, the settlements are on privately owned land, on some of which rent is paid. The development of these has been slow and piecemeal, but there are many cases of planned "invasions" of vacant land. In such an instance makeshift homes are constructed, often overnight, with materials collected in advance and in accordance with a general plan for land occupance. The intent is to make it both morally and physically difficult to be dislocated by authorities.

Although some dwellings in squatter settlements are of cinder block, many other dwellings are constructed of whatever materials are available— scrap wood, cardboard, and flattened tin cans. Public services are scarce, with few sources of water, little or no paving, no sewer lines, no garbage collection, and only limited provisions of electricity. Sanitation conditions in shantytowns are therefore marginal, and rats abound. Over time, however, the tendency is for the dwellings to become more substantial as the residents acquire better building materials and a modicum of public services is provided.

The occupants of the squatter settlements are generally employed or underemployed low-income families, since the creation of squatter settlements is more a consequence of the housing shortage than it is a problem of unemployment. Indeed, as high as 90 percent of the potential labor force in such settlements is employed as artisans, street peddlers, shopkeepers, construction laborers, mechanics, and general laborers. For many, these slum conditions offer hope and are viewed as an early stage in the long process of material progress.

More and more common to the major cities of Latin America are the related problems of traffic congestion and environmental deterioration. The narrow colonial streets of the center city, highly unsuited to modern cars and buses, are greatly overburdened, given the vitality of the downtown business district in the Latin American metropolis. In some cities continued observance of the long midday *siesta* creates an extra set of daily traffic peaks as people go to their homes for lunch, but this custom is now on the decline as cities grow larger and make the two extra journeys too time consuming and costly.

In response to the traffic problem, a few cities have turned to rapid mass transit. Buenos Aires was the first city to employ the subway (1913); Mexico City inaugurated its first line in 1970. Caracas, Rio de Janeiro, São Paulo, and some other cities are presently either considering or installing subways. Most cities, including those with subways, rely on the overburdened bus, however. Only a few trolley lines are still in operation, and suburban train service is limited to a very few of the larger cities.

Growing traffic volumes, fires for cooking and waste disposal, and the growth of industry are major contributors to an increasing level of air pollution. The dissipation of pollutants occurs in most cities through normal air circulation; all are becoming larger *heat islands*, and some are subject to serious smog conditions, including Santiago de Chile, Mexico City, São Paulo, and Rio de Janeiro.

The Latin American city is being engulfed by the unrestrained growth on its periphery of the residential *barrio*, the squatter settlement, and the industrial tract. Concurrently comes an inability to finance adequate public services, a growing traffic congestion problem, and a housing crisis of proportions that even the best of public housing policies could not handle effectively. Inadequate parks and a shortage of open space for new parks and playgrounds gives the gridiron pattern an even glummer appearance. All in all, indications are that conditions are worsening over time and that the Latin American city is in a crisis situation. Poverty, disease, crime, corruption, and political instability are all exacerbated by the unceasing growth of the cities.

Too Many Big Cities?

It is a common and true observation that most countries of Latin America are characterized by an urban hierarchy wherein one city sharply dominates the others in terms of population and economically, socially, and politically. Such a condition is termed *primacy*, and the dominant cities are known as *primate* cities. Virtually all of the Caribbean islands have only one major city and, except in Colombia, Brazil, and Ecuador, the condition has long been characteristic of the mainland. In Colombia rugged terrain and varied economic bases have historically made regional interaction difficult and fostered the growth of Bogotá and Medellin. In Brazil coffee gave impetus to São Paulo as an important competitor to Rio de Janeiro, and the entry of Ecuador into world commerce has brought the port of Guayaquil to the fore at the expense of traditionally more important Quito. São Paulo surpassed Rio in population sometime in the 1960s, while Guayaquil overtook Quito about 1940. The dominance of a few cities was, of course, a characteristic of Latin America from the very beginning of the colonial period and a feature of its mercantile system. The major administrative centers such as Mexico City and Lima and the major ports clearly dominated the urban network just as the commercial-industrial-political centers do today.

Some feel this primacy is now to be deplored, arguing that the primate city hinders the growth of the smaller regional centers because it draws off capital, skilled labor, and the educated to the major city. In addition to this "parasitism" and "brain drain," it is argued that the largest cities cannot provide urban services as economically as smaller cities can. It is also felt that the large cities compound environmental problems more than smaller cities do.

On the other side, primacy offers some advantages, including the availability of goods and services that smaller cities cannot offer because of an inadequate market size. The larger the city, the greater the number and the broader the variety of goods and services. The larger city is also given credit for helping to modernize society, enhance the social integration of the masses, and provide better educational opportunities than smaller cities or rural areas. It is also maintained that they provide better health services and otherwise represent a viable concentration of scarce resources. It is only when the largest, or *primate*, city reaches a size where "diseconomies of scale" in the form of traffic congestion, long journeys to work and shop, extremely high land values, environmental pollution, and so forth outbalance the advantages that the value of directing growth to smaller centers becomes apparent.

To date, there is no effective way to determine an optimum size for cities; in any case, the optimum will vary from region to region, depending on its range and wealth. Optimum city size will also vary over time, related to changing technology and its application and variations in consumer real income.

Nonetheless, there is some justification in believing that large cities such as Mexico City, São Paulo, Rio de Janeiro, and Buenoes Aires have now reached a point where more is lost than gained by increased centralization of commerce, industry, and population. Elsewhere, it is not so clear that the optimum size has been attained: who can argue that the primate cities of the various Caribbean islands, much of Central America and Paraguay, Bolivia, or Uruguay are too large? Without at least one large city in each of these countries, many of the higher-order goods and services could not be economically provided. These dominant centers are industrial growth poles and the only viable site for many cultural, educational, and health facilities. On balance, there is perhaps a strong case in favor of the strong primate city in some Latin American countries.

Prospects

One would have to blend a large portion of naiveté with Pollyanic optimism to conclude that the problems of the Latin American city will be significantly ameliorated in the future. Instead, a careful reading of past processes and future trends indicates that the urban landscape—an expression of the broader economic and social framework of a country—will continue to deteriorate.

There is every reason to forecast increasing *urbanization*. The effect of urbanization will be to place additional pressures on the urban housing market and continue to overtax public utilities such as water, sewers, and streets. Underemployment and unemployment will remain high; street vendors hawking shoestrings, lottery tickets, or shoe shines may strike the visitor to the Latin American city as picturesque, but they are in reality symbols of *underemployment*, where a worker is engaged in activities well below his or her potential and the only alternative is unemployment.

As the cities get larger, traffic congestion and air pollution in the narrow streets of the colonial central business district will worsen as automobile ownership rises and bus systems expand their fleets. No alternative to the bus exists in most cities; while this results in an admirable network of routes, travel times slowly creep upward as congestion increases. The high cost of land in the densely built-up central portion of the city reduces the potential for an adequate network of boulevards and freeways.

The housing crisis promises to become even more critical than it is today. The Romans were said to have partly vented their discontent with crowded tenements by turning thumbs down on the gladiators. It is very likely that a share of the urban terrorism in Latin America is traceable to the frustrations of modern urban life as well as the nationwide political and social inequities that become so apparent in a city where all socioeconomic spectrums can be easily observed and compared. But most Latin Americans compensate in more passive forms. Neighborhood bars, plazas, and streets are important social outlets for both tenement and shantytown dwellers, and professional soccer replaces the gladiator. Bullrings are found in a few countries of Latin America, notably Mexico, Venezuela, Colombia, and Peru.

Many affluent city residents who are not apartment dwellers have a private patio or backyard as a compensation for public parks that tend to be inadequate in number, size, facilities, and maintenance. In this aspect of urban life, like so many others, there is little prospect for improvement because of tight city budgets. Indeed, entire new suburban *barrios* are virtually without basic services such as water and sewers, and the streets are commonly unpaved, unpatrolled, and unswept by the city.

To this must be added the real prospect of long-lasting two-digit or even three-digit inflation that eats up low salaries, reduces the incentive to save, increases speculative investments by higher-income groups in apartments and land, and raises the price of raw land on the periphery, putting it out of the reach of most city dwellers. Fragile economies and corrupt governments often add to the instability and precariousness of urban life in much of Latin America.

Although a number of Latin American cities have instituted zoning and practiced urban planning since the 1930s, the planning agencies are as inefficient as their U.S. counterparts because of the inability actually to *implement* effective long-range plans. Additionally, planning is often devoted to aesthetics more than to urban problems, municipal government is often weak, and planning is usually in the hands of architects who lack a true background in urban planning.

If there is little reason to look forward to the continued rapid population growth and physical expansion of the major cities, one is allowed guarded optimism in anticipating the growth of middle-sized cities and the changing hierarchy of cities within regions. New areas, such as the Amazon Basin, could become occupied parts of the national territory as they are settled, and they will hopefully be a positive element in the agricultural and industrial growth of the country. In the process, they could become areas in which to decant some of the population from overcrowded cities and poorer regions. There are few such large virgin areas left, however, and the potential of Amazonia and other similar, if smaller, regions should not be overrated. They could prove to be environmental and agricultural disasters.

One can anticipate the growth of towns at all levels of the existing urban hierarchy as a consequence of high birthrates and increasing urbanization of the population. Small towns in all but the most marginal of areas will become small cities, providing new services and enhancing life-styles in districts removed from the larger cities. The growth of the primate city is probably inevit-

Table 6-2   Population of the Major Cities of Latin America in 000's

City	1880	1905	1930	1950	1960	1970	1980	2000
Mexico City	250	450	900	3,419	5,000	8,605	13,625	22,492
Guadalajara	70	110	150	461	735	1,445	2,331	3,627
Monterrey	15	70	100	411	600	1,167	1,883	3,086
Guatemala City	50	90	120	337	380	1,067	1,430	3,021
Managua	10	30	35	109	190	385	662	1,604
San Salvador	30	50	110	213	230	565	858	1,939
Tegucigalpa	10	20	30	72	105	295	406	974
San José	30	30	60	146	220	401	508	920
Panama City	15	35	70	217	255	520	794	1,568
Havana	200	300	600		1,220	1,681		
Kingston	40	60	120		380	505		
Port-au-Prince	25	100	120	143		385		
Santo Domingo		20	35	182	365	671		
San Juan	20	40	80		590	700		
Caracas	55	100	200	686	1,355	2,058	3,208	4,969
Maracaibo	20		100	252	455	682	1,037	1,541
Bogotá	40	110	170	607	1,125	2,540		
Guayaquil	20	80	110	260	450	855		
Quito	75	70	120		315	550		
Lima-Callao	100	150	250	1,229	1,965	3,318	4,679	8,176
Santiago	150	300	600	1,350	1,700	2,850	3,902	6,200
Valparaiso	100	195	240		380	480		
Buenos Aires	290	1,200	2,000	4,722	6,765	8,353	10,240	12,870
Rosario	30	160	400		670	795		
Montevideo	90	300	450	609	860	1,500		
Rio de Janeiro	350	800	1,500	3,044	4,675	6,847	9,619	14,825
São Paulo	25	400	1,000	2,336	4,430	7,838	12,273	20,714
Belo Horizonte	130	250	350	409	655	1,505	2,279	
Salvador	130	250	350	396	655	1,067	1,563	
Brasilia	0	0	0	0	130	538	1,082	

Sources. J.P. Cole, Latin America, London, Butterworths, 1975. R.W. Fox, Urban Population Growth Trends in Latin America, Washington, D.C., I.A.D.B., 1975. Statistical Abstract of Latin America, 1978.

Note: Population statistics often have an error margin of 5 to 10 percent, sometimes more. Comparability is difficult, but general trends can be identified from the data. Different sources also disagree on population figures.

able and sometimes desirable. The development of many planned new towns is unlikely, since the capital and economic infrastructure for the development of new towns is unavailable to most countries.

Cities have been a reality in Latin America since the *conquistadores* arrived. Indeed, the large Indian cities of the Aztecs and Incas predate the Europeans. Another reality, however, has been unbalanced resource distribution, debilitating climate in some areas, recurrent natural disasters, a strong dependence on foreign markets and capital, increasingly unfavorable terms of trade, and the curse of the *kakistocracy*—government by the petty and the corrupt. There is little reason, unfortunately, to anticipate any significant change in these realities. Instead, rapid population growth promises to exacerbate the situation. The consequence will be a growing urban crisis.

BIBLIOGRAPHY

Beyer, G. (ed.), *The Urban Explosion in Latin America*, Ithaca, N.Y., Cornell University Press, 1967.

Cornelius, W. A., and R. V. Kemper (eds.), "Metropolitan Latin America: The Challenge and the Response," *Latin American Urban Research*, Vol. 6, Beverley Hills, Calif., Sage, 1977.

Davis, K., "Colonial Expansion and Urban Diffusion in the Americas," *International Journal of Comparative Sociology*, Vol. 1, 1960, pp. 43–66.

Deffontaines, P., "The Origin and Growth of the Brazilian Network of Towns," *Geographical Review*, Vol. 28, 1938, pp. 379–99.

Delson, R. M., *New Towns for Colonial Brazil; Spatial and Social Planning of the Eighteenth Century*, Ann Arbor, Mich., University Microfilms International, 1979.

Hauser, P. M., *Urbanization in Latin America*, New York, Columbia University Press, 1961.

Houston, J. M., "The Foundation of Colonial Towns in Hispanic America," in R. P. Beckinsale, and J. M. Houston (eds.), *Urbanisation and its Problems*, Oxford, Blackwell, 1968, pp. 352–90.

Katzman, M. T., *Cities and Frontiers in Brazil*, Cambridge, Mass., Harvard University Press, 1977.

Mangin, W., "Latin American Squatter Settlements: A Problem and a Solution," *Latin American Research Review*, Vol. 2, 1967, pp. 65–98.

Morse, R. M., *From Community to Metropolis: A Biography of São Paulo, Brazil*, Gainesville, University of Florida Press, 1958.

_____ (ed.), *The Urban Development of Latin America, 1750–1920*, Stanford, Calif., Center for Latin American Studies, Stanford University, 1971.

Sargent, C. S., *The Spatial Evolution of Greater Buenos Aires, Argentina, 1870–1930*, Tempe, Arizona State University, 1974.

Sauer, C. O., *The Early Spanish Main*, Berkeley, University of California Press, 1966.

Vance, J. E., *The Merchant's World*, Englewood Cliffs, N. J., Prentice-Hall, 1970.

CHAPTER 7

Mining and Manufacturing

Alan Gilbert

Mining in Latin America has a long history and the area today contains several of the world's major mineral-producing countries. For example, Brazil is a significant producer of iron ore, Peru and Mexico extract large quantities of lead, Chile is notable for copper production, and Bolivia is known for tin. Venezuela and, more and more, Mexico rank high in terms of oil production. Manufacturing, by contrast, has neither the same long history nor the same world importance. Even so Brazil and, to a lesser extent, Argentina and Mexico, have developed widely diversified industrial structures.

Several Latin American countries have failed to develop mining or manufacturing beyond a rudimentary level. In Bolivia manufacturing generates less than 15 percent of the gross national product and employs only a tiny fraction of the work force. Paraguay produces few minerals; among the Central American republics, only Honduras exports minerals in any quantity. One of Latin America's major industrial characteristics, indeed, is this diversity. Several countries are industrializing rapidly, while others possess only the simplest consumer-goods industries. Chile regularly earns over 90 percent of her foreign exchange from copper, while Paraguay and Costa Rica rely entirely on agricultural exports. Some nations, such as Venezuela, exploit minerals that have faced buoyant world prices for many years; others, such as Bolivia with its tin industry, have experienced wide fluctuations in prices and foreign earnings.

Such diversity, however, does not preclude generalizing usefully about the processes of mineral and manufacturing development. It is strange how discussions on these sectors follow such similar lines in such different countries. Latin Americans feel strongly about mining and manufacturing and the role these activities play in national development. Such feelings overlap into specifically geographical phenomena such as the "overconcentration" of industrial activity, the "enclave" nature of so many industrial and mining companies, and the rights and wrongs of industrial dispersal. Discussions of all these problems are merging more often into a similar analytical framework. The problems of mining and industrial development, the spatial phenomenon of urban "primacy," the ownership of industry and the "underdevelopment" of Latin America are to be explained in similar terms. The orientation of Latin American economies toward the world economy, and specifically the "dependency" relationship that has evolved, is seen as the principal and continuing cause of underdevelopment. To understand fully the processes of industrial location and mineral development, it is impossible to divorce them from the wider issues of economic development. Before discussing the spatial tendencies and related policy responses, therefore, it is important to examine the historical processes of industrial and mineral development in the continent.

THE STRATEGY OF IMPORT-SUBSTITUTING INDUSTRIALIZATION

Mineral exploitation has long been a vital element in the process of Latin American development. Without the lure of gold and silver the Spanish and Portuguese conquests would have followed very different lines. The high civilizations of precolonial America made extensive use of silver and gold; these societies received the brunt of Spanish interest in the New World. The silver mines of Mexico and upper Peru sustained the weak Spanish economy, the gold of Minas Gerais that of Portugal and, indirectly, both gold and silver helped the development of British trade and industry (Stein and Stein, 1970; Furtado, 1970).

After independence interest in mining and the extractive industry became more widespread both in terms of the range of products and the countries and areas involved. Political and economic elites in Latin America during the nineteenth century and up to 1930 saw economic growth as a direct consequence of export development. In Argentina and Uruguay prosperity followed from the development of agricultural products, wool, mutton, beef, and wheat for export, and in southern Brazil and Colombia from the development of coffee. In other areas export activities centered on minerals.

In the late nineteenth and early twentieth centuries world demand increased, and the Latin American mineral sector boomed. As the development of more deposits became economic, foreign companies came in search of mineral wealth, and more countries became involved in large-scale mining activity. In Mexico copper, oil, and lead were first developed during the rule of President Diaz (1876–1910), Bolivian tin was exported in large quantities after 1900, Chile's second copper boom got under way during World War I, and Venezuela's petroleum was heavily exploited only after 1920. As a consequence of mineral development, several countries, or certain groups within these countries, prospered. Venezuela became a major recipient of foreign investment after the discovery of petroleum and, from the 1920s on, foreign capital and revenues poured into the country. In most nations, however, the results of mineral development, while pronounced, were disappointing; employment in mining was limited, foreign revenues fluctuated wildly, and governments failed to use their foreign resources effectively (Stein and Stein, 1970).

Gradually, doubts began to accumulate about whether economic diversification would occur on the basis of mineral and other primary exports. An answer was seen to lie more and more in the development of manufacturing industry. Several of the larger countries started to industrialize during the world depression of the 1930s as governments strove to overcome the difficulties caused by the sudden fall in export revenues. Industrial development accelerated during World War II, when the markets of urban Latin America were isolated from the developed countries and their manufactured exports. Most countries were only partially affected by these events but, during the 1950s, all responded to the new development strategy propounded by Raul Prebisch in 1949 (UNECLA, 1951).

Prebisch diagnosed the economic problems of Latin America in terms of its dependence on primary export products and its deteriorating terms of trade. The developed countries had discovered new techniques to produce a more complex and ever-changing basket of manufactured exports, but Latin America continued to produce only mineral and agricultural products. Over time, the prices of manufactured goods had risen relative to the prices of the primary products; the result was that Latin American countries received less in the way of manufactured goods from the developed countries for each ton of primary products they produced. The differing demand and supply characteristics of these two kinds of products and the ownership by foreign companies of so many mineral operations had led to the price terms of trade turning against the continent in favor of the developed countries. Prebisch's solution to the dilemma was that Latin America must begin to build its own manufacturing industry so that changing world technology could bring benefits instead of losses to Latin America. This could only be achieved if every government began to protect its market from certain imported products and replace them with locally produced substitutes. This strategy was strongly advocated by the United Nations Economic Commission for Latin America and, under its tutelage, by many Latin American governments. The 1950s and 1960s were characterized by the widespread adoption of this policy; quotas and import restrictions were established, and several governments set up industrial institutes to encourage manufacturing development (UNECLA, 1966).

As a result of the strategy, industrial investment and production increased rapidly. In the largest countries it was successful insofar as it permitted the development of a highly diversified industrial sector; by the 1960s Mexico, Brazil, and Argentina contained most kinds of manufacturing activity. In the medium-sized countries—Colombia, Venezuela, Peru, and Chile—intermediate-goods industries and even plants producing steel and automobiles were established. The establishment of a manufacturing industry was less effective in the rest of the continent. In the smallest and poorest nations the combination of small populations, low per capita incomes, and acutely concentrated distributions of income meant that markets were too limited for most kinds of industry to develop. Industrial development seldom went beyond the establishment of consumer-goods industries. A basic problem was that the strategy of substituting imports was soon exhausted in all except the six largest nations. A further difficulty, however, affected all nations without exception; while production often increased rapidly, employment did not. The reason was simple; modern capital-intensive technology was being used that raised productivity and used relatively little manpower. For example, between 1958 and 1967 industrial value-added in Colombia doubled while employment increased only by one-quarter. This was a critical problem in countries where the population was often expanding at an annual rate of 3 percent. Admittedly, industrial development usually grew more quickly than national or even urban populations but, because of the small base on which expansion was occurring, it absorbed very few workers. One consequence was that both unemployment and underemployment in the cities continued to grow.

Another dilemma was that instead of improving the balance-of-payments situation, industrial development often led to a deterioration. The substitution of imported products, for example, created a demand in the new factories for intermediate and capital goods with which to make the substitutes. Thus, while the structure of imports changed, the total import bill rarely declined. A further pressure on the balance of payments was that many of the new products used foreign patents and techniques on which royalties had to be paid. This tendency was exacerbated by the fact that many of the new industries were subsidiaries of foreign or multinational companies. Naturally, these companies required a return on their investments and repatriated considerable sums to their head offices abroad. A further drain on foreign exchange was the repayment of loans; both private industrialists and national governments borrowed money to establish plants and economic infrastructure. The combination of all these processes often meant that a deterioration occurred in the foreign trade situation.

The result of the import-substitution process, therefore, was an industrial sector that solved neither unemployment nor the foreign trade deficit of most

Latin American countries. Worse still, many companies were highly inefficient, especially where the market was small or where too many companies
produced similar products. Multinational and foreign companies were problems in that many repatriated high shares of their profits. Even where national
governments encouraged companies to reinvest in the local economy, difficulties arose. With ready access to capital and technology, foreign subsidiaries
were highly competitive and bought out many national companies. Gradually,
their share of the industrial sector grew, and this process began to worry national governments, which feared that control over the national economy was
passing into foreign hands.

Such dilemmas still face most Latin American countries. Industrialization
has worked to a degree but has not resolved the recurrent problems of unemployment and balance-of-payments deficits. This situation has arisen from
what is generally known today as "dependent development." The economy is
no longer undeveloped, but it has evolved in such a way that it is more closely
tied than ever to foreign sources of finance and technology (Furtado, 1970,
1972–1973; Sunkel, 1969).

Most Latin American governments have been looking for a way out of
this situation for some time. Several possibilities exist, but few promise to provide a general solution, especially for the problem of widespread unemployment. The Brazilians and, to a lesser extent, the Colombians have tried successfully to stimulate manufactured exports by regular devaluations of their
currencies. Many of these exports, especially semiprocessed goods such as tex-
tiles·and chemicals, have been sold to developed nations (Winpenny, 1970).
But the techniques used to produce these goods have continued to be capital-
intensive and the strategy has created too few jobs. A related approach has
been to encourage international integration within Latin America. Various
groups were established from 1958 onwards, notably the Latin American Free
Trade Area, the Central American Common Market and, most recently, the
Andean Pact (Dell, 1966). These schemes are considered in Chapter 8, but it is
fair to say that they have failed to resolve the dilemmas inherent to industrialization. Indeed, LAFTA and CACM can no longer be seen as effective forces
toward integration. Even though the Andean Pact, before the departure of
Chile, made some progress in avoiding the problems posed by national jeal-
ousies and differing interpretations of development, its members still face the
intractable problems posed by dependent industrialization.

MINING

Mining activity in Latin America has had a long and highly controversial history. The reasons why are not difficult to establish. First, it is a sector that can
produce immense wealth for a country quickly. In very few years major miner-

al exports can be created that will transform the whole national economy. In Peru, for example, the *guano* boom in the 1850s and 1860s and the expansion of nitrates up to 1879 generated large foreign exchange earnings that transformed the city of Lima, the size of the government bureaucracy, and the whole relationship between national and provincial economies (Levin, 1960; Romero, 1949). Similarly, in Chile the growth of the nitrate economy after the War of the Pacific (1879–1884) and especially the second copper boom after 1910 brought prosperity to many groups in Chilean society and caused the government's budget to expand rapidly (Blakemore, 1974; Blakemore and Smith, 1971; Mamalakis and Reynolds, 1965). Unfortunately, while mining revenues could suddenly soar, they could decline equally quickly. The discovery elsewhere of alternative mineral supplies, a change in manufacturing technology, or the discovery of an acceptable substitute could plunge a national economy from prosperity to penury. Fluctuations both temporary and permanent have plagued Latin America.

Second, not only has national prosperity been linked to the prices paid on world markets but, until quite recently, the bulk of mineral exploitation in most countries has been in the hands of foreign companies. Large, multinational companies such as Kennecott and Anaconda were involved in the Chilean copper industry and Standard Oil and Shell in the exploitation of petroleum in Venezuela and Mexico (Odell, 1974; Odell and Preston, 1973; O'Connor, 1962). Such foreign involvement in activities that have been the main source of export earnings and that have sometimes generated as much as one-third of the gross national product has been tailored for controversy, especially since many foreign companies established highly profitable deals with unsophisticated and often corrupt national governments. The history of petroleum deals in Venezuela before 1958 is scandalous and the experiences of Bolivia up to 1952 little better (Lieuwen, 1960; Osbourne, 1964; Klein, 1965). Gradually, control over foreign companies has tightened; in many cases the state has taken over mining activities. The Mexicans nationalized their petroleum industry in 1938, although few other governments followed. Since World War II, however, and especially since the late 1960s, the pace of nationalization has quickened. The Bolivian tin industry was nationalized in 1952, the Peruvian petroleum industry in 1968, Chilean copper in 1973, and Venezuelan oil in 1976. This whole process has been fraught with tension and argument.

Third, the very nature of the mining process has not eased the relationship between mining companies (whether foreign or state owned) and the nation as a whole. Mining activities tend to be highly organized, large-scale, capital-intensive activities and in Latin America are superimposed on very poor economies. In the past they have been run by foreign companies almost as separate states. But even today they are distinctive, since they create huge revenues but employ few workers and generate few input-output linkages. Only recently has

Bolivian tin been smelted in that country. Venezuelan petroleum is processed locally or on nearby Caribbean islands but has created few other forward industrial linkages. This "isolation" from the rest of the national economy has been magnified by the physical location of many mining activities. Most of the copper of Chile and Peru comes from mines distant from the main population centers of those countries (Warren, 1973); petroleum reserves in Venezuela, Ecuador, Colombia, and Peru were discovered in areas away from the main cities. Add to these features the common situation where the miners are better paid and politically more active than most other groups in the country, and the "enclave" view of these activities can be understood (Odell and Preston, 1973).

Despite the inevitable clashes that arise in the mining sector, few Latin American governments are foregoing the opportunities to develop their mineral resources. Increasing control over profit repatriation by foreign and multinational companies and higher levels of state ownership mean that the worst difficulties can be avoided and more wealth can be channeled into national development. The 1960s and 1970s have seen more and more countries involved in mining activity. Since the middle 1960s, large new deposits of iron ore have been exploited in Peru and Brazil, copper in Peru, Chile, and Mexico, nickel in Colombia, and petroleum in Ecuador, Bolivia, and Mexico. Throughout the continent new reserves of different kinds of minerals are being discovered. Only coal seems lacking in large quantities, although Colombia is belatedly developing the large and accessible reserves in the coastal Guajira region.

Mining activities clearly will continue to influence the economic and geographical structures of Latin American countries. Levels of per capita income will continue to vary widely both internationally and internally, partly because of fortuitous discoveries of "key" minerals. The ability of governments to introduce more widely based programs of social development will depend, partly, on their ability to finance them and therefore indirectly on the exploitation of mineral resources. But the nature and impact of mineral development will vary according to the mineral developed. Nowhere are the geographical consequences of different minerals better shown than in the experiences of two countries—Venezuela and Bolivia.

By comparison with the results in most Latin American countries, mining in Venezuela has been highly successful. Since the 1920s, when petroleum began to be exploited in large quantities, this product has contributed consistently somewhere over 90 percent of Venezuela's foreign exchange and has been the main cause of the country's high gross national product (Table 7-1). The current position, with world oil prices at an all time high, has accentuated the situation. While Venezuela's oil reserves remain limited and costs of production continue to be high in world terms, current OPEC policies seem to guarantee that future solutions to the nation's development problems will not be held back principally by the shortage of income or foreign exchange.

Table 7-1   Venezuelan Oil Production, 1920-1974 (Average Annual Production in
Million Barrels)

1920-1929	37.9
1930-1939	150.8
1940-1949	311.5
1950-1959	782.1
1960-1969	1,412.5
1970-1972	1,275.7
1978	2,100.0

Source. Venezuela, Ministerio de Fomento Anuario Estadistico.

Venezuela has been highly favored with its petroleum wealth, but reading
its modern history tends to create the impression that its oil legacy has been a
liability (Lieuwen, 1965; Travieso, 1972). This dichotomy is explained by the
controversial relationships that have existed between national government and
foreign companies since the 1920s and by the failure of the majority of Venezuelans to share in the proceeds of oil exploitation. This history is a supreme
example of many of the problems just discussed. Venezuela became a major
producer in 10 years. Overgenerous concessions to the major oil companies
and huge reserves under Lake Maracaibo enabled the country to become the
world's second oil producer and its leading exporter by 1928 (Lieuwen, 1954).
Under the auspices of the Gomez government (1910-1935), one of Latin
America's least enlightened dictatorships, Venezuela became rich, but most of
its people remained poor. Petroleum changed the economy radically without
adding to its productive potential. The country became almost wholly dependent on foreign supplies of manufactured goods and even food.

Some changes were made after Gomez's death in 1935. Oil laws less favorable to the foreign companies were gradually introduced, and the first plans
were laid to diversify the Venezuelan economy; oil revenues were to be used to
increase agricultural production, accelerate industrial growth, and build social
and economic infrastructure. A new oil law was signed in 1943 that set the
ground rules for the next 30 years. After the fall of the Medina dictatorship in
1945 the criteria of a fair deal from the companies and investment in other economic sectors underlay government policies. This brief period of relative
enlightenment soon faded, however, with the rise of a new dictator, Perez Jimenez. The favorable treatment of Venezuelan labor was forsaken, vast new
concessions were granted to major oil companies, and foreign earnings poured
in. Unlike earlier regimes, not all this money went to the president and his associates. Large investments were made in developing the iron industry and
building roads. But the most notable "development" goal was turning Caracas into a national showpiece. Half of the government's revenues were spent in
the city. The government bureaucracy increased, skyscrapers proliferated, urban motorways were extended, and the city's population grew from 695,000 in
1950 to 1,348,000 in 1961.

The return to democratic government in 1958 affected the relationship between oil and the national economy in degree but not in kind. Deals between the foreign companies and the government favored the latter more and more, but it was not until 1976 that the oil industry was nationalized. More funds were invested in development projects—in transport links, in the Ciudad Guayana program, in building up industry, and in agricultural colonization—but the basic relations between the foreign oil companies, the dependent middle class, the national government bureaucracy, and the poor remained unaltered (Travieso, 1972). These failures have been due primarily to government policies.

Even so, it has to be said that the nature of the oil economy has been a problem. Oil has always been an enclave in Venezuela and, although direct control by foreign companies has ended, it is likely to remain so. First, oil extraction employs very few people. In 1971 mining generated one-fifth of the gross national product but employed only 36,513 workers—1.3 percent of the national workforce. Second, petroleum creates little related manufacturing employment. In 1974 about 40 percent of crude petroleum was processed in the country, but the 12 refineries employed less than 5000 workers (Karlsson, 1975). Nor does the industry create much in the way of forward or backward linkages. Venezuelan industry uses little crude oil or petroleum derivatives except as fuel, and most of the inputs to the petroleum industry are imported. Third, the main oil-producing regions—Zulia to the west and the *llanos* area to the east (Figure 7-1)—are isolated from the dynamic regions of the country. During the oil boom, Maracaibo grew from a small town to the country's second city but, since 1950, has grown more slowly than most other large Venezuelan cities.[1] Most industrial and commercial activities are concentrated in the Caracas-Valencia area and are continuing to locate there. The western oil capital, in fact, has been gradually losing importance, and recent improvements in transportation are reducing its influence even over petroleum (Odell and Preston, 1973).

The last point leads to an interesting geographical paradox. Apart from the initial expansion of the petroleum economy in Maracaibo and later in the *llanos*, the principal regional beneficiaries from oil have been the cities of Caracas, Maracay, and Valencia. All three cities benefited during the Gomez period as funds were directed almost exclusively toward them, but the most spectacular "transfer" of funds occurred between 1948 and 1957. Perez Jimenez not only boosted government revenues that helped the national capital, but he initiated a policy to make Caracas one of the world's great showpieces. Distant

[1] Population Growth Rates (percent)	1950–1961	1961–1971
Maracaibo	5.5	4.4
National urban population	6.8	7.1

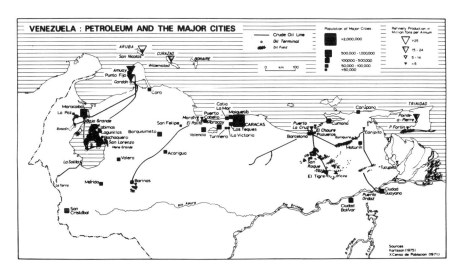

Figure 7.1

from the oil fields, Caracas is the first and foremost beneficiary from the oil revenues; its bureaucracy, industrial sector, and large middle-class population have all grown on this basis.

If Venezuela has a prosperous mineral economy, Bolivia has the very opposite. While Venezuela has continued to benefit from the rising demand for petroleum, Bolivia has suffered from fluctuating tin prices and severe competition from countries such as Malaysia. From the early years of the century, when tin was first exploited in major quantities, Bolivian export production rose rapidly to a peak of 47,087 tons in 1929 (Table 7-2). From that peak it fell to 14,957 tons in1933, and today exports fluctuate around the 30,000-ton level.

Table 7-2 Bolivian Tin Production, 1897-1973 (Average Annual Production in Metric Tons)[a]

1897-1899	3,907
1900-1909	14,912
1910-1919	24,710
1920-1929	33,205
1930-1939	25,843
1940-1949	38,821
1950-1959	28,733
1960-1969	24,760
1970-1973	30,341

Sources. R. Ruiz Gonzalez, *La economia boliviana y el comercio exterior*, Bolivia–Ministerio de Hacienda y Estadistica, 1955, and *United Nations Statistical Yearbook*, 1974.

[a]1897-1966 export volume; 1967-1969 production; 1970-1973 ore production plus exports of refined ore.

This fundamental difference can be seen from a comparison of the revenues accruing to each nation from petroleum and tin. In 1970 Venezuela earned $2,380 million compared to Bolivia's income of $191 million from tin. By 1974, even though tin prices had risen sharply, the OPEC agreements had boosted Venezuelan revenues dramatically; in that year Venezuela's oil revenues were $10,319 million, Bolivia's a mere $229 million. This explains many of the differences between the two economies and especially those between their per capita incomes; with a 1973 per capita income of $1260 dollars, Venezuela is one of the richest nations in Latin Ameria; Bolivia is one of the poorest with only $230 (ECLA, 1975).

Despite this major difference and its consequences, certain strands do link the mining experiences of the two countries. Like Venezuela, Bolivia's tin industry has failed to create widespread employment. Even in 1956, at the peak of postnationalization overmanning, the number of miners working for COMIBOL was only 36,558 (less than 3 percent of the labor force) (Fox, 1967; Zondag, 1966). Similarly, tin has failed to create employment in linked industries. Tin ore has traditionally been smelted in Britain or the United States and, until recently, most ores were merely passed through a concentration process in Bolivia. In the late 1960s a tin smelter was built at Oruro capable of producing 7500 tons of refined tin and designed eventually to produce 15,000 tons. Employment in the smelter apart, few other jobs are created except on the railways that ship the ore to the Pacific ports.

As in Venezuela certain population centers grew with the development of mining. Oruro, the closest city to the main mining centers, experienced a growth in population from 14,000 to 45,000 between 1914 and 1937. More recently, as the tin economy has stagnated, Oruro and other towns dependent on tin have found themselves peripheral to the main centers of dynamism in the Bolivian economy. Like Venezuela's oil centers, they now seem to be candidates for decline; Oruro and Potosí are certain to decline compared to cities such as Cochabamba, Santa Cruz, and La Paz.

A final partial similarity rests in the political influence of mining interests in the Bolivian and Venezuelan economies. Foreign interests soon became integrally associated with the development of Bolivia's tin industry and did so in a particularly high-handed and exploitive fashion (Klein, 1965). The revolution of 1952 changed much of this and led to the nationalization of the main mines and the establishment of COMIBOL, the national mining corporation. Nationalization stimulated considerable controversy, especially since production costs and manpower levels soon began to rise. It was recognized that the industry was overmanned when tin was being subsidized up to 30 percent of its production costs by the central government. A fundamental problem was that the tin workers were a politically powerful and homogeneous group. The bloodshed and strikes in the tin mines of Bolivia had their parallel in the oil strikes in

Venezuela. In both countries the mining and refining industries have played an important role in national development, and their workers represent relatively well-off groups among the national working class.

These similarities apart, Bolivia's tin industry differs fundamentally from the oil industry of Venezuela. In addition to fluctuating world tin prices, Bolivia has suffered from major supply difficulties. The tin reserves have long been depleted of their best ores, are expensive to develop by world standards, and are also difficult to refine. Furthermore, Bolivian tin has the major disadvantage of a long haul to the major ports; this situation is made still more difficult because Matarani, Arica and Antofagasta are located beyond the national frontier in Peru or Chile (Figure 7-2). Despite recent improvements to these

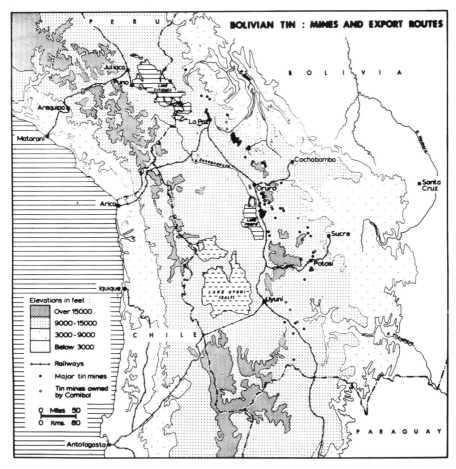

Figure 7.2

ports and in the railway links to them, transportation costs remain high (Fifer, 1972; Livesey and Henderson, 1969). Bolivia's tin industry can well do without such additional problems!

Within Latin America the mining industry has played an important economic, political and, indeed, geographical role. What both the Venezuelan and the Bolivian experiences show is that these consequences depend greatly on the nature of the mineral and the ways in which the revenues are used. The benefits from mining usually have been highly concentrated in a few hands. Certain middle-class groups have benefited, government revenues have boomed, and even the miners have participated to a certain degree; the majority of the population has been excluded. Geographically, too, the benefits have been concentrated: rapid initial growth in the mining areas and then a gradual decline as employment and sometimes production failed to increase further; outside, little impact at all except for the major recipient, the national capital. Perhaps this is a fundamental feature of mining on Latin American geography; the principal effect of mining enterprise often located in inaccessible parts of the continent has been to boost the expansion of the primate cities. Bolivia and, to a supreme extent, Venezuela illustrate this process perfectly.

INDUSTRIAL LOCATION

The geographical pattern of manufacturing activity is strongly linked to the nature of the manufacturing sector and to the socioeconomic environment in which the industrialization process occurs. Thus the many changes that have occurred during the twentieth century have brought a multitude of changes in the distribution of industry in most Latin American nations (Dickenson, 1974; Gilbert, 1974a).

Before the turn of the century and, in the smaller countries, even up to 1950, most industrial production was in the hands of artisan producers. Small companies operated in the food, drink, and clothing sectors, generally supplying local markets and using local materials. Certain cities held an advantage in particular kinds of products through the possession of either resource advantages (e.g., sugar and tobacco) or through the emergence of more efficient industrial enterprise. Industrial concentrations existed in the larger cities, especially in rich resource areas and port centers. But industry and artisan production generally were more widespread than today.

The rise of the manufacturing industry in the late nineteenth century in Argentina and southern Brazil and in the early twentieth century in Mexico, Chile, Peru, and Colombia altered this pattern. The new plants were oriented toward markets located in the largest cities, and they tended to establish themselves in those centers. Thus textile, tobacco, and cement factories were established in or near most of the larger cities. In addition, certain plants were concerned with processing export products and were located in the port cities; in Argentina and Uruguay large meat-slaughtering and refrigeration plants were established. There were still numerous cases when factories were set up in small cities, but this was normally confined to industries that used location-specific materials such as agricultural and mineral products. Generally, the trend toward spatial concentration had begun.

However, it was not always the capital cities that grew most rapidly. In three cases spectacular developments took place in smaller cities that initially left the capitals struggling behind. In Mexico, Monterrey with its iron and coal reserves was the main industrial center of the country by 1920 and remained so up to World War II (Balan, Browning, and Jelin, 1973; Megee, 1958). Similarly, in Colombia entrepreneurs in Antioquia established a series of large, efficient textile plants long before industrial activity developed fully in Bogotá (Parsons, 1949; Ospina, 1955). Even though the city lacked natural resources and faced endless transport difficulties, Medellin was the main manufacturing center of Colombia until the 1960s. Finally, in Brazil, São Paulo developed industry more rapidly than Rio, mainly because of the capital and enterprise generated by the booming coffee economy (Morse, 1958). But while none of these centers were capital cities, all were major cities; they therefore represent interesting variations instead of a contradiction to the basic tendency toward spatial concentration. Indeed, by 1930, whether in the capital cities or in other centers of the country, industry was highly concentrated.

The process of import-substituting industrialization emphasized this trend still further, so that today more and more industry has come to be concentrated in Latin America's largest cities: in Brazil the proportion of industrial workers employed in the state of São Paulo increased from 38.6 percent in 1950 to 48.0 percent in 1970; in Colombia the three largest cities increased their share of employment from 45.7 percent in 1945 to 66.5 percent in 1973. And in Mexico, the Federal District and the neighboring state of Mexico increased their share of employment from 29.5 percent in 1930 to 46.1 percent in 1965.

This industrial concentration trend was accompanied at the regional scale by a general movement of industry toward the fringes and toward the rural areas surrounding the larger cities. The forces of rising land prices, local taxes, and often traffic congestion, plus the growing force of local government land use planning, has encouraged this process. Thus Mexico City is surrounded by industry on the main routes out from the city, and industry in Argentina is spreading out from Buenos Aires to the smaller cities of the River Plate estuary.

Both tendencies have occurred in many developed countries in the past. The spatial concentration of industry, however, was probably never so marked as it has become in Latin America. For this reason it is interesting to examine the processes operating in Latin America to see why this level of concentration has developed.

The early stages of import substitution led to the development of industries for which markets had already emerged. These markets, which had previously been supplied by imports, tended to be concentrated in the foodstuff, textile, and consumer durable sectors and catered mainly to a limited urban-based population. Their "natural" location was in the major cities—a tendency emphasized by the highly concentrated distribution of income in most Latin American countries. Encouraging this pattern further was the fact that most other markets could be supplied easily from the larger cities because of the orientation of the transport network. Buenos Aires, for example, was an ideal point from which to supply most of the Argentine population; as central marketing points, Santiago, Lima, and Caracas were even more favored. Consequently, the market-oriented industry, which was characteristic of this stage of development, concentrated in the major centers.

The distribution of infrastructure also favored the growth of major cities, since few small urban centers and certainly no rural areas were provided with adequate electricity, water, or sewage systems. Labor supplies were another factor. Supplies of unskilled labor were probably of less importance than those of managerial, professional, and skilled manpower. Among the latter group, few lived and, perhaps more important, were prepared to live outside the main centers. Such environmental preference undoubtedly influenced locations of companies wishing to establish outside the big cities and wishing to hire good employees and of the entrepreneurs who made the location decisions.

In many cases inputs could be obtained more readily in the larger cities. Many large Latin American cities are located near the coast so that for companies importing 70 or 80 percent of their materials a port or near port location was an important consideration. And, as import substitution became more advanced and national industries began to supply more of the inputs required by other industries, the advantages of the major industrial centers became more marked. Industrial linkages, both material and nonmaterial, became more important as industrialization proceeded. And, since the original concentrations of industry were located in the major cities, new companies supplying those original plants tended to locate nearby. Of course, there were numerous exceptions where industry required location-specific materials—state-owned iron and steelworks such as Huachipato or Paz del Rio located close to ore supplies and cement plants near to good supplies of limestone—but most industry was not of this kind. One of the ironies of Latin American industry is that so-called footloose industry is more strongly concentrated in the capital cities of Latin America than other kinds of industry (Gilbert, 1974b).

If further explanation of this tendency toward concentration is required, it lies in the role played by national governments. Import-substituting industrialization was encouraged and indeed directed by government agencies. Complex systems of quotas and import licenses regulated and determined which materials would be imported and which companies would be protected from manufactured imports. Governments made available finance and capital for industrial development and established agencies to promote small industry, assist companies in specific sectors, and encourage export production. As the industrial sector became larger and trade unions more powerful, governments became more involved in the control of prices, wages, monopolies, transport rates, social security, and other related matters. When superimposed on traditional Latin American political and business procedures, the increasing links between business and government constituted a strong centralizing force. Managers found themselves in negotiations with one or another branch of government several times a week. The traditional failure in Latin America to delegate authority meant that minor matters were determined in face-to-face meetings at the executive level. Many managing directors whose companies could, in strictly economic terms, have been located in provincial cities decided that their meetings with top government representatives were of such importance that the plants and/or the head offices were established in the capital city. In certain countries noncapital cities are sufficiently large that ministers and high government officials visit frequently. This precludes the need for companies to locate in the capital city; examples are São Paulo, Rio de Janeiro, and Guayaquil.

These various concentrating tendencies have had a pronounced effect on the distributions of industry and in turn on the development of the national city hierarchies. Most cities with more than 200,000 inhabitants have developed industry over the past 20 to 30 years. Small provincial towns such as Arequipa, Manizales, Bucaramanga, Puebla, and Toluca have all experienced periods of rapid industrial growth. But, throughout the continent, the strongest tendency has been for industry to concentrate in cities at the very top of the city hierarchy.

INDUSTRIAL DECENTRALIZATION

The trend toward industrial concentration in Latin America was paralleled by the spatial tendencies of most other economic activities. As economic development occurred, commercial, business, and government activities were centered in the larger cities. The growth in employment opportunities encouraged migration that, together with high rates of natural increase in these cities, led to dramatic rises in large city populations. Between 1950 and 1970 Mexico City grew from 3,419,000 to 8,605,000 and São Paulo from 2,336,000 to 7,838,000 (Fox, 1975). Growth on this scale began to worry many national governments. Everywhere urban expansion was associated with larger numbers of people living in slums and squatter settlements. Local governments became alarmed by their inability to service the growing populations: the youth of the populations caused schooling to become a major problem; traffic congestion worsened; and air pollution began to be noticed. In certain cities local factors emphasized particular problems and focused attention on the question of urban diseconomies. In Mexico City air pollution and the provision of water were more serious problems because of the topography and climate of the city area. The location of Caracas in a narrow valley increased the value of land, magnified the problems of physical growth, and encouraged the extensive growth of squatter settlements on hillsides subject to landslides.

National governments were also aware that the concentration of economic activities in the major cities was associated with the failure of economic development to bring benefits to the poorest parts of their countries. The stagnation and poverty of areas such as the Peruvian *sierra* or the Brazilian northeast was shown in stark contrast with the expansion of Lima, São Paulo, and Rio de Janeiro. Sometimes this contrast was underlined by political controversy in the poor regions. In northeast Brazil the recurrent droughts and consequent starvation demanded a political response (Hirschman, 1965). One possible solution for these poor regions (and also a means for slowing migration to the larger cities) was a policy of economic decentralization.

Parallel to these developments came a change in thinking about planning, During the 1950s and 1960s, international organizations such as the United Nations Development Program (UNDP), the United Nations Economic Commission for Latin America (UNECLA), the Organization of American States (OAS), and the World Bank were emphasizing the need for planning, initially at a national scale but later also at a regional level. The establishment of national planning offices in the late 1950s and the 1960s was soon followed by a realization of the need for some form of regional development programming.

The combination of these processes led to efforts in several countries to decentralize economic activity. The emphasis and amount of energy put into programs naturally differed from government to government but, by the late 1960s, most governments had adopted some form of regional development planning and instigated some effort at economic decentralization. A common element in these efforts was the dispersal of industrial activity away from the large and primate cities.

Dispersing the industrial sector was a natural corollary. For several years industrialization had been seen as the principal means by which high rates of economic growth and development could be achieved. The industrial sector was growing rapidly compared to most other sectors, so its dispersal might bring dynamism to the poorer regions. It was a sector that was heavily concentrated in the major cities but one that could operate in the provinces if appropriate services were provided. Finally, it was the sector on which regional policies in most European countries had been used. Nevertheless, it is surprising that other employment sectors were neglected. Agriculture was an obvious candidate for policies to help the poorest regions but received limited attention, partly for political reasons related to the issue of land reform. The largest employer in most economies—the tertiary sector—also played a minor role.

It is only relatively recently that governments such as those in Colombia, Venezuela, and Brazil have considered decentralizing ministries and agencies as a means of spreading employment opportunities. Throughout the continent, the main agent for regional development and employment dispersal was the industrial sector.

The range of schemes employed in Latin America to disperse industry is too long to detail. Sometimes the government acted directly and established state companies in poorer regions. This approach often embraced related national development motives such as the wish to exploit natural resources, as in the case of Ciudad Guayana—a steel and power complex in Venezuela. Direct government action has the major virtue that it guarantees industrial development will take place. Schemes that rely on the private sector are far less predictable. But direct action has been an exceptional response in most countries. More common are efforts to provide the main provincial cities with basic infrastructure in the hope that private industry will locate in the area. Setting up industrial estates is very common throughout the continent and is clearly an intellectual legacy from European planning practice. Some governments have built factories (e.g., in Mexico at Ciudad Sahagun), but most provided only services such as water, roads, drainage, and telephones. Industrial estates of this kind have been built in practically every Latin American country.

Often the establishment of industrial estates has been supplemented by tax incentives. Industry is persuaded to move to the poorer regions by the promise of not paying income tax for a certain number of years; Mexico, Puerto Rico, Peru and, currently, Venezuela have adopted this method. An interesting variation is the Brazilian 34/18 mechanism, which offers existing companies tax relief if they will invest the unpaid taxes along with new funds in poorer areas of the country (Hirschman, 1968; Goodman, 1972). The scheme at first embraced only the northeast but was later extended to include the Amazon region. Finally, Chile in the 1950s and very recently Colombia and Venezuela have experimented with industrial licensing. Specific industries are banned from the largest cities, most foreign companies from Bogotá, Medellin, and Cali, and most new industries with more than 150 workers from Caracas. The Venezuelan government in 1975 introduced what seem to be very strict controls on the growth of Caracas and lesser controls on the growth of cities such as Maracay and Valencia.

Many of these programs are recent and their impact is yet to be felt. However, a number have been operating for several years, and certain lessons can be learned from their experiences. First, many governments have been successful in building their own plants in the backward regions or in persuading private companies to move there. The Brazilian government indirectly has spent a lot of money but has succeeded in stimulating industrial development in the northeast and Amazon regions. Recife, Fortaleza, Salvador, Belem, and Manaus have been major beneficiaries of the regional program. Large petrochemical plants have been built near Salvador, a steel mill is being built in Manaus, and major jeep, paint, and refrigerator manufacturers have located in Recife. The Mexican government has persuaded many North American companies to take advantage of cheap labor and free-trade facilities on the Mexican side of the border (Baerresen, 1971, 1975). Admittedly this is a special case; not every Latin American country has such a rich neighbor, but it is a further example of how industry can be attracted to poorer regions. Clearly, where there is a strong political or economic motive, governments can disperse industry.

Whether industrial decentralization makes economic sense and whether it helps the poorer regions are different questions. Undoubtedly, problems can arise from industrial dispersal. In certain circumstances major sources of inefficiency can be created. Arica is a case in point. In 1958 the Chilean government decreed that all automobile plants should be established in the northern port. At first, despite protests, the decree was successful and producers established in Arica. They imported parts from abroad and shipped the finished vehicles to the main markets in the south. Later, however, problems became apparent as increasing numbers of parts were produced in Chile. Most of the engineering companies that made car components located in or near Santiago. The consequence was that a double transport haul was required; components were shipped from Santiago almost 1300 miles (over 2000 kilometers) to the south, assembled in Arica, and hauled back to the central region. The inefficiency was wholly undesirable, and it was not long before the decree was lifted. Immediately four car manufacturers shifted their plants to the central region. Certain types of companies just do not have the kind of operation to be decentralized successfully.

The fundamental question about industrial decentralization, however, is whether or not it helps to reduce income disparities and poverty in the regions receiving assistance. Apart from reducing congestion in the major cities, the prime rationale for decentralizing industry is that it will create employment in the poorer regions. It may create employment both directly within its own plant and indirectly through forward and backward linkages. Unfortunately, the evidence suggests that both direct and indirect employment effects are usually very limited. In northeast Brazil, a great deal of industrial investment has taken place but relatively little employment created, especially when it is realized that certain forms of investment have modernized local plants but displaced workers (Goodman, 1972). In the Amazon the declaration in 1967 of Manaus as a free-trade zone led to the immediate establishment of 30 industries, including an oil refinery and a steel mill, but little employment (Kleinpenning, 1975; Henshall and Momsen, 1974).

In light of our earlier discussion, of course, this result should not cause surprise. Since most new Latin American industry is capital-intensive, plants established in poor regions are likely to share this characteristic. Unless greater financial incentives are given to more labor-intensive industries, which is rarely done, the national dilemma of fast-rising productivity and slowly increasing employment is transferred to the poor region.

The industrial employment effects are little different. One reason is that since few people are employed in the new plants, they generate little additional income in the region. Another reason is that many of the linkages of dispersed industry are with foreign companies or with plants in the large cities. A study of Arequipa, for example, showed that 34 percent of all industrial inputs were imported and a further 25 percent came from areas outside southern Peru (Waller, 1974). The consequences for regional development are obvious. First, the poor region does not benefit from linkage effects. Second, industries in the major cities will grow rapidly through their links with the regions. The outcome is that interregional disparities and, more important, poverty within the poor regions do not decline. The solution in these circumstances is to introduce industry into poorer regions that can create stronger local linkage effects. Industries that can stimulate local agriculture, industries that can encourage instead of crush local artisan production, and companies that use local material supplies are the kinds of activities essential for an effective program.

Nowhere are these issues better illustrated than in Venezuela's Ciudad Guayana program. This ambitious project was intended to help the region by incorporating it more firmly into the national economy and the nation by exploiting the region's huge mineral and power resources and thereby accelerating the growth of the economy (Friedmann, 1966; Rodwin, 1967). Certainly, the physical development of the city and the manufacturing sector has been impressive by any standards. Major plants producing 600,000 metric tons of steel and 50,000 metric tons of aluminum ingots have been erected and are currently being extended. The Guri Dam and its related hydroelectric complex produce a high percentage of Venezuela's electricity. Associated with these industrial and infrastructural projects has been the breathtaking growth of the city itself. Santo Tomé de Guayana was a *pueblo* of 3803 inhabitants in 1950, had only 29,497 inhabitants in 1961 and, by 1971, had grown to be a major city with 143,540 people.

Unfortunately, the growth of the city has not been free from problems. Perhaps the most important difficulty is that industry has not created as many jobs as had been anticipated by the planners. According to one early estimate, the city was expected to have around 30,000 manufacturing workers in 1971 whereas it actually had 8825. By comparison, rates of population growth have been much nearer to the planning targets (61 percent of the target compared to 29 percent for employment); the clear implication is that unemployment and underemployment have remained consistently higher than had been hoped. Indeed, unemployment rates have remained around the 12 to 14 percent level since the early 1960s (Macdonald and Macdonald, 1968). Quite simply, rates of migration have maintained unemployment in Ciudad Guayana at a level similar to those in most other large Venezuelan cities. Similarly, the city's formal housing program has been unable to keep pace with the growth of the city. It had been hoped that most workers would be housed in the new city by the middle 1970s. In fact, the majority are still housed in the shanty settlements on the San Felix side of the river.

It was also hoped that Ciudad Guayana would act as a growth center for the surrounding rural areas and that growing industrial consumer markets would stimulate the rural economy, especially since the related agricultural, forestry, ranching, and mining activities, were planned in the "zone of principal development." As Figure 7–3 shows, however, this has not occurred. Most of the surrounding *municipios* have grown quite slowly, and several have not even matched the national population growth rate. Only La Paragua, close to the main iron ore deposits, and Santo Tomé de Guayana itself have grown at an annual rate of more than 4 percent. Few industrial linkages have benefited the local area. Most have been felt outside the Guayana region, some in Caracas and in the Maracay-Valencia area, some outside Venezuela altogether (Travieso, 1972, 1975).

Some commentators have argued that these characteristics mean that Ciudad Guayana has been a failure. Travieso (1975) has classed it "an error not to be repeated," since it has simply "replicated all the characteristic problems of the traditional cities." While this is especially harsh criticism, it does forcefully underline the problems that regional planners face in creating jobs in less developed areas. Ciudad Guayana demonstrates once again that "dependent," capital-intensive industry is not the sole answer for regional development. A similar argument can be made on the basis of the experiences of northeast Brazil. Recife is one of the principal cities of the region and has received around one-quarter of the total industrial investment from the 34/18 mechanism. As such, it is one of the major beneficiaries of the northeast program, and welfare

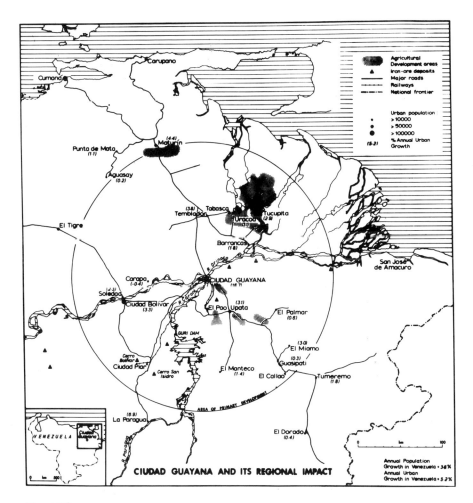

Figure 7.3

levels should reflect this position. Unfortunately, recent evidence seems to indicate otherwise. Specifically, family-budget surveys carried out from 1960 to
1962, and 1967 to 1968 showed that per capita income during that period rose
annually by only 1.5 percent. Worse still was the fact that per capita income
among the poorer two-thirds of the population actually fell from 37.8 to 36.8
cruzeiros. In addition, *prima facie* evidence suggests that between 1960 and
1968 starvation and malnutrition in the city increased (Gilbert and Goodman,
1976). This situation was worsened by continuing in-migration from the surrounding area. Nevertheless, the point is clear; industrial decentralization is insufficient in itself to resolve severe regional problems.

CONCLUSIONS

What conclusions can we draw from such evidence about the decentralization of industrial activity? Unfortunately, planners are far from agreement on this matter. Many writers argue that industrial dispersal is irrelevant to the needs of the poorer regions and to the wider process of national development. Others suggest that regional development and industrial dispersal still have a role to play both in limiting the growth of the larger cities and in helping the poorer areas.

The many critics of employment dispersal policies are far from agreement in their views; some argue that national economic growth will accelerate if resources are concentrated in the major urban areas, and others emphasize the social advantages to be gained from spatial concentration. Among the first group are several urban economists who have noted that while urban diseconomies afflict large cities, their incidence is less connected to size than to the social and spatial organization of those cities (Alonso, 1971; Richardson, 1973); thus levels of crime, for instance, are more a reflection of society than the size of the city.

In addition, they have argued that urban economies normally rise more rapidly than urban diseconomies; benefits to industrial companies, say, from agglomeration outweight the costs to the city of traffic congestion or air pollution. A clear implication of this argument is that planning efforts should be directed less toward industrial dispersal than to organizing the future development of the large cities. Others have supported this argument by offering suggestions as to how large cities might best be planned; Smulian and Turner (1971) have argued the case for "new towns" and Currie (1975) the case for semiautonomous subcenters within large cities. Currie, indeed, has argued that urban development provides a means for stimulating the national economy in a less developed country; his ideas for stimulating the construction industry were incorporated into the Colombian national development plan between 1972 and 1974 (Gilbert, 1976a).

The second group of critics of employment dispersal argue the case from a completely different ideological perspective. Rofman (1974) and Corragio and Geisse (1972), for example, have argued that to encourage industrial dispersal ignores the nature and causes of underdevelopment. Establishing industrial activity in provincial cities will merely create at the provincial level the national problems of dependent development. Elite and middle-class groups in the provinces will gain, but the diffusion of benefits to the rest of the provincial population will be limited. Much more can be done to help the poorest groups by helping them in the larger cities. In countries such as Argentina where almost 50 percent of the population live in greater Buenos Aires and Chile where over 50 percent live in greater Santiago, their argument makes a good deal of sense. It is especially pertinent where the dispersal policies embrace only industrial activity and neglect other forms of regional development such as agricultural investment and infrastructural provision.

Is there no case to be made for decentralization? Under certain circumstances and providing that definite kinds of policies are introduced, I believe there is. First, certain cities are facing major congestion problems. Caracas, confined to its narrow valley, and Rio de Janeiro, confined by the mountains and the sea, cannot expand without adopting expensive engineering solutions. Satellite towns could be an answer, and the Venezuelan and the Brazilian governments are in the process of establishing them. In such circumstances, and especially since there are very poor regions in these countries, decentralization might be encouraged.

Second, the advocates of big cities and centralization accept that planning of some kind is essential; the worst urban diseconomies must be avoided and the maximization of urban economies must be encouraged. But is planning sufficiently sophisticated or are politicians sufficiently interested in planners' recommendations to implement those plans? It seems to me that there is plentiful evidence, from Latin America and elsewhere, that planning has not been a major success in big cities (Cornelius and Kemper, 1977; Gilbert, 1976b). If it is accepted that smaller cities are easier to plan and that the probability of their suffering from severe crises is less than that of large cities, the implications are clear: decentralize economic activity to slow the growth of the big cities and give more time for other solutions to be developed.

Third, despite arguments to the contrary, decentralizing employment can assist poorer regions. The fact that the strategies so far adopted in Latin America have failed to solve the more trenchant difficulties is no argument against helping areas such as the Brazilian northeast or the Peruvian *sierra*. What is required, perhaps, are regional policies more geared to the creation of employment and the redistribution of income. Such policies might be achieved by encouraging the growth of local artisan industry, by land redistribution, by establishing local education facilities, or even by decentralizing sections of the national bureacracy. It may be that the tools employed and not the strategy are at fault. If this argument is wrong, the implications are clear: the only effective solution is to encourage large-scale emigration from the poorest regions.

Finally, there is a strong argument for decentralization in terms of resource development. Latin American nations possess many mineral and agricultural resources. One way of developing these resources is to foster regional development. Of course, industrial or employment dispersal is only one form of regional development; there are many others, but the dispersal of economic activities designed to assist in the stimulus of agricultural production can surely only help.

Arguments can clearly be made on both sides, but their validity depends a great deal on the objectives of different national governments and the geographies of their different regions. If the Brazilian government is presently unconcerned with social inequality it is hardly likely to introduce an equity component into its regional policies. If the Cuban government wishes to spread "development" widely among the population it may achieve this with or without decentralization. Ideology and value judgments enter the discussion firmly at this point. Similarly, the validity of dispersing economic activity and, indeed, the case for regional development in general will vary with the spatial structure of the country. The larger the geographical area, the larger the major cities and the more trenchant their problems; the greater the disparities between rich and poor areas and the greater the resources to be found in the provinces, the better the case is for regional development and some element of industrial and employment decentralization. In different circumstances the case is less strong.

Therefore government reactions to dispersal policies must be flexible. The spatial concentration of industry in certain cities may not be a problem. Perhaps no city in the world has yet reached its optimal size. Perhaps industry should be allowed to locate in Mexico City and São Paulo. In addition, various governments that decide that the poorer regions of their countries must be helped may not achieve this goal through industrial dispersal if the dispersed industry is inappropriate to the needs of the region. The only indisputable lessons from past experience are that unless action is taken industry will continue to concentrate in the larger cities and that past efforts to help poor regions by dispersing industry have not helped much in raising the living standards of the poor. Other strategies must be implemented.

BIBLIOGRAPHY

Alonso, W., "The Economics of Urban Size," *Papers and Proceedings of the Regional Science Association*, Vol. 26, 1961, pp. 67–83.

————, *Industrial Location and Regional Policy in Economic Development*, Berkeley, Calif., Center for Planning and Development Research, No. 74, 1968.

Baerresen, D. D., *The Mexican Border Industrialization Program*, Lexington, Mass., Heath Lexington, 1971.

————, "Unemployment and Mexico's Border Industrialization Program," *Inter-American Economic Affairs*, Vol. 29, 1975, pp. 79–90.

Balan, J., H. L. Browning, and E. Jelin, *Men in a Developing Society*, Austin, Texas University Press, 1973.

Blakemore, H., and C. T. Smith (eds.), *Latin America: Geographical Perspectives*, London, Methuen, 1971.

Blakemore, H., *British Nitrates and Chilean Politics, 1886–1896: Balmaceda and North*, London, Athlone Press, 1974.

Brodersohn, M., "Regional Development and Industrial Location Policy in Argentina," in *Industrial Location and Regional Development*, UNIDO, New York, United Nations, 1971, pp. 474–552.

Colombia, D. N. P., *Las Cuatro Estrategias* Bogotá, Departamento Nacional de Planeacion, 1972.

_____*Ciudades Dentro de la Ciudad*, Bogota, Tercer Mundo, 1974.

Cornelius, W. A., and R. V. Kemper (eds.), "Metropolitan Latin America: The Challenge and the Response," *Latin American Urban Research*, Vol. 6, Beverly Hills, Calif., Sage, 1977.

Currie, L. L., "The Interrelations of Urban and National Economic Planning," *Urban Studies*, Vol. 12, 1975, pp. 37-46.

Dell, S., *A Latin American Common Market?*, London, Oxford University Press, 1966.

Dickenson, J. P., "Imbalances in Brazil's Industrialization," in B. S. Hoyle (ed.), *Spatial Aspects of Development*, London, Wiley, 1974, pp. 291-306.

Fifer, J. V., *Bolivia: Land, Location, and Politics Since 1825*, Cambridge, Cambridge University Press, 1972.

Fox, D. J., *The Bolivian Tin Mining Industry: Some Geographical and Economic Problems*, London, International Tin Council, 1966.

Fox, R. W., *Urban Population Growth Trends in Latin America*, Washington, D.C., Inter-American Development Bank, 1975.

Friedmann, J., *Regional Development Policy: A Case Study of Venezuela*, Cambridge, Mass., M.I.T. Press, 1966.

Furtado, C., *Economic Development of Latin America: A Survey from Colonial Times to the Cuban Revolution*, Cambridge, Cambridge University Press, 1970.

_____, "The Post-1964 Brazilian 'Model' of Development," *Studies in Comparative International Development*, Vol. 8, 1972-1973, pp. 115-127.

Geisse, G., and J. L. Corragio, "Metropolitan Areas and National Development," in G. Geisse and J. E. Hardoy (eds.), *Latin American Urban Research*, Vol. 2, Beverly Hills, Calif., Sage, 1972, pp. 45-59.

Gilbert, A. G., *Latin American Development: A Geographical Perspective*, Harmondsworth, Penguin Books, 1974(a).

_____, "Industrial Location Theory: Its Relevance to an Industrialising Nation," in B. S. Hoyle (ed.), *Spatial Aspects of Development*, London, John Wiley, 1974(b), pp. 271-289.

_____, "Urban and Regional Development Programs in Colombia Since 1951," in W. A. Cornelius and F. M. Trueblood (eds.), *Latin American Urban Research*, Vol. 5, Beverly Hills, Calif., Sage, 1976(a), pp. 241-276.

_____, "The Argument for Very Large Cities Reconsidered," *Urban Studies*, Vol. 13, 1976(b), pp. 27-34.

Gilbert, A. G., and D. E. Goodman, "Regional Income Disparities and Economic Development: A Critique," in A. G. Gilbert (ed.), *Development Planning and Spatial Structure*, London, Wiley, 1976, pp. 113-141.

Goodman, D. E., "Industrial Development in the Brazilian Northeast: An Interim Assessment of the Tax Credit Scheme of Article 34/18," in R. J. A. Roett (ed.), *Brazil in the Sixties*, Nashville, Vanderbilt University Press, 1972, pp. 231-74.

Grunwald, J., and P. Musgrave, *Natural Resources in Latin American Development*, Baltimore, Johns Hopkins Press, 1970.

Henshall, J. D., and R. P. Momsen, *A Geography of Brazilian Development*, London, Bell, 1974.

Hirschman, A. O., *Journeys Toward Progress*, New York, Anchor Books, 1965.

_____, "Industrial Development in the Brazilian Northeast and the Tax Credit

Scheme of Article 34/18," *Journal of Development Studies*, Vol. 5, 1968, pp. 1-28.

Karlsson, W., *Manufacturing in Venezuela: Studies on Development and Location*, Stockholm, Institute of Latin American Studies, 1975.

Klein, H. S., "The Creation of the Patino Tin Empire," *Inter-American Economic Affairs*, Vol. 19, 1965, pp. 3-24.

Kleinpenning, J. M. G., *The Integration and Colonization of the Brazilian Portion of the Amazon Basin*, Nijmegan, Katholick Universiteit, 1975.

Lavell, A. M., "Regional Industrialization in Mexico: Some Policy Considerations," *Regional Studies*, Vol. 6, 1972, pp. 343-62.

Levin, J. V., *The Export Economies: Their Pattern of Development in Historical Perspective*, Cambridge, Mass., Harvard University Press, 1960.

Lieuwen, E., *Petroleum in Venezuela: A History*, Berkeley, California University Press, 1954.

———, *Venezuela*, 2nd ed., London, Oxford University Press, 1965.

MacDonald, J. S., and L. E. MacDonald, "Motives and Objectives of Migration: Selective Migration and Preferences Toward Rural and Urban Life," *Social and Economic Studies*, Vol. 17, 1969, pp. 417-434.

McGinn, N. F., and R. G. Davis, *Build a Mill, Build a City, Build a School: Industrialization, Urbanization, and Education in Cuidad Guayana*, Cambridge, Mass., M.I.T. Press, 1969.

Mamalakis, M., and C. W. Reynolds, *Essays on the Chilean Economy*, Homewood, Ill., Irwin, 1965.

Megee, M. C., *Monterrey, Mexico: Internal Patterns and External Relations*, Chicago, University of Chicago Press, 1958.

Morse, R., *From Community to Metropolis, a Biography of São Paulo*, Gainesville, Florida University Press, 1958.

Odell, P. R., *Oil and World Power: A Geographical Interpretation*, Harmondsworth, Middlesex, Penguin, 1970.

Odell, P. R., and D. A. Preston, *Economies and Societies in Latin America: A Geographical Interpretation*, London, Wiley, 1973.

Osborne, H., *Bolivia*, London, Royal Institute of International Affairs, 1964.

Ospina Vasquez, L., *Industria y Proteccion en Colombia 1810-1930*, Medellin, Editorial Santa Fe, 1955.

Parsons, J. J., *Antioqueno Colonization in Western Colombia*, Berkeley, California University Press, 1963.

Richardson, H. W., *The Economics of Urban Size*, Westmead, Saxon House, 1973.

Rodwin, L., et al., *Planning Urban Growth and Regional Development: The Experience of the Guayana Program of Venezuela*, Cambridge, Mass., M.I.T. Press, 1969.

Rofman, A. B., *Dependencia, Estructura de Poder y Formacion Regional en America Latina*, Buenos Aires, Siglo XXI, 1974.

Romerò, E., *Historia Economica del Peru*, Buenos Aires, Ed. Suramericana, 1949.

Stein, S. J., and B. H. Stein, *The Colonial Heritage of Latin America: Essays on Economic Dependence in Perspective*, New York, Oxford University Press, 1970.

Sunkel, O., "National Development Policy and External Dependence in Latin America," *Journal of Development Studies*, Vol. 6, 1969, pp. 24-48.

Travieso, F., "Cuidad Guayana: Polo de Desarrollo?," *Guadernos de la Sociedad Venezolana de Planificacion*, 1971, pp. 77–92.

———, *Ciudad, Region y Subdesarrollo*, Caracas, Fondo Editorial Comun., 1972.

———, "Ciudad Guayana: Una Evaluacion," *Resumen*, No. 86, 1975.

Turner, A., and J. Smulian, "New Cities in Venezuela," *Town Planning Review*, Vol. 42, 1971, pp. 3–27.

United Nations Economic Commission for Latin America, New York, United Nations, 1951, 1966, 1975.

Waller, P. P., "The Spread Effects of a Growth Pole—A Case Study of Arequipa (Peru)," in F. M. Helleiner and W. Stöhr (eds.), *Spatial Aspects of Development*, Proceedings of the I.G.U. Commission on Regional Aspects of Development, Vol. 2, Toronto, Allister, 1974.

Warren, K., *Mineral Resources*, Harmondsworth, Penguin Books, 1973.

Winpenny, J. T., "Prospects for Latin American Manufactured Exports," *Bank of London and South America Review*, Vol. 4, 1970, pp. 420–428.

Zondag, C. H., *The Bolivian Economy, 1952–1965*, New York, Praeger, 1966.

CHAPTER 8

Latin America and the World Scene

Brian W. Blouet

Since 1492, a major theme in the history of Latin America has been the creation of transatlantic and transpacific linkages. It is a highly complex theme involving the establishment of routeways and trade connections, the migration of peoples, and contact between cultures. The intrusion of the Iberians brought Western European and pre-Columbian cultures into contact and conflict. Several indigenous cultures, including the Incan and the Aztec, were destroyed or badly damaged in the process of exploration, conquest, and settlement. However, innumerable pre-Columbian cultural traits have survived and have contributed to the evolution of a distinctively Latin American cultural realm.

The "black legend" of the Iberian conquest has always made a good story, and the tales of relatively small armies of *conquistadores* subduing and exploiting the indigenous inhabitants has not lacked chroniclers. But the Iberians were not only destroyers. They, too, had traits to contribute to the new culture realm that was being created in Middle and South America.

The introduction of Spanish eventually gave the region a *lingua franca*. The Europeans transferred many valuable plants and animals to the region: wheat, vines, coffee, sugar, citrus fruits, cattle, sheep, pigs, and horses. Similarly, the indigenous cultures contributed traits to the present-day life of the region together with plants that have diffused into many parts of the globe. Maize (corn), tobacco, cacao, the potato, and many species of beans and squash are examples of domesticated plants widely used by farmers in regions far removed from Latin America.

Although abundant New World sources of gold and silver may have been bad for the economy of Spain in the long run, the mines of Mexico and Peru provided additional quantities of circulatable wealth at a critical period in the economic growth of the North Atlantic region. The additional coinage, which came into circulation in the sixteenth century, proved to be inflationary, but it stimulated trade, capital investment, and the growth of financial institutions. These factors contributed to the eventual emergence of capitalized, industrial societies in Europe.

The imperial structures of Spain and Portugal only linked a tiny proportion of the inhabitants of the region to the economic circulations of the Atlantic and the Pacific, although there were plantation and mining regions intensively involved in production for export. Spain and Portugal were not early industrializers, but the use of Latin America as a source of raw materials that were to be consumed in the industries of Western Europe intensified in the nineteenth century, when Britain became particularly active as an investor and trader in the region.

The United States became interested in the resources of the area later but, by the end of the nineteenth century, was the largest trading partner of many Latin American countries. The United States subsequently has come to dominate aspects of the economic life of the region. Politically, too, the United States has insisted on a measure of control. The Monroe Doctrine of 1823 declared that Latin America was not to be the object of colonial activity by European states. The immediate impact of this assertion was not great but, by the end of the century, America was having a major influence on the foreign affairs of the region. During the 1890s the United States initiated arbitration between Venezuela and Britain concerning the Venezuela-Guiana boundary dispute. In the Spanish-American War (1898) Spain was deprived of all remaining possessions in the Western Hemisphere, and the United States became the predominant power in the Caribbean. Puerto Rico was acquired, and the right to interfere in the internal affairs of Cuba and the Dominican Republic was assumed. In 1903 the British bowed to the inevitable and reduced naval strength in the Caribbean, and in 1904 the Canal Zone was leased from Panama.

United States political pressure and direct interference were asserted mainly in the lands around the Caribbean, but economic activity knew no such bounds in the twentieth century. United States investment, on a vast scale, has touched every country in the hemisphere. The well-known examples are the development of sugar estates in Cuba, banana growing in Central America, oil exploration in Venezuela, Peru, and Colombia, copper in Chile, and iron ore in Venezuela. This investment in the production of industrial raw materials and agricultural commodities was important, but it was only the beginning.

United States corporations and individuals invested in banks, import-export companies, shipping lines, railroads, manufacturing plants, and retail outlets. The region became an important, but not exclusive, outlet for the export of U.S. capital and goods, and a source of commodities that could be utilized in the United States.

In many ways this economic interchange has been excellent in that it has provided Latin America with capital, technology, business, expertise, and general contact with the largest economy in the world. The United States has benefited in having an outlet for investment and sources of raw materials in the Western Hemisphere.

Perhaps inevitably the size and strength of the United States and of its major corporations came to be resented. The United States was seen by Latin Americans as being too ready to support American corporations, too ready to interfere politically, and capable of taking economic reprisals against countries that were thought unfriendly. Even observers sympathetic to the United States find many of its actions hasty when dealing with Latin American countries. In Guatemala in 1954, after a left-wing government began to take land away from the United Fruit Company, in exchange for government bonds, the United States supported a right-wing takeover. The U.S. part in the 1961 "invasion" of Cuba is not applauded, and the sending of marines to the Dominican Republic (1965), again to oust a left-wing faction, is not well regarded. Supposed interference by the United States in the internal affairs of many Latin American countries has received heavy criticism.

Until recently the terms on which Latin America traded with the United States always seemed to favor the richer region. Latin American currencies tended to be weak against the dollar, the cost of imported manufactured goods went up faster than the price of exported raw materials, and large, multinational corporations were apparently able to find cheaper sources of commodities elsewhere in the world, without great difficulty. Since 1973 some of this has changed. The dollar is frequently under pressure, raw materials, such as oil, are no longer glutting the market, and prices have risen. However, it is still true that the more diversified economies of the advanced manufacturing countries, like the United States, are better able to cope with economic stress than Latin American countries, which rely heavily on the export of a few raw materials.

There is a feeling held by many informed Latin Americans that, while there are economic benefits to be gained from proximity to the United States, the very strength of the U.S. economy has slowed the process of diversification within Latin American countries. It was to overcome this problem that the Argentine economist, Raul Prebisch, advocated the establishment of a Latin American common market. More will be said about this later in the chapter; the basic idea was that if the countries of the region combined to create a larger market area, the process of industrialization might be speeded up, at least within countries such as Argentina, Brazil, and Mexico, which have been relatively successful in establishing broadly based manufacturing regions.

ECONOMIC CHANGE WITHIN LATIN AMERICA

Latin America is effected by global economic forces that are controlled by factors generated beyond the region. At the same time, and interlocked with worldwide trends, profound economic change is taking place within the countries of the region; this change carries with it major social consequences. Superficially, economic change seems similar to the process of industrialization that has already taken place in Western Europe and North America but, apart from the cultural distinctions indicated in the introduction, there are important differences in the type of development and the timing of development.

Industrialization is normally accompanied by the agglomeration of manufacturing plants, people, and services at emerging nodes in the transportation system. The nodes that gain initial advantages in the agglomeration process are determined by a complex of factors, including chance. The relative value of the factors has altered historically, and the late industrializers have been subject to a different weighting of factors as compared to the countries that enjoyed early industrial revolutions. The first industrial revolutions took place when the only major form of power production—other than animal power, water, gravity, and wind—was the steam engine, a device that in its paleotechnic form was voracious in its consumption of coal relative to the work it did in driving machinery. The need for cheap coal was a prerequisite of factory location, and the availability of coal became a major locational force, at least until the construction of railroads, which allowed fuel to be moved around more cheaply. As a result of the early importance of coal, nascent industrial regions in Britain and Belgium, which were on or close to this source of fuel, acquired initial locational advantages that were to be retained long after other forms of power became available and coal had ceased to be an overriding consideration. The distribution of industry in countries that industrialized early still bears the marks of the early technology of steam engines. Interestingly, Germany, industrializing at a time when steam engines and railroads were more advanced, found that manufacturing was less dependent on the availability of coal. Other locational factors, such as market considerations, played a more important part in the distribution of industry at an earlier stage in the development process. As a result, German industry was less tied to coal fields than British and Belgian industry.

Not only has Latin America started economic development late, but the whole process has come about largely as a result of economically advanced regions connecting Latin America to the North Atlantic economy. The North

Atlantic area, which includes Western Europe and North America, has provided, at a price, much of the industrial technology. The economies of Western Europe and North America have also been sources of capital, manufactured goods, and markets for Latin American countries.

A series of spatial consequences have followed on late development and on economic transformation that was, in many important respects, heavily influenced by what had already happened in the North Atlantic region. Later industrialization has meant industrialization at a time when the pull of raw materials and fuels, as a locational factor, has decreased. Improved methods of power transmission and bulk transportation of raw materials have freed many production units from the necessity of locating at the source of these commodities.

Because economic development in Latin America depended on what was happening in more advanced economies, location in relation to the North Atlantic was of major importance. The regions and cities that were well placed to act as connecting links with the North Atlantic prospered. Cities in this category include Buenos Aires, Montevideo, and Rio de Janeiro. Such centers became ports for the entry of technology, capital, and manufactured goods and conduits for the export of raw material and foodstuffs. They acquired a momentum, attracted increasing populations to work in new economic activities, and became, in their own right, manufacturing centers producing some goods for the local market. The more important connecting links were all on, or close to, the eastern side of Latin America. Santiago, Valparaiso, Lima, Guayaquil, and Buenaventura enjoyed nothing like the importance of Buenos Aires, Rosario, Montevideo, Santos, Rio, Barranquila, and Veracruz.

Economic development has tended to take place earlier in the east than the west and, to this day, the countries possessing well-diversified industrial regions—Mexico, Brazil, and Argentina—are those that were first linked with the industrial countries of the North Atlantic and derived initial, regional, economic advantages from the experience.

Late industrialization has resulted in differing emphases. In the early phases of industrial revolution in Western Europe basic manufacturing industries were important. In Latin America there has been a tendency to bypass this phase and emphasize industries producing consumer goods and service industries.

Late industrialization has therefore had an influence on the spatial distribution of economic activity and on the structure of economies. The countries that have industrialized after the advanced economic regions were already in existence have, among other things, found world markets extremely competitive. The inability to compete in export markets may well be part of the explanation of why manufacturing industries have grown less rapidly than service industries in Latin America. However, if the present high demand for raw materials such as oil, iron ore, and bauxite continues, we may see a greater development of basic, heavy industry in Latin America with more oil refining, iron and steelmaking, and aluminum refining for export as countries in the region exploit the resource base more fully.

If a higher degree of economic independence is to be obtained for the region there will have to be more in the way of political and economic cooperation among the countries of Latin America. It is probably unrealistic to think that the level of interdependence can reach that displayed by the Western European nations through their common market (E.E.C.), but the Latin American states have shown a desire to establish, at least, a free-trade area that includes the major countries of the region. Unfortunately, Latin America has a long history of national rivalries and unresolved boundary disputes that constantly produce frictions between countries. To outsiders, Latin America may seem to have a community of interests to which all countries subscribe but, in practice, this is far from the case. Virtually all adjoining countries in the region have disputes concerning their boundaries and, for instance, in economic terms the gap between the needs of Argentina and Paraguay is greater than the gap between any two Western European countries. The histories and traditional interests of countries vary greatly.

THE ORIGINS OF STATES IN LATIN AMERICA

At the end of the eighteenth century, there were four major divisions in Spanish America; the viceroyalties of New Spain (created 1535), New Granada (1717), Peru (1542), and Rio de la Plata (1776). Yet these powerful units, with their seats at Mexico City, Bogotá, Lima, and Buenos Aires, respectively, did not become the exclusive cores of emergent nation states in the nineteenth century. Instead, the fracturing into new units took place along lines roughly coincident with the limits of jurisdiction of the *audiencias*, or royal law courts. A major reason for this has been outlined by Phelan (1967, p. 38) as follows: "The Spanish concept of the state was essentially medieval in that administration of justice, not legislative or executive authority, was regarded as the highest attribute of sovereignty." Thus, when the Spanish Empire collapsed, *audiencias* became the bases of the independent nation states.

There were *audiencias* at Santa Domingo (erected 1526), Mexico City (1527), Panama (1535), Lima (1542), Guatemala (1543), Guadalajara (1548), Bogotá (1549), La Plata (1559) (with its seat at what is now Sucre in Bolivia), Quito (1563), Santiago (1609), Buenos Aires (1661), Caracas (1786), and Cuzco (1787). Not all these *audiencias* became the cores of states. Guadalajara and Cuzco did not give issue to independent nations. The *audiencia* of Guatemala, while maintaining coherence for a time, eventually became the republics of Guatemala, El Salvador, Honduras, Nicaragua, and Costa Rica. In the cases of Paraguay and Uruguay *audiencias* were lacking but, in these instances, the "buffer" qualities of the regions, between Spanish and Portuguese spheres of influence, go a long way to explaining their separate existence.

In the early nineteenth century the Portuguese section of Latin America evolved into the United States of Brazil, but the Spanish sphere fragmented into 15 independent nation-states. Although these states in theory succeeded to the territory of the preexisting *audiencia*, it was in practice difficult to define the limits of jurisdiction of the royal courts. To overcome some of the difficulties, most of the states involved embraced the principle of *uti possidetis, ita possideatis* (as you possess, so you may possess) (Cukwurah, 1967). Under this concept, the new states were regarded as succeeding to the territory of the preexisting colonial administrative division on which the emergent nation had been based. To help remove misunderstandings, "critical dates" were recognized, so that in South America the administrative boundaries operative in 1810 were to become the basis of the new states, while in Central America the date was fixed at 1812. Useful as the adoption of the *uti possidetis* principle has proved to be, difficulties have arisen simply because it has frequently been impossible to establish the boundaries of administrative divisions at the critical date. The maps or descriptions on which divisions had been based were often inaccurate or ambiguous, while the *de facto* and *de jure* boundaries of the administrative units were not always coincident.

It is clear that there are a number of potential causes for boundary disputes in Latin America—unoccupied lands, strategic considerations, ambiguously defined or poorly demarcated boundaries and, of course, the discovery of new resources, which make it worthwhile for a state to search for exploitable ambiguities in the hope of territorial expansion. It is not possible here to examine all the past and present boundary disputes in Latin America, but the dispute between Peru and Ecuador over a part of Amazonia illustrates some of the problems with which successor states have had to contend in the definition of boundaries. The *audiencia* of Quito enjoyed jurisdiction over the coastal lowlands and the *sierra* and over an extensive tract of Amazonia stretching well beyond the present southern and eastern borders of the Ecuadorian *oriente*. In 1720 the *audiencia* was detached from the viceroyalty of Peru and became part of the newly created viceroyalty of New Granada. However, in 1802 the provinces of Mainas and Quijos were transferred by the Spanish crown from the New Granada viceroyalty to that of Peru. Thus, under the *uti possidetis* principle, at the critical date of 1810 these provinces were part of the unit that eventually became Peru. However, the Ecuadorians suggested that the transfer of territory had never been affected and, in any case, the whole question had been settled in 1829 in the treaty between Peru and Gran Colombia, of which Ecuador was then a part, when Peru had recognized the boundaries of Gran Colombia as of the 1720 situation. In international law, then, the

Ecuadorians had a good case but, as time passed, Peruvians became more active in the trade and settlement of the disputed regions and began to establish *de facto* control in a region to which Ecuador had *de jure* claims. Attempts were made to arbitrate the issue in the nineteenth century, and the two countries negotiated the question in 1924 and 1936 but, in 1941, Peruvian forces invaded Ecuador and control of the disputed territory was ceded to Peru under the Protocol of Rio de Janeiro (1942). Ecuador still hopes to regain lands that, although sparsely populated, are seen as having considerable economic potential. In recent years there have been several incidents between Peru and Ecuador, and the border dispute has threatened to provoke armed conflict between the countries.

The foregoing is just one example of a type of boundary dispute that has been common in Latin America. Such disputes are a potential cause of international conflicts as the recent problems between Chile and Argentina over the ownership of territory around the Straits of Magellan show. Such stresses may make economic cooperation difficult. For example, the opening up of Amazonia may bring economic benefits to Brazil, Venezuela, Colombia, Ecuador, Peru, and Bolivia but, considering the long history of Brazilian expansion in the area at the territorial expense of adjoining states, some of the less powerful states may be reluctant to engage in cooperative regional development.

INTERNATIONAL ECONOMIC GROUPINGS IN LATIN AMERICA

In spite of rivalries between states in Latin America there has been a movement in the 1960s and 1970s toward the establishment of international economic organizations within the region.

The countries of the Third World that aspire to higher levels of economic development (and most of them do) have examined the experience of the economically advanced nations in search of lessons and principles that might be applied to their own situation. Not surprisingly, it has been concluded that a closer degree of economic cooperation, as exemplified by the European Common Market, might help to accelerate regional industrial development, improve terms of trade, and increase diplomatic influence. In the 1960s and 1970s nascent groupings of states for economic purposes appeared in Latin America, Africa, and Asia. Within Middle and South America the Central American Common Market (1960), the Latin American Free Trade Association (1961), the Caribbean Free Trade Association (1968), and the Caribbean Common Market (1974) have come into operation, and nearly all states in the region are members of, or are linked to, a supranational economic organization.

Three major types of international cooperative economic grouping may be recognized: the free-trade area, the customs union, and the common mar-

Figure 8.1

ket. A free-trade area consists of two or more states that agree to remove tariffs and other restrictions on trade between them, although the partners are at liberty to trade with nonmember states on their own terms. A customs union involves a group of states consenting to remove restrictions on trade between them and additionally in the establishment of common external tariffs, which are applicable to all members of the union. A common market provides for the removal of restrictions on trade between the nations involved, the establishment of common external tariffs, and the creation of economic policies and business laws that apply equally to all the member states. In short, the attempt is made to create a multinational region with common business operating conditions.

The aim of a free-trade association, a customs union, or a common market is the creation of larger market area in which investment will be stimulated, competition will promote efficiency, economies of scale will be gained, and the process of economic development accelerated.

Politically, there is an increasing degree of commitment from a free-trade association to a common market and, in the latter case, a central authority may be empowered to make decisions that are currently arrived at by national governments. International economic groupings in Latin America can only emerge as successful operating entities after lengthy negotiation, leading to the reconciliation of numerous national interests. Before the benefits of unity can be obtained and equitably distributed, many difficulties must be surmounted, some of which are geographical.

Latin America lacks a regional transportation network, and it is not possible to envisage the large-scale movement of a wide range of goods over the region. This basic disability renders unrealistic much of the talk of promoting a larger volume of intraregional trade. Although there is seaborne trade in raw materials between some states of the region, the rail and highway networks, which are necessary to promote significant flows of manufactured goods, do not exist.

Perhaps the largest difficulty to be overcome is the fact that the countries of Latin America, and regions within countries, have markedly different levels of economic development. Around the middle of the nineteenth century Brazil (Graham, 1968), Argentina (Ferns, 1969), and Mexico (Cumberland, 1968) were able to establish a number of initial economic advantages in the region that are continuing to serve them well in the present century.

As the world economy expanded in the nineteenth century, Brazil, Argentina, and Mexico attracted outside investment and slowly established areally limited economic systems that in many ways mirrored the North Atlantic industrial societies and acted as bridgeheads of industrialization and modernization. The attraction of foreign interest and investment was not, of course, a matter of chance. Mexico is contiguous to a major economic system and, in Latin American terms, is relatively close to Europe. As explained earlier, Brazil and Argentina are on the ''accessible side'' of South America, and the areas of both countries that attracted interest are subtropical or temperate. Although not subscribing to a physical determinist view of events, Europeans and North Americans have found it easier to transfer their personnel and techniques (agricultural and industrial) to temperate and subtropical lands than to the tropical world. Even though other Latin American countries have developed their bridgeheads, the largest and most important industrial centers are still in the temperate and subtropical parts of the region, which are accessible to the North Atlantic.

A quickening of the rate of regional economic growth may now mean a relatively higher rate of advancement in the already advantaged countries, whether or not the states of the region are members of a free-trade association or a common market. The less fortunate partners in a free-trade area or a common market are likely to appreciate these facts and demand a redistribution of the benefits coming to Argentina, Brazil, and Mexico, who are aware of the situation and are extremely cautious about committing themselves deeply to any cooperative project, such as a common market, that would evolve common policies for redistributing wealth.

In the early stages of economic development growth is notoriously unequal. This produces strains between regions within countries and between countries if they are linked in an economic association. The whole process of economic development implies a reevaluation of resources, relocation of population, and reappraisals of positional advantages and disadvantages. Such problems are part of the normal growing pains of economic development, but they are readjustments with political repercussions. Areas within a nation that experience migratory outflows and fail to attract new industrial investment are liable to feel aggrieved as their relative importance and prosperity decline. Within a country the strains can usually be contained but, when the adjustments are between states, disadvantages to one can produce antagonisms that may harm international relationships.

ECONOMIC GROUPINGS IN LATIN AMERICA

The Latin American Free Trade Association (LAFTA)

LAFTA was established by the Treaty of Montevideo (1960) and became operative in June 1961 in the hope of gradually liberalizing trade between member states. The treaty was originally signed by Argentina, Brazil, Chile, Mexico, Paraguay, Peru, and Uruguay, although other Latin American states subsequently acceded to it. The member nations and their population totals are shown in table 8-1.

Table 8-1   Members of LAFTA

Country	Estimated Population, 1979 (in millions)
Argentina	26.8
Bolivia (acceded February 1967)	5.2
Brazil	124.4
Chile	10.9
Colombia (acceded October 1961)	26.1
Ecuador (acceded October 1961)	7.8
Mexico	66.1
Paraguay	3.2
Peru	17.3
Uruguay	2.9
Venezuela (acceded September 1966)	16.5

The total number of persons residing within the free-trade area is over 300 million. For comparative purposes it can be stated that the combined populations of the member countries of the European Common Market (E.E.C.) number just over 260 million. Comparisons of LAFTA and the E.E.C. in terms of populations have little validity in a commercial sense, because purchasing power in the greatest part of Latin America is considerably less than in Western Europe, while populations and therefore markets are usually more widespread.

The treaty of Montevideo stated that within a period not exceeding 12 years from the date of entry into force (June 1961) "the contracting parties shall gradually eliminate, in respect of substantially all their reciprocal trade, such duties, charges and restrictions as may be applied to imports of goods originating in the territory of any contracting party." Elimination was to be achieved by means of negotiation, but the negotiations were so complex that the removal of restrictions was not achieved in 12 years.

Establishing a free-trade area within Latin America is an extremely complex operation simply because the countries of the region are at markedly different stages of economic development. Some countries have so little trade that there can be few advantages to them in eliminating tariffs (and the revenue these produce) unless some compensations are provided. Other countries with developing industries fear exposure to competition from the more efficient plants of the relatively developed nations of the region.

For these reasons it was necessary to proceed slowly and to write into the treaty a considerable number of saving clauses and exceptions besides providing for the weaker states. A member could reimpose restrictions on imported goods "if these products are imported in such quantities or under such conditions that they are liable to have serious repercussions on specific productive activities of vital importance to the national economy." The treaty included clauses in favor of countries at a less advanced stage of economic development, allowing them to adopt the treaty at a slower pace and to use certain protective measures. Bolivia, Paraguay, and Ecuador were recognized as less advanced. After the treaty had been in operation for some time, it became clear that another group of countries—Chile, Colombia, Peru, Venezuela, and Uruguay—were suffering certain disadvantages in comparison with the more advanced industrial states; they were granted an intermediate status and allowed to slow the process of tariff reduction.

The treaty contained special provisions concerning trade in agricultural produce. Agricultural imports could be limited to the amounts of produce required to meet deficits in national production, and dues were imposed to equalize the price of the imported and domestic product. These clauses excluded agricultural produce from the provisions of the free-trade treaty.

A commonly voiced criticism of the Treaty of Montevideo was that it did not contain provisions to insure that the poorer states would receive a fair share of the benefits occurring from the creation of a free-trade area. In particular, the treaty lacked mechanisms whereby regional development schemes could be initiated to guide a proportion of new development into the less advanced areas.

The Andean Group

The inability of LAFTA to achieve its initial aims and progress toward the establishment of a common market strengthened the desire of some countries to form subregional organizations. The Andean countries have been anxious to coordinate their development and, since 1966, have been moving toward closer economic ties while remaining within the LAFTA framework. In 1969 Colombia, Ecuador, Peru, Bolivia, and Chile agreed to establish a customs union, coordinate economic policies, and build a regional communications system. Venezuela joined the organization in 1973, but Chile has since left.

There is much sense in the Andean group. The countries share many of the same problems; some of them (e.g., transportation) will be more successfully tackled in unison. The disparity in levels of development is not so great, and the number of member states (five) is likely to mean that there are fewer interests to be reconciled, while the area, just over 17 million square miles, and population (over 70 million) is manageable within relatively straightforward administrative devices. The position of the smaller nations is improved; countries such as Ecuador and Bolivia are not completely outranked by larger states. In the case of Ecuador (which was peripheral to the LAFTA territory), a smaller member gains a nodal position within the Andean group from which economic benefits may be derived. The group has established an Andean Development Corporation (1968) that has the authority and finance to undertake regional projects that individual states would have difficulty completing from their own resources. In 1975, under the Cartagena Agreement, the development of an integrated petrochemical industry in each of the member countries was established.

Problems remain. The economic hardships of Bolivia look no more tractable within this organization than in the context of LAFTA, although the long-term prospects for development of the Bolivian *oriente* are probably improved. Economic differentials within the group are not as great as those found in LAFTA, but they exist nevertheless. Colombia, by virtue of size, resources, industrial structure, and position, enjoys a number of advantages that are enhanced by relatively low manufacturing costs. Venezuela, too, enjoys advantages that may allow her to dominate aspects of the group's economic existence, even though higher wage rates may retard the growth of exports. Of course, the friction between Peru and Ecuador could endanger the stability of the group.

At a conference in Acapulco in June 1980, the member states decided that LAFTA should be replaced by a Latin American Integration Association designed to operate a system of bilateral and generalized trade preferences that would take into account the different levels of economic development. The Andean group will continue to operate along the existing lines. The integration association represents a less ambitious effort to bring about international economic cooperation in Latin America and suggests that any successful attempt to promote a regional common market is many years away.

The Central American Common Market

The Central American Common Market was established by the Treaty of Managua (1960). The member states, together with population totals, are shown in Table 8-2. Panama is not a member, since it is generally more prosperous than the other Central American republics, and this makes it difficult to accommodate Panama within a common market.

Although the common market is small, approximately 20 million persons in all, it was successful until 1969 when the El Salvador-Honduras war severely damaged intraregional trade. The reasons for success are readily apparent: (1) the member states were at about the same level of economic development; (2) they form a relatively compact unit; (3) the regional transportation network, while not fully developed, had established the initial linkages in a system that was capable of further growth; and (4) the members were reaching the point where the development of import substitution industries might be profitable and the profits would be greater within an enlarged market area. And so it came to pass, at least for a time. Investment in small-scale manufacturing plants was stimulated, intraregional trade expanded at a rate of about 7 percent per year, of which just over one-sixth could be directly attributed to the common market system.

The establishment of the common market coincided with a period of rapid expansion in manufacturing industry. However, industrial growth was unevenly spread and so, as intraregional trade increased, the disparity in the trading position of the partners widened. El Salvador and, to a lesser extent,

Table 8-2 Members of the Central American Common Market

Country	Estimated Population, 1979 (in millions)
Costa Rica (acceded 1962)	2.2
El Salvador	4.6
Guatemala	6.8
Honduras (membership currently in abeyance)	3.6
Nicaragua	2.5

Guatemala by virtue of population size, a better economic infrastructure, and existing industrial investment were able to attract a disproportionate share of the new manufacturing plants established in the region. This naturally gave rise to resentment and was a factor in starting the short 1969 war between El Salvador and Honduras. The conflict has proved to be the first of a series of dislocations in the region that have disrupted the common market. The internal troubles in Nicaragua and El Salvador are not conducive to promoting trade.

The pace of economic growth in Latin America will not be wholly, or even largely, determined by the success or failure of international economic groupings. Such organizations can speed or retard the rate of growth, but they do not in themselves control economic development. The economies of many countries are becoming more diversified and less dependent on outside forces, but basically Latin America is a region that is greatly influenced by world economic trends. However, more regional economic integration would probably provide a greater degree of economic self-sufficiency.

SUMMARY

All countries of the Third World that are striving to modernize and produce a higher standard of living face similar problems. Everywhere there is a conflict between traditional value systems and the new life-styles that development may bring. Many Third World countries are attempting to integrate isolated territory into the effectively administered national space. Another problem is the need to give distinct ethnic groups an effective place in national life. Most Latin American countries have Indian populations that have the dilemma of either hanging on to established life-styles in isolated areas or leaving a traditional community and adopting the Spanish or Portuguese language and other cultural traits. Admission to the modernization process is obviously done at considerable social cost. Some Latin American governments (e.g., Mexico) do have policies that try to preserve Indian communities, but it is hard to see how more national unity can be attained without some use of the "melting pot."

Most countries of the world have problems concerning international, economic relationships. The United States and Britain have balance-of-payments difficulties, manufacturing industries are seeming less competitive, and currencies fluctuate too much on the international exchanges. All of these problems are greatly magnified for most less developed countries. Latin American countries generally suffer high rates of inflation, find it difficult to export manufactured goods into world markets, and are prone to rapid fluctuations in the value of their currencies. Reliance on a few commodities to make up the bulk of exports is a major cause of currency instability. For example, if the price of tin is high, Bolivian international earnings go up and the currency strengthens. On the other hand, if the market for bananas is weak, the currency of a number of countries, including Ecuador and Guatemala, may be adversely affected.

The fluctuation of commodity prices is not entirely a product of supply and demand. Speculative activity plays a major role, as we know from the price history of silver in 1980. Speculators attempted to corner the market, for a time were extraordinarily successful, and drove the price to five times the previous level. Then the corner was broken and prices quickly subsided to somewhere near their previous level.

Speculation in the future price of commodities, which can be done whether the price trend is down or up, illustrates how Latin America lies on the margins of world economic activity. Most of the speculative trading is done in the existing financial centers, at exchanges in London, Paris, Brussels, New York, Chicago, and Tokyo. The profits (and, at times, big losses) are taken outside of the region of production by dealers, who rarely take delivery of the commodities traded. If the price of copper or coffee is rising it is certain that a good percentage of the increased value will accrue to dealers and institutions at the heart of the world's economic system. The result is that less money is available to finance economic activity in the area of production. Not only Latin America suffers from this economic core-economic periphery relationship. African nations have the same problems, as do many poorer areas within economically advanced countries. This core-periphery relationship is at the bottom of much of the economic resentment that Latin American countries feel toward the richer nations because it seems that no matter what happens, an apparently unfair proportion of the profits from international trade end up, through multinational corporations and commodity dealers, in financial institutions in New York, London, or Zurich.

Latin American history of the last 500 years may have been a story of increasing contact with the wider world, but the region is still spatially peripheral to the major centers of economic activity. As a late-developing region, Latin America tends to have a higher degree of dependency on external economic forces than older, established industrial regions, such as Western Europe. It may be that if the rise in raw material prices continues, there will be a transfer of some wealth from North America, Japan, and Europe to Latin America. However, if continued price rises for materials such as oil produce a major recession in the economically advanced countries, the effects would be quickly felt in Latin America as the demand for all commodities slackened.

We must not close on a pessimistic note. Observers have been talking for the last 20 years about the evils of economic dependency, but they have frequently failed to note that many countries in Latin America, including Mexico, Brazil, and Venezuela, have been sustaining impressive rates of industrial growth that, in percentage terms, are much higher than those being achieved by North Atlantic countries. Mexico now produces over 80 percent of the consumer goods bought in the country, and Brazil has impressive machine tool, automobile, and electronics industries. In short, several countries in the region seem to have reached a critical mass that will allow a more independent form of economic development.

BIBLIOGRAPHY

Cumberland, C. C., *Mexico: The Struggle for Modernity*, New York, Oxford University Press, 1968.

Cukwurah, A. D., *The Settlement of Boundary Disputes in International Law*, New York, Oceana, 1967.

Dell, S. S., *A Latin American Common Market?*, London and New York, Oxford University Press, 1966.

Ferns, H. S., *Argentina*, New York, Praeger, 1969.

Graham, R., *Britain and the Onset of Modernization in Brazil 1850–1914*, New York, Cambridge University Press, 1968.

Grunwald, J. (ed.), *Latin America and the World Economy: A Changing International Order*, Beverly Hills, Calif., Sage, 1978.

Hilton, R. (ed.), *The Movement Towards Latin American Unity*, New York, Praeger, 1969.

Krause, W., and J. Mathis, *Latin America and Economic Integration; Regional Planning for Development*, Iowa City, University of Iowa Press, 1970.

Maritano, N., *A Latin American Economic Community: History, Policies and Problems*, Notre Dame, Indiana, University of Notre Dame Press, 1970.

Phelan, J. L., *The Kingdom of Quito in the Seventeenth Century: Bureaucratic Politics in the Spanish Empire*, Madison, University of Wisconsin Press, 1967.

Index